INDIA
Resources and Development

By the same author

South Asia

Place, People and Work in Japan

Bangladesh

INDIA
Resources and Development

B. L. C. JOHNSON

Professor of Geography
Australian National University

HEINEMANN EDUCATIONAL BOOKS · LONDON

BARNES & NOBLE · NEW YORK
10 East 53rd St., New York 10022
(a division of Harper & Row Publishers, Inc.)

To my friends of the Indian road.
'I met a hundred men on the road to Delhi and they are all my brothers.'

Published by Heinemann Educational Books Ltd
48 Charles Street, London W1X 8AH
ISBN 0 435 35487 6

First published 1979

Published in the U.S.A. 1979 by
HARPER & ROW PUBLISHERS INC.
BARNES & NOBLE IMPORT DIVISION
ISBN 0-06-493348-2

Library of Congress Cataloging in Publication Data

Johnson, Basil Leonard Clyde.
India, resources and development.

Bibliography: p.
Includes index.
1. India – Social conditions – 1947– 2. India – Population. 3. India – Economic conditions – 1947– 4. Agriculture – India. 5. India – Industries.
I. Title.
HN683.5.J58 1978 309.1'54'04 78-15402
ISBN 0-06-493348-2

Filmset in Monophoto Times and printed in Great Britain by
Cox & Wyman Ltd, London, Fakenham and Reading

CONTENTS

PREFACE

India in its thirtieth year of independence is a vast and complex country. With a population of over 600 million, it is the world's second largest state. This book is an attempt to provide in a limited compass the essential facts of India's present stage of development as seen in the perspective of the country's achievements since independence, and in the context of a nation striving fully to utilize its physical and human resources.

It is written with the general reader in mind as well as the student in any discipline that has an interest in India. Numerous maps and tables are used as vehicles for presenting data in a readily intelligible form. Academic jargon has been assiduously avoided so that any reader may have access to knowledge and understanding of the most critically poised country in the developing world.

ACKNOWLEDGEMENTS

Thirty five years of contact with India makes it impossible for me to remember by name everyone who has contributed to my knowledge and understanding of India and to my affection for that land and its peoples. They are very numerous and come from every major community and state of the Indian Union, as well as from among my professional colleagues in the most friendly world-wide fraternity of geographers. After my own Australian National University who granted me the study leave which made this book possible, I am immediately most indebted to the Director of the Institute for Social and Economic Change, in Bangalore, Dr V. K. R. V. Rao, who offered me the hospitality of the Institute's library; to my old friend and colleague Dr V. L. S. Prakasa Rao, Head of the Department of Human Geography at I.S.E.C. and to Dr J. P. Singh, Research Fellow in its Department of Agricultural Economics, on both of whom I inflicted sections of this book, but who are in no way responsible for its imperfections; to Mr Selwyn Cornish of the Department of Economic History in the Australian National University who made valuable suggestions for the content of the section on the economy; to Dr R. Ramchandran of the Delhi School of Economics, Professor C. D. Deshpande and Mrs Sita Dasibhatla of the University of Bombay, Mr T. Basak of the Calcutta Metropolitan Planning Department, and Miss Ranjna Hanspal of I.S.E.C. Bangalore, all of whom helped me obtain census maps and material on their respective cities; to Dr P. T. Malshe who showed me round Kolhapur and Ratnagiri; to Mr Walter Sharpe of Wallardie Tea Estate, Kerala for giving me an unforgettable experience of plantation life and hospitality; to Mr Kevin Cowan and Mrs Val Lyon who with great patience drew the maps and to Mrs Margaret Scrivenor who cast her critical and constructive eye over them; to Mrs Anne Coutts, Research Assistant at the A.N.U. Canberra; to my old friend and fellow Indianist Professor Andrew Learmouth who made valuable suggestions; to Mr J. C. Ajmani, High Commissioner for India in Canberra, who kindly read the manuscript and pointed out some factual inaccuracies; and by no means least to my wife who for a while in India helped organize the masses of data and then wisely accepted grass-widowhood in Australia during the book's difficult gestation in Bangalore. Its blemishes are mine alone. The dedication is borrowed from an Indian proverb used similarly by Rudyard Kipling.

Bangalore, India: February–May 1976
Australian National University, Canberra:
June–August 1976 B. L. C. J.

Photographs

Thanks are due to the Indian High Commission, Canberra, for permission to reproduce photographs 4, 48, 53, 66, 70, 71 and 72; and to Margaret Scrivenor for providing photographs 17, 21 and 55. The remaining photographs were taken by the author.

LIST OF TABLES

LIST OF FIGURES

INTRODUCTION

A country is at once a part of the earth's surface and a part of humanity. How a people support themselves in the land they occupy, how they adjust to their environment, how they use, mis-use, or neglect to use the resources and talents with which they have been endowed by nature and their ancestors, – all these matters are of abiding interest to their fellow humans. India is among the world's most extensive countries and second only to China in the number of its people. Since becoming independent in 1947 India has been conducting an experiment in democracy at a hitherto unheard of scale and despite having a largely illiterate population. Traditional *mores* have been respected while at the same time belief in a democratic socialist ideal has become the cornerstone of national policy.

As a geographer, the author tries to present an holistic view of India since independence, appraising the country's environmental characteristics, the way India is currently using its 'lands, airs, waters and fires', the latter the sun's energy, to support human life, and how these may be used in the future as demands on them expand in quantity and quality.

The author sees it as the geographer's craft and responsibility to portray to the world as true and vivid a picture as he can of the world as seen through eyes trained particularly to appreciate the subtleties of man's relationship to the land. In that it cannot be a catalogue nor a gazeteer, his record is of necessity selective of those aspects that have claimed his interest over the years. To that extent the geographer practices an art rather than a science, but within the limits of selectivity he tries to take as balanced a scientific view as any environmentalist. Time, space and cost set severe limitations, and he craves the reader's indulgence if specific questions appear to have been neglected.

The first two chapters explore the political and economic realities of independent India against the background of the diversities of social and cultural levels and the complex patterns of languages and religions.

Agriculture as the mainstay of the country's economy is dealt with from several viewpoints. Water, both from direct rainfall and obtained indirectly from irrigation sources is of the utmost importance as is underlined in the two sample studies of critical droughts that resulted in severe scarcity. The 'green revolution' is studied in the broader context of agricultural modernization. Crop distribution and crop associations are analysed over the whole country, a separate chapter serving to synthesize them in a number of representative transects.

Industry is crucial to India's development. Resources for industry are surveyed, and the mixed system of village, small-scale and 'organized' manufacturing industry, encompassing as it does traditional crafts and the most advanced technologies, is described.

The chapter on population distribution focusses on change since independence, the rapid growth of urban centres and the degree of progress towards a more urbanized society. Eight towns and cities, four of them of 'millionaire' status, are examined to illustrate the character of the Indian city, a palimpsest of many centuries of change.

Finally, development achievement is briefly summarized and we hazard a look into the future.

PART I
The People and Their Needs

CHAPTER ONE

THE PEOPLE AND THE NATION

SUMMARY

The cultural heritage that constitutes the nucleus of modern India's unity is of great antiquity. Hinduism and Buddhism are indigenous religions long predating the introduction of Christianity by trading settlers in the first century AD, and that of Islam by conquering invaders from the west. Those religions were adopted, absorbed and adapted by populations themselves the progeny of a variety of peoples migrating into the Indian sub-continent and mingling genetically though selectively over several millenia. Racially the Indian population contains several strains including Mediterranean and Mongoloid, overlain probably on less clearly discernable elements of Proto-Australoid and Negrito representing still earlier 'aboriginal' folk.

Religious traditions and possibly racial characteristics form strands in the complex fabric of India's highly stratified society. Despite constitutional assertions of secularity, Hindu culture provides the unifying concept for a political federated patchwork of states, many of which find their identity through a language distinct from that of their neighbours.

India provides the remarkable phenomenon of a state highly diverse in its cultural elements. It is characterized by extremes of economic sophistication and backwardness, by technological and intellectual advancement and primitive and unlettered archaism, by social conservativism at all levels in the community alongside professed ideals of equity and social justice. These latter, with painful slowness, may be beginning to engender the fundamental changes that will create a truly modern nation.

HUMAN AND CULTURAL BACKGROUND

India came into being in 1947 on the partition of the former British Empire of India between the new nations of India and Pakistan. It then achieved for the first time within its present borders political unification independent of alien authority. However, India is not simply the Asian successor to part of the colonial territory of a European nation, which in turn had acquired it piecemeal from the disintegrating empire of the invading Moghuls. India is the inheritor of one of the world's great ancient civilizations, predating those of Greece and Rome, and for a time contemporaneous with those of Mesopotamia, Egypt and China, and having cultural intercourse with all of them. The size of the debt of Western civilization to Indian philosophy through Graeco-Judaic Christianity is beginning to be appreciated. Unlike Buddhism, Christianity or Islam, the origins of Hinduism cannot be dated or attributed to a particular historic individual. As an amalgam of beliefs, customs and practices incapable of precise definition Hinduism is the result of many centuries of absorption into a more philosophically structured religion of the spiritual concepts of various primitive groups. The most important of several religions to develop from Indian Hinduism was Buddhism which carried elements of pre-existing Hinduism via Sri Lanka to much of Southeast Asia, China and ultimately Japan.

It is not surprising that in a country as vast as India, political cohesion as we understand it today was not achieved simultaneously over the whole country until British rule imposed from outside an infrastructure of communications and adminis-

1 The sanctity of the cow is deeply rooted in Hindu religious tradition: It is expressed with great charm in this life-sized carving of a farmer milking his cow while she cherishes her calf. This forms but part of a complex sculpture of scenes from the life of Krishna. 8th Century A.D. Pallava style; Mahabalipuram, Tamilnadu.

2 Fresh milk, modern style: cows and a calf tethered outside a milk bar in Mysore City. The problem of keeping milk fresh in a community where refrigerators are a costly luxury often produces this kind of solution. The greenery hanging above the shop sign is decoration to mark a Hindu festival.

3 Indian mythology carved from the solid granite: the leading elephant is about three metres tall: 7th century Pallava art, Mahabalipuram, Tamilnadu.

tration of a scale previously unknown in the civilized world. Even their predecessors, the Moghuls, controlled less than the whole of India in a loosely feudal style often disturbed by the disloyalty of rival rulers nominally owing allegiance to the great Moghul in Delhi.

Early Muslim rule and all British domination were alien, so that when India gained independence it was after some seven centuries of colonial rule, which while it introduced fresh cultural elements from foreign civilizations, stunted the development of indigenous culture. Before the Delhi Sultans began to extend Muslim rule and influence from the early thirteenth century, India had produced considerable kingdoms of its own, the most extensive probably being that of Asoka whose Mauryan Empire, ruled with Buddhist tolerance, stretched from Orissa to Gandhara (in Pakistan's northwest frontier province) and south to Karnataka in 274 BC. Another powerful kingdom, Vijayanagar, based in Karnataka, included Tamilnadu and Kerala and extended its power overseas to southeast Asia. Such centrifugal movement was, however, exceptional, and inward rather than outward invasions have been the rule.

India has for millenia been a region to which peoples have been attracted from the harsher lands beyond its mountain fringe. The main flow of peoples and cultures has been from the northwest, entering the sub-continent from Persia and Turkestan through Afghanistan and the vale of Peshawar, to follow the Himalayan piedmont plain southeastwards into the Ganga basin, the cultural hearth of Hindu India. Lesser streams from the Chinese cultural realm came over the Himalayan ranges to exert their influence on the hill peoples, but stopped short of the plains, while in the east the upland tribal cultures of Southeast Asia dominate the marchlands on the Burma border. Not all migratory waves have been overland, and India's island territories have been peopled from the sea: the Andaman and Nicobar Islands lying closer to Malaysia and Indonesia than to India, by folk of southeast Asian culture; Lakshadweep (the Laccadive, Amindivi and Minicoy Islands in the Arabian sea, 300 km off the coast of Kerala) by Arab seafarers from the west, who also made an important contribution to the southwest coast of the mainland.

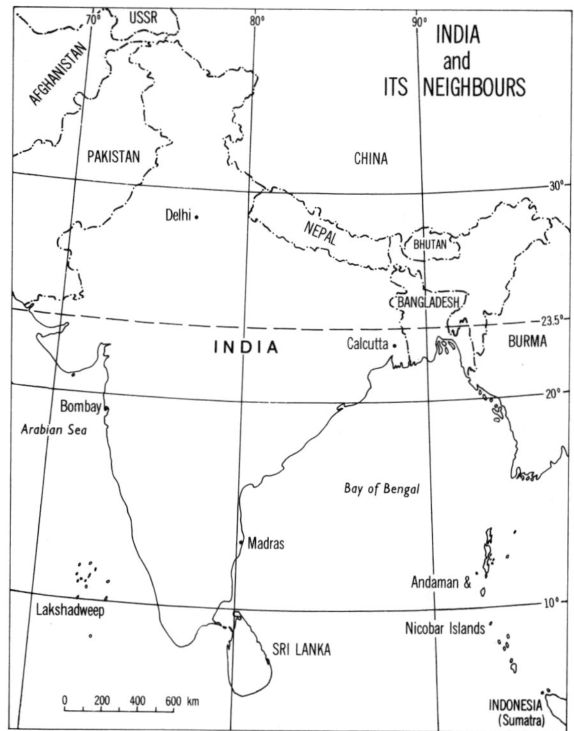

FIG. 1.1

Ancient and obscure as many of these migrations were, they leave clear evidence in the cultural map of modern India, difficult as this may be to interpret with any confidence. Until the Christian era it is impossible to say with certainty which migrant groups brought what cultural elements to the Indian melting pot (see Figure 1.5).

The earliest occupants of the region may be represented today by the Negrito of the Andamans and possibly in Kerala, and by Proto-Australoid populations among the tribes of Peninsular India. The location of some of these elements suggests that their forebears retreated to inaccessible hill country or at least were able in such country to preserve something of their cultural identity while those who remained in the path of the newcomers were absorbed by them. It is thought (following Guha) that two main waves of migration may be recognized in the present population, both coming from the northwest: a Palae-Mediterranean people, relatively dark-skinned, who preceded, probably by several millenia, a second wave of lighter-skinned Mediterraneans. The Palae-Mediterraneans formed the basic stock of the south Indian peoples of Dravidian culture. Their earlier extent was more widespread, but the later Mediterraneans probably displaced them from the better lands of the north. Which of these peoples created the first urbanized civilization in the sub-continent, the Indus civilization with cities at Harappa and Mohenjodaro in Pakistan, but extending into western India, is a matter for speculation, but from 2500 BC there was contact with the older centres of urbanization in the civilizations of Mesopotamia and Egypt.

Guha identifies Alpine racial elements mainly in western India, and Nordic elements in the northwest as later arrivals, whose cultural impact was more significant than their genetic contribution.

As civilization advanced, the mass migration of groups of more or less primitive subsistence pastoralists and cultivators gave place to military conquest and the establishment of empires by invading forces. Early among such groups were the Greeks, who under Alexander the Great in the fourth century BC ruled for a while an empire extending as far east as the river Chenab. The impact of the Muslims was more extensive over time and space, culminating in the Moghul empire which was eventually displaced by British rule. The Portuguese and the French also contributed to the alien elements in the Indian scene. While the effect of these invaders on the racial character of the Indian peoples was minimal, their cultural influence is writ large over modern India.

THE RELIGIOUS FACTOR

When the All-India Congress Party accepted partition as the price of independence it was with reluctance, since it had always sought freedom for the whole country on a secular basis. Despite the considerable number of Muslims in the Congress Party who preferred that policy, Jinnah, and the Muslim League which he led, insisted on a separate Pakistan and so occurred the dismemberment of what could have become a unitary or possibly a federal state. Religion was the basis for partition. The boundaries between India and the two wings of Pakistan were broadly drawn to give to Pakistan the contiguous districts with Muslim majorities and to India those with non-Muslim (Hindu plus Sikh) majorities. Lord Radcliffe had to arbitrate the final boundary within those areas formerly ruled directly by the British. The princely states were to opt to join either India or Pakistan.

Religion, then, was the primary factor in delineating the new India, contrary as this principle was to the tenets of the nation's founders. India is predominantly Hindu. Nearly 500 million Hindus constitute 83 per cent of the population. Over 60 million Muslims make up 11 per cent, the largest minority group, Christians account for 2.6 per cent, Sikhs for almost 2 per cent, and there are about 4 million Buddhists (0.7 per cent) and three million Jains (0.5 per cent). One should not exaggerate the cultural differences between these

4 The strong demand for images of Hindu Deities for domestic shrines provides continuing stimulus for a flourishing craft industry. Here castings are being touched up before sale.

religious groups. To a degree, a way of life deriving from Hinduism permeates all religions in India. Hinduism was itself considerably influenced by the reforming movements that led to Buddhism and Jainism in the sixth century of the pre-Christian era.

The Muslim religion has been least compromising, but the fact that it was largely imposed by invaders on Hindus and Buddhists guaranteed the survival by fusion of some non-Islamic traits in the culture of Indian Muslims. Islam was brought to India in the tenth century AD mainly by invaders from the northwest, and was the religion of the Moghuls who established their rule over a large part of India by the beginning of the seventeenth century. Figure 1.2 shows the present distribution of Muslims, which in large measure reflects the strength of the Moghul Empire in the Ganga plains, particularly from Delhi through Uttar Pradesh and Bihar to Bengal, where their high proportions in east Bengal led to its partition as east Pakistan, with the addition of the Sylhet district of Assam. The large proportion of Muslims in the Assam valley came by migration from Bengal

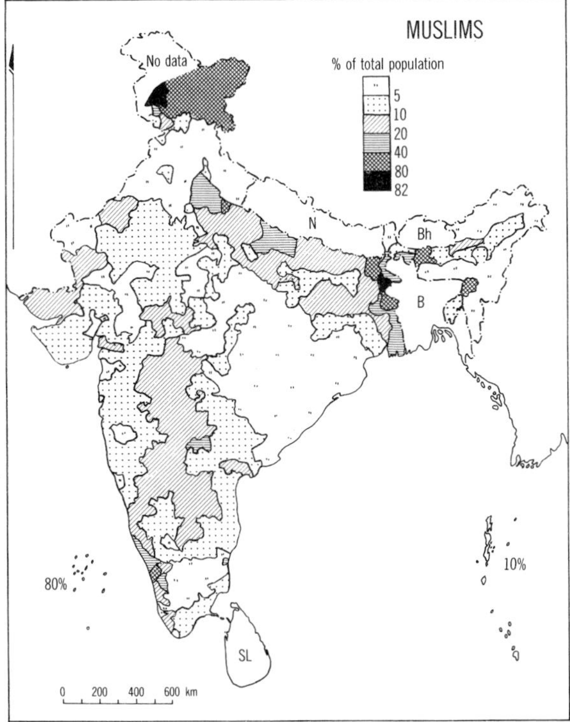

FIG. 1.2 N Nepal; Bh Bhutan; B Bangladesh; SL Sri Lanka.

over the last hundred years. Muslims are quite numerous through the Deccan, especially in those parts of Andhra Pradesh and Maharashtra that had formed the Dominions of the Nizam of Hyderabad, a Muslim ruler of a princely state under the British. The concentration of Muslims in northern Kerala and in the islands of Lakshadweep is attributable to sea-borne contacts between these areas and southwestern Asia. Such contacts predate Islam, as is evidenced by the presence in Kerala of a small Jewish community tracing its origins back to the first century AD and of the very large Christian population of that state adhering to the Syrian Churches, which claim to have been converted by the apostle St Thomas. In the far northwest of India, Muslims exceed 80 per cent of the population in parts of Jammu and Kashmir, and reach 66 per cent in that state as a whole. When the Hindu Maharaja of Jammu and Kashmir opted to join with India at the time of partition, Pakistan objected that the state, being predominantly Muslim, should have become part of its territories, and in 1947–48 tried by invasion to take control. The attempt failed but Pakistan did not withdraw from the areas occupied when United Nations brought about an armistice, since when a cease-fire line has separated Indian Jammu and Kashmir from the Pakistan-occupied territory. India now administers Jammu and Kashmir as a fully-fledged state within the Indian Union.

In West Bengal and Assam there remain districts with large Muslim populations close to the borders of Bangladesh (formerly East Pakistan). By contrast, in Punjab and Haryana, Indian states created out of the former British Indian Province that included what is now Pakistan's Punjab, Muslims generally fail to reach five per cent of the population. It was here that the huge uprootings and migrations of Muslim minorities from India into Pakistan and of Hindu and Sikh minorities from Pakistan into India took place. The relatively small number of Muslims remaining bears witness to the stronger intercommunal bitterness in this corner of India. In Bengal a common Bengali culture helped transcend religious differences and consequently migration was on a much smaller scale.

Partition came very near to separating Amritsar, the sacred city of the Sikhs, from their main areas of settlement in Indian Punjab and Haryana.

Large numbers of Sikhs in what became Pakistan's Punjab gave up their lands and migrated east. Some settled on farms abandoned by Muslims, others found a new life as city dwellers, creating by their customary initiative vigorous industrial enterprises in towns like Ludhiana. The Sikh religion originated in the Punjab in the fifteenth century. In a sense it was a reforming faith from within Hinduism, notable for its militancy and its lack of rigid caste. When Moghul power began to crumble in the eighteenth century, the Sikhs seized control of the Punjab, thus becoming embroiled in wars with the British. They subsequently served with distinction in the Indian Army both under the British and since independence. Figure 1.3 shows where Sikhs constitute more than five per cent of the population of districts. In Punjab and the adjacent districts of Haryana, they are predominantly agriculturists, as they are also in the *terai* districts of Uttar Pradesh, notably in Nainital. There they account for 9 per cent of the total population and they are an important element in a string of districts from Dehra Dun to Kheri where they have settled as cultivating colonists on Government projects aimed to rehabilitate refugees on the newly cleared jungle lands.

Apart from their reputation as successful farmers the Sikhs are well known for their enterprise in business and mechanical engineering. The map shows their spread in the urban areas outside the districts where they form five per cent or more of the population, and it is clear how they are attracted to centres of industrial development like Meerut, Kanpur, Indore, Bombay, Pune (Poona) and Calcutta, and the heavy industrialized districts of the Damodar Valley and Singhbhum in West Bengal and south Bihar.

Like Islam, Christianity was partly brought to India from overseas, following early trade links between southwest Asia and the coast of southwest India, and part the result of missionary activity under the protection of the British Raj, (and locally of the Portuguese, as at Goa). Christianity was notably successful among the hill tribes of the northeast, with the result that Nagaland and Mizoram are predominantly Christian, while it is the leading religion in Meghalaya, and that of 26 per cent of the people of Manipur (Figure 1.4).

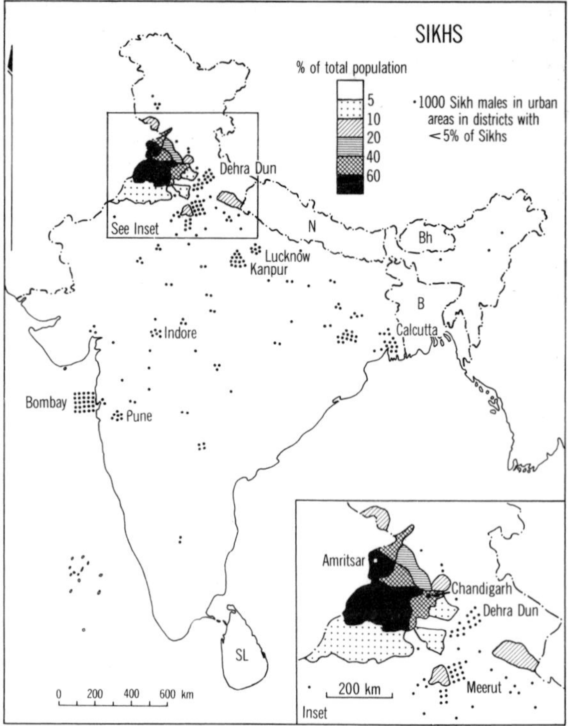

FIG. 1.3 Abbreviations as in Figure 1.2.

FIG. 1.4 Abbreviations as in Figure 1.2.

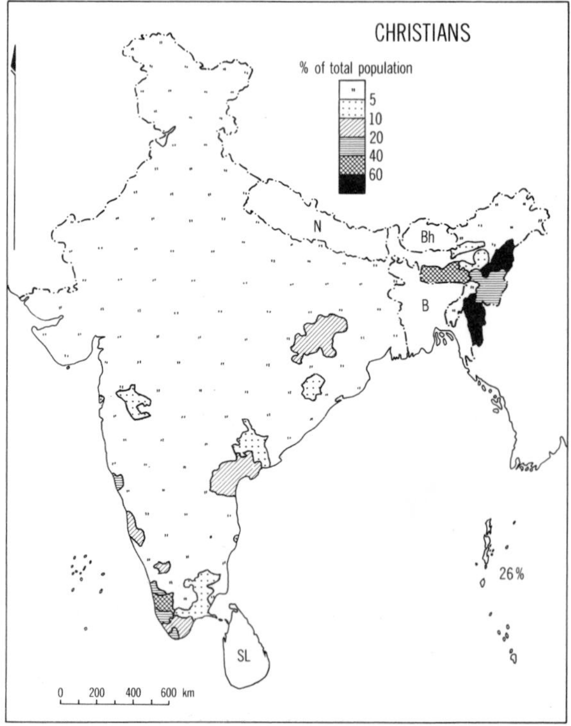

Missionaries were active in tribal areas of Orissa and adjacent districts in Bihar and Madhya Pradesh, and in coastal Andhra Pradesh. The most substantial Christian population outside Kerala, however, is in Tamilnadu where 2.4 million make up nearly six per cent of the total, and are fairly widely spread throughout the state, with a concentration of 39 per cent in Kanyakumari on the borders of Kerala. The size of Christian communities in the Assam Valley and in the hill country of Kerala and Tamilnadu is related to some extent to the long association of settled British plantation managers who lived in a closer and more permanent relationship to their work force than did most of their compatriots in government service or commerce.

Buddhism, which had its origins in Bihar was probably for some centuries the dominant religion of India, northwards from Orissa and Maharashtra. It spread beyond the present boundaries of India to the far northwest where in synthesis with elements of Greek culture brought by followers of Alexander the Great it flourished for several centuries in Gandhara, whence it was taken to China. It also spread southwards to Sri Lanka from which it was carried eastwards to become established in Burma and Thailand.

In its Lamaistic form it persists in Tibet. While its reforming influence on Hinduism remains, as a popular religion it is confined to a few areas. The Lamaistic Buddhists of the Himalayan districts of Ladakh and Lahul and of Spiti in the west and of Sikkim and Darjiling in the east, are really overflows southwards from Tibet. Burmese Buddhism is found among tribes on the northeast frontier. 'Indigenous' Buddhism is largely limited to Maharashtra, where once it flourished under the inspiration of teachers from centres like Ajanta and Ellora, and has recently enjoyed some revival among the Hindu 'scheduled caste' Harijan population following Dr B. R. Ambedkar's movement. In central and eastern Maharashtra Buddhists now form between 10 and 16 per cent of the population in eight districts, and they make up 6.5 per cent of the total in the state as a whole, their 3.3 million (1971) accounting for 87 per cent of all India's Buddhists. Ambedkar, himself a Harijan, saw in Buddhism an escape from the discrimination suffered by the scheduled castes at the hands of orthodox Hindus. Between 1951–61 some 3.5 million followed his example and became converts to Buddhism.

The other religion commanding a substantial number of adherents is Jainism, with 2.6 million followers, again mainly in Maharashtra (27 per cent of the total) and the other western states: Rajasthan (20 per cent), Gujarat (17 per cent), Madhya Pradesh (13 per cent) and Karnataka (8 per cent). Jains are predominantly urban dwellers, forming an influential group in banking, money lending and commerce.

Within India today religion is not in general a divisive political factor, except in Punjab. Here adherents to the Sikh religion are Punjabi speakers using the Gurmukhi script in which their holy book is written. Language has been the cultural matrix of the individual Indian states which are held together by a national secular ideal. The constitution provides for freedom of conscience, the rights of minorities to preserve their culture and language, equality before the law and the prohibition of discrimination on grounds of religion, race, caste, sex or place of birth.[1] Yet M. N. Srinivas, writing on the nature of the problem of Indian unity comments: 'The concept of the Unity of India is essentially a religious one'.[2] It is tolerance, a fundamental characteristic of Hinduism, that makes it possible for non-Hindus to live comfortably among them. That such a medley of linguistic groups can find national unity he explains in part by their adherence to a religion that encourages pilgrimage to its holy places, often taking masses of people across linguistic boundaries and thus maintaining their awareness of the cultural diversity within their heritage.

LANGUAGES

Language may be seen as the major sub-division of culture in India. Figure 1.5 is simplified from Schwarzberg's map of the cultural regions of South Asia.[3] If the various genetic groups that migrated into and moved within India are conceived of as

[1] See *India, a Reference Annual*, Ministry of Information and Broadcasting, 1975, p. 19.

[2] M. N. Srinivas, *Caste in Modern India*,

[3] J. E. Schwarzberg, 'Prolegomena to the study of South Asian Regions and Regionalism', in R. I. Crane, (ed.) *Regions and Regionalism in South Asian Studies: an Exploratory Study*, Duke University, Durham N. C., 1967.

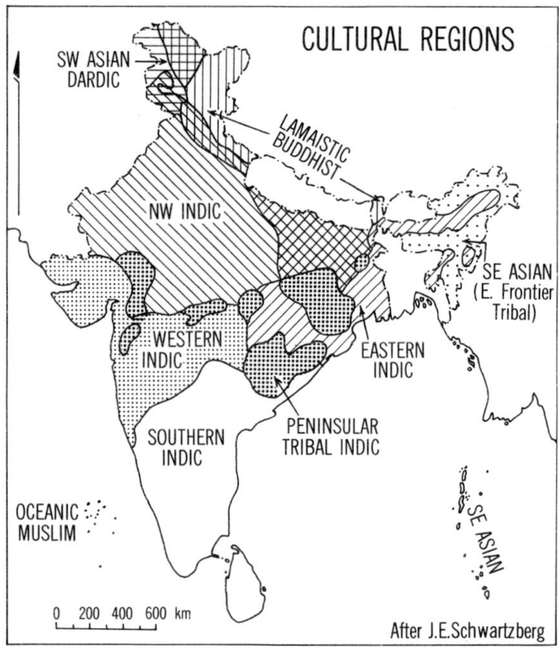

FIG. 1.5

FIG. 1.6

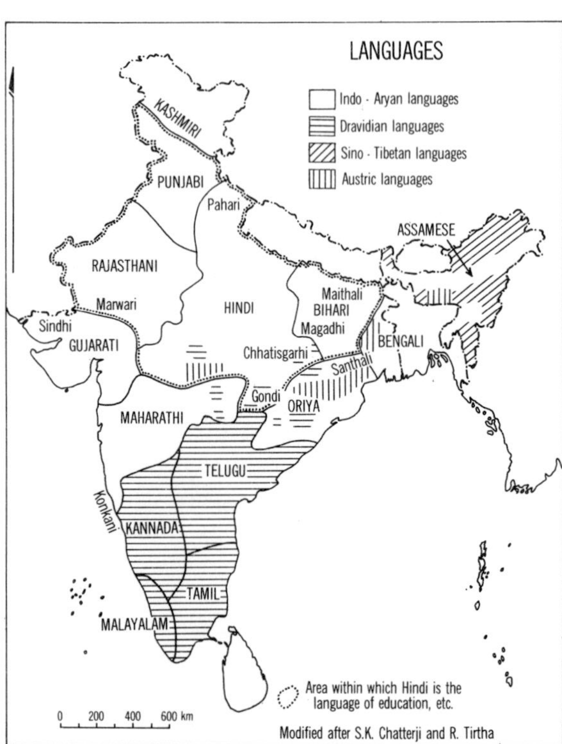

the vehicles of culture, a rough correlation can be made between the basic racial and cultural elements. Figure 1.6 of Indian languages reflects closely the broader cultural regions. Several hundred languages and dialects are spoken in India. The census of 1961 enumerated 1652 'mother-tongues', of which 82 were each spoken by more than 100,000 people in 1971. Numbers speaking the 23 principal languages which cover 96 per cent of the population are shown in Table 1.1 in order of size. Those specified in the constitution are asterisked, and those forming the basis for the differentiation of states are printed in bold type. Education, literature and cultural affairs generally, in languages specified in the constitution are encouraged by the Central Government.

TABLE 1.1
Principal Languages
(Millions and per cent of total population)

	No.	*%*
1. **Hindi***	163	30
2. **Bengali***	45	8
3. **Telugu***	45	8
4. **Marathi***	42	8
5. **Tamil***	38	7
6. Urdu*	29	5
7. **Gujarati***	26	5
8. **Malayalam***	22	4
9. **Kannada***	22	4
10. **Oriya***	20	4
11. **Punjabi***	16	3
12. Bhojpuri (Bihari)	14	2.6
13. **Assamese***	9	1.6
14. Chhatisgarhi	7	1.3
15. Magahi/Magadhi	7	1.3
16. Maithili	6	1.1
17. Marwari	5	0.9
18. Santhali	4	0.7
19. Kashmiri*	2	0.4
20. Rajasthani	2	0.4
21. Sindhi	1.7	0.3
22. Gondi	1.5	0.3
23. Konkani	1.5	0.3

Source: Languages asterisked, from Census of India 1971 Pocket book of Population Statistics, (1972): remainder are from Appendix II of Census of India 1971, Census Centenary Monograph No. 10, Language Handbook on Mother Tongues in Census.

Note: In addition to those asterisked, Sanskrit with 2,212 speakers only is also 'specified' in the Constitution on the grounds of its cultural, mainly religious, significance.

In the 1961 Census Chhatisgarhi was grouped with Hindi, Magahi/Magadhi and Maithili with Bihari, and Marwari with Rajasthani though neither Bihari nor Rajasthani are specific languages, but rather regional groups of closely related tongues.

Four distinct major language families are represented in India, though the vast majority of its languages fall within two of these. The oldest languages are those of the Austro-Asiatic sub-family of the Austric family, spoken by some tribal groups in the northeast peninsular interior and Nicobar Islands. They include Santhali, in the Munda Branch, and Khasi and Nicobarese in the Mon-Khmer Branch spoken by about six million. The second family is that of the Tibeto-Chinese languages used by over three million mainly tribal people of Mongoloid stock in the Himalaya and Northeastern Hills.

The earlier but lesser of the two families spoken by the mass of the population is the Dravidian family of south India. This includes Telugu in one branch, Kannada and the more closely related and to some extent inter-intelligible Tamil and Malayalam in another, with Gondi in an intermediate group. The Indo-Aryan branch of the Aryan sub-family of the Indo-European family, shares a common distant ancestry with most European languages, and covers the major tongues of northern India among which there are varying degrees of inter-intelligibility. Linguists group together in an inner sub-branch, western Hindi, Punjabi, Rajasthani, Gujarati and Pahari, with an 'outer sub-branch' around them, Sindhi to the west, Marathi to the south, eastern Hindi (Bihari), Oriya, Bengali and Assamese to the east. Kashmiri belongs to the Dardic branch of the Aryan sub-family.

As is shown on Figure 1.6, Hindi is the *lingua franca* of much of northern India, losing general currency only at the margins of the Indo-Aryan region, where variations in script (even though traceable back to a common source) tend to exaggerate and perpetuate differences. Urdu spoken by 29 million people does not appear on the map of Indian languages. Only in Jammu and Kashmir is it the official language. Urdu and Hindi have much in common, so that in practical terms they are highly inter-intelligible. Urdu has its own script deriving from Persian, from which it also has its literary and poetic traditions. It was the former language which evolved by interaction between Hindi and Persian, the language of the Moghul rulers and their courts and administration, and consequently is widely disseminated throughout their former empire, along with the Muslim religion. Thus even in south India there are considerable pockets of urban dwellers who regard Urdu as their mother tongue, rather than a Dravidian language: over three million in Andhra, and almost as many in Karnataka, speak Urdu, mainly in areas formerly in the Nizam's State of Hyderabad.

LINGUISTIC STATES

At independence India inherited a complicated political map (Figure 1.7). Apart from the small enclaves of French and Portuguese territory, all of which today retain, as Union Territories, a status separate from the states they adjoin, Britain administered two political systems within the Indian Empire. The 'native' or princely states covered about 42 per cent of the area of present-day India and 22 per cent of the population. They were ruled, with varying degrees of democratic representation, by the Indian princes (with British Resident advisers) under individual treaties made before 1857 when the British Government took over the responsibilities of the East India Company, and

FIG. 1.7

Fig. 1.8

with them most of the existing agreements with the princes. Some princely states, like Mysore were models of sound administration; others were little more than feudal manors in size and level of development. The provinces of British India were ruled directly by British Governors, assisted as time went on, by councils which included representatives of the provincial population. While some of the princely states, like Mysore and Travancore and the Sikh states of the Eastern Punjab, had a fair measure of linguistic homogeneity in their populations, by and large the provinces were not delineated with this factor in mind, though adjustments that were made paid some attention to the principle laid down by a Commission in 1918, that it was administratively desirable to have in a province homogeneity of language, race, religion and economic interest. Long before independence the Congress Party was demanding the reorganization of provinces to recognize linguistic unity.

The first task facing the administrators of newly independent India was to absorb the princely states. Later they had to arbitrate on the fervent and sometimes fanatical demands and counter-demands of linguistic groups seeking self-determination as states within the Indian Union. With the dismemberment of the Dominions of the Nizam of Hyderabad, Andhra Pradesh was the first new state to win recognition in 1953 for the Telugu language (Figure 1.8). The new state was constituted from eight districts of Hyderabad, eleven from north Madras, three from south Madras and portions of the Central Provinces and Orissa. Despite justification on linguistic majority grounds, the Central Government refused to deprive the

Tamil region of their traditional capital Madras, which it may be noted, is most eccentric to the state it now administers. Tamilnadu, Mysore (now re-named Karnataka) and Kerala were shaped respectively for their Tamil, Kannada and Malayalam speakers from the remnants of Madras, the princely states of Travancore-Cochin and Mysore, and parts of the former Bombay Presidency and Hyderabad. Among the educated in the four Dravidian language states, English is the *lingua franca*, and there is resistance to pressures from the North to establish Hindi as the single national language of India. Hindi remains as the official language of the Union but the law provides for the use of English 'for all purposes for which it was being used immediately before 1965 and also for the transaction of business in Parliament.[1]

Some of the states using Indo-Aryan languages followed closely the administrative divisions established by the British. Bihar remained unchanged; Orissa lost some Telugu districts to Andhra Pradesh; West Bengal comprised the districts of partitioned Bengal remaining to India. In Assam and the Northeastern Hills country, there has been progressive reorganization to give hill tribal communities a measure of autonomy as states. Tripura, Manipur, and Nagaland have become fully-fledged states. Meghalaya has been cut out of Assam to form a separate state. Mizoram and Arunachal Pradesh are Union Territories, the latter replacing the old Northeast Frontier Agency. Assam remains with its problem of a substantial minority of Bengali speakers and a high degree of linguistic rivalry between the indigenous Assamese, and the economically, politically and socially more advanced 'foreign' Bengalis who have been colonizing the Assam Valley for generations. UP, the United Provinces, conveniently changed its name to Uttar Pradesh, the 'northern province', without undergoing much-needed political surgery: as a state of over 90 million people it outnumbers many sovereign nations (e.g. all the European states outside USSR) and suffers from administrative cumbersomeness. New states were created, Madhya Pradesh ('Midland Province') to cater for the mainly Hindi areas of the Central Provinces and adjacent princely states of the Central India Agency, and Rajasthan for those of the Rajputana Agency. For a while what remained of the former Province or Presidency of Bombay, together with the Marathi-speaking portions of Hyderabad and the Gujarati-speaking princely states of western India were incorporated in Bombay State. Both linguistic groups sought recognition in States of their own, but the rich multi-lingual city of Bombay remained a stumbling block. A proposal by the States Reorganization Commission that neither should have Bombay, but that it should be centrally administered pleased no one, and after some bloody rioting the present states of Maharashtra (capital Bombay) and Gujarat (capital Ahmadabad, and later Gandhinagar) were established. It was a difficult decision, since Gujarati commercial traditions and interests had spread long since from the Gulf of Cambay ports to Bombay, following the shifts of the focus of East India Company activity on the west Coast from Surat to the new port city of Bombay. The militant Marathas, sharing with the Sikhs the distinction of rising to oust the Moghuls, and subsequently fighting the British and then serving them as soldiers, derived their regional consciousness from the Deccan Plateau rather than from the Coast, but Bombay was a prize too rich to let go.

In the northwest, the state of Jammu and Kashmir is a special case. Apart from the Pakistan-occupied areas beyond the cease-fire line and some border areas occupied by China, India administers as one of its States the whole of this former princely state. Adjacent to it, the small hill state of Himachal Pradesh incorporates some diminutive princely states, and several sub-montane districts of the former Punjab State, inherited at the time of the latter's partition in 1966. The States Reorganization Commission had probably its most knotty problem in the demand by the Punjabi-speaking Sikhs for a separate state. India had received as part of its share of the partitioned British Indian Punjab, the areas of the newly established Punjab State, incorporating the Patiala and East Punjab Union of Sikh princely states (PEPSU). The Commission had resisted, as a danger to Indian unity, the concept of a state based on religious communal homogeneity. The Sikh

[1] India, a Reference Annual 1975, p. 22.

argument that they spoke Punjabi and wrote it in their own peculiar script, won the day despite the obvious fact of religious homogeneity. Haryana became the Hindi-speaking (Hindu majority) state absorbing the plains districts to the east of the reduced Punjab. The brand new capital Chandigarh, designed by le Corbusier to replace the lost Lahore in Punjabi affections, became a centrally administered territory while remaining the capital of both Punjab and Haryana.

Table 1.2 summarizes the political divisions of the Republic of India, with their population and main languages.

TABLE 1.2

Administrative Divisions of India

States	*Population (millions)*	*Main languages*
Uttar Pradesh	88	Hindi, Urdu
Bihar	56	Hindi, Bihari
Maharashtra	50	Marathi
Andhra Pradesh	44	Telugu
West Bengal	44	Bengali
Madhya Pradesh	41	Hindi, Gondi, etc.
Tamilnadu	41	Tamil
Karnataka	29	Kannada
Gujarat	27	Gujarati
Rajasthan	26	Rajasthani, Hindi
Orissa	22	Oriya
Kerala	21	Malayalam
Assam	15	Assamese, Bengali
Punjab	14	Punjabi
Haryana	10	Hindi
Jammu & Kashmir	5	Kashmiri
Himachal Pradesh	3	Hindi, Pahari
Tripura	1.6	Bengali, Tripuri, Manipuri
Manipur	1.1	Manipuri, Bengali
Meghalaya	1.0	Khasi, Jaintia, Garo
Nagaland	0.5	Various tribal

Union territories	*Population (thousands)*	
Delhi	4,066	Hindi, Urdu, Punjabi
Goa, Daman, Diu	858	Marathi, Kannada
Pondicherry	472	Tamil
Arunachal Pradesh	468	Various tribal
Mizoram	332	Various tribal
Chandigarh	257	Punjabi, Hindi
Andaman & Nicobar Islands	115	Andamanese, Nicobarese
Dadra & Nagar Haveli	74	Gujarati, Marathi
Lakshadweep	32	Malayalam

Note: Sikkim with a population of about 230,000 was incorporated as the twenty-second state of the Union in 1975.

GOVERNMENT

As a Union of States India is governed by the President elected by an electoral college of the Houses of Parliament of the Central Government and the Legislative Assemblies of the states. The President is advised by a Council of Ministers, led by the Prime Minister, who are responsible to the House of the People, the Lok Sabha, which is elected by universal adult franchise, its membership being approximately proportionate to the population of the states. There is an Upper House, the Rajya Sabha or Council of the States, which has a 'rotating' membership mostly elected by the members of the State Legislative Assembly of each state, which body is directly elected by the people. In turn each state has a Legislative Council composed partly of elected members of the Assembly and partly of non-members representative of local government, educational and cultural interests. The Lok Sabha holds final control of money matters, and may in times of emergency intervene in areas normally reserved to the states.

Most revenue is collected by the Centre which distributes funds to the states, which, within the plans approved by the Centre, are responsible for executing schemes for development and for the day-to-day running of their administrations. The Centre is directly responsible for administering the Union Territories in most of which there are Legislative Assemblies with powers, however, less wide than those of the State Legislatures.

India's system of government is, then, a federal one, similar in many respects to that of Canada or Australia. The states are very dependent on the Centre and tend to be dominated by it. Although subjects such as agriculture, education, co-operatives, industry and health are state responsibilities under the constitution, the policies the states should adopt are dictated by the Centre which holds the purse strings. The dominance of a single party at the Centre from independence to 1977 is seen as contributory to this situation in which the Planning Commission has become very powerful and 'ubiquitous' in its role.[1]

The strength of the system lies in its broadly democratic basis. Among its weaknesses is the risk that states may receive development finance for

[1] W. H. Morris-Jones, in M. Venkatarangaiya and M. Shiviah (Eds), *Indian Federalism*, New Delhi, 1976.

political reasons rather than to meet purely economic and social ends, and the real difficulty of compelling a reluctant state legislature which probably draws its power from the landed and wealthier classes, effectively to implement legislation such as land reforms which strike at their own power base.

Intermediate between the Centre and the states are five Zonal Councils, Northern, Eastern, Western, Southern and Northeastern, whose function is to discuss matters of common interest among the states and Union Territories within the zone. The Northeastern Council covers Assam, and the smaller states of Manipur, Meghalaya, Nagaland and Tripura, plus the Union Territories of Arunachal Pradesh and Mizoram. These are grouped together for the co-ordination and unification (where appropriate) of planning. With these responsibilities and powers of review of security measures within the zone, the Northeast Council has the character of a decentralized executive body of the Centre.

Within the states there is generally 'grass-roots' democratic government exercised by elected local bodies. Village assemblies or Gram Sabhas elect Panchayats which have wide responsibilities for the economic and social welfare of the community. They detive funds from house and land taxes, levies on markets and fairs, sales taxes, etc. While broadly democratic they are required to ensure that the scheduled caste and tribal population of the village are directly represented, and also the women. A group of Panchayats constitutes a Block and above this is the District, with democratic representative committees at each level. Members of State Civil Services provides full-time expertise and executive responsibility.

Urban areas are administered by Corporations, Municipal Committees or Councils, depending on their size, and these embody principles similar to those underlying Panchayat Raj or rule.

PROBLEMS OF UNITY IN DIVERSITY

The creation of linguistic states has met the demand for regional identity but carries with it the potential for disunity, since it is a move possibly counter to the development of a stronger sense of national unity. States jealous of their rights within the Union, especially the non-Hindi speaking states, tend to become inward-looking and may unwittingly inhibit intercourse between states by insisting on the use of the state language in high schools and universities. Barriers are thus erected to the free flow of educated job-seekers between states. Within states, particularly those with substantial tribal populations, such as Madhya Pradesh, Orissa and Gujarat, the tribal people are placed at some disadvantage when the state insists on its own language, doubly so when that is other than Hindi. An aspiring tribal Gond in Maharashtra needs to be tri-lingual or even quadra-lingual to reach the highest levels in the Union; he must have, in addition to his mother tongue, his state language Marathi, the national language Hindi and (if he goes far in education at tertiary level) English. Variation of scripts between states makes travel difficult; the Hindi-speaking literate from Haryana is faced with sign posts in Gurmukhi as he crosses the border into Punjab, and similar problems face the inter-state traveller arriving in Maharashtra from Karnataka.

The demands of linguistic majority groups for recognition have been met largely by the creation of the 'linguistic' states, but in a country of so many languages it is impossible to cater for everybody without excessive fragmentation of the body politic. Despite the widespread occurrence of bilingualism, large populations, of several states cannot speak the official language of their own state. The problem reaches its largest dimension in Madhya Pradesh which has a great number of tribal groups constituting 20 per cent of the population. The 1961 Census enumerated not only the mother-tongue but the second language where spoken, and from the tables it is possible to make a rough estimate of how many people in each state were unable to speak its official language (or a language close enough to it to be regarded as inter-intelligible for practical purposes.) In Madhya Pradesh almost a quarter of the people were in this situation, in Karnataka 21 per cent, Maharashtra 16 per cent, West Bengal 14 per cent and Orissa 11 per cent. Most but not all of these represent tribal groups in the areas so shown in Figure 1.5. In Maharashtra and West Bengal the industrial conurbations of Bombay and Calcutta have of course attracted numbers of non-Marathi and

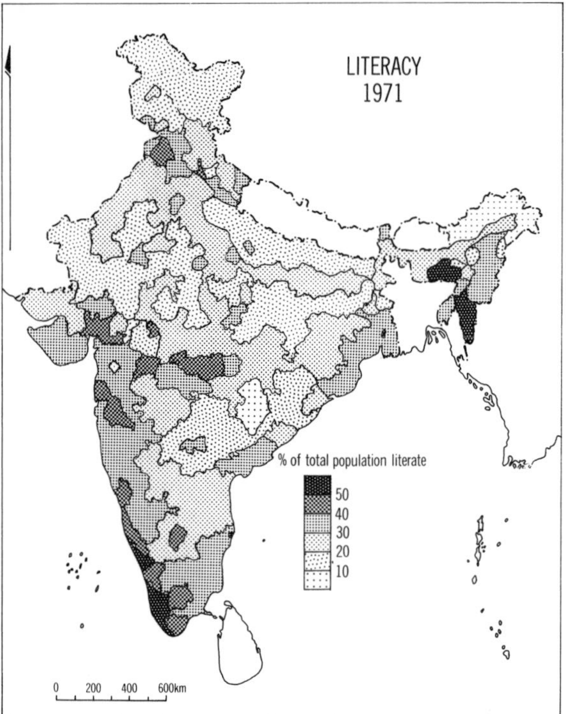

Fig. 1.9

non-Bengali speakers respectively who may well not yet claim to understand the language of their state of adoption. In the remaining states of the Peninsula the proportion of 'non-speakers' runs from Andhra Pradesh with 8 per cent to Tamilnadu with seven, Kerala with four, Gujarat six and Rajasthan 5 per cent. Only in the states of the Indo-Gangetic plain do the figures fall to negligible levels: 1.4 per cent in UP, 0.7 in Bihar and 0.2 in Punjab-Haryana, reflecting at once the relative homogeneity and stability of the populations in these Hindi-Punjabi core areas. The polyglot character of many large cities is illustrated by the cinemas of Bangalore which advertise films in as many as six languages (see Figure 1.6).

A quite different dimension of language which is very important in its implications for modernization and social change, is literacy. Of the total population, 29 per cent were recorded as literate in 1971: 39 per cent of the males were literate and 19 per cent of the females. Allowing for a quarter of the total population being under ten years of age (below which literacy is of limited immediate impact) the literacy rate is rather better than the figures suggest at first sight, and would be 39 per cent of the population ten years old and over. Figure 1.9 shows the percentage of literacy by districts. Apart from the major urban areas like Bombay, Calcutta, Madras and Delhi, the highest rates are found in Kerala, which has 60 per cent literate overall (equivalent to 80 per cent of the population aged 10 or more). That there may be a strong positive correlation between literacy and adherence to Christianity (implying missionary educational activity) is suggested by a comparison of Figures 1.4 and 1.9. However it may well be argued that there is little general correlation between literacy and the level of economic advancement. A glance at Figure 2.5 on page 34, showing the percentage of the population living below the poverty line, finds Kerala, Tamilnadu and Orissa among the poorest states.

The highest levels of literacy and with it awareness of the political and economic affairs of the nation may be gauged from the circulation of newspapers and periodicals which totalled 25.6 million in 1970. Table 1.3 below shows the dominance of English over Hindi publications, and the considerable strength of some but not all of the regional languages.

Table 1.3

Circulation of papers and periodicals (thousands)

English	6,270
Hindi	5,117
Tamil	2,918
Malayalam	2,046
Gujarati	1,744
Marathi	1,705
Urdu	1,492
Bengali	1,286
Telugu	937
Kannada	705
Punjabi	293
Oriya	193
Sindhi	119
Assamese	95
Sanskrit	11

The figures approximately parallel literacy rates, understandably, with the Hindi papers having to serve the literate of several northern states.

It is generally accepted that elementary education is lagging far behind the need, especially in rural areas, and the low level of literacy in the densely populated plains of UP and Bihar reflects badly on the administrations of these the most populous states of the union. A new means to reach the masses and so to outflank in a sense the slow processes of formal education, is the SITE project (Satellite Instructional Television Experiment) by which a satellite stationed over India has been relaying educational programmes direct to villages equipped with dish receiving aerials and TV sets for communal use. The scheme has great potential for communicating directly to the illiterate, most backward and sometimes depressed sections of the isolated rural community their rights as citizens and the aspirations of their political leaders on their behalf.

SOCIAL JUSTICE AND THE BACKWARD CLASSES

Of recent years the five-year plans have stressed as objectives the dissemination throughout the nation of social justice, and the improvements of the lot of the 'backward classes', a term now used to include the scheduled castes (the 'Untouchables' or Harijans), the scheduled and other tribes, and others in the population constituting the lowest 20–30 per cent in economic terms. There are 80 million in the scheduled castes (almost 15 per cent of the total population) and 38 million (almost 7 per cent) in scheduled tribes (see Figures 1.10, 1.11).

The scheduled castes and tribes are those so determined for each state, or even for a particular district or tahsil within a district, by the President acting under Articles 341 and 342 of the constitution. A group scheduled in one area may be unscheduled in another. Membership of a scheduled caste or tribe entitles a person to certain privileges, varying from state to state, aimed at reducing the disabilities with respect to education and employment that he may previously have suffered.

The 1961 Census listed for Orissa 94 castes and 62 tribes in the schedule, and for Rajasthan 114 and 28 respectively. Thus it will be appreciated that the terms Harijan or Adi-Dravida for a scheduled caste member, or Adivasi for a scheduled tribesman are gross generalizations for a very complex reality.

Caste is probably the strongest element in the Hindu way of life, and despite some weakening of its former rigidity and strength, particularly in the cities, it still permeates rural society, and inhibits its weaker, lower caste, members from asserting their constitutional rights and raising their socio-economic status. Caste is basically a system of functional stratification of the society maintained

FIG. 1.10

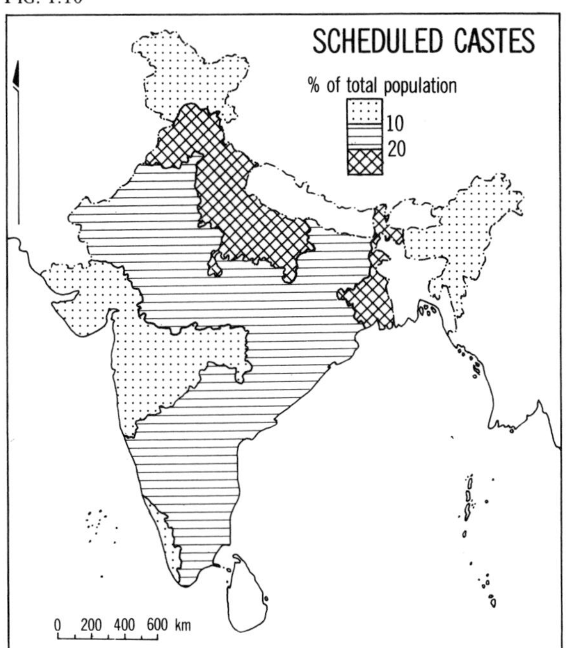

FIG. 1.11

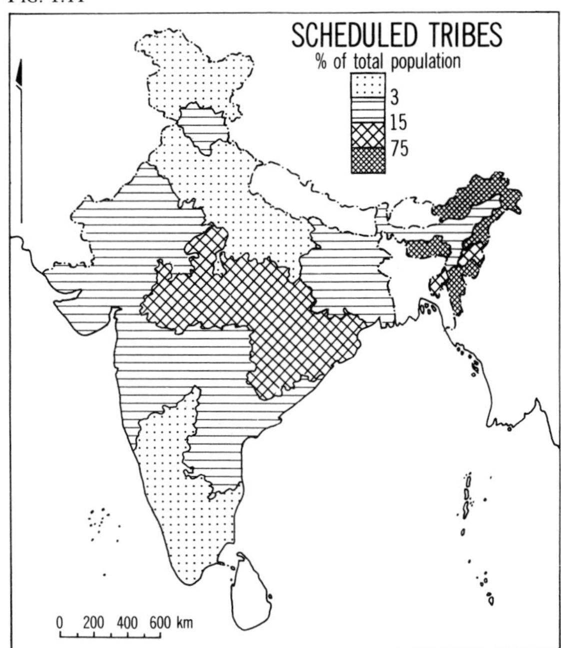

by religious sanctions. It seems to have its origins in the domination of tribal populations by immigrant groups, and so had some genetic basis, though despite theoretical prohibitions on inter-caste marriage, the racial identity of caste or tribe has long since disappeared.

There are basically three groups of castes. At the apex of the system are the Brahmins, the priestly caste of the Hindu religion, themselves divided into three main exogamous sub-castes: the highest are scholars of the Hindu religious books, while ranking below them are the temple priests and the priests who perform religious rites for the non-Brahmins. In practice Brahmins may be land owners, or belong to a variety of professions. As a general rule they are well-educated and seldom poor. The second and largest group are the non-Brahmin caste Hindus, including landowning castes, cultivators, traders, moneylenders, artisans like potters, goldsmiths and carpenters, and castes rendering services to Brahmins and caste non-Brahmins, such as barbers and washermen. Below these are the group of untouchable castes, the Harijans, who nonetheless live in association with the higher caste groups as labourers and menials, sweepers, disposers of dead animals, human excreta and so forth. They were formerly (and in practice still sometimes feel themselves) debarred from temples and from streets occupied by Brahmins. Under the village *jajmani* system the rights, responsibilities and obligations of each caste group towards the others are clearly established in practice by tradition, and caste committees may extract penalties from those who fail to observe the rules.

The tribal Adivasis have generally remained outside the congeries of castes described above, but when they do come into socio-economic association it is at a very low rank in the hierarchy. Although caste is said to exist among Muslim and even Christian communities, the constitution recognizes only Hindu and Sikh castes.

Caste is perhaps best understood by seeing it as simultaneously a social unit and a system. As a social unit, Atal[1] sees its basic attribute as endogamy (marriage restricted to within the caste), other common attributes being membership by heredity, a common occupation, and regulation of the behaviour of its members by a caste panchayat. Often a person's caste may be identifiable in his name, and sometimes in the style or detail of his dress or a superficial design in paste applied to the forehead. As a system, caste comprehends a plurality of interacting endogamous groups, hierarchical in character, and generally representing a traditional division of the labour functions of the rural community.

Another authority sums it up thus: 'Each caste is a complete society within a society, a kingdom within a kingdom. A caste has its own gods, its own temples, its council which regulates social behaviour, its hereditary occupation and status, its own customs about food, dress and marriage.[2] The enormous social injustice of caste, in the eyes of all but the most orthodox high caste Hindu, is its rejection of the Harijans from common social intercourse and their relegation, in perpetuity, to the lowliest tasks and a condition of total subordination. Following, but at a snail's pace, the inspired admonitions of Mahatma Gandhi who spent his life trying to awaken the conscience of the Hindu community, legislators have banned 'untouchability' and each successive five year plan makes possible some improvement in the outcaste's lot.

Although the scheduled castes are now equal to other citizens in the sight of the law, it is not surprising that the attitudes inculcated over many centuries of repression and indignity cannot be erased with the stroke of a legislator's pen. It will take at least another generation before the backward classes can begin to stand on their own economic and social feet. Meanwhile much is being done to help them. The first stage in the eradication of their disabilities is taking place with the diminution of the strictly caste factor in their situation; for example, places are reserved for them in colleges and the government service. Socio-economic status as understood in western countries is beginning to replace caste stratification, although social mobility within the system will be extremely sluggish while ingrained habits and deferential attitudes rooted in caste persist in the community.

[1] Yogesh Atal, *The Changing Frontier of Caste*', New Delhi, Natural Publishing House, 1968.

[2] K. W. Kapp, *Hindu Culture, Economic Development and Economic Planning in India*, Bombay, Asia Publishing House, 1963.

The impact of caste is still discernible in most rural areas. The sketch maps showing the layouts of four villages in widely separated parts of India (Figure 1.12) have been much simplified and standardized from originals in the 1961 census. They demonstrate some common features of caste segregation. Occupational terms have been substituted for the regionally variable caste names, so that several castes may be included under the description 'agricultural'.

Local segregation of castes within a village is thus common. Often the Harijans are excluded from the main street and relegated to living outside the main village, commonly in much inferior dwellings of thatch and matting. Although in some states improved housing is being built for Harijans it is located still away from the rest of the community. In other areas any attempt on the part of Harijans to improve their lot is frowned upon, and one reads of cases of caste Hindus punishing

FIG. 1.12 Caste in four villages (Thakar is a Brahmin sub-caste). After the *Census of India 1961:* Part iv – A (iii).

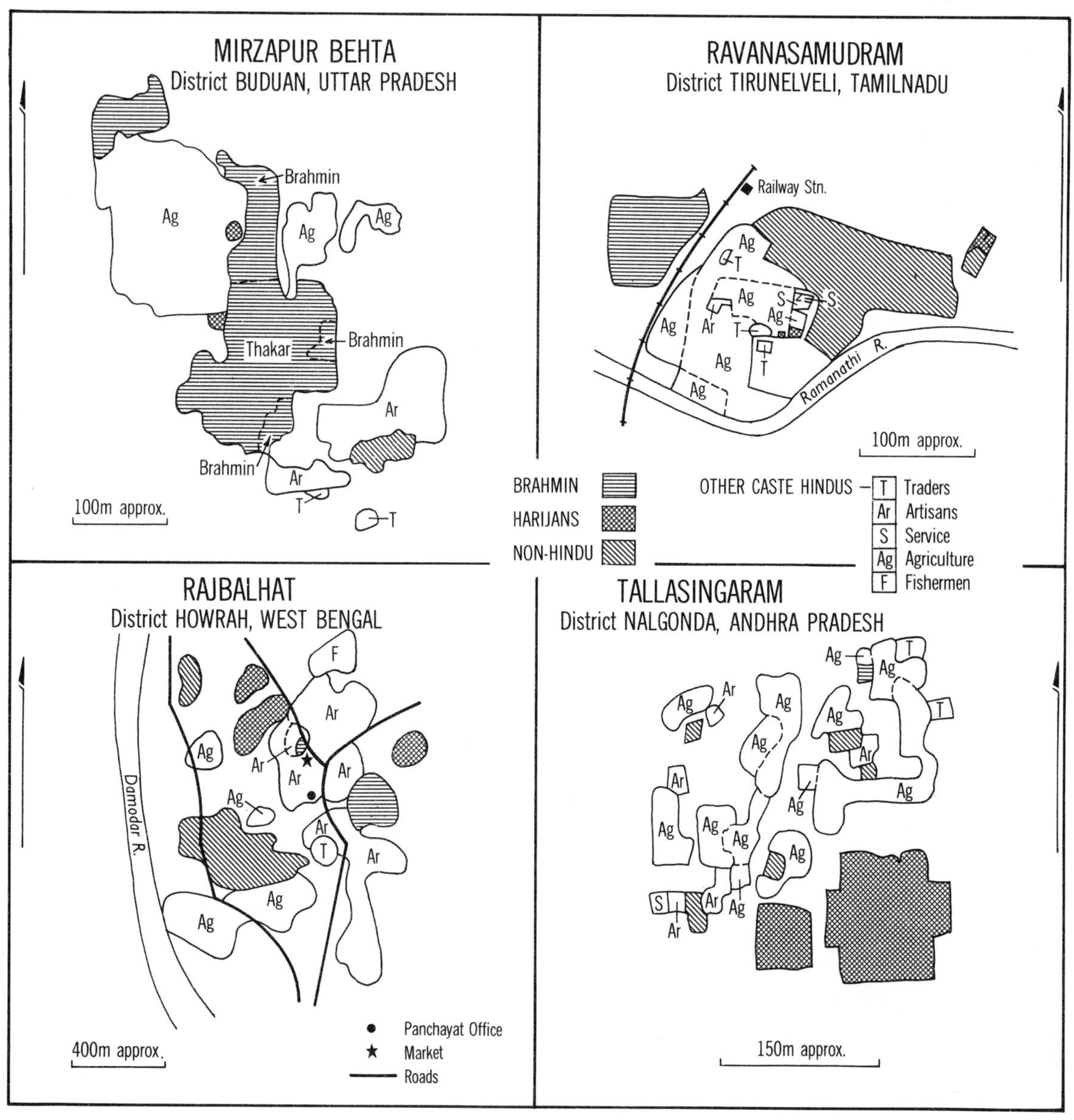

physically, or damaging the property of, a Harijan who exceeded the traditional limits on his behaviour; for example, by using a caste group's well, or by building himself a better house. Such happenings are now reported in the press in the spirit of a warning to the caste Hindus that times are changing, and in many cases legal action is taken to punish such oppression. In towns and cities extreme physical segregation is impracticable, for while the caste system maintains any semblance of its basis in the division of labour, the services of barbers, washermen, sweepers, gardeners, and so forth are required to be available close to the more privileged.

In the traditional village, now fast disappearing, the caste system provided a full range of crafts and services to the land owners and to each other for grain paid at harvest time or for mutual services rendered. As in Medieval Europe obligations were honoured, and the wealthy accepted their responsibilities. Now increasingly the labourer and specialist is paid a money wage or fee, and the ties of tradition are weakening. An insidious aspect of caste which will take a long time to eradicate, however, is the enmity, or at least the antipathy, that sometimes pervades the relationships between one caste Hindu and another, let alone between caste Hindu and Harijan, and which makes difficult the kind of co-operation needed for mutual benefit in agriculture; e.g. combining to share a pump, or allowing a neighbour to take an irrigation ditch across a field that separates one of his fields from his source of water.

A recent study in Rajasthan[1] describes how land reforms have enabled some former tenants to become rich and start moneylending businesses, and how former 'polluting' low castes have changed occupation and improved their position in the caste hierarchy. Despite these changes, the relative power and status of groups within the community have changed little, but caste status as such is being replaced by socio-economic status deriving from the superior education and economic enterprise that produce wealth.

Similarly in the city traditional relationships based on caste are weakening and the kind of socio-economic class distinctions common in western countries are beginning to appear. The change from caste prejudice to nepotism in business appointments may be imperceptible, and a universal meritocracy remains a distant ideal, but a considerable amount of social modernization is taking place.

At the present time the reduction of the disabilities of the Harijans and scheduled tribes seems to be encouraging their identification as different from the rest of the community rather than removing their present social distinctiveness. At least until 1980 they have special representation in the Lok Sabha and state legislatures. The central and state public services reserve a proportion of posts for scheduled castes and tribes, and carry this principle into promotion, making it easier for such officers to gain advancement.

The backward situation of the tribal populations in India is in part due to their long identification by Hindus as outside the caste system proper, and in

[1] K. L. Sharma, *The Changing Rural Stratification System*, Bangalore, 1976.

5 Houses to resettle Harijans (outcasts) on the fringe of a Tamilnadu town, built by the State Government. Formerly such mainly landless labourers would have lived in poor thatched huts outside the village. Their segregation persists but in better dwellings.

part to their location in inaccessible areas such as the Vindhyan and Orissa Hills and the forests of the Bastar Plateau. With the scheduled tribes the problem is rather to accelerate their economic progress lest they fall far behind the community at large, while protecting them from exploitation by the economically more powerful and less scrupulous. The education and economic development of the tribal peoples is being undertaken more energetically under the Fifth Plan than ever before. The case of the Gond Block at Utnur in Adilabad District in the northernmost corner of Andhra Pradesh illustrates some of the processes and problems of this kind of development.

Utnur Tribal Development Block

The block comprises 169 villages in the east of Adilabad District. A little over half of the 94,000 population belong to scheduled tribes, mainly Gonds, but five other scheduled tribes and two 'denotified' tribes are represented. Denotified tribes are not officially recognized as tribes in this area, but under the legislation to assist backward classes generally, the old distinctions based on tribal affiliation are weakening. Until recently the condition of all these people and their agriculture was backward – agriculture was rudimentary and at the subsistence level, the community being forced into collecting forest products, or into labouring during periods of seasonal scarcity. Villages are still administered for religious, social and petty legal purposes by hereditary headmen, patels, assisted by hereditary dewaris. Under the new panchayat raj, villagers elect the patel to their panchayat committee.

The development being undertaken covers many aspects of life and economy. Agriculture, the mainstay of the economy, is being raised to more efficient levels by instruction and on-site demonstration and supervision by the hard-pressed Block Development Officer and his staff. New strains of jowar, maize and cotton requiring fertilizer and pest control are being introduced, and diesel pumps to raise water from the streams to irrigate the roughly levelled fields have been made available. A great deal is done free at first, but farmers are quickly introduced to the meaning and operation of credit from the bank. Many of the farms are of 'marginal' size, and are grouped into informal co-operatives for the purpose of sharing pumps and so on. Cattle are being improved through veterinary dispensaries and breeding centres.

Both producer and consumer co-operatives are being established and assisted, and alternative occupations to farming are being encouraged through a training scheme for carpenters, metal workers, weavers, potters and cane furniture makers. More formal education is being fostered through primary schools and through a high school in Utnur to which selected boys and girls from outlying areas can go by boarding in hostels built for them. Midday meals are provided in primary schools as an incentive to parents to let their children attend. Medical services are rather more rudimentary, though Utnur has a small 'bush' hospital, and there are four primary health subcentres in the block.

At the very least, a start has been made in a variety of directions. One can only admire the enthusiasm and hard work demanded of the small staff in order to catalyse into action a population easy-going and lethargic in their traditional poverty.

6 Brickmaking in Kerala: after sun-drying, the bricks are fired using timber fuel. The clay for making bricks is dug from the paddy fields.

CHAPTER TWO

THE PEOPLE AND THE ECONOMY

SUMMARY

India already with 600 million people appears poised on the brink of demographic change. While mortality rates have been declining over many decades under the impact of modernization in public health and protective medicine, the maintenance of a very high birth rate has resulted in a rise in the rate of population growth from one census to the next. After a decade or so of vigorous propaganda it seems that family planning is beginning to influence the population equation. It is essential for the success of national economic planning, for food self-sufficiency and for better standards of living that this should come about as soon as possible.

Poverty is endemic throughout India, and with it both qualitative and quantitative deficiencies in the diet. Adequate food properly distributed throughout the society is an essential prerequisite to creating a population physically and mentally energetic enough to tackle the problems of development. At the national level there has been since independence a continuous struggle to grow enough food to meet demand and so to become independent of food imports. In years of drought imports have exceeded 10 million tonnes; in good years less than half a million tonnes has been needed, and current hopes are that 1975–76 marked the beginning of an era in which the government controls sufficient stocks of grain to meet year-to-year fluctuations and so keep prices stable and imports to a minimum.

At independence India was severely handicapped by the poorly integrated 'colonial' structure of its economy. It had to set about replanning the economy. The country's substantial physical and human resources had to be developed in the fashion best suited to India's needs: self-sufficiency in food; better standards of living for the masses through a higher level of economic activity; the capacity to earn foreign exchange through exports which should contain as large an input of Indian labour as possible. The several five-year plans mark the progress in the national economic strategy towards these goals.

As measured by per capita gross national product and by its average growth rate, India is still near the bottom of the table of the world's large nations despite the enormous efforts that have been made. Population growth has devoured too much of the increase in resources and so poverty continues to stalk the land. Some optimism can be gleaned in the wide variation in per capita income from state to state which suggests that vigorous agricultural and industrial enterprise *can* succeed. Over time the balance of economic activity has been shifting away from the primary, mainly agricultural sector towards secondary industry, particularly manufacturing, and the tertiary sector. This is in accordance with the planners' hopes, but many more jobs need to be created in the industrial sector if it is ever to reduce the inevitable surplus of labour in agriculture. As yet women make up only 17 per cent of the total workforce. It is the effective harnessing of India's huge resources of human energy and potential skills that poses the greatest challenge to the government and its economic planners.

The pattern of export trade has been changing, if slowly, to give more emphasis to processed and manufactured commodities and goods. In imports, the position of foodstuffs long at the head of the list has been taken by petroleum since the worldwide energy crisis precipitated when the oil-producers put up their prices. Despite this threat to India's expectations that external trade might be brought into balance, India has been able to convert a trade deficit of Rs 12,160 in 1975–76 to a surplus of Rs 720 million in 1976–77.

THE NUMBERS OF THE PEOPLE

The 1971 census showed 547.9 million people in India, an increase of 24.8 per cent over the 1961 total, and over 51 per cent or 186.8 million more than in 1951, the first census following independence. By the end of 1975 the population had passed 600 million, and was heading towards 700 million by some time in the 1980s. At the rate of increase experienced during the inter-censal decade 1961–71, the figure would be reached by 1982. The five-year planners take a more hopeful view of the possibilities for family planning becoming effective sooner rather than later, and estimate that 700 million will be reached in 1986. Ten years is a short time in the context of planning an economy which has to be able to feed this number and provide jobs for its workforce. Figure 2.1 summarizes the vital demographic statistics.

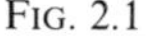

In terms of the theory of the demographic transition the first turning point in India's population history came after World War I. Up to that time India had experienced high birth rates and equally high death rates; the former fairly constant, the latter fluctuating with the incidence of epidemic disease, with or without accompanying famine. The total population increased only slowly, some decades registering near static or even slightly falling numbers. From the 1920s, public health measures including mass-inoculation against smallpox and the increasing application of preventive and curative medicine, had a dramatic impact on the death rate, which as the graph shows, plummeted through the inter-war years and continued falling after independence. The immediate effect of this is vividly demonstrated in the lengthening of the life-span. In 1921 an Indian could expect to live to be 20 (on average); by 1941 this expectation at birth had risen to 32, which remained the span at the time of independence. Subsequently the increase has continued, to 41 by 1961 and 47 by 1971. The Draft Fifth Five Year Plan projects the increase to 54 by 1978 and 56 by 1983. All this is due to reducing both infant and adult mortality.

Death rates, then, can be expected to continue to fall, but at a diminishing rate, to reach an annual rate of perhaps 10 per thousand in the middle 1980s and thereafter inevitably to rise a little as the population as a whole begins to have a larger proportion of ageing people.

The birth rate on the other hand has not yet changed appreciably. It had fallen from its traditional levels in the high 40s to the low 40s per thousand by about the time of independence. Effectively it had remained static since then, at between 40 and 42 per thousand. Apparent falls

FIG. 2.1

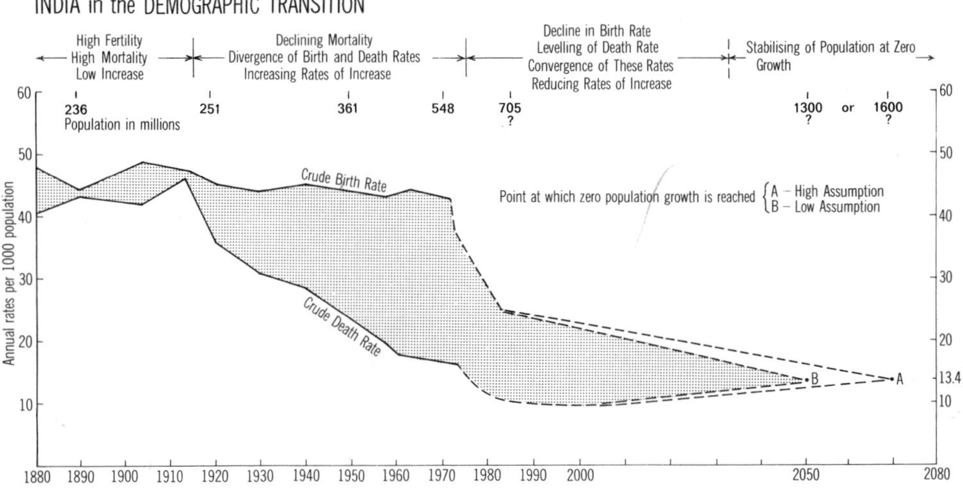

7 This auto rickshaw in Madras, carries family planning sign as an extra 'Stop' signal! The auto-rickshaw was probably made in Pune, Maharashtra. A Hindu roadside shrine behind the cyclist.

in the past have been reflections of the larger total population (due to falling death rates) rather than to any real change in reproductive habits. The planners see some glimmerings of change in the sample surveys of 1972 which gave an overall rate of 36.6, compounded of a rural rate of 38.4 and an urban rate of 30.5. Grasping at these straws, they are bold enough to forecast a continuing downward trend to less than 30 by 1978 and about 25 by 1983. It is true that the changes in attitudes to family planning, and its effective practice, can come about very rapidly indeed. The question is whether this point has now been reached in a sufficient proportion of the Indian population for the strategic planners to be justified in their optimism. If they are right, India may have arrived at the most significant turning point in the course of the demographic transition, where after a period in which the death and birth rates diverge, with alarming consequences for the total number of the people – the population explosion in fact – these trend lines begin to converge, so that each year the rate of natural increase in the population diminishes. It is greatly to be hoped that this is indeed the case, for otherwise the planners' hopes of modest development within the present five-year plan will certainly be frustrated, and their projected increases in production will go, as so often in the past, merely to feed the new mouths instead of bringing a better standard of living to a population in control of its numbers. There can be little doubt that most of the people know of the possibility of controlling conception. There is a constant flow of propaganda to limit the family to two, and to seek sterilization thereafter, for which opportunities are provided by travelling surgical teams in the rural areas. The inverted red triangle which is the family planning symbol is seen widely; in the streets of Madras the three-wheeled auto-rickshaws often carry the red triangle and its 'ideal family' of two parents with two children vividly depicted below their red rear stop light!

Ultimately, however, it is likely that parents and not government will decide the issue. India is still a very long way from being a welfare state. A man looks to his family and particularly his sons as his only prospect of security in old age or ill health. There is no old-age pension, not even the 'work house' for the aged destitute. For the lowest labouring classes children are potential bread-winners even if for eight or nine years they are additional mouths to be fed. To their parents the case for family planning cannot be argued in the unanswerable logic that convinces politicians. There is a high probability that some of their children will die before becoming economically useful, and their concern to ensure there will be sons to maintain them justifies their large families. While this social pattern persists, and until the health and survival of the children of the poor can be assured, the authoritarian imposition of family limitation might be seen by them at least, as a grievous injustice. The problem is complex and hardly susceptible to armchair academic solution.

India's demographic experience is summarized in the population pyramid (in Figure 2.2a). It is a broad-based pyramid characteristic of the less developed countries (LDCs). In the highly developed countries (HDCs) where infant mortality rates are low and life expectancy is high there is little tapering in the pyramid until middle age, where mortality begins to thin out the age groups. The age-sex pyramid for Sweden (Figure 2.2b) is characteristic of a mature HDC.

The proportion of couples in India using family planning methods has been estimated as 14 per cent, but it varies widely between states. Maharashtra claiming 23 per cent, Kerala and Punjab 19 per cent, Tamilnadu 18 per cent, Gujarat and Haryana 17 per cent and Orissa, are all above average performers; below the line are Madhya Pradesh with 12 per cent, Karnataka and West Bengal 11 per cent, Himachal Pradesh, Assam and Jammu and Kashmir 8 per cent, with those frequent tail-enders, Uttar Pradesh and Bihar on 7 per cent. For some states sheer inaccessibility may explain the position, but this can hardly be claimed for the last two. There the sheer magnitude of the task of informing and assisting a huge population of village-dwellers is formidable indeed. The problem in the more urbanized states is less difficult: it is significant that four of the six states at the head of the table for family planning also lead the table of per capita income (Table 2.8). This is the kind of correlation the government must hope will stimulate the laggards. The relative size of the states' population may be checked in Table 1.2 on page 12 and their levels of urbanization in Figure 12.2 on page 165, where the distribution of population is more fully examined.

Family planning, particularly by such drastic measures as sterilization, tends to be undertaken too late in the reproductive history of a couple to be effective in rapidly reducing the rate of increase: sterilization is accepted after 4.5 children on average, IUCD (intra-uterine contraceptive device) after 3.8.[1] Over the ten years to 1976, 17 million sterilizations have been performed, 5.7 million IUD have been inserted, and about 2.5 million couples are protected by conventional contraceptives. One authority estimates that it will be 2026 AD before a net reproductive rate of unity can be achieved through at least 60 per cent of couples being effectively protected against conception.

[1] J. P. Ambannavar, *Second India Studies: Population*, New Delhi, South Asia Books, 1976.

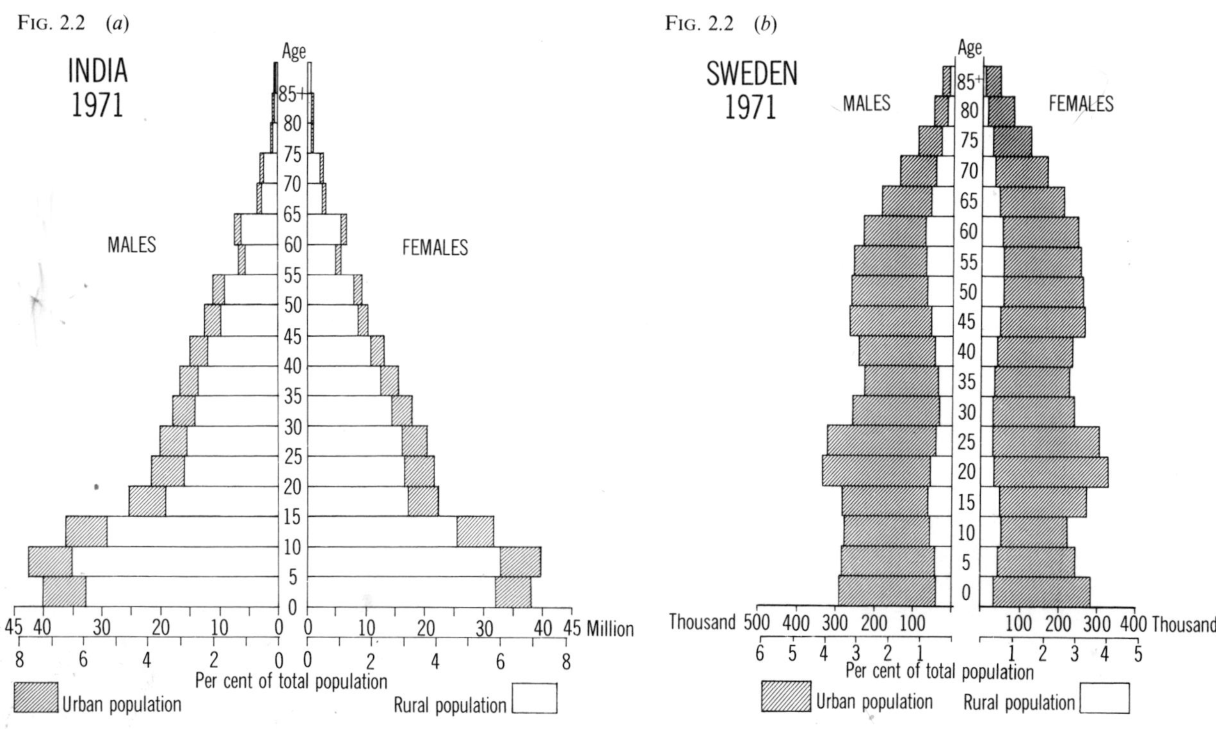

FIG. 2.2 (*a*)

FIG. 2.2 (*b*)

In its determination to tackle the problem the central government has increased the marriageable age from 15 to 18 for women and 18 to 21 for men. Positive incentives are offered to encourage sterilization. In the first half of 1976 almost one and a quarter million people were sterilized. It is estimated that in the first six months of 1976, 1.5 million sterilizations were carried out.

The 'green revolution' in agriculture, discussed in Chapter Six, gives India a brief respite in which to bring about effective population control. The ultimate objective must be to reach a low fertility stage of the demographic transition, with birth and death rates converging to meet at a level of 13.4 per thousand. United Nations demographers calculate that this level can maintain zero population growth, in a population with a life expectancy of near 75 years and a family size averaging 2.08 children per woman.[1]

In such a population the dependency ratio would be 58; or in other words, 100 people aged 15–64 would support 58 persons, aged 14 years and less, or over 65. In 1973 the dependency ratio in India was estimated as 77, boosted principally by some 42 per cent of the population being under 15, and although there are many economically active children and old people in the community it would be better for the country's long-term future if all that quarter of the total population aged 5–14 were at school. Dependency ratios in developed countries lie commonly in the range 58 (northern and western Europe) to 61 (Australia) and 62 (North America). The achievement of zero population growth is still a long way off, realistically seen by Indian experts as happening a century hence, between 2071–81, by which time India's population could have stabilized at around 1600 million, three times the present total. The UN demographers, perhaps unaware at the time of the hopeful signs of a downward turn in the birth rate, expected the population to *quadruple* before it stabilized.

There is hope that the zero growth point will be reached sooner than one hundred years hence, for every year less of continuing increase will reduce the size of the ultimate problem. The year 2071 is given as a 'high' assumption. If changes now in train were to take place very rapidly, zero growth might be reached by about 2051, when the total could be of the order of 1300 millions. These figures are of course to a large degree speculative, but their general tenor is not to be denied. The only factors that could radically change the direction and magnitude of current demographic trends are those comprehended in the phrase 'Malthusian checks' – war, pestilence and famine – operating to restore the death rate to levels that would bring about temporarily, and with untold misery, zero growth. That is the alternative that faces the surplus children of the reproducing couples of India today and is one which the economic planners have to assume will not come about. What technological innovations and institutional changes will have to occur to make it possible for India to feed, clothe, house and educate four times its present population can only be surmised. Present populations must assume currently available solutions to their problems.

The Draft Fifth Five-Year Plan opens with these words: 'Removal of poverty and attainment of economic self-reliance are the two strategic goals that the country has set for itself.' The primary task is to become self-sufficient in food, but equally important is to ensure that work is available to make it possible for every breadwinner to earn the means to purchase it.

FOOD NEEDS

There are two kinds of food needs to be met to ensure a healthy population. There is a quantitative need, which if not met results in undernourishment, and in extreme circumstances, starvation. There is also a qualitative need, which if not met produces malnutrition and deficiency diseases. Malnutrition is the more insidious for its sufferers may be unaware of the cause of their debility or of the disease to which they are prone. However, malnutrition is rare when quantitative needs are met. The National Institute of Nutrition at Hyderabad, in its *Diet Atlas of India* (1971) sets out separate balanced dietary scales fulfilling the basic needs for calories and protein for strict vegetarians, who make up some 28 per cent of the population, and for non-vegetarians (Table 2.1). The 'average' diet

[1] UN Department of Economic and Social Affairs: *Concise Report on the World Population Situation in 1970–75 and its Long-Range Implications.*

TABLE 2.1
Daily Dietary Needs in India (in grams)

	Vegetarian diet		*Non-vegetarian diet*		*Average per capita need*	*Average per capita availability (1970)*
Cereals	369.5		369.5		369.5	395
Pulses	68.9	78.4	52.2	64.7	68.6	51
Groundnuts	9.5		9.5			
Leafy vegetables	107		107		107	10
Other vegetables	125		125		125	53
Fruits	37		37		37	44
Milk	241		154		178	108
Oils, fats	35		39		38	10
Flesh foods	—		49		35	12
Sugar/jaggery	40		40		40	46

available provided 1945 calories against an estimated need for 2357, and 49 grams of protein against a need for 44.3. Too much of the protein is second class vegetable protein however.

Cereals play a much larger part in the diet than they do in the more developed countries, and the overall provision of calories and proteins is much lower. Western Europeans and particularly North Americans consume an excess of both calories and protein; Indians by and large need more and better protein (especially as children) than they get, and more calories in total. The net food supplies to an Indian citizen are compared in Table 2.2 with those available to his British and American counterparts.

TABLE 2.2
Net Food Supply: India, UK, USA (grams per head)

	India (1970)	*UK (1967–68)*	*USA (1967)*
Cereals	395	200	177
Potatoes etc.	44	283	133
Sugar etc.	46	135	133
Pulses, nuts	51	16	23
Vegetables	46	173	269
Fruit	46	139	239
Meat	4	204	295
Eggs	1	44	51
Fish	7	26	17
Milk	108	600	665
Fats, oils	10	60	61
Total protein	49	87.5	95.6
Animal protein	5.5	53.8	68.6
Calories	(1,945)	(3,150)	(3,200)

In the Indian diet about two thirds of the calories come from the cereal foods, in western countries only one third, the remainder being derived from sugars, fats, oils and meat. In 1970, a good year as far as crop production was concerned, the average Indian had 17.5 per cent less than the desirable level of calories. Very many in the poorer section of the community must have had much less than this. Studies in Maharashtra in the 1960s showed that the poor consumed only 1120 calories, while the rich exceeded 3000. The needs of westerners, 2600 calories on average, are higher than those of Indians because their generally colder climate requires a greater intake of heat-providing food, but also because their greater bodyweight demands higher inputs for efficient performance. As Indian diets improve, succeeding generations will be bigger boned and heavier, and their food needs will therefore increase.

The overall extent of under-nourishment in the Indian population is difficult to gauge, but P. V. Sukhatme writing in 1965 considered that between a third and a quarter had too little food. Malnutrition he thought was more widespread and affected half the people. The lack of a properly balanced diet is a major factor reducing resistance to disease, and several specific maladies may be traced to the lack of some mineral or vitamin in the diet. Retarded growth in children is often due to protein deficiency, and Indian diets are notoriously lacking in first class animal protein. Pulses provide second class protein, but it is thought that children in particular need to be able to take in their

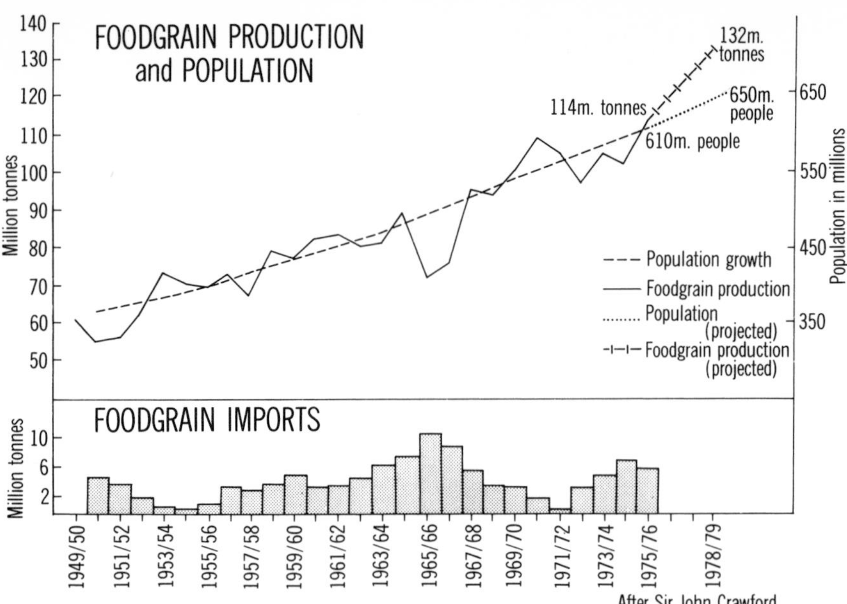

FIG. 2.3

protein requirements without having to consume an excessive quantity of calories in pulses and cereals in order to do so. The outstanding deficiencies in the average diet are of vegetables and milk, both important sources of protective vitamins and minerals, and both relatively easy to supply from Indian agricultural resources if properly developed. The realization of the vital role these elements should be playing in the diet must come through formal education and propaganda; once demand is stimulated, the Indian farmer has shown that he is capable of meeting it. In the case of milk supplies, it is recognized that despite the huge numbers of working cattle bred each year, their mothers are generally poor providers of milk.[1] The local breeds belong to the family *Bos indicus*, among whom it is difficult to develop as high milk yields as are commonly obtained from the European stock, *Bos taurus*. Successful acclimatization of European types in the more temperate areas of India has taken place, and breeding research is seeking to develop crosses of *indicus* and *taurus* that will combine the work capacity, docility, and resistance to disease and climatic stress characteristic of Indian breeds, with the milk productivity of some *Bos taurus* breeds. Successful crosses have been established in tropical and sub-tropical Australia in order to produce disease-resistant milking cattle. The Australian Milking Zebu (AMZ) is one example which might meet Indian needs.

[1] Of 179 million cattle, 22 million were in milk in 1972, and 75 million formed the workforce. Buffaloes, better producers of milk, are costlier to keep and more difficult to breed. Milking buffaloes numbered 15 million, against 8 million work animals.

The average intake of 1945 calories masks not only variations between rich and poor, but also quite significant regional differences, as Table 2.3 demonstrates for thirteen states over the period 1960–69.

The ranking of these states for per capita income is shown in order to dispel any suspicion that wealth might be an over-riding factor accounting for the regional differences. The well-fed states seem to be those where a wheat diet predominates together with a high level of protein intake. In Jammu and Kashmir rice, maize and wheat are eaten, and the high level of calorie consumption reflects the climatic stress of its winters, colder than elsewhere. The ragi, jowar and bajra eaters, supplementing their millet with wheat or rice as the case may be, come in the middle, with the rice eating states at the bottom of the list. There is a rough correspondence of rank in protein intake with calorie consumption, as is also the case with fats and oils. In terms of meeting need, calorie intake appears to diminish southwards and eastwards into warmer regions in a general sense, but only two states overtop the estimated minimum level, and if the overall calorie intake in Tamilnadu is as stated, the degree of food deficiency among the poor in that state must indeed be severe.

TABLE 2.3

Per capita Consumption of calories, proteins, fats and oils by states

Rank for calories	*State*	*Calorie intake*	*Protein intake (g)*	*Animal protein*	*Rank for proteins*	*Oils, fats*	*Rank for per capita income (to 1971)*
1.	Punjab-Haryana	2,831	84	16	2	52	3
2.	Madhya Pradesh	2,779	98	7	1	45	11
3.	Uttar Pradesh	2,307	66	5	5=	32	8
4.	Maharashtra	2,281	68	6	4	30	1
5.	Jammu & Kashmir	2,265	63	1	7	25	9
6.	Karnataka	2,220	66	3	5=	18	7
7.	Rajasthan	2,044	77	5	3	34	12
8.	Andhra Pradesh	2,040	53	5	10	21	10
9.	West Bengal	1,927	48	7	11	24	2
10.	Bihar	1,865	56	3	8	13	13
11.	Kerala	1,842	47	11	12	25	6
12.	Gujarat	1,612	54	2	9	13	4
13.	Tamilnadu	1,498	36	4	13	12	5
	INDIA	1,985	55	6		24	
	Estimated need	2,400	44				

A recent report delves deeply into the nutrition habits in Tamilnadu. *The Tamil Nadu Nutrition Study* by Sidney M. Cantor Associates Inc. (1973) found that if the satisfaction of even 80 per cent of the calorie needs was an acceptable level of nutrition, then half the families in the state were below this level. The study covered 2500 families throughout the state, and included anthropological investigation of the eating habits of the family and of its members individually, by caste, occupation, age, sex, etc. Proteins were found not to be deficient to the degree that calorie foods were, and the main conclusion was that just *more* of the same foods as were at present consumed would meet basic needs. However certain groups were identified as particularly at nutritional risk because of traditional attitudes and family feeding habits. These were, in order of need, the weaning child, the pregnant mother, the nursing mother and the adolescent female. The practice of the males in the family eating their fill before the female members dine off the remnants is normal, and obviously militates against the proper nutrition of females, the more so in families where the total food availability is low.

8 Transplanting paddy seedlings into irrigated fields for a dry season crop, near Goa. Some of the cultivators probably find employment in the iron mines lying beyond the ridge in the background.

On average younger pregnant or lactating women got only 60 per cent of their calorie needs. That the small children suffer is supported by the finding that out of 1000 live births only 555 survive to be six, though not all child mortality is due to malnutrition. The corresponding figure for Europe and North America is 950. Malnutrition thus currently contributes effectively to limit population. The consequence of the child mortality levels in Tamilnadu being on the same level as those of the west would be an enormous and rapid increase in population unless the change were accompanied by effective birth control. The assurance that children born have a good prospect of survival is an essential element in any campaign to encourage family planning.

TRENDS AND TARGETS IN FOOD SUPPLY

The problem of balancing food production and demand even in years of good rainfall has been ever present since independence, varying only in the degree to which it has been necessary to spend foreign exchange on imported food grains. Production has increased overall, but as the figures in Table 2.4 indicate, it has fluctuated, with an inevitable impact on imports. Persistent population increase makes it difficult to close the gap, and harder still to build up the buffer stocks that are essential to insure against seasonal scarcity and to guard against economic scarcity due to prices rising under manipulation by hoarders. A. M. Khusro suggested a minimum buffer stock of 7 million tonnes, 5 million in store and 2 million in the 'pipe line' as appropriate to these purposes.[1]

Foodgrain stocks reached a record level of 20 million tonnes in 1976 following the bumper kharif and rabi crops of 1975–76 and a normal harvest in 1976–77. Supplies indeed outran storage capacity and school buildings and old palaces had to be pressed into service as well as improvised outdoor stackyards. In times of shortage, inter-state movement of foodgrains is strictly controlled by central and state governments, and may even extend to movements from local collecting centres. The Centre has been asserting its control increasingly in order to be able to mobilize surpluses accumulated in one state to meet deficiencies in another. Understandably states who see themselves as liable to shortage are reluctant to part with stocks for fear that prices will be forced up in their own region, creating premature scarcity.

In the inter-censal decade 1961–71 population rose by 24.8 per cent, and because of the bumper harvest of 1970–71, food production at 36.5 per cent above that of 1960–61 seemed to have gone ahead. There was a setback however, so that in 1972–73, the population 30.2 per cent above the 1961 level had food available from home production only 20.8 per cent above that level. Food self-sufficiency, achieved in 1976–77 despite increasing population was the central aim of the Fifth Five-year Plan, which anticipated somewhat conservatively an end of plan 1979 population of 637 million, a figure almost certain to be reached early in 1978. The projected production figures for the major food crops are appended to the table of

[1] A. M. Khusro, *Buffer Stocks and Storage of Foodgrains in India*, 1973.

9 Modernization in agriculture requires scientific control of pests and diseases. Here insecticide spray is being prepared for a paddy crop in the Godavari Delta, Andhra Pradesh.

TABLE 2.4

Total Cereal Production and Imports (million tonnes)

Year	*Rice*	*Wheat*	*Jowar*	*Bajra*	*Maize*	*Total all cereals*	*Total food-grains*	*Imports*	*Popula-tion (millions)*
1950–51	22.1	6.8	6.3	2.7	2.4	45.8	55	2.1	361
1960–61	34.6	11.0	9.8	3.3	4.1	69.3	82	3.8	442
1961–62	35.7	12.1	8.0	3.6	4.3	71.0	82	2.4	452
1962–63	33.2	10.8	9.7	4.0	4.6	68.6	80	3.0	462
1963–64	37.0	9.9	9.2	3.9	4.6	70.6	81	3.3	472
1964–65	39.3	12.3	9.7	4.5	4.7	76.9	89	6.9	483
1965–66	30.6	10.4	7.6	3.8	4.8	62.4	72	7.7	493
1966–67	30.4	11.4	9.2	4.5	4.9	65.9	74	10.4	504
1967–68	37.6	16.5	10.0	5.2	6.3	83.0	95	8.7	515
1968–69	39.8	18.7	9.8	3.8	5.7	83.6	94	5.7	527
1969–70	40.4	20.1	9.7	5.3	5.7	87.8	99	3.9	539
1970–71	42.2	23.8	8.1	8.0	7.5	96.6	108	3.6	547
1971–72	43.1	26.4	7.7	5.3	5.1	94.1	105	2.1	559
1972–73	38.6	24.9	6.4	3.8	6.2	87.1	97	0.4	569
1973–74	44.0	30.0	9.5	6.5	5.6	93.9	105	3.6	581
1974–75*	40.3	24.2	10.2	3.2	5.7	90.7	101	4.9	600
1975–76*	–	–	–	–	–	–	121	6.8	–
1976–77*	–	–	–	–	–	–	110	6.5	–
1978–79†	54.0	38.0	11.0	8.0	8.0	126.0	140‡	Nil	637

* Estimate
† Plan target
‡ Subsequently revised downwards to total of 125 million tonnes

actual cereal production, Table 2.4 (and see Figure 2.3). The variations in production are discussed further in Chapter Five while some of the major problems to be overcome in achieving the plan target are the content of Chapter Six.

PLANNING AND ECONOMIC DEVELOPMENT

At the time of independence, India inherited an imperfectly integrated part of the former British Indian colonial economy, which for a long time had been tied to that of Britain. Indian exports, of agricultural products for the most part, paid for imports of manufactured goods, mainly from Britain, to which also flowed the interest on investments in railways and in those areas of industrial development permitted by the British, such as jute and cotton textiles. These were not allowed to encroach too far on the higher quality market reserved for British mills. There had been some development of heavy iron and steel manufacturing in Bihar and Bengal, but on a modest scale in relation to the real needs of the subcontinent. Aggravating this situation were the disruptions and imbalances caused by the Second World War which, while it had some stimulating effect in that India was called upon to provide the military needs of armies in the Middle East, and in Southeast Asia, the disruption of communication starved established industry of spare parts and replacement machinery. Whatever advantages might have flowed from this stimulus were largely dispersed by the partition of British India into India and Pakistan.

Independent India had to set about the task of achieving economic independence to parallel its newly won political independence, and to bring about higher living standards for its people. Economic independence does not of course mean economic isolation and complete self-sufficiency. No country can be expected to 'pull itself up by its own boot straps'. All countries have a measure of dependence on others through the economies of division of labour operating at an international level. India had to decide what pattern of economy was capable of achievement; what factors among its own resources could best be advanced both to increase national wealth internally, and to provide goods and services for sale to others in order to earn foreign exchange. Foreign exchange is needed to purchase those goods and services which, for the time being at any rate, others are better able to provide. At the outset Indian planners had at their disposal vast resources of land, materials and manpower, but a dearth of capital, experience, enterprise and technological know-how.

The problems facing Indian planners were, and continue to be formidable though much has been achieved in thirty years. In summary they have to activate the human resources to produce what the nation needs in the way of food and other raw materials from the soil, and to produce a surplus of such commodities as can profitably be exported; to establish and expand industries upon which future economic growth can be erected; to create employment opportunities for the millions of unemployed and under-employed; to raise the general level of economic activity so that people have the means and the opportunity to buy more of the necessities for a better standard of living; and at the same time to bring about agricultural, industrial, and demographic revolutions as quickly as possible so that the population explosion does not devour the whole substance of whatever increases in production can be achieved. No other country of comparable size has attempted so much within a society committed to parliamentary democracy.

THE FIVE-YEAR PLANS

The policy for development and the broad strategy to be followed by Central Government ministries and by the states in carrying out the policy are laid down in the five-year plans. To paraphrase the terms of reference of the Planning Commission as

TABLE 2.5

Five Year Plans: Proportionate Outlay in Major Divisions (as per cent of total)

	First Plan 1951–2 to 1955–6	*Second Plan 1956–7 to 1960–1*	*Third Plan 1961–2 to 1965–6*	*Fourth Plan 1969–70 to 1973–4*	*Fifth Plan 1974–5 to 1979–80*		
					(a)	*(b)*	*(c)*
Agriculture	14.8	11.7	12.7	16.9	12.7	18.3	14.4
Irrigation, flood control	22.2	9.2	7.8	7.4	7.2		5.0
Power	7.6	9.7	14.6	17.8	16.3	0.6	11.8
Village and small industry	2.1	4.0	2.8	1.5	1.6		
						38.7	28.4
Industry and minerals	2.8	20.1	20.1	18.5	22.4		
Transport and communications	26.4	27.0	24.6	18.4	19.2	11.6	16.8
Education	7.6	5.8	7.7	5.6	4.6	0.6	3.5
Health and family planning	5.0	4.6	2.9	3.6	4.6	0.1	3.3

(a) Public sector; (b) Private sector; (c) Total outlay.

10 Techniques for threshing grain crops are many and various, often reflecting local resources, as here. Near Mysore, Karnataka, granite is abundant, and is used to make rollers for threshing rice.

deriving from the constitution, the aim is to bring about a socialist pattern of society in which both public and private enterprise have a place, but in which the concentration of wealth or power in the hands of a few is to be avoided, and the lot of the more backward and underprivileged in the community is to be raised. The proportionate outlay of public funds to achieve these aims under the various plans is summarized in Table 2.5 and Figure 2.4. Under Plan V, public sector outlays are under (a), private sector outlays under (b), and the total outlays, public and private, under (c).

FIG. 2.4

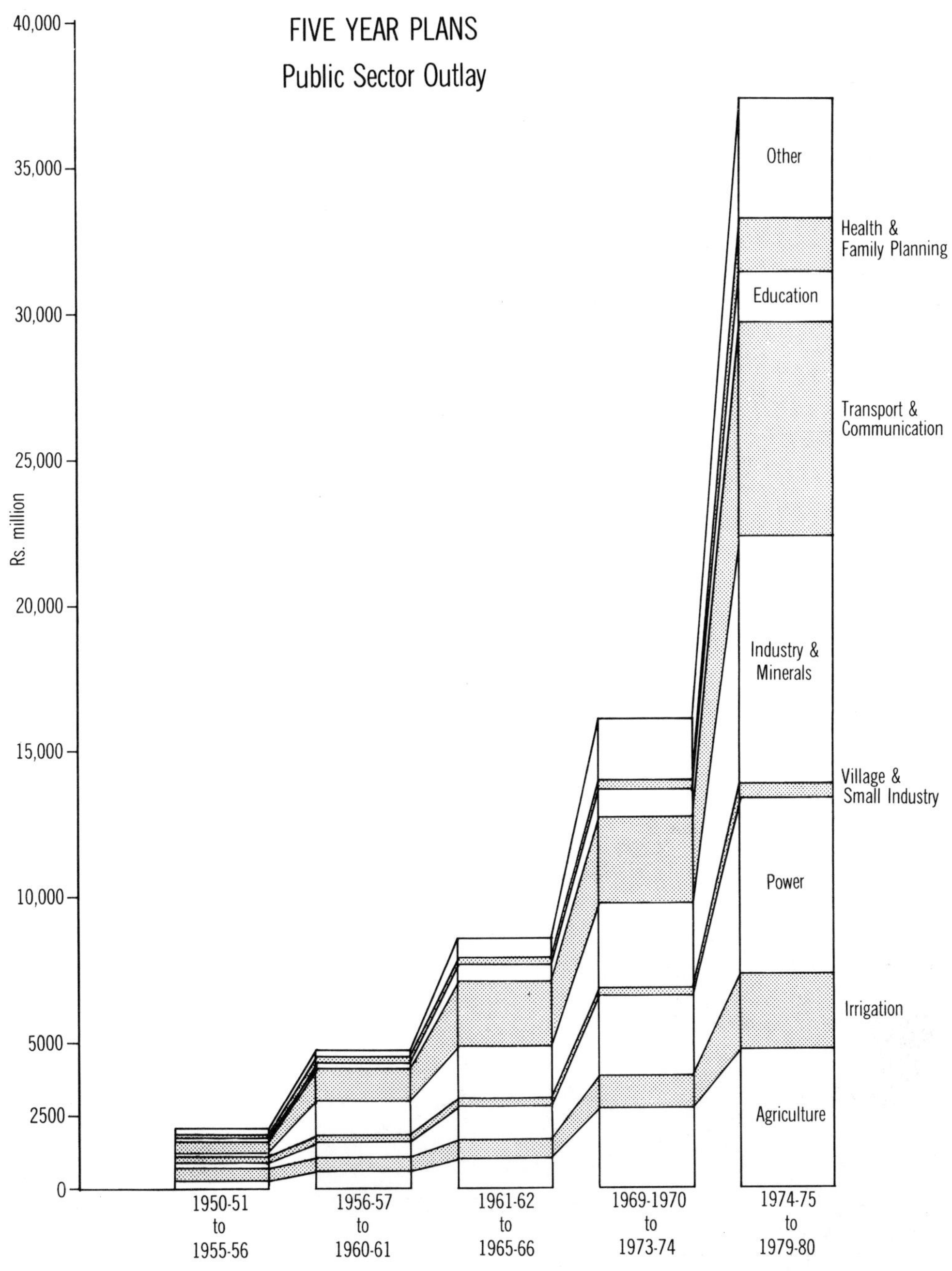

The private sector accounts for 30 per cent of the total of Rs 534, 110 million.

In the First Plan agriculture and irrigation received most attention. The necessity to import food had already appeared, caused partly by the loss following partition, of the food surplus regions of the Pakistan Punjab and Sind. Transport and communications had also to be rehabilitated in the aftermath of the run-down during the war years followed by the disruptions to the system occasioned by partition. The plan aimed to raise the National Income by 12 per cent, a level which was in the event exceeded at 18 per cent (see Table 2.6). Per capita income rose 9 per cent during the plan period. The First Plan was very much an interim measure. The country's leaders were fully stretched coping with the political and administrative reorganization of the new nation; the constitution itself had barely been adopted.

In the Second Plan the ultimate shape of the economy became clearer. Heavy industry and power dominated thinking, rather as they had in the planning of development in the USSR. The establishment of iron and steel industries, heavy chemicals (including fertilizers), and heavy machinery and engineering industries was meant to lay the foundations for future industrial growth.

TABLE 2.6

Trends in National and per capita Income

(a) Per cent increase over plan period

	First plan	*Second plan*	*Third plan*	*Annual plans period*	*Fourth plan*
National Income	18	20	14	14	15
Per Capita Income	9	11	no change	7	2.5

(b) Per capita income in Rupees (at 1960–61 Prices)

1950/51	1955/56	1960/61	1965/66	1968/69	1969/70	1970/71	1971/72	1972/73	1973/74	1974/75
253	276	306	311	332	343	352	348	337	340	341

Although the Plan made reference to the need to expand employment opportunities, it has been criticized for over-emphasizing heavy industries. These are not immediately job-producing, i.e. their spread effects are minimal in the short run, and they take a long time to mature to the stage where they start generating more labour-intensive kinds of manufacturing. Aiming at an increase of 25 per cent in National Income, the plan achieved 20 per cent.

11 Human muscle may be the cheapest means of threshing, as here in Tamilnadu, where labourers beat rice sheaves against a stone.

An interesting aspect of the Third Five Year Plan, and one which persists into subsequent plans, is the emphasis given to power development, urgently needed for agriculture (for irrigation pumps) and for industry alike, not to mention the demands of the urban public now enjoying some degree of modernization of their traditional life-style. Self-sufficiency in foodgrains is an objective that has recurred in every plan thereafter, but proves difficult to achieve while the number of mouths to feed persists in increasing at a greater pace. Similarly the need to increase jobs and to reduce disparities in wealth are recurrent themes. Industrial growth on a wider front absorbed a fifth of the outlay, and made good progress with annual growth rate of 8–10 per cent over the first four years, 5 per cent in the last. National income showed a similar relapse following high hopes, and ultimately increased by 14 per cent, well below the target of nearly 30 per cent for the plan period. The cause of these slumps in performance was the war with Pakistan, which not only diverted resources away from more productive avenues, but also led the USA to withdraw its financial support of India's development programmes. Severe droughts in the last year of the plan put a further strain on capital resources which had to be used to purchase imported food. Such was the economic crisis provoked by these events, that the Fourth Plan could not be introduced, there being insufficient funds for investment. In three years that followed, from 1966 to 1969, ad hoc annual plans were implemented with whatever funds could be made available, and a fresh Fourth Five Year Plan period began in 1969.

Outlays under the Fourth Plan were more in balance than previously, allowing that the investment in power was to benefit both rural agricultural and urban industrial sectors. There was much stress placed on the need to uplift the condition of the backward groups and to ensure them social justice, a campaign that gained ground in the Fifth Plan. Performance in the Fourth Plan was handicapped by sluggishness in industry, much capacity being under-utilized. National income rose 15 per cent, but with population growing faster than ever, per capita income advanced only slowly, by 2.5 per cent in the period. Industrial unrest, 'invasion by refugees' from East Pakistan and the short war that followed with Pakistan, did not help.

In the current Fifth Five Year Plan the mixture of outlays is much as before, but the data as tabulated obscure the growing integration between industry and agriculture; with the prosecution of the green revolution, fertilizers and pumps are in increasing demand and are to be supplied substantially from domestic production. Overall economic self-reliance at long last appears to be an achievable goal, if, as has been said earlier, the birth rate really has taken a downward trend. Taking up the call made in earlier plans, but most strongly in the Fourth, the needs of the more backward 30 per cent in the population are singled out for special attention, implying not only investment but a vigorous pursuit of programmes to implement land reforms and to broaden the availability of rural credit.

STRUCTURE OF THE ECONOMY

Poverty is the outstanding economic characteristic of the Indian population. In terms of per capita share of Gross National Product as calculated by the World Bank, India in 1973 ranked close to the bottom of the table in the company of Pakistan and Sri Lanka. A selection from that table is given in Table 2.7 to show the enormous disparity between India and the highly developed countries.

This table refers to the year at the end of the Fourth Plan during which India's per capita income remained substantially unchanged at Rs 850 at current prices (Rs 340 at 1960–61 prices). Measurement of GNP is a much less certain undertaking in a country like India where the subsistence element in agriculture remains so high, than in more economically sophisticated countries with totally monetized economies. Furthermore it must be remembered that the per capita figure is a gross average. Expressed otherwise, using as a basis the distribution of personal disposable income through deciles of the population as estimated for 1964–65[1] and applying it to income data for 1973–4, we find the average disposable

[1] J. P. Singh, *Changing levels of living in rural India*, Report in preparation: Institute for Social and Economic Change, Bangalore.

TABLE 2.7

Gross National Product per capita (1973) and Annual Average Growth Rate (1965–73) for Selected Countries $ US)

USA	6,200	2.5	USSR	2,030	3.5	Indonesia	130	4.5
W. Germany	5,320	4.0	Spain	1,710	5.3	India	120	1.5
Australia	4,350	3.0	Malaysia	570	3.7	Sri Lanka	120	2.0
Japan	3,630	9.6	China	270	4.6	Pakistan	120	2.5
UK	3,060	2.3	Egypt	250	0.8	Bangladesh	80	- 1.6

Source: World Bank *Atlas of Population, Per Capita Production and Growth Rates*, 1975.

income of the poorest 30 per cent of the people to be Rs 303 (of the poorest tenth, Rs 227) while the uppermost 30 per cent have Rs 1464 (and the richest tenth Rs 2498) on average. This is a measure of the glaring inequality in levels of living that the present government is trying to reduce by fiscal and social legislation. Another way of measuring living standards is by the wage rates of factory workers. Assuming even that their wages have to support the 'ideal' family of four, the per capita income ranges from Rs 424 in Jammu and Kashmir to Rs 789 in Maharashtra. The median figure for 18 states and Delhi is Rs 683.

J. P. Singh (op. cit.) has calculated that for the 1950s and 1960s the percentage of the population living below the poverty line remained consistently around 40, with some regional variation. According to the National Sample Survey Draft Report 269, relating to 1970–71, a total of 245 million, or 45 per cent of the population lived below this level, having in rural areas Rs 28 or less and in urban areas Rs 43 or less per month for consumer expenditure. Half the states have 45 per cent or more of their people in poverty. As will be seen in Figure 2.5 these states form a large central block extending south to Kerala and Tamilnadu. The major rice eating states are included, excepting those in the Brahmaputra Valley, and the belt continues west through UP and Madhya Pradesh into the arid zone in Rajasthan. Gujarat and Karnataka are just above the average level, and Maharashtra well over it, in all three cases industry being of some importance. The least poor are the irrigated Punjab, and Assam where population pressure is not yet excessive. The NSS also identified destitution and severe destitution, the latter with expenditure below Rs 21 (rural) or Rs 28 (urban). Almost 120 million fell into this group – 22 per cent of the population. Of the states having 45 per cent or more in poverty, only Andhra escapes being in the group with over 22 per cent in severe destitution.[1]

According to J. P. Singh, on average the poor spend three quarters of their available wealth on food, and increase the amount when their income permits. Their power to purchase the products of manufacturing industry is pitifully weak, yet it is to their general economic uplift that the nation's efforts and ingenuity must be directed if the urban-industrial as well as the rural-agricultural sectors are to realize the planners' aspirations.

[1] 'The Third World and Destitution', *Monthly Commentary on Indian Economic Conditions*, Vol. XVII, 5, 1975, Indian Institute of Public Opinion.

FIG. 2.5 After *National Sample Survey*, by NSS areas.

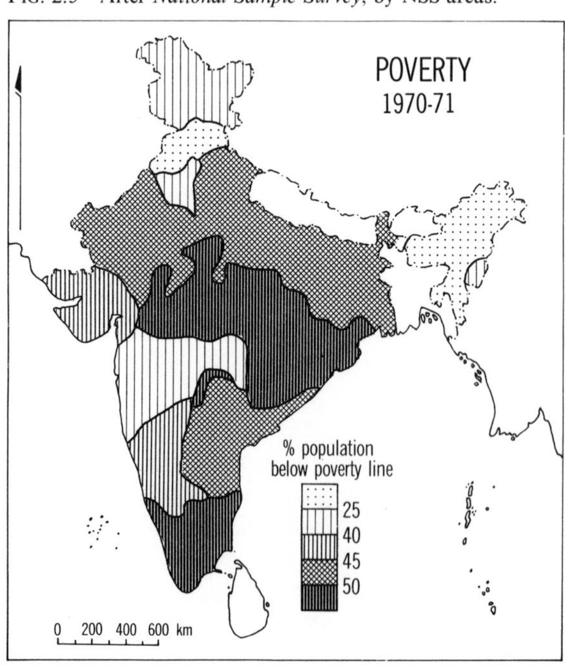

Across the country the average per capita income varies considerably as Table 2.8 demonstrates (see also Figure 2.6). By analogy with the argument in the preceding paragraph, the Bombay (Maharashtra) rich may be that much richer, and the Bihari poor that much poorer than the national average for their group.

TABLE 2.8
Per capita Income by States (1972–73 or latest) in Rupees, current prices

Rank	*State*	*Income*
1.	Maharashtra	1,075
2.	Punjab	1,054
3.	Haryana	906
4.	Gujarat	856
	India Average	*698*
5.	Uttar Pradesh	652
6.	Tamilnadu	644
7.	Madhya Pradesh	632
8.	Andhra Pradesh	631
9.	Rajasthan	630
10.	Kerala	579
11.	Assam	571
12.	Karnataka	570
13.	West Bengal	568
14.	Himachal Pradesh	563
15.	Jammu & Kashmir	513
16.	Orissa	511
17.	Manipur	424
18.	Bihar	403

FIG. 2.6

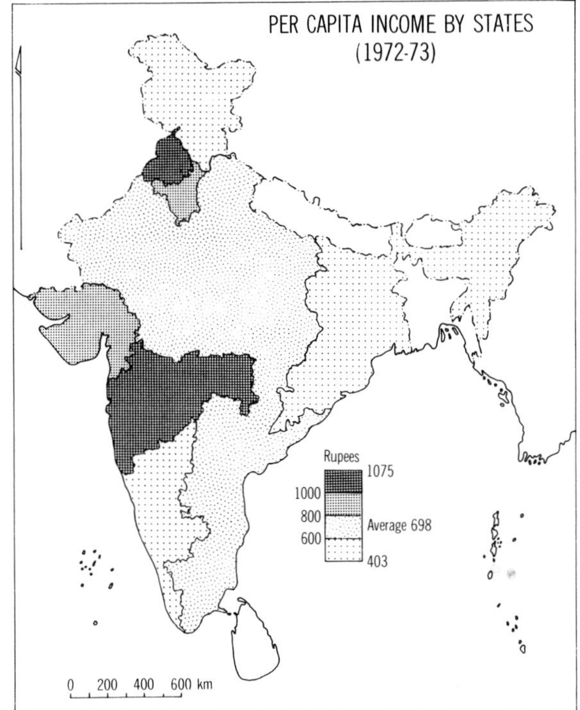

Many factors enter into an explanation of the ranking and range of disparity shown above. Urbanization, industrialization, irrigation, community structure, history of land tenure, politics, religion and cultural backwardness are but a few obvious elements of any explanation, and there are some intriguing contradictions to almost every theory one might try to formulate on any single criterion.

India's Domestic Product is still predominantly from the primary sector, though the secondary and particularly the tertiary sectors have been making substantial gains in the last decades. This is an indication of modernization in the economy as a whole. The position is summarized in Table 2.9 (see also Figure 2.7).

These trends are expected to continue into the Fifth Plan period. The planners see the sectoral composition of the gross domestic product as likely to change as in Table 2.10 in which it will be noted that only agriculture shows a relative decline.

The creation of new employment opportunities, and the intensification of real employment in existing jobs are needed to absorb the unemployed and under-employed in the existing population and the increasing numbers joining the employable age group. It is hoped that the employment of juvenile labour may cease as the economy develops and that education can absorb all children between 6 and 14 years. This target is far from attainment at present. The importance to poorer families of the small income that children can contribute, often working alongside their parents, may be gauged indirectly from the fact that while 80 per cent of the 6–11 age group was enrolled in school in 1971 (43 per cent in 1951) the proportion fell markedly in the 11–14 age group, to 35 per cent in 1971 (13 per cent in 1951). However some progress is being made, as the change since independence indicates. The planners considered that by 1973–74 *all* boys aged 6–11 would be at school, and 66 per cent of the girls to give a total of 84 per cent, while in the later age group, 11–14, 48 per cent of the boys, 22 per cent of the girls and 36 per cent of the total would be enrolled. Twenty-two per cent of the 14–18 age group (31 per cent of boys,

TABLE 2.9

Structure of Net Domestic Product by Sectors (per cent of total at 1960–61 prices)

	1950–51	*1960–61*	*1965–66*	*1970–71*	*1973–74*
Agriculture	54.1	49.3	40.4	42.7	39.6
Forestry and fishing	2.0	1.9	2.2	2.0	2.0
Mining	0.9	1.0	1.2	1.1	1.2
TOTAL PRIMARY SECTOR	57.0	52.2	43.8	45.8	42.8
Manufacturing	11.7	13.9	16.8	15.6	16.0
Construction	4.5	4.7	5.7	5.5	5.2
Public Utilities	0.2	0.5	0.8	1.0	1.2
TOTAL SECONDARY SECTOR	16.4	19.1	23.3	22.1	22.4
Transport, storage, communications	3.6	4.3	5.1	5.1	5.4
Trade, hotels	8.5	9.7	11.1	10.5	10.7
Banking, insurance	0.9	1.2	1.5	1.6	1.9
Real estate, etc.	3.1	3.0	2.9	2.4	2.4
Public administration and defence	3.6	4.0	5.4	5.9	7.3
Other services	6.9	6.5	6.9	6.6	7.1
TOTAL TERTIARY SECTOR	26.6	28.7	32.9	32.1	34.8
Total (million Rs)	91,220	133,350	152,340	192,190	199,100

FIG. 2.7

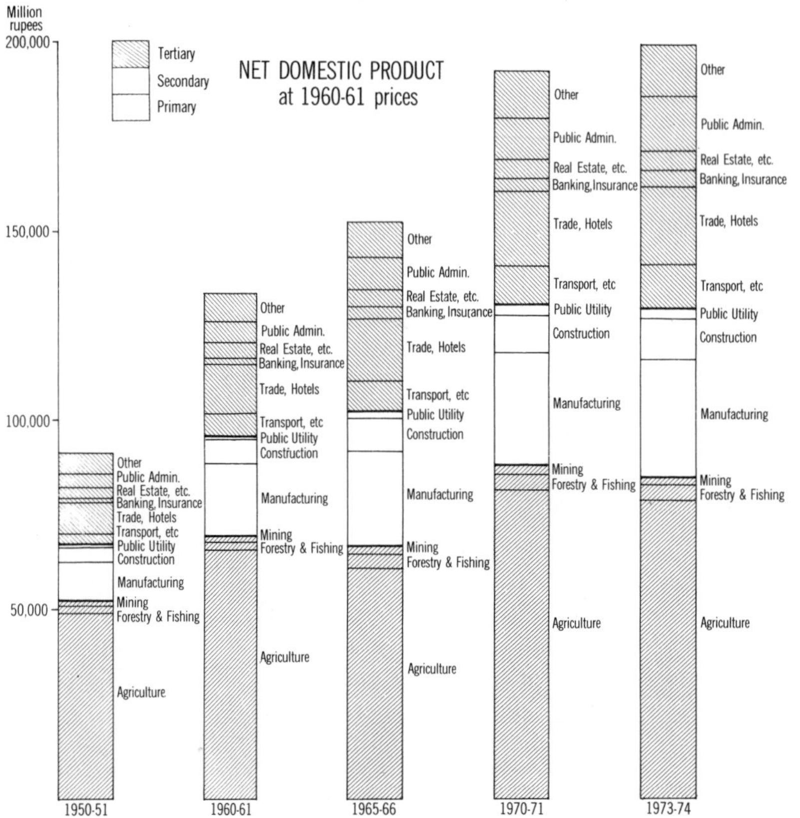

TABLE 2.10

Sectoral composition of Gross Domestic Product 1973–74 and 1978–79

	Agri-culture	*Mining*	*Manu-facturing*	*Elec-tricity*	*Cons-truction*	*Transport*	*Services*
1973–74	45.7	1.0	14.4	1.1	5.6	4.4	27.7
1978–79 (planned)	42.4	1.2	16.2	1.4	6.5	4.4	27.9

12 per cent of girls) would be at secondary schools. Expansion of education will not only keep children out of the workforce longer, but will also provide jobs for some of the swollen numbers of university and college graduates who find themselves unemployable at present. Education is at present in a depressed condition. Changes in curricula towards a content more relevant to children whose future should be in the rural sectors is urgently needed to avoid adding to the frustration of 'qualified' graduates who find themselves qualified for nothing the community needs.

The planners comment that 'Employment is perhaps going to be the most important challenge to development planning during the perspective period.' Even if population increases at a diminishing rate, for at least 15 years hence the children of the population explosion will be entering the workforce.

The 1971 Census categorized the working population as shown in Table 2.11 (see also Figure 2.8). Of the working population thus enumerated,

TABLE 2.11

Distribution of Working Population by Occupation, 1971 (percentage of each item represented by females in parentheses, numbers in millions)

Total population	548 (48.2)
Total workers	180 (17.4)
Total workers as percentage of total population	32.9

Workers by occupation	*Number*	*Per cent of total workers*	*Females as per cent of group*
Primary sector	**130**	**72.0**	**27.2**
Cultivators	78.2	43.3	11.8
Agricultural labourers	47.5	26.3	42.1
Livestock, forestry, fishing, plantations, etc.	4.3	2.4	18.2
Secondary sector	**20.2**	**11.1**	**12.4**
Mining, etc.	0.9	0.5	13.4
Cottage industry	6.4	3.5	20.9
Manufacturing industry	10.7	5.9	8.1
Construction	2.2	1.2	9.2
Tertiary sector	**30.2**	**16.7**	**9.7**
Commerce	10.0	5.6	5.5
Transport, communications	4.4	2.4	3.3
Other services	15.8	8.7	14.1

FIG. 2.8

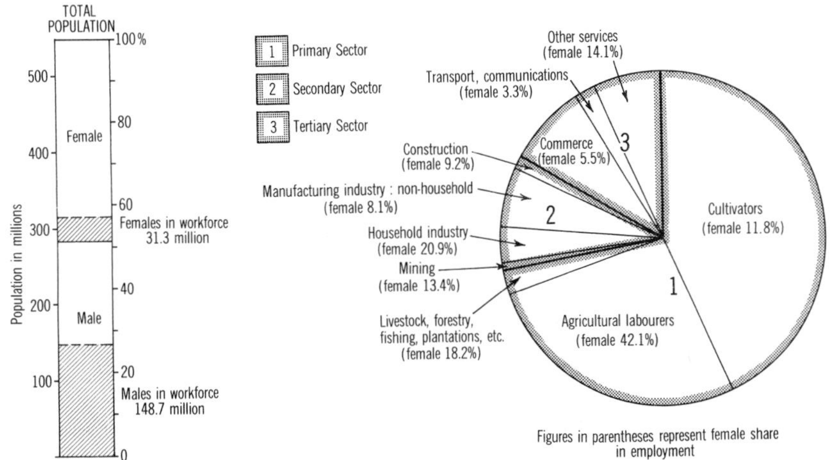

only one tenth is employed in the 'organized sector', meaning the more or less modernized part of the economy in which employment is generally full time. The distribution of this section of the work-force is as under (Table 2.12 and Figure 2.9).

The very high percentage of employment in the public sector outside manufacturing and plantations reflects the policies of the government in the direction of public ownership and socialization. While planners can apply to the organized sector the conventional yardsticks used in developed economies, these must be used with caution in appraising the capacity of the 'informal' or traditional sector of the economy, in the rural areas particularly, to create employment or to absorb the surplus of man-hours available. For example, the 43.3 per cent of the working population described as cultivators are self-employed family groups as a rule, whose labour is fully utilized for very long hours during planting and harvesting seasons, when extra hands will generally be hired from the pool of agricultural labour. The capacity of the cultivator to absorb more labour depends on how much land he utilizes, and the intensity with which he is able to farm it, which depends in turn on his access to credit for the necessary inputs. For the present decade at any rate, it will fall to this group more than any other to provide employment both for its own increase in numbers, and for the increase in the traditionally landless labourers. With 38 million more expected in the labour force within the period of the Fifth Plan, and 65 million by 1984 at the end of the Sixth Plan, it is obvious that the 'organized sector', which at present engages a mere 19.3 million, cannot possibly triple in five years let alone expand five times in ten years to take in the 'surplus'. Any rural-urban flow that might result from the development of less labour-intensive agricultural technology would add to the urban unemployed. For the foreseeable future, rurally based small scale and cottage industries will have to be encouraged and continue to receive protection from the 'organized' industrial sector, and ways need to be found for the self-employment of the large proportion of the agricultural labour force who are seasonally unemployed. It is much to the credit of the Indian people that they have not in the mass adopted the material aspirations that commonly motivate the worker in the developed countries, even though they accept, in its appropriate place, the science and technology of the most advanced. There is still an underlying respect for the practice of craftsmanship, for the dignity of labour, and for a way of life characterized by modesty, simplicity and the avoidance of ostentation in material things.

TABLE 2.12

Distribution of the Workforce in the Organized Sector 1975

Occupation	*Number (million)*	*Per cent of total*	*Per cent in public sector*
Forestry, plantations	1.222	5.7	28.2
Mining:	.8	4.1	84.4
Coal mining*	(.513)		
Manufacturing:	5.203	26.7	21.1
Cotton textiles	(.859)		
Construction	1.074	5.5	89.2
Electricity	.593	3.0	93.1
Commerce	.804	4.1	58.3
Transport, communications	2.448	12.5	96.8
Other services	7.464	38.3	84.8
TOTAL	19.506	99.9	65.1

*January 1975 †July 1975

FIG. 2.9

DISTRIBUTION OF THE WORKFORCE IN THE ORGANISED SECTOR 1975

Total in Workforce - 19.5 million

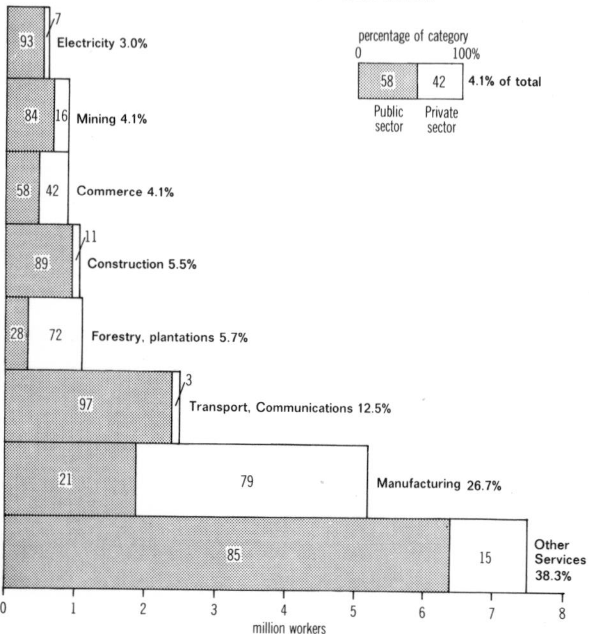

12 Cattle treading out pulses in Tamilnadu: dry sloping fields beyond the coconut and palmyra palms.

EXPORTS, IMPORTS AND THE BALANCE OF PAYMENT

However India decides to apportion wealth and power among its citizens, in so far as it lives within an international economic community, it must pay due regard to maintaining sound financial relationships with the rest of the world. Payment for imports must be balanced by earnings from exports, or the shortfall met from reserves or from loans and grants in aid from friendly nations.

From a relatively simple colonial economy at independence, dominated by a few trading partners within the British Commonwealth and covering a narrow range of mainly agricultural exports and manufactured imports, India's external economy has grown to embrace the whole world. A far wider range of exports and imports reflects the capacities and needs of an expanding mixed economy. Tables 2.13 and 2.14 list the principal exports and imports in 1950–51 and 1974–75 (see Figure 2.10).

The value of exports has grown from Rs 6000 million in 1950–51 to Rs 32,986 million in 1974–75. Despite the development of secondary industry, there has been a comparative drop in the export value of processed agricultural products (coffee and leather being notable exceptions). Part of the reason for this is the growth of domestic

TABLE 2.13
Exports
(Per cent of total: t less than 0.05 per cent)

Item	*1950–51 Rs 6,006 million*	*1974–75 Rs 32,986 million*
Jute manufactures	18.8	8.8
Cotton and other textiles	26.4	6.5
Clothing	—	4.1
Woollen carpets, etc.	0.9	1.3
Tea	13.3	6.8
Coffee	0.2	1.6
Leather	4.2	4.1
Oil cake, etc.	—	3.1
Vegetable oils	4.2	1.0
Sugar	t	10.3
Total processed agricultural products	**68.0**	**47.6**
Raw cotton	0.8	0.5
Raw wool	1.3	0.3
Fruits and nuts	1.8	3.7
Crude vegetable materials	2.3	3.5
Tobacco	2.3	2.4
Hides and skins	1.6	0.4
Total agricultural raw materials	**10.1**	**10.8**
Iron and steel	0.5	2.6
Metal manufactures	—	4.8
Petroleum products	t	0.4
Machinery, transport equipment	—	6.4
Total mineral-based manufactured goods	**0.5**	**14.2**
Iron ore, etc.	t	4.9
Coal, coke, etc.	0.6	0.2
Non-ferrous ores etc.	t	0.9
Total mineral raw materials	**0.6**	**6.0**
Total of items listed	**79.3**	**78.6**

demand, particularly for cotton textiles and foodstuffs, as population has grown. The export of iron and steel has been made possible by the considerable expansion of the industry, but it will be noted comparing Tables 2.13 and 2.14 that there is on balance an import under this head, covering items not manufactured in India. Partial data for 1975–76 show India is now a net exporter of iron and steel products. Mineral raw materials, especially iron ore, have become a vital export, mainly to Japan, but their importance and that of the agricultural raw material section, which remains proportionately static but greatly expanded in real terms, reflects sadly on the difficulty the developing countries have in escaping from the patterns of economic activity inherited from their colonial past. The developed become richer and more developed, while the less developed have to run ever faster, seemingly to stay in the same place. It may be tempting to strive to emulate the high living standards of the successful advanced countries, but in India saner counsels seem to prevail in the present policies of self-reliance.

As Table 2.15 and discussions elsewhere indicate, the import of foodgrains is a very variable but sometimes crushingly dominant element in the import accounts. The share of imports made up by wheat and rice has varied according to seasonal conditions in India.

Of recent years, petroleum and its products have caused concern when the oil producers raised their prices throughout the world on 1 January 1974. Petroleum had been an increasing burden on import expenditure, particularly from 1968–69, culminating in the crippling level of 25.9 per cent of the total in 1974–75.

Paralleling exports, the total value of imports has escalated from Rs 6500 million in 1950–51 to Rs 44, 681 million in 1974–75. The more sophisticated manufactured goods make up a greater share of the total, while (setting aside the variable foodstuffs item) industrial raw materials and semi-manufactured goods increasingly within India's capacity to produce have tended to decline in importance.

The direction of trade has changed over the years since independence. The main feature in the case of both exports and imports is a reduction in the concentration of trade with the UK and USA.

TABLE 2.14
Imports
(Per cent of total: t = less than 0.05 per cent)

Item	*1950–51 (Rs 6,502 million)*	*1974–75 (Rs 44,681 million)*
Wheat and rice	23.5	17.1
Fruits and nuts	1.5	1.4
Oilseeds	0.4	0.2
Vegetable oils	0.5	0.3
Milk products	0.5	0.6
Total foodstuffs	**26.4**	**19.6**
Petroleum and products	8.3	25.9
Non-ferrous metals	2.7	3.4
Raw cotton	15.4	0.6
Wool	0.9	0.6
Jute	t	t
Total industrial raw materials and fuels	**27.3**	**30.5**
Iron and steel	2.2	9.3
Metals, manufactured	2.1	4.6
Chemicals	1.4	4.0
Fertilizers	t	10.1
Pharmaceuticals	1.5	0.8
Coal tar, dye stuffs	1.8	t
Textile yarns	2.3	0.2
Paper	1.6	1.3
Total manufactured materials	**12.9**	**30.3**
Machinery	10.3	8.9
Electrical machinery	3.4	3.4
Transport equipment	5.4	2.8
Total machinery etc.	**19.1**	**15.1**
Total of items listed	**85.7**	**95.5**

TABLE 2.15
Changes in Value of Food and Petroleum Imports (per cent of total)

	1950/51	*1965/66*	*1966/67*	*1967/68*	*1968/69*	*1969/70*	*1970/71*	*1971/72*	*1972/73*	*1973/74*	*1974/75*
Wheat and rice as per cent of total imports	23.5	21.8	24.3	45.3	16.6	15.3	12.4	6.6	3.2	16.0	17.1
Petroleum and oil products as per cent of total imports	8.3	4.8	3.0	3.7	7.0	8.7	8.3	10.6	10.9	19.0	25.9

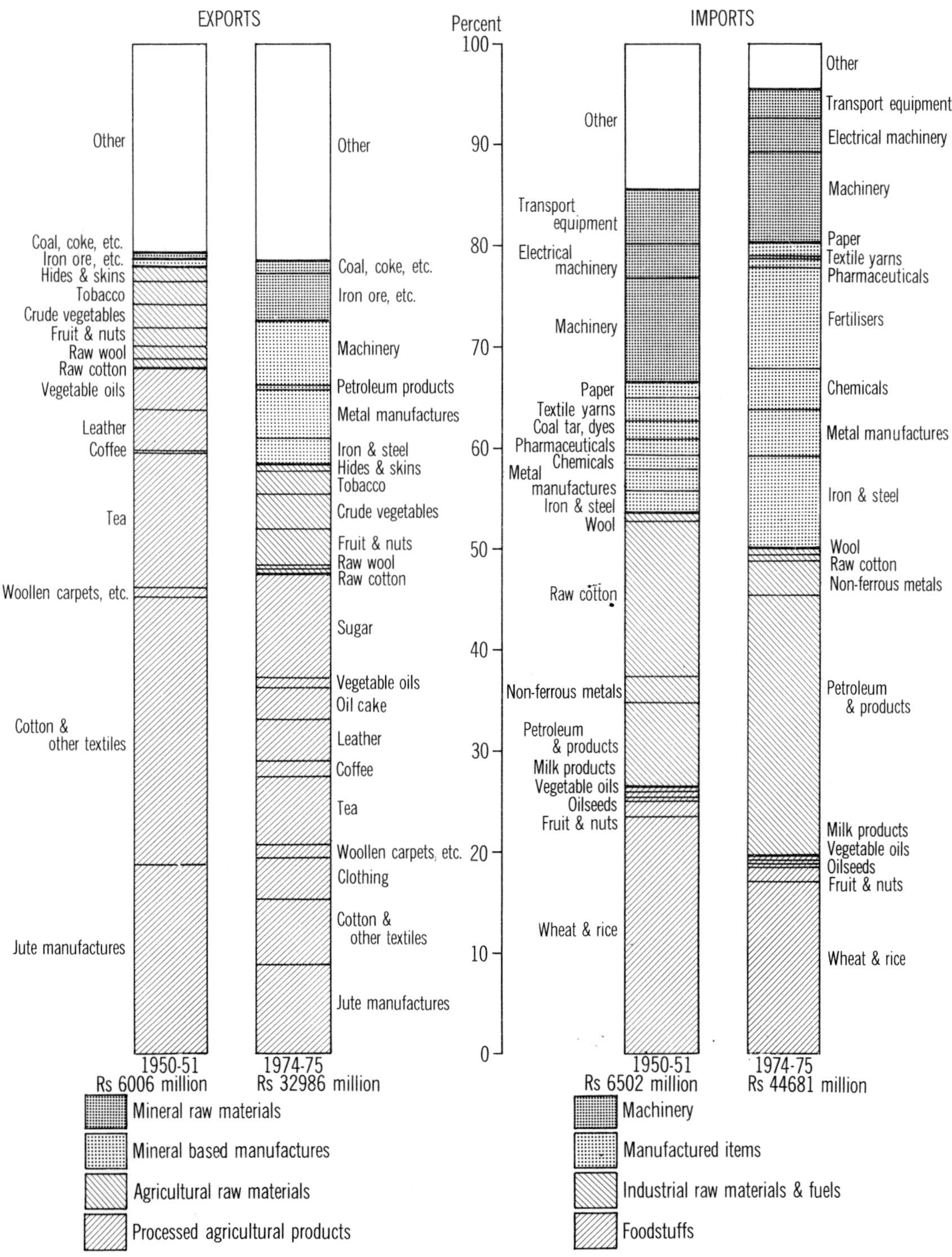
FOREIGN TRADE
1950-51 and 1974-75
EXPORTS
Percent
IMPORTS
100
90
80
70
60
50
40
30
20
10
0
Other
Coal, coke, etc.
Iron ore, etc.
Hides & skins
Tobacco
Crude vegetables
Fruit & nuts
Raw wool
Raw cotton
Vegetable oils
Leather
Coffee
Tea
Woollen carpets, etc.
Cotton & other textiles
Jute manufactures
1950-51
Rs 6006 million
Other
Coal, coke, etc.
Iron ore, etc.
Machinery
Petroleum products
Metal manufactures
Iron & steel
Hides & skins
Tobacco
Crude vegetables
Fruit & nuts
Raw wool
Raw cotton
Sugar
Vegetable oils
Oil cake
Leather
Coffee
Tea
Woollen carpets, etc.
Clothing
Cotton & other textiles
Jute manufactures
1974-75
Rs 32986 million
Other
Transport equipment
Electrical machinery
Machinery
Paper
Textile yarns
Coal tar, dyes
Pharmaceuticals
Chemicals
Metal manufactures
Iron & steel
Wool
Raw cotton
Non-ferrous metals
Petroleum & products
Milk products
Vegetable oils
Oilseeds
Fruit & nuts
Wheat & rice
1950-51
Rs 6502 million
Other
Transport equipment
Electrical machinery
Machinery
Paper
Textile yarns
Pharmaceuticals
Fertilisers
Chemicals
Metal manufactures
Iron & steel
Wool
Raw cotton
Non-ferrous metals
Petroleum & products
Milk products
Vegetable oils
Oilseeds
Fruit & nuts
Wheat & rice
1974-75
Rs 44681 million
Mineral raw materials
Mineral based manufactures
Agricultural raw materials
Processed agricultural products
Machinery
Manufactured items
Industrial raw materials & fuels
Foodstuffs

FIG. 2.10

Significant new trading partners are West Germany and USSR and trade with Japan has expanded considerably with her purchases of iron ore and sales of machinery and fertilizers. The purchasers of India's exports and providers of its imports are listed in Tables 2.16 and 2.17 respectively.

Since independence India's balance of payments has almost invariably been in deficit, imports exceeding exports by from 25 to 29 per cent of total trade (imports plus exports) in the period 1960–68. The deficit reached Rs 9218 million in 1966–67. In recent years the trade deficit has been reduced, and even reversed in 1972–73, but the oil crisis has swung the terms of trade heavily against India with a record deficit of Rs 10,970 million in 1974–75. The deficit has had to be balanced by borrowings and grants, and by dipping into reserves. One asset India had at independence was a reserve of about $2,000 million accumulated during the Second World War, and this was invaluable during the years of stagnation and slow growth of the First and Second Five Year Plans. With the running down of these reserves foreign aid came to the rescue to help the country through the drought years, and to provide the means for investing in development. Loans have ultimately to be repaid, and the costs of servicing have tended to loom larger in the budget every year. The Fourth Plan and again the Fifth, have aimed to reduce the burden of aid, progressively. A rough guide to the size of this burden is that the estimated debt service payments in 1972–73 were approximately one quarter of the value of exports that year. In other words, India may be approaching the stage when energetic promotion of exports and reduction of imports by vigorous development of import-substituting industries could close the trade gap in a normal year and dispense with the need for aid. But for the oil crisis this might have occurred sooner.

TABLE 2.16

Countries receiving India's Exports
(per cent of total)

Country	*1950–51*	*1974–75*
USSR	0.2	12.7
USA	19.3	11.3
Japan	1.7	8.9
UK	23.3	9.2
Bangladesh	—	1.3
West Germany	—	3.2
Italy	2.5	1.6
France	1.5	2.5
Czechoslovakia	1.7	1.8
Netherlands	1.7	2.2
Egypt	1.0	1.6
Canada	2.3	1.3
Australia	4.9	1.8
Sudan	0.7	2.0
Iran	—	6.4
Total listed here	60.8	67.8

TABLE 2.17

Countries providing India's Imports
(per cent of total)

	1950–51	*1974–75*
USA	18.3	16.3
Iran	5.7	10.5
Japan	1.6	10.1
USSR	—*	9.0
West Germany	—*	6.9
Saudi Arabia	0.1	6.7
Iraq	—	5.6
UK	20.8	4.8
Canada	3.4	2.9
Australia	5.1	2.6
Belgium	1.4	2.3
Poland	—	2.1
France	1.7	1.8
Italy	2.5	1.7
Kuwait	—	1.4
Netherlands	1.1	1.1
Egypt	5.1	0.5
Sudan	1.2	0.1
Total listed here	68.0	86.1

Source: Monthly Statistics for Trade of India: March 1975.
* West Germany had 8.1 per cent and USSR 5.8 per cent in 1964–65.

Table 2.18 summarizes the debt owed by the Government of India in 1971–72, and Table 2.19 the sectorwise longterm foreign investment in corporate industrial and commercial enterprises in 1968, with 1948 data for comparison. The figure for the petroleum industry will have fallen somewhat following recent nationalization of some oil companies.

A World Bank Report on the Indian Economy issued in May 1976 provides an appropriate tailpiece to this chapter:

> It is one of the world's poorest countries with a per capita income of $130, but it has the world's tenth largest Gross National Product and is the world's fourth largest foodgrain producer. Whole millions of farmers use primitive technology.

India is the world leader in wheat research, has a nuclear research capacity and its medical research is at the frontier of reproductive biology. In short India is an immense, culturally diverse and contradictory country rich in potential yet slow to develop the potential.[1]

[1] Deccan Herald, Bangalore, May 17, 1976.

TABLE 2.18

Government Debt raised outside India 1971–72 (Rs million)

USA	24,827
UK	6,470
W. Germany	4,080
USSR	3,540
Japan	2,530
Canada	1,700
International Bank	2,450
Int. Development Association	8,340
Total	**70,270**

TABLE 2.19

Foreign Investments: 1948 and 1968 (Rs million)

		1948		*1968*
Plantations		520		1,230
Mining		120		100
Petroleum		220		1,960
Manufacturing		710		8,210
Textiles	280		660	
Transport equipment	10		850	
Food	100		440	
Machinery	10		500	
Electrical eng.	50		650	
Metals	80		1,550	
Chemicals	80		2,410	
Miscellaneous	100		1,150	
Services		1,080		3,930
Construction, Transport etc.	320		2,220	
Financial	160		960	
Trading	430		540	
Miscellaneous	180		210	
Total		2,650		15,430

Source: 'India a Statistical Outline', India, Ministry of Food, Agriculture, Commodity Development and Cooperation.

13 Elephant working timber in the hills on the Kerala-Tamilnadu border. India's fine timber resources are continually under threat from encroachment by cultivators in search of land and by unauthorized exploiters of forest products. Sustained yield policies are pursued by the state forestry departments.

PART II

Agriculture and Its Environments

CHAPTER THREE

THE PHYSICAL ENVIRONMENTS OF AGRICULTURE

The aspects of the physical environment most affecting the cultivator tilling the land in a particular place are climate, soil and slope. To a limited extent these elements may be modified but only at some cost either to the farmer or to the community. In India the most important environmental modification has been irrigation, by means of which the time and space relationships of rainfall, the ultimate source of moisture, can be manipulated to the farmer's advantage. Sparse precipitation can be collected from a wide catchment to be concentrated on a smaller area of crops. Water can be stored from the rainy season so that crops can be irrigated during a dry period. Storage may be in man-made dams, or water may be recovered from natural groundwater reservoirs. The farmer can do little to modify temperature. In developed countries winter cold can be avoided by the creation in a greenhouse of an artificial environment for products of high value. In India the problem is rather to mitigate the dessicating effects of excessively high temperature and direct insolation. In the case of perennial crops like coffee and tea, trees are planted to provide shade and to act as wind-breaks. At the level of the microenvironment, annual field crops of different heights and habits may be interplanted to provide mutual protection. Soils are more difficult to alter physically, but increasingly man is able at relatively small cost by using artificial fertilizers or natural composts, to compensate his crops for any deficiencies there may be in soil nutrients. Some amelioration of soil texture may be achieved by ploughing in village garbage and green manure crops.

The physical nature of the soil is related in part to its parent material, often the weathered rocks of the land over which it has developed during millenia as a superficial film, rarely more than a metre or two thick. Over large areas of India the soil is formed of alluvial material transported originally to its present location by rivers, and in coastal areas, perhaps re-sorted by marine tides and waves. The quality of alluvium where it occurs and the thickness and quality of soils developed *in situ* are related to physiographic and climatic processes (themselves inter-linked to a degree) working on the surface of the earth.

Also related to these processes is the slope of the land on which the farmer lays out his fields. This again he may modify at some cost, and must so do, by levelling and bunding for example, if he wants to grow wet rice, for which an even depth of standing water is needed. For other crops he may be content merely to reduce the slope thereby concentrating the soil somewhat to create a deeper medium to absorb more moisture and provide ample space for crop roots to develop. By and large however, agriculture has to be practised on the slopes and soils as nature made them, and under climatic conditions as they are. Man is far from controlling his environment, however impressive may be his efforts to exploit its elements and to mitigate the effect of extreme occurrences such as droughts and floods.

14 Women threshing jowar (seen behind), a man winnows grain and another records the yield at a crop sampling near Aurangabad on the Deccan Lavas of Maharashtra.

Fundamental to an understanding of the soils that the Indian farmers cultivate is some knowledge of the country's geology and morphology. India consists of three basic structural features (see Figures 3.1 and 3.2); the geologically ancient and now stable 'shield' of Peninsular India; the relatively young mountain chains of the Himalaya, still a region of considerable geological instability; and between them the extensive alluvium-filled depression occupied by the three great river systems, Indus, Ganga and Brahmaputra. The rocks of the Peninsula include some of the oldest known, the early Pre-Cambrian or Archaean formations. Granites and gneiss are widespread, but there are also metamorphosed sedimentary and igneous rocks with which India's main mineralized belts are associated. Countersunk, as it were, into the Archaean formations are remnants of sedimentary rocks of two major phases of geological history. First younger Pre-Cambrian and Early Palaeozoic formations, the Cuddapah and Vindhyan respectively, may be taken together. Their metamorphosed slates and quartzites form impressive scarplands in Andhra Pradesh, the Nallamallai and

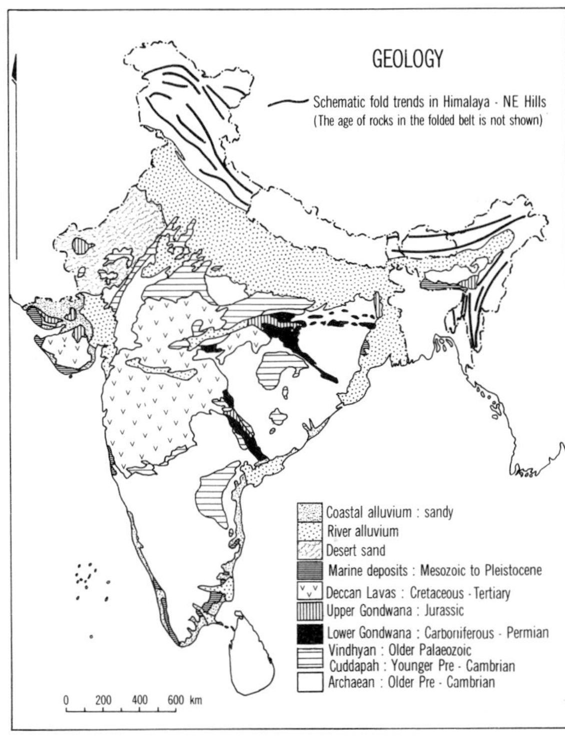

FIG. 3.1 After Wadia and others.

15 Treading out grain and winnowing on the Deccan Lavas near Aurangabad, Maharashtra.

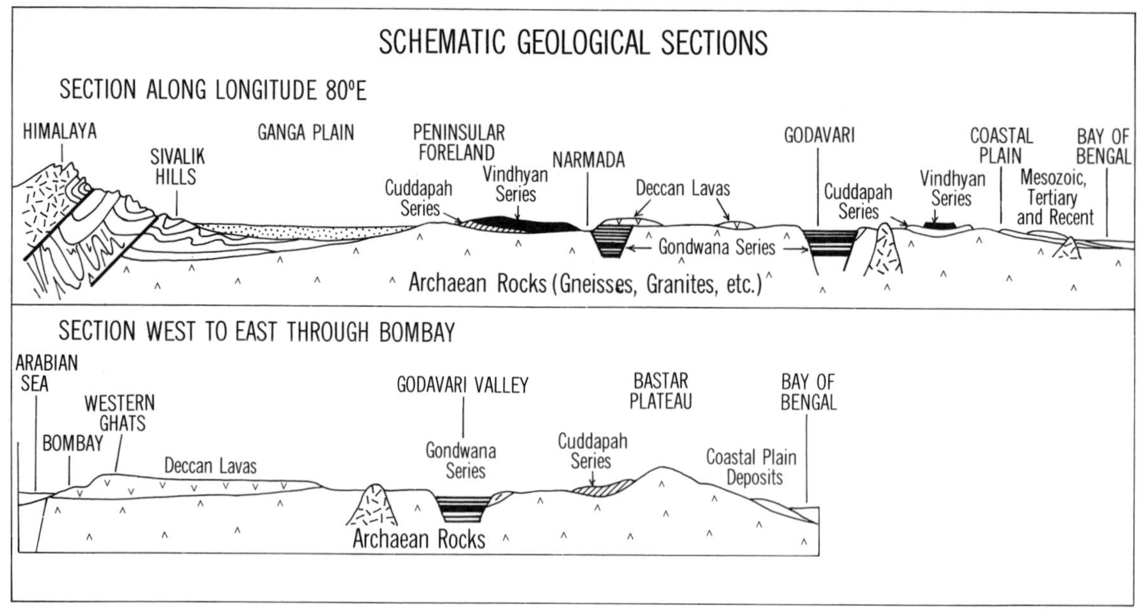

FIG. 3.2

Velkonda Ranges, and the close-ribbed agriculturally forbidding Peninsular Foreland in Madhya Pradesh. A later and very different geological episode is represented in the Gondwana rocks, of Carboniferous to Jurassic age. These are continental deposits including important coal seams, which have been preserved in fault-bounded rift-like troughs which are still followed by major drainage lines, notably the Damodar and the lower Godavari.

It seems that for the whole of Mesozoic and Tertiary time the Peninsula remained a landmass exposed to weathering and erosion. Only here and there on its coastal margins do marine formations indicate limited incursions of the sea. There was however geological activity of a different kind over almost a third of the region. In late Cretaceous and early Tertiary time there occurred fissure eruptions of lava on an immense scale which buried the northwestern part of the Peninsula beneath thousands of metres of basalt.

As a structural element the Peninsular Shield does not end abruptly at its surface junction with the Indo-Gangetic alluvium but beneath the latter extends northwards and westwards from the Aravalli Ranges, outcropping in rocky inliers in recent superficial deposits in Delhi and Rajasthan. To the northeast its rocks reappear to form the Meghalaya Plateau beyond the Ganga Delta.

Through eons of geological time the Peninsular Shield to the south and a continental mass lying in central Asia to the north poured sediments into a broad deepening trough, part of an ancient sea that extended from southern Europe into Southeast Asia. Ultimately, in Tertiary time the continental masses or 'plates' moved inwards, thrusting upwards in what became the Himalayan ranges the sedimentary strata of the intervening geosyncline. The process continued for a long time, and as the mountain chains rose, erosion fast worked upon them, and rivers carried vast quantities of coarse material into the marine gulfs that separated them from the Peninsula. Continued uplift and fracturing incorporated some of these deposits into the outer Himalayan chains, e.g. the Sivaliks which in turn were exposed to vigorous erosion. As the marine gulfs were filled in, conditions were locally favourable at various times to the formation of coal seams and petroleum, and to the accumulation of salt.

As the cross-section in Figure 3.2 indicates, the sub-Himalayan depression of the Indo-Gangetic plains is a structural element of a lesser order compared with the Himalaya and the Peninsular Shield which although separated on the surface are in contact beneath the alluvial infill. This alluvium has itself been subjected to structural movement and base-level change. In broad terms,

FIG. 3.3

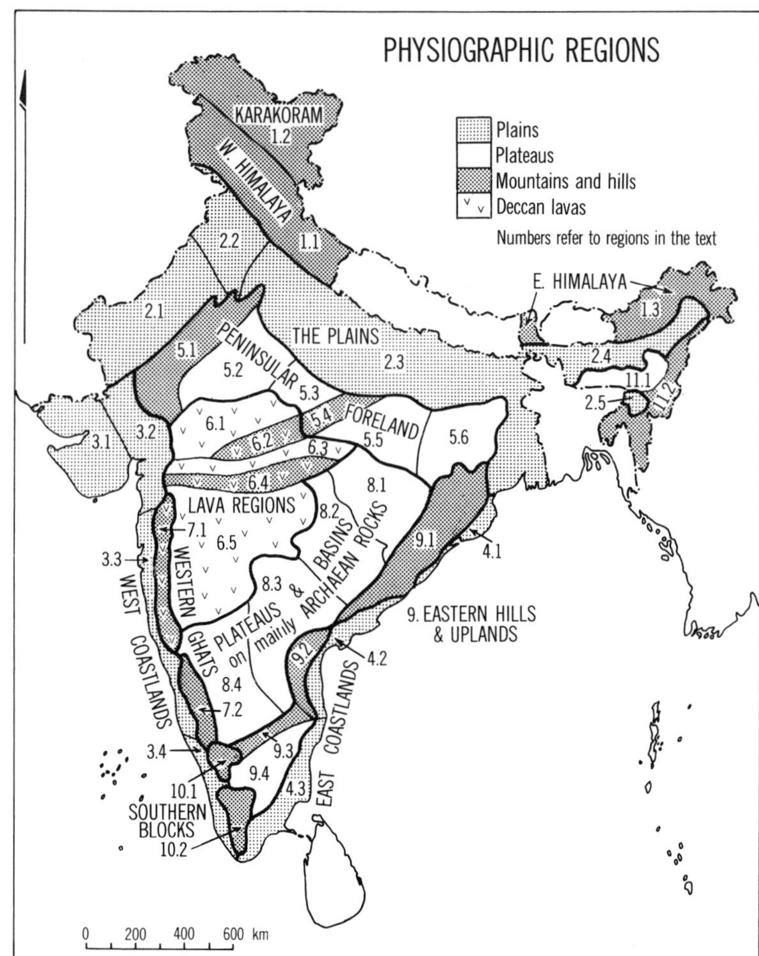

TABLE 3.1
Physiographic Regions (refer to Figure 3.3.)

1 Himalaya-Karakoram
1.1 Western Himalaya
1.2 Karakoram
1.3 Eastern Himalaya
2 The Plains
2.1 Rajasthan Plains
2.2 Punjab-Haryana Plains
2.3 Ganga Plains
2.4 Assam Valley
2.5 Surma Valley
3 West Coastlands
3.1 Kutch and Kathiawar
3.2 Gujarat Plains
3.3 Konkan-Karnataka Coast
3.4 Malabar (Kerala) Coast
4 East Coastlands
4.1 Orissa Coast
4.2 Andhra Coast
4.3 Tamilnad Coastal Plain
5 Peninsular Foreland
5.1 Aravalli Range
5.2 Chambal Basin
5.3 Bundelkhand
5.4 Vindhyan Scarplands
5.5 Baghelkhand
5.6 Chotanagpur Plateau
6 The Peninsular Lava Country
6.1 Malwa Plateau
6.2 Vindhyas
6.3 Narmada Valley
6.4 Satpura Ranges
6.5 Deccan Lava Plateau
7 Western Ghats
7.1 Western Ghats: Lava section
7.2 Western Ghats: Archaean section
8 Plateaux and Basins on mainly Archaean Rocks
8.1 Chhatisgarh Plain
8.2 Dandakaranya Plateau
8.3 Telangana Plateau
8.4 Karnataka Plateau
9 Eastern Hills and Uplands
9.1 Orissa Hills
9.2 Nallamallai Hills
9.3 Balaghat
9.4 Tamilnad Plateau
10 Southern Blocks
10.1 Nilgiri Hills
10.2 Southern Ghats
11 Hills and Plateaux of the Northeast
11.1 Meghalaya Plateau
11.2 Northeastern Hills

the plains consist of a number of coalescent alluvial fans deriving their sediment from Himalayan rivers. Accordingly the sediments tend to be most coarse along the Himalayan Piedmont. Much less material is offered by the rivers draining northwards from the Peninsular block, with the result that the major rivers, the Yamuna and Ganga, follow courses close to the southern edge of the alluvium.

The end-product of Indian structural and erosional history may best be summarized in the map of physiographic regions (Figure 3.3), and the accompanying key, Table 3.1. These also provide a frame of reference for subsequent discussions on a number of themes. The relevance of geology and physiography to the character of soils is examined below, following an examination of climate, as it affects agriculture (in part of course through its role in soil formation).

Agriculture is the mainstay of the Indian economy, and is likely to remain so for the foreseeable future. Of all the factors involved in crop production by far the most important in India is rainfall. By comparison, the other major climatic element, temperature, is of small significance, It is a limiting factor to plant growth in winter but really only in the north, particularly in the hills, and at the other extreme it everywhere promotes high rates of evaporation in summertime. Figure 3.4 shows some significant isotherms. Effectively, low temperature causes a serious hiatus to plant life only at high elevations in the Himalaya and its inter-montane plateaux and valleys. Even here temperatures permit the cultivation of autumn sown wheat, which lies dormant through the freezing winter. The plains of Punjab and Haryana have occasional ground frost, but in lowland India generally the only major constraint exerted on agriculture by low winter temperatures is on some rice varieties which may not mature in December and January north of the tropic. As the map shows, most of India enjoys a pleasantly warm winter, comparable to the ideal summer of many a temperate land. Fig. 3.6 shows temperature regimes for representative stations. In only two cases, both stations over 1,500m above sea level, do absolute minima fall below freezing point.

Average daily maxima lie generally within the comfortable 20s, only Pune and Bellary in the Peninsular interior, and Cochin on the Kerala coast in the far south among the stations illustrated, exceeding 30°C. (See also the tabulated climatic data in Table 3.2 on pages 50–52.) The isotherm for 20°C would parallel closely that for 10°C which follows the Himalayan foothills.

Summer isotherms (Figure 3.5) suggest more homogeneous conditions than in winter. Setting aside the mountains where elevation reduces shade temperatures appreciably (note the maxima for Leh and Simla in Table 3.2 and Figure 3.6) it is only in the near-equatorial south, along the west coast, and around the head of the Bay of Bengal that average daily maxima fail to top 38°C (100°F). The effect of continentality is clear. Absolute maxima at stations well inland, like New Delhi, Jodhpur and Allahabad, lie in the 40s for five or six months.

FIG. 3.4

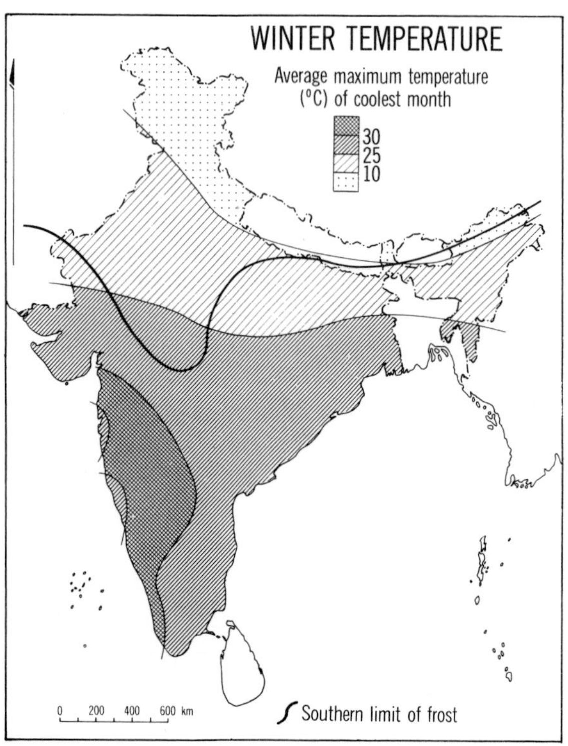

FIG. 3.5

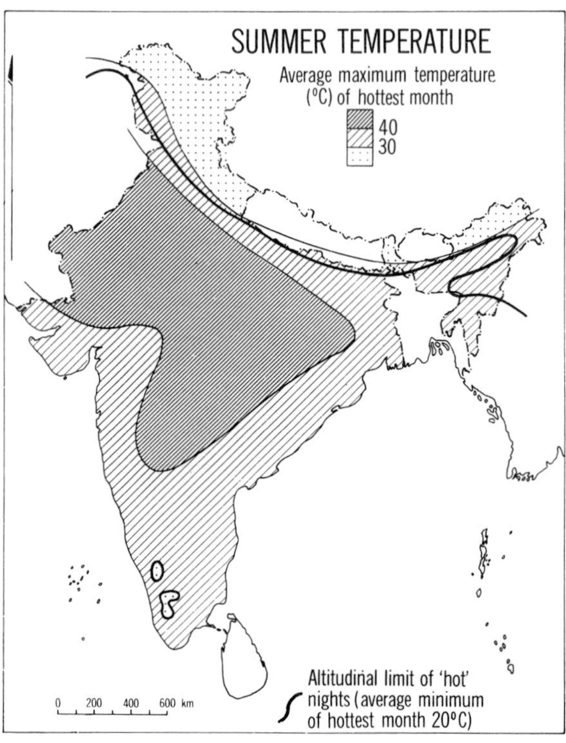

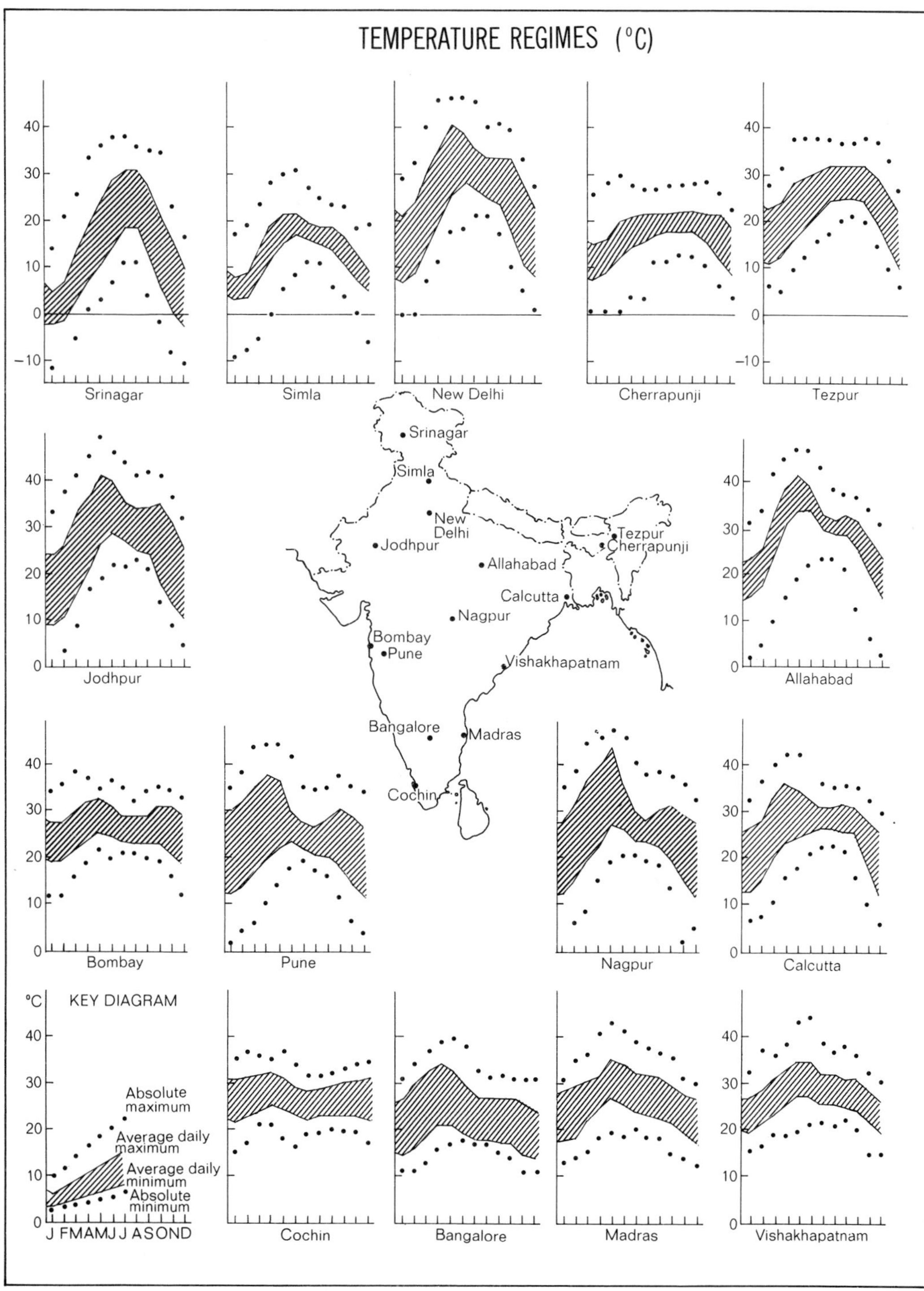
TEMPERATURE REGIMES (°C)
Srinagar
Simla
New Delhi
Cherrapunji
Tezpur
Jodhpur
Allahabad
Bombay
Pune
Nagpur
Calcutta
Cochin
Bangalore
Madras
Vishakhapatnam
KEY DIAGRAM
Absolute maximum
Average daily maximum
Average daily minimum
Absolute minimum
J F M A M J J A S O N D

FIG. 3.6

TABLE 3.2
Climatic Data (Temperature 0°C, Rainfall in mm)

Region Station (Altitude in metres)	*No. of years recorded.*	*Jan*	*Feb*	*Mar*	*Apr*	*May*	*June*	*July*	*Aug*	*Sept*	*Oct*	*Nov*	*Dec*	*Per year*
Cold Dry														
1. *Leh* (3,514)														
Av. daily max.		−1	+1	7	13	16	20	25	24	21	15	8	2	
Av. daily min.	23	−13	−12	−6	−1	1	7	10	10	6	0	−7	−11	
Av. temperature		−7	−6	0	6	9	14	18	17	14	8	1	−4	
Av. rainfall	23	10	8	8	5	5	5	13	15	8	3	2	5	116
Humid (10 wet months)														
2. *Simla* (2,202)														
Av. daily max.		8	9	14	18	22	23	21	19	19	17	14	11	
Av. daily min.	30	2	3	7	11	14	16	16	15	14	11	7	4	
Av. temperature		5	6	11	15	18	20	19	17	17	14	11	8	
Av. rainfall	75	61	69	61	53	66	175	424	434	160	33	13	28	1,574
3. *Kodaikanal* (2,343)														
Av. temperature	10	13	13	15	16	16	16	14	15	15	14	13	12	
Av. rainfall		43	21	73	231	169	96	129	122	157	263	237	123	1,664
4. *Cherrapunji* (1,313)														
Av. daily max.		16	17	21	22	22	22	22	23	23	22	19	17	
Av. daily min.	35	8	9	13	15	16	18	18	18	18	16	12	9	
Av. temperature		12	13	17	19	19	20	20	21	21	19	16	13	
Av. rainfall		18	53	185	666	1280	2695	2446	1781	1100	493	69	13	11,437
5. *Darjiling* (2,265)														
Av. daily max.		8	9	14	17	18	18	19	18	18	16	12	9	
Av. daily min.	25	2	2	6	9	12	13	14	14	13	10	6	3	
Av. temperature	30	6	8	11	14	16	17	18	18	17	15	11	8	
Av. rainfall	60	22	27	53	109	187	522	713	573	419	116	14	5	2,760
Humid (8–9 wet months)														
6. *Tezpur* (79)														
Av. daily max.	20	23	24	28	28	31	32	32	32	32	30	27	24	
Av. daily min.	19	11	13	17	19	22	25	26	26	25	22	16	12	
Av. temperature		17	19	23	24	27	29	29	29	29	26	22	18	
Av. rainfall	20	13	28	58	158	252	305	366	366	208	107	18	5	1,880
7. *Cochin* (3)														
Av. daily max.		32	32	33	33	32	29	29	29	29	31	31	32	
Av. daily min.	43	22	23	25	26	26	24	23	24	24	24	24	23	
Av. temperature		27	28	29	30	29	27	26	27	27	28	28	28	
Av. rainfall	60	23	20	51	125	297	724	592	353	196	340	171	41	3,106
Humid (6–7 months)														
8. *Calcutta* (6)														
Av. daily max.		27	29	34	36	36	33	32	32	32	32	29	26	
Av. daily min.	60	13	15	21	24	25	26	26	26	26	23	18	13	
Av. temperature		20	22	28	30	30	30	29	29	29	28	24	20	
Av. rainfall		10	31	36	43	140	297	325	328	252	114	20	5	1,582
9. *Mormugao* (62)														
Av. daily max.	30—	29	29	31	32	32	31	29	28	28	29	30	29	
Av. daily min.	29	21	22	24	26	27	25	24	24	24	24	23	21	
Av. temperature		25	26	28	29	30	28	27	26	26	27	27	25	
Av. rainfall	30	2	2	2	18	66	752	793	404	241	97	33	5	2,413
10. *Vishakhapatnam* (3)														
Av. daily ax.	45	27	28	31	32	33	33	32	32	31	31	29	27	
Av. daily min.		19	22	24	26	27	27	26	26	26	25	22	20	
Av. temperature		23	25	28	29	30	30	29	29	29	28	26	24	
Av. rainfall	40	10	23	13	18	51	104	112	132	165	198	119	15	944

Humid (4–5 wet months)														
11. *Allahabad* (98)														
Av. daily max.		24	26	33	40	42	40	33	32	33	32	28	24	
Av. daily min.	30	8	11	16	22	27	28	27	26	25	19	12	8	
Av. temperature		16	19	25	31	35	34	30	29	29	26	20	16	
Av. rainfall	60	23	15	15	5	15	127	320	254	213	58	8	8	1,032
12. *Bombay* (11)														
Av. daily max.		28	28	30	32	33	32	29	29	29	32	32	31	
Av. daily min.	60	19	19	22	24	27	26	25	24	24	24	23	21	
Av. temperature		24	24	26	28	30	29	27	27	27	28	28	26	
Av. rainfall		10	18	15	15	20	224	371	290	203	56	20	13	2,078
13. *Nagpur* (310)														
Av. daily max.		28	32	37	41	43	37	31	31	32	32	29	27	
Av. daily min.	28	13	16	20	24	28	16	24	24	23	20	16	12	
Av. temperature		21	24	29	33	36	32	28	28	28	26	23	20	
Av. rainfall	60	10	18	15	15	20	224	371	290	203	56	20	13	1,251
Humid (4–7 wet months)														
14. *Madras* (16)														
Av. daily max.		29	31	33	35	38	38	36	35	34	32	29	29	
Av. daily min.	60	19	20	22	26	28	27	26	26	25	24	22	21	
Av. temperature		24	25	28	31	33	33	31	31	30	28	26	25	
Av. rainfall		36	10	8	15	25	48	91	117	119	305	356	140	1,233
Sub Humid (normal)														
15. *New Delhi* (216)														
Av. daily max.	89	21	24	31	36	41	39	36	34	34	34	29	23	
Av. daily min.	65	7	9	14	20	26	28	27	26	24	18	11	8	
Av. temperature		14	17	23	28	34	34	32	30	29	26	29	16	
Av. rainfall	75	23	18	13	8	13	74	180	173	117	10	3	10	715
16. *Bangalore* (921)														
Av. daily max.	32	27	30	33	34	33	29	28	28	28	28	27	26	
Av. daily min.	33	14	16	18	21	21	19	19	19	18	18	17	15	
Av. temperature		21	23	26	28	27	24	24	24	23	23	22	21	
Av. rainfall	60	5	8	10	41	107	74	99	127	170	150	69	10	924
17. *Ahmadabad* (55)														
Av. daily max.		29	31	36	40	42	38	34	32	34	36	34	30	
Av. daily min.	23	14	15	19	23	26	27	26	25	24	22	18	15	
Av. temperature		22	23	28	32	34	33	30	29	29	29	26	23	
Av. rainfall		2	3	3	2	10	109	285	206	94	15	3	2	804
18. *Pune* (559)														
Av. daily max.		31	33	36	38	37	32	28	28	29	32	31	29	
Av. daily min.	24	12	13	17	20	22	23	22	22	21	19	15	12	
Av. temperature		22	23	27	29	30	28	25	25	25	26	23	21	
Av. rainfall	60	2	2	2	15	28	114	168	89	135	89	28	3	715
Sub-Humid (Summer drought)														
19. *Pamban* (11)														
Av. daily max.		28	29	32	33	33	32	32	32	32	31	29	28	
Av. daily min.	50	24	24	25	27	27	27	26	26	26	26	24	24	
Av. temperature		26	27	29	30	30	30	29	29	29	29	27	26	
Av. rainfall	60	66	23	18	46	25	3	13	15	28	216	297	193	922
20. *Bellary* (449)														
Av. daily max.		31	34	37	39	39	34	32	32	32	32	31	29	
Av. daily min.	30	17	19	23	26	26	24	24	23	23	22	19	17	
Av. temperature		24	27	30	33	33	29	28	28	28	27	25	23	
Av. rainfall	60	3	5	5	20	48	43	41	61	125	107	51	3	511

Summer and Winter Transitional														
21. *Ludhiana* (247)														
Av. temperature	85	13	16	21	27	33	34	31	30	30	26	20	15	
Av. rainfall		35	35	29	11	9	54	191	173	136	35	3	14	725
22. *Srinagar* (1587)														
Av. daily max.		5	7	14	19	24	29	31	31	28	22	16	9	
Av. daily min.	30	−2	−1	3	7	11	14	18	18	12	5	−1	−2	
Av. temperature		1	4	9	13	18	22	25	24	21	14	8	4	
Av. rainfall	60	73	72	104	78	63	36	61	63	31	28	20	36	665
Semi Arid														
23. *Jodhpur* (224)														
Av. daily max.		24	27	32	37	41	40	36	34	34	35	31	26	
Av. daily min.	23	9	11	16	21	26	28	27	25	24	18	13	10	
Av. temperature		17	19	24	29	34	34	32	30	29	27	22	18	
Av. rainfall	50	3	5	3	3	10	36	102	122	61	8	3	3	364
Arid														
24. *Jaisalmer* (242)														
Av. daily max.														
Av. daily min.														
Av. temperature		16	19	25	29	34	34	32	31	31	28	22	17	
Av. rainfall	10	3	1	3	3	5	8	90	86	14	1	5	3	216

Sources: Wernstedt, F., *World Climatic Data*, Climate Data Press 1972, for Jaisalmer.
US Dept of Commerce, *World Weather Records*, 1951–60 Vol. 4 Asia 1967 for Ludhiana and Kodaikanal.
Great Britain, Meteorological Office, *Tables of Temperature, Relative Humidity and Precipitation for the World*, Part V: Asia, 1966, for the remainder.

As a rule the hottest months precede the onset of the rains and their extremely high temperatures tend to off-set the beneficial effects of the pre-monsoon rains that may fall in April-May-June. May or June is usually the time of peak temperature, from which it falls quite sharply with the arrival of the monsoon, to a modest plateau in July-August and September. It declines further with the approach of winter when clear skies allow night-time radiation to bring a higher diurnal range.

A distinctive characteristic of the Indian climate, sensibly if not meteorologically, is its threefold division into (i) the cool and mainly dry winter from November to February; (ii) the hot and mainly dry season from March or April into early June, and (iii) the wet monsoon, which 'bursts' in June (Figure 3.7) and lasts into September or later. This seasonality is as much a function of the rainfall as of the temperature regime.

The cool season, the *rabi* season of the agriculturalist, is one of general atmospheric stability. Clear dry days succeed one another, interrupted only in the northwest by occasional passing depressions which move eastward bringing light but valuable rains to Punjab and Haryana, and more rarely as far east as Patna. In the extreme southeast the end of the 'retreating monsoon', which is further discussed below, delays the dry season somewhat.

With the passing of the March equinox it becomes evident that the cool season is over. Temperatures rise day by day, and one looks forward to afternoon cloud to reduce the build-up of heat in buildings and so moderate the evening temperature. In April, thunder showers bring temporary respite. By May the Intertropical Convergence zone, the ITC, with which is associated heavy equatorial convectional rainfall, begins to move gradually northwards across India, bringing with it the 'break' of the monsoon.

The southwest winds which give the summer monsoon its prefix, are the resultant of cyclonic airflows within the monsoon air mass. This, as the dates of its first burst indicate is moving more directly northward. The southwest monsoon winds sweep across the Western Ghats bringing torrential orographic rain to the steep scarp and the coast at its foot. The air stream recovers stability as it descends across the Deccan, which thus lies in typical rainshadow relationship to the Ghats. In eastern India the monsoon drives from the south towards Bengal, one part swinging up the Ganga

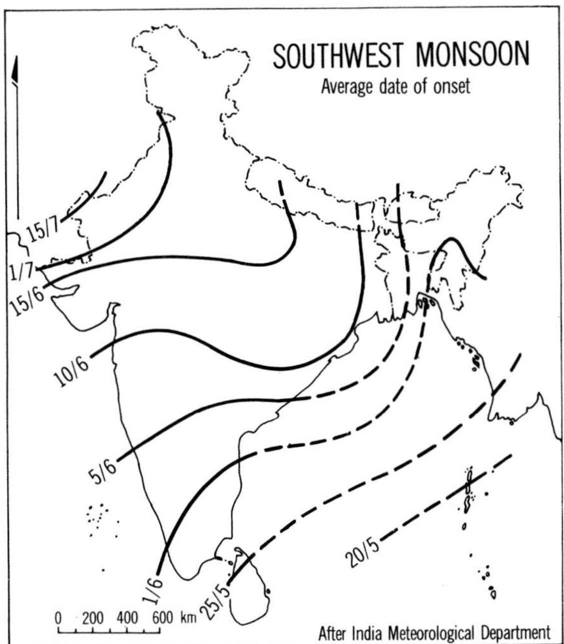

FIG. 3.7

16 Drying jowar on the hot smooth bitumen road near Mahabalipuram.

Valley as a southeast stream under the deflective influence of the Himalaya. Another part moves as a converging and ascending air stream between the Northeastern Hills and the Meghalaya Plateau, dousing in its wake the hill town of Cherrapunji, whose sole claim to fame is as holder of the world's average rainfall record of 11,437 mm. A daily downpour of as much as 924 mm has occurred in June, when the normal total for the month is almost 2700 mm. The other air stream, travelling up the Ganga Valley, spreads heavy rain along the Himalayan ranges. It loses moisture and thickness as it goes, arriving over the Rajasthan Desert only 500 metres thick and inhibited from releasing its remaining load of moisture by an overriding 'lid' of warmer westerly air originating in the mid-latitude subtropical high pressure cell that stands semi-permanently over the Sahara and extends a ridge across Iran-Afghanistan and the Indus Valley. When on occasion this lid retreats westward, the desert receives one of its rare soakings.

Through the monsoon, dynamic waves in the ITC cause the characteristic pulsations in the weather, bringing periods of heavy rain interspersed with brief respites of clear but unpleasantly sticky conditions, which increase in duration through August to become the dominant feature of September's weather. Thereafter settled conditions return in the north, and the ITC retreats southwards, continuing to allow a measure of convergence and precipitation over a diminishing area of southern India. In the Bay of Bengal the effect of this 'retreating monsoon' in bringing an autumnal maximum to the Tamilnadu coast is reinforced by the occasional occurrence of tropical cyclones, which move westwards across the Bay to trace arcuate clockwise courses along India's east coast and the delta fringe of Bangladesh. Tropical cyclones are responsible for heavy rainfall in October–November, and sometimes for considerable devastation and loss of life particularly in Orissa. As in Bangladesh, storm surges associated with cyclones heading into the shallowing and narrowing waters at the head of the Bay of Bengal can sweep sea water inland.

The amount of rainfall and its seasonal incidence are the most significant facts influencing agriculture in India. Figure 3.8 shows annual average rainfall. The influence of the Western Ghats and the Himalaya, Maghalya Plateau and Northeastern Hills in stimulating precipitation is clear, as are also the rainshadow in the Deccan, and the diminution of total rainfall up the Ganga Valley. It may be noted that the 1000 mm isohyet divides the country into two roughly equal parts, a division that carries into agricultural regionalization as the boundary between rainfed rice cultivation and that of wheat or millets. Different aspects of rainfall incidence are depicted in Figure 3.9, showing the length of wet and dry seasons, in Figure 3.10 of rainfall incidence and in the rainfall dispersion diagrams for individual stations (Figure 3.11). The concept

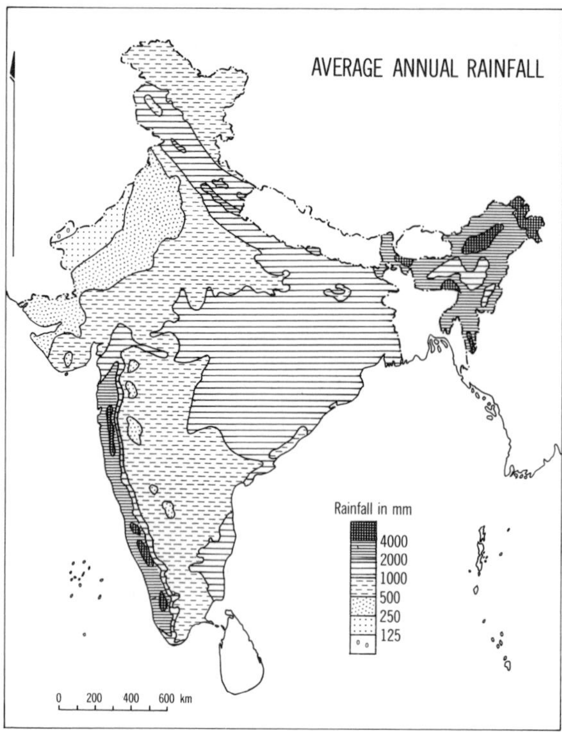

Fig. 3.8

Fig. 3.9

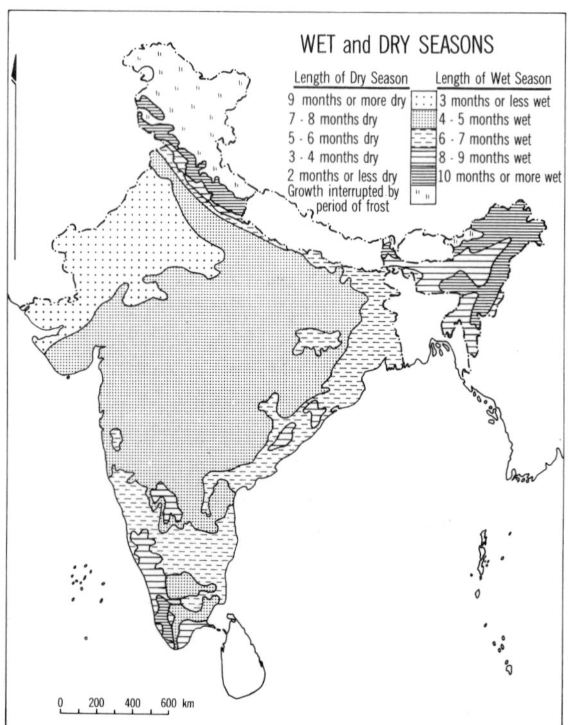

Fig. 3.10

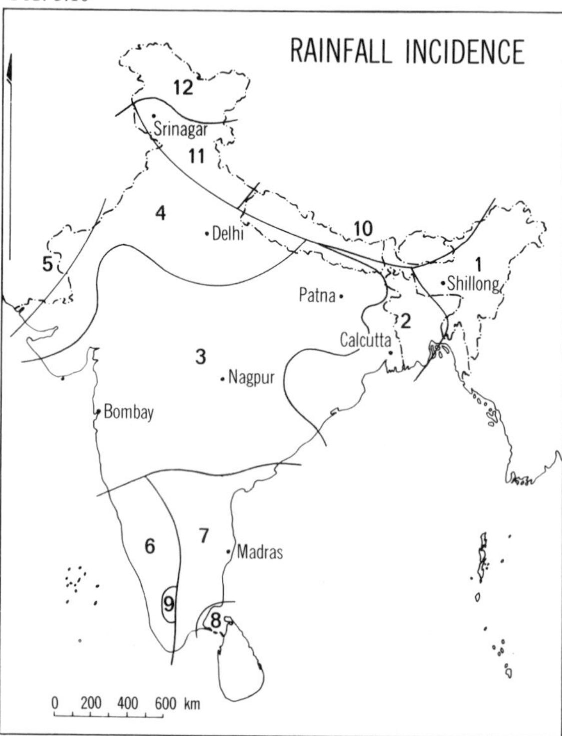

Type	Wet Months (Pmm>2T°C)											
	J	F	M	A	M	J	J	A	S	O	N	D
1 Assam		-	—	—	—	—	—	—	—	—	-	
2 Bengal - Orissa				-	—	—	—	—	—	—	-	
3 Central India						—	—	—	—	-		
4 NW India							—	—	-			
5 Desert							—					
6 Kerala - Karnataka				-	—	—	—	—	—	—	-	
7 Tamilnadu - S. Andhra							-	—	—	—	-	
8 Palk Bay	—	-								—	—	—
9 Nilgiris	—	—	—	—	—	—	—	—	—	—	—	—
10 E. Himalaya	—	—	—	—	—	—	—	—	—	—		
11 W. Himalaya	—	—	—	—	—	—	—	—	—	—	—	—
12 Inner Kashmir	—	—	—	-								—

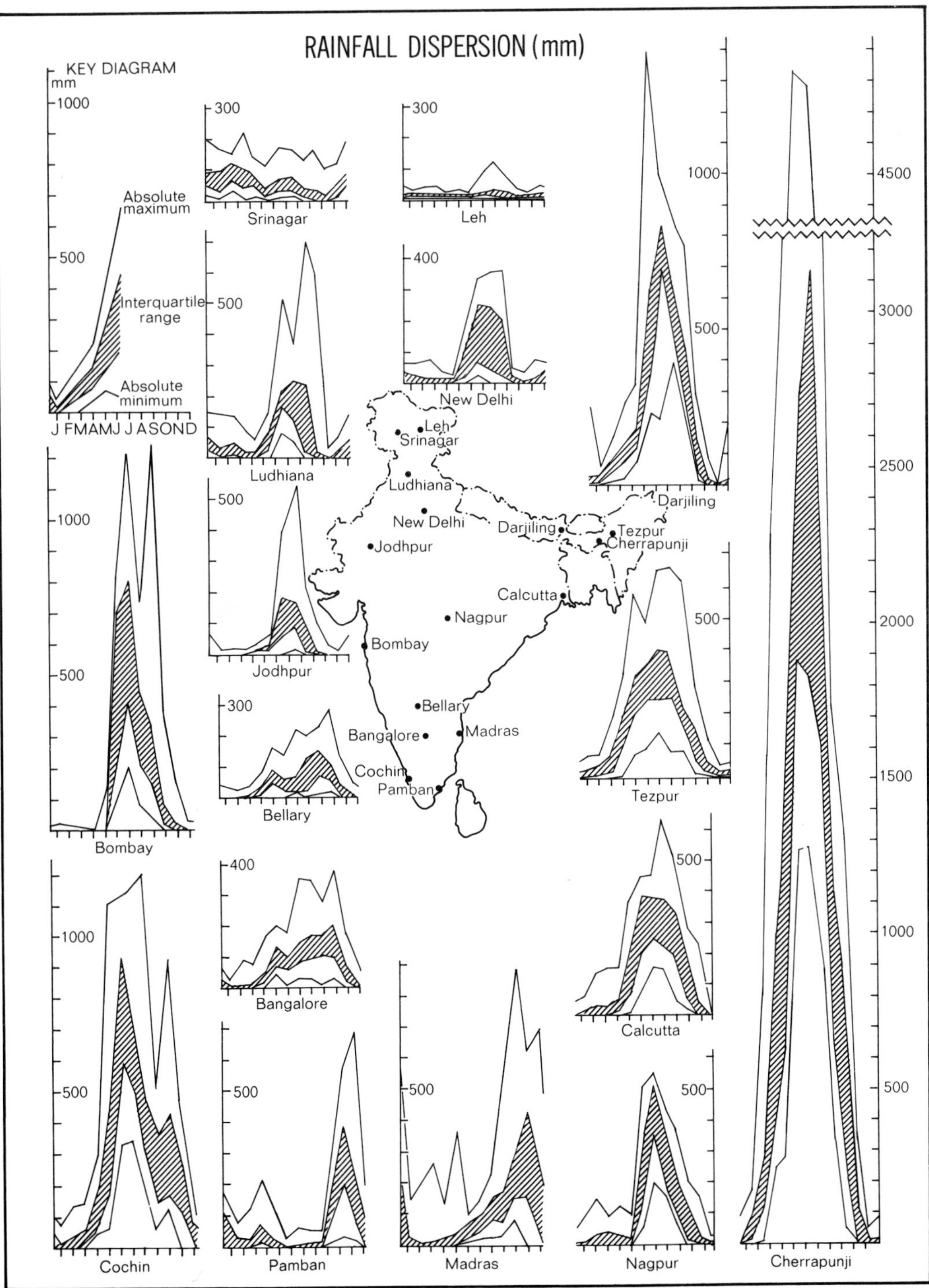
RAINFALL DISPERSION (mm)
KEY DIAGRAM
mm
1000
Absolute maximum
500
Interquartile range
Absolute minimum
J F M A M J J A S O N D
Srinagar
Leh
Ludhiana
New Delhi
Jodhpur
Bombay
Bellary
Bangalore
Cochin
Pamban
Madras
Nagpur
Calcutta
Tezpur
Darjiling
Cherrapunji
Leh
Srinagar
Ludhiana
New Delhi
Jodhpur
Darjiling
Tezpur
Cherrapunji
Calcutta
Nagpur
Bombay
Bellary
Bangalore
Madras
Cochin
Pamban
300
400
500
1000
1500
2000
2500
3000
4500

Fig. 3.11

of a 'wet' month is derived from the work of French geographers at the Institut Français at Pondicherry, which resulted in a series of maps of vegetation and of 'bioclimates'. They evolved a simple formula which identifies as a dry month, one in which precipitation (in mm) does not exceed twice the average temperature (in degrees Celsius). This value was found to approximate satisfactorily to conditions of stress in vegetation in India.[1]

The rains arrive earliest and last longest in Kerala and coastal Karnataka in the southwest, and in northeastern India from Orissa to Assam. The highest parts of these regions, and the Western Himalaya, have no true dry season, though the regime of their rainfall is clearly monsoonal. The western Himalaya and Kashmir, with the Karakoram lying beyond, have a substantial winter precipitation from depressions arriving from the west. Central India, with four to five wet months from June to October embodies the average characteristic of the Indian Monsoon. To the northwest the wet season is reduced to two or three months starting in July. The desert, notoriously erratic in its rainfall, tends to receive whatever it gets in July at the time the monsoon breaks. In the southeast, Tamilnadu and adjacent parts of Andhra although in the path of the monsoon as it passes over the Peninsula from the southwest are in a rainshadow due to the subsidence of the dynamic stream. They have some rain, but their major falls come from August onwards into November when the doldrum conditions of the retreating monsoon settle over this region and Kerala. A small coastal strip around Palk Bay, represented by Pamban (Figure 3.11) has four wet months starting in October. Only this area of India can be said to benefit substantially from the so-called northeast monsoon, which as a flow of air across the Bay of Bengal is, for four or five months, the assertion of the Northeast Trades, the typical wind in oceanic areas at this latitude. It does not set in until January as a rule, and cannot be credited, (despite common belief), with the rainfall more properly assigned to the retreating monsoon.

[1] H. Gaussen, 'The vegetation maps', *Travaux de la Section Scientifique et Technique*, Inst. Francais de Pondichery, Tome I, Fasciscule IV, 1959, p. 170.

The duration of both wet and dry seasons, are shown in Figure 3.9. Although a small proportion of annual rainfall comes outside the monsoon period, the latter accounts for around 80 per cent of the total. The length of the dry season gives a fair indication of the need for irrigation if agriculture is to be carried on outside the rainy season. Frequent reference to this map will illuminate the subsequent sections on agriculture. Similarly, Table 3.2 may be found helpful.

Figure 3.12 showing climates, brings together the essential climatic elements of concern to the cultivator: temperature, and the amount, duration and incidence of rainfall. Cold climates, where average temperatures below freezing for a month or more are a severe constraint on agriculture, are limited to the Himalaya and Kashmir. The inner regions of Kashmir, the upper Indus Valley and the Karakoram, are distinguished from the Hima-

17 Bullock cart convoy, Kolhapur, Maharashtra. Under the fodder straw were stacks of jaggery (raw sugar) blocks.

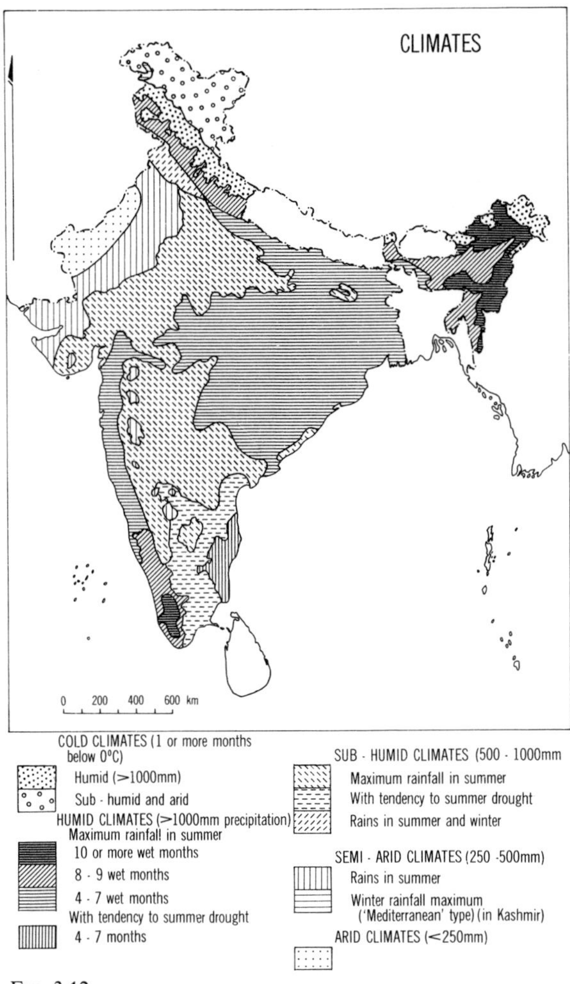

FIG. 3.12

laya by their aridity (see data for Leh in Table 3.2). Altitude of course has an important bearing on temperature, but latitude and the probably equally significant topographical situation must not be overlooked when comparing data from climatic stations. Simla and Darjiling stand on hills, and although they show absolute minima below freezing, air drainage prevents such places, despite their elevation at over 2100 m, from suffering such cold for long. Srinagar, further north and at lower elevation (1587 m), lies in the Vale of Kashmir into which cold air from the surrounding snow-clad ranges can drain to give below freezing average minima from November to February. Nevertheless these stations do not come strictly within the category of cold climates.

For the rest, rainfall rather than temperature is the basis for division, reasonably in that in the plains temperature is not an absolute deterrent to plant growth. Relative terms are used to distinguish four climatic types: *humid* for those with more than 1000 mm of rainfall per year, *sub-humid* for those with between 500 and 1000 mm, *semi-arid* between 250 and 500 mm, and *arid* with below 250 mm. The length of the rainy season (as already defined) within the two relevant regimes, the one with summer rains and the other tending to summer drought, gives five regional types which are agriculturally distinctive. The sub-humid climates may be separated on the basis of regime (or its absence in areas of equable distribution). The semi-arid and arid climates do not merit sub-division within India.

On the whole the pattern of climates calls for little further comment. Attention may be drawn to certain features which may not be obvious at the scale of the map, but which are of local agricultural relevance. The Ganga Plain, despite the funneling of the monsoon stream along the valley from the Bay of Bengal, gains less rain than the mountains and plateaux that flank it, so that a small area of sub-humid climate occurs in western Bihar-eastern UP, the location of some notorious famines. The Assam Valley is in a slight rain-shadow, but here this means an escape from superfluity of rainfall rather than a threat of drought. The severity of drought in another less welcome rainshadow lying immediately east of the Western Ghats may be picked out in patches of semi-arid climate while a narrow strip along the coast of Andhra Pradesh north of the Godavari delta has a sub-humid climate possibly due to the monsoon flowing parallel to that coast before turning northward over Orissa and the Ganga delta.

While the cultivator looks to the clouds for the rains which will enable him to plant his crops, the soil in which he plants them is itself a product of the interaction of climate upon the materials of the earth's surface. Probably the least affected by climate is alluvium, much of which is too young to have undergone the processes that lead to the development of distinct horizons in the soil profile. On such geologically recent alluvium, the farmer is mainly interested in the texture, which influences workability, and the water-holding capabilities of

18 Shoeing a working draught bullock by the roadside near Mysore, Karnataka.

the ploughed field, which affect his ability to grow wet rice. It is the nature of alluvium, laid down by the changing courses of rivers meandering in their flood plains, to vary in texture both laterally and vertically since the most coarse sands are laid down closest to the most energetic current, while finer silts and clays are deposited away from the main channel. What lies beneath the surface concerns the farmer as well as what he sees as he ploughs. He may be fortunate to find good aquifers below his land from which by sinking wells he can draw water for irrigation. He will be less fortunate if his surface loams are underlaid with impervious clays which accelerate waterlogging as he applies irrigation. Characteristically alluvium in all but the most humid parts of India contains *kankar*, concretions of lime that accumulate through the fluctuation of water in the soil. Kankar is a valuable source of building lime and whitewash in the Indian village, and is most prevalent in the older areas of alluvium where the process of its formation has been going on for thousands of years. This older alluvium is generally darker and of a more clayey texture than younger alluvium, and is widespread on the broad interfluve areas of the Ganga Plain for example. In more humid regions as in Assam, Meghalaya and West Bengal, the older alluvium has been subjected to intense leaching, producing lateritic soils, reddish in colour and fine textured, but 'droughty' as far as field crops are concerned.

Younger alluvium tends to be more sandy and lighter in colour, but may be very fertile on account of the annual replenishment of plant nutrients by flood waters. Figure 3.13 shows the distribution of the major soils, though the pattern of older and younger alluvium is too complex to map at this scale. Along the foot of the Outer Himalaya in Uttar Pradesh and eastwards, a narrow strip of *terai* soils is shown. Here the alluvial material of confluent fans grades from gravel to clay as the surface slopes with diminishing gradient towards the Ganga Plain. Water sinks into the coarse soils of the *bharbar* tract close to the hills, to reappear in springs and swamps in the terai.

FIG. 3.13 After *Irrigation Atlas, Survey of India.*

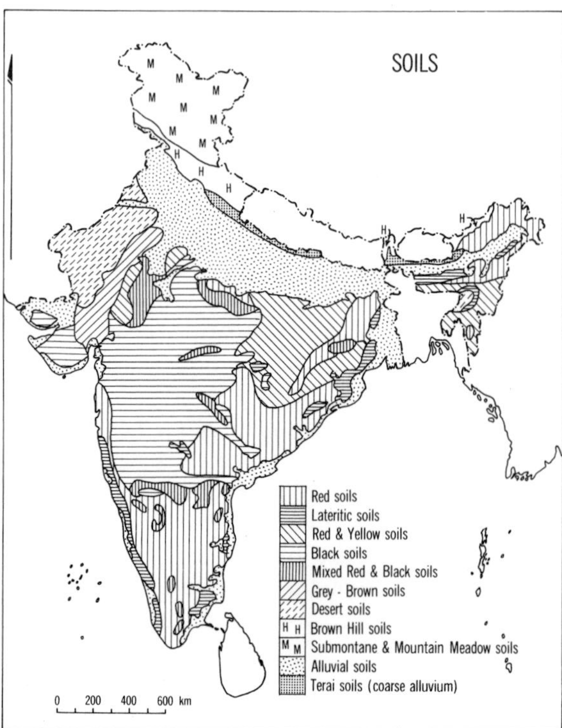

19 Threshing jowar on the open road: passing traffic does the job. Near Mysore, Karnataka.

Near the sea coastal alluvium merges with river alluvium, and the two cannot easily be separated. Too fine a distinction should not therefore be read into their mapping. In Gujarat the wide expanse of coastal alluvium reflects this area's relatively recent and probably continuing emergence from the sea bed, while along the seaward margin of the Ganga delta the tidal reworking of river alluvium is involved.

In addition to the lateritic soils found on the old alluvium in the northeast, there are narrow zones of laterites significantly most in evidence on what appear to be marine-cut raised platforms around the more humid coastlands of the Peninsula. Thus they are found southwards from Ratnagiri in Maharashtra into Kerala on the west coast, and in patches usually adjoining alluvial lands on the borders of West Bengal and Orissa, and near the Orissa and Andhra coast almost as far south as Tamilnadu. That some of these areas are today probably less humid than would be necessary for laterization to occur suggests that such laterites may be the product of past climatic conditions. Other laterite areas however, occur in the sub-humid central Deccan, indicating more clearly the influence of past climate in their formation. Agriculturalists have found these areas unattractive, and even the more humid coastal platforms are relatively difficult to exploit, yielding better returns under tree crops like cashew nuts than can be had with shallower rooted field crops.

Red and red-and-yellow soils cover extensive areas of upland India. The red soils of the moderate rainfall and sub-humid tracts of South India are generally developed on gneisses and schists of igneous and metamorphic origin. Although they are usually deficient in plant nutrients, particularly calcium, potassium and phosphorus compounds, the red soils possess a texture that makes them an ideal medium for irrigated cultivation. Under irrigation this very lack of minerals, potential salt-producing elements, becomes one of its virtues. The red and yellow soils are found also towards the more humid northeast, generally in hilly country.

The other major soil of the Peninsula is *regur*, the black soil often associated with the Deccan Lava country, but found also in admixture with red soils on the margins of, and well away from the lavas themselves. The thickest black soils and those best exhibiting the group's characteristics are found on the Deccan in Maharashtra. Typically, regur is a heavy clay that cracks deeply into intractable clods when it dries. In contrast to the red soils, it is rich in potash and phosphorus and generally is littered with calcareous kanker. These features render it liable to produce alkali patches when irrigated, but as if by compensation, its capacity to hold moisture is considerable. The latter quality is exploited by the farmer, who often prefers to take a crop such as rabi jowar, sown just before the soil becomes intractable towards the end of the monsoon, and which can then grow when the evapo-transpiration rates are at their lowest during the cool season. The cropping pattern of the Deccan is greatly influenced by this factor. Farmers on the thinner black soils have to adhere to the more usual practice of kharif cropping during the rainy season. Within the black soil region thickness of soil is generally a function of site within a catenary gradation from medium to thin on interfluves, through thin and stony on slopes, to thick in valley floors, where they may be as much as 6 m deep.

In the northwest of the Peninsula, the soils grade with increasing aridity through grey-brown to desert soils, generally sandy and alkaline, but capable of high productivity under careful irrigation. This however, is possible on the basis of local water resources in only a few areas close to the Aravalli Hills, though the development of the Rajasthan Canal deriving water from the Himalayan rivers is transforming the northern margins of the desert.

The humid Himalaya, because of their steep slopes, support either brown forest soils or simply colluvium, immature soil constantly in movement down slope. At higher levels skeletal soils are usual, but these areas are generally climatically inimical to agriculture anyway. The interior intermontane plateaus and high valleys of Kashmir have mountain meadow soils, valuable as the name suggests as summer pasture for yaks and sheep.

CONCLUSION

We may now attempt briefly to categorize India's surface in terms of its intrinsic qualities as agricultural land, though later sections will amply indicate that physical characteristics are only part of the explanation of the patterns of cultivation. In particular man has shown great ingenuity in moderating total or seasonal aridity by irrigation.

Firstly regions of extreme difficulty from the cultivator's point of view may readily be identified in the high cold mountains of the Himalaya and Karakoram and their associated intermontane plateaux. Sheltered valleys at moderate altitude and floored with accumulated alluvium may provide specially favoured niches for agriculture on a small scale. The Vale of Kashmir is exceptional in its extent.

Steepness of slope rather than absolute altitude is a more prevalent constraint on agriculture, though again man has expended enormous effort in some areas cutting terraces for his fields. The Himalaya, the Northeastern Hills and the steep and rugged country flanking the Peninsular plateaux to west and east are extensively uncultivatable because of slope.

Aridity in the extreme west of Rajasthan is another type of absolute deterrent to cultivation, except where exotic sources of irrigation water can be tapped.

Setting aside these regions of more or less extreme difficulty we are left with the greater part of India, moderately well watered by highly seasonal and often variable rainfall, and displaying a range of soil quality. Three broad regional types may be identified. Over the plateau country of much of Peninsular India soils derive from parent materials in the Archaean and Early Palaeozoic formations, with gneisses, granites and metasediments predominating. Alluvial soils are limited to flood plains which in the undulating terrain form only a small proportion of the total area. Non-alluvial soils are often thin and stoney, particularly in sloping areas. They tend to be poor in plant nutrients but where thick enough respond well to irrigation, notably in the case of the red soils group. A second regional type is the lava-covered Deccan which carries some remarkably rich and productive soils. The thick black soils have the best capacity to retain moisture, allowing them to be cropped during the dry season. There are however considerable tracts where the lava soils are thin and full of rock fragments. The third and by far the most important category of region from the point of view of agriculture is that covering the alluvial soils, most extensive in the Indo-Gangetic Plain and the deltas of the Peninsular rivers. Where these soils can be irrigated from their own groundwater reservoirs or from canals and tanks the constraints of seasonally deficient rainfall can be overcome.

CHAPTER FOUR

MAN AND THE HYDROLOGICAL CYCLE

SUMMARY

Man in India has for many centuries interfered in the hydrological cycle in order to overcome the deficiencies he found in the natural environment, notably the regular alternation of wet and dry seasons and the extreme variability of rainfall in many areas. Water is a limited resource the efficient use of which is of increasing importance as the demand expands from agriculture, industry and a water- and power-using population with rising living standards. India cannot afford to allow water to run to waste and must strive to bring under control as much of its water resources as possible. As their development proceeds the options remaining to India within her own borders diminish and the long-term future for utilizing effectively the flow in many of the Himalayan rivers will depend on international co-operation between India and Nepal and China, the countries in whose territories sites for storage reservoirs are located. In the Peninsula the major rivers have been harnessed to the extent that few opportunities remain for future development of surface water.

Meanwhile the main prospects for improving the efficiency of water use lie in the continued development of groundwater through sinking traditional open wells and modern tube-wells. The relative importance of well irrigation has increased greatly since independence.

Already 30 per cent of India's hydroelectric potential has been brought into use. Installed capacity of power stations is almost equally distributed between the Himalayan rivers and those of the west and east flowing rivers of the Peninsula. Future prospects are best in Kerala and Karnataka in the south, and in the Eastern Himalaya, all regions with long heavy rainy seasons and steep slopes for power generation.

In several river basins the total volume of water used exceeds the total surface flow, indicating the re-use of water through the exploitation of groundwater reservoirs and the re-cycling of surface drainage through canal and tank systems. Multipurpose river development is the rule, though problems do arise from the competing demands of industry for electric power and process water on the one hand and agriculture for irrigation water on the other. Such conflicting demands cannot always be resolved to everybody's satisfaction. In order to improve the utilization of power and irrigation potential several major rivers have been or are in process of being diverted: the Beas to supplement the Bhakra-Nangal scheme on the Sutlej; the Periyar away from its westerly course to water a dry area in Tamilnadu to the east, producing power on the way; the Koyna from its easterly course to generate power over the Western Ghats. Inter-state problems of development and utilization underline the need for the Centre effectively to control water resources in the national interest. The partition of the Indus tributaries between India and Pakistan is now past history. Currently the only international problem relates to the Farakka Barrage on the Ganga which Bangladesh sees as a threat to her own dry season agriculture. This problem is discussed below.

As water use intensifies, the problems of controlling salinity and waterlogging in canal irrigated areas and of maintaining water quality at a non-toxic level for downstream users, are likely to increase, particularly in the drier parts of the country. Imaginative plans to transfer excess monsoon flow from the Ganga and Brahmaputra systems for use in the Peninsula may well begin to be implemented before the end of the century. Any

20 Maithon Dam, Bihar, part of the Multi-purpose Damodar Valley project. Storage of water for industry is as important as power generation. Flood control is an incidental boon, with irrigation an objective of lesser priority.

such schemes would need to be designed to assure adequate supplies to Bangladesh through which both rivers reach the sea. The recent political tensions between India and Bangladesh over the Farakka Barrage are a reminder that development of one part of a river system inevitably affects areas downstream.

THE HYDROLOGICAL CYCLE AND IRRIGATION

Precipitation of moisture from the atmosphere may be taken as the starting point of the hydrological cycle. When rain (and snow) fall to the ground a part of this moisture percolates into the soil, part becomes surface flow moving down the slope towards the ocean or a centre of internal drainage. Evaporation returns some of the moisture to the atmosphere directly from the falling rain, from snow fields, from water surfaces of every kind – river, lake and ocean – and from the interface between moist soil and the air. Evapo-transpiration transfers water vapour to the air from growing plants which have drawn it from the soil. Moisture not so returned moves down through the soil to become groundwater, eventually rejoining the cyclic system by appearing at the surface as spring water, or joining the surface or sub-surface flow of rivers.

Man in India has been interfering with the hydrological cycle for many centuries in order to improve the supply of water for his own needs. The urban concentrations of the Indus Civilization (2500 BC) in semi-arid northwestern India were undoubtedly made possible by flood-channel irrigation of crops along the rivers and the wells and tanks that abound throughout the sub-continent are probably of at least equal antiquity. In Peninsular India tanks are shallow storages ponded behind earth and masonry dams across minor rivers. In deltaic West Bengal they are excavated ponds which fill with rainwater or groundwater seepage. Devices for raising water have evolved through time to suit local conditions, and some powerful rulers, notably during the Moghul period, using skills developed in Persia and Afghanistan, undertook elaborate engineering works to bring irrigation and drinking water by canal to their settlements, palaces and pleasure gardens.

Modern irrigation practices involve no new principle. They merely apply greater amounts of capital and managerial skill to the age-old problems of diverting, storing transporting, raising and delivering water. The main difference lies in modern man's command of inanimate sources of energy, enabling him to achieve and to operate irrigation systems at a speed and on a scale unthinkable when the only sources of mechanical energy were the muscle power of the farmer and of his domestic animals. One of the major achievements of independent India has been to make available to the cultivator inanimate power to drive a small pump, less impressive though this may appear in comparison with the mighty high dams, barrages and wide canals of a Bhakra-Nangal Scheme. However water resources are a finite quantity and each completed project brings nearer the time when no more rivers or groundwater reserves remain to be exploited. Each new scheme has to tackle more difficult and more expensive problems than the last. The continuing rise in the demand for food, for power and for water for domestic and industrial use underlines the need, now widely recognized, to understand better how to use the available water for the greatest good, and how to create the new institutional infrastructure needed to carry out this aim.

The marked seasonality of Indian rainfall generally, and its variability in many areas, makes irrigation advantageous everywhere and essential for high productivity in some regions. Table 4.1 summarizes the development of irrigation since independence. Almost a quarter of the total area sown is now irrigated, representing an increase of almost 17 million ha or 83 per cent since independence.

It may be noted that whereas canals and tanks have almost held their share of the area under irrigation, the land under well irrigation has increased substantially, a trend likely to continue as surface water resources become more fully utilized. In terms of the movement of water through the hydrological cycle, canals are an extension of the route river-water must take towards the sea, while tanks delay the flow within a river system. In both cases the channels, storages and the fields themselves on which the water is ultimately spread, supply more water by percolation to the groundwater reserves which in turn may be further exploited by wells. Under certain conditions, all too commonly met in sub-humid areas, irrigation is responsible for the groundwater becoming saline, a problem which is discussed in more detail below.

Tables 4.2 and 4.3 break down the gross figures of Table 4.1 into five regional groupings. Table 4.2 shows how regional shares of the total area under canal, tank, well and other forms of irrigation have changed over time. Table 4.3 shows the changing proportional contribution made by the different irrigation sources within each region.

In these tables attention is drawn to the above average increase in total irrigation in the Northwest and West Central regions. In the Northwest big canal projects have been undertaken on the basis of water from the Sutlej and Beas Rivers, but it is interesting to note that well irrigation's share of the regional total has advanced at the expense of that of canals. The large proportionate increase in the West Central area is related to a small total, but again the rise of well irrigation is impressive. The same trend is seen in the other three regions despite their lesser overall expansion. Canal irrigation shows above average expansion only in the Northeast Region, where the Damodar and Mayurakshi developments are mainly responsible. Tank irrigation has always largely been the preserve of the Southeast, particularly of Andhra and Tamilnadu, where this traditional method continues to thrive. The high percentage increase in tanks in the Northwest relates to rugged Rajasthan where the technique is appropriate, and that of the West Central region to Maharashtra and Madhya, but in neither region do tanks loom large in the total picture.

TABLE 4.1

Irrigation since Independence (thousand ha)

	1947–48	*Per cent of total*	*1969–70*	*Per cent of total*	*Per cent of change*
Net Area Irrigated from					
Canals	7,996	42	12,265	40	+ 53
Tanks	3,234	17	4,448	15	+ 38
Wells	5,069	27	11,146	37	+120
Other	2,577	14	2,490	8	− 10
Total	**18,876**	**100**	**30,340**	**100**	**+ 61**
Irrigated more than once	1,417	8	6,876	23	+385
Gross area irrigated	20,293		37,216		+ 83
Net area irrigated as per cent of net area sown		19		22	
Gross area irrigated as per cent of gross area sown		18		23	
Net area sown	99,354		138,700		+ 40
Gross area sown	112,565		163,800		+ 46
Area sown more than once	13,211	13	25,100	18	+ 90

TABLE 4.2

Irrigation: Regional percentages of irrigated areas by sources, 1947–48 and 1969–70

		Total		*Canals*		*Tanks*		*Wells*		*Other*	
Region	*Period**	% Indian net irrigated area	% Increase	% Indian canal irrigated area	% Increase	% Indian tank irrigated area	% Increase/decrease	% Indian well irrigated area	% Increase	% Indian 'other' irrigated area	% Increase/decrease
1. *Nortwest*											
Haryana Himachal Pradesh,											
Jammu and Kashmir, Punjab,	1947–48	12		27		2		22		4	
Rajasthan, Delhi	1969–70	22	94	27	50	5	300	28	177	5	21
2. *North Centre*	1947–48	34		27		19		47		49	
Bihar, Uttar, Pradesh	1969–70	30	41	26	48	12	−11	38	80	42	−19
3. *Northeast*											
Assam, Manipur,											
Meghalaya, Nagaland,	1947–48	8		6		13		—		16	
Tripura, West Bengal	1969–70	7	41	11	183	8	−18	—	60	21	27
4. *West Centre*											
Gujarat, Madhya	1947–48	8		10		3		13		3	
Pradesh, Maharashtra	1969–70	13	150	10	47	10	410	20	248	6	129
5. *South & Southeast*											
Andhra Pradesh, Kerala,											
Karnataka, Orissa,	1947–48	32		29		64		18		28	
Tamilnadu	1969–70	27	37	26	39	66	41	13	63	26	−10
		100	61	100	53	100	38	100	120	100	−4
		100		100		100		100		100	

* Correspondence between periods is approximate only.

21 Reclaiming rice land from coastal backwaters near Cochin, Kerala. Coconuts are established as a cash crop on the embankments. Sluices enable the farmer progressively to remove salt water from the 'polder'.

TABLE 4.3

Irrigation: Percentages of total net irrigated area by regions and sources, 1947–48 and 1969–70

Region	*Period**	*Canals*	*Tanks*	*Wells*	*Other*	*Total*
1. *Northwest* Haryana, Himachal Pradesh, Jammu and Kashmir, Punjab, Rajasthan, Delhi	1947–48 1969–70	63 49	2 3	32 46	3 2	100 100
2. *North Centre* Bihar, Uttar Pradesh	1947–48 1969–70	34 36	10 6	37 47	20 11	100 100
3. *Northeast* Assam, Manipur, Meghalaya, Nagaland, Tripura, West Bengal	1947–48 1969–70	30 60	27 15	.6 .7	27 24	100 100
4. *West Centre* Gujarat, Madhya Pradesh, Maharashtra	1947–48 1969–70	50 29	5 11	41 56	4 4	100 100
5. *South & Southeast* Andhra Pradesh, Kerala, Karnataka, Orissa, Tamilnadu	1947–48 1969–70	38 39	34 35	15 18	12 18	100 100
		42 40	17 15	27 37	14 8	100 100

* Correspondence between periods is approximate only.

22 Canal bank, Alleppy, Kerala. The small crafts are poled along. On the quayside are stacks of tapioca tubers and bricks, with copra drying on the ground between.

The category 'other' in respect of irrigation sources covers the pumping of water from rivers particularly during the dry season, and channel bed diversions, the latter inevitably of a temporary nature as river floods will destroy the small scale structures engineered by the farmers. The most substantial developments of this kind have been undertaken in West Bengal and Assam, but over India as a whole the category is declining in relative importance. Table 4.4 provides details by states and gives an impression of the magnitude of the irrigated area and its importance within agriculture.

For India the average percentage of irrigated to total sown area is 27. The states which better this figure fall into two groups: one extends from Jammu and Kashmir through Punjab to Bihar; the other consists of Andhra Pradesh and Tamilnadu. All these are areas of ample alluvial plains. The better watered states in the northeast (Orissa, West Bengal, Assam, etc.) and south (Kerala) fall below the average. So also do those of the drier lands of the plateau interior and the west, from Karnataka to Rajasthan. Even with the completion of irrigation projects already sanctioned which will bring the average to 33 per cent, the pattern will remain effectively the same, only Orissa rising above average level. Three maps show the distribution of areas under canal, tank and well irrigation (Figure 4.1, 4.2 and 4.3 respectively).

In Table 4.5 an attempt has been made to draw up a water balance for India's major river basins grouped in surface flow regions (see Figures 4.4

TABLE 4.4

Net Area Irrigated by Source (1969–70) by States

Region	*Thousand ha and percentage of state total*									*% of India*	*Gross area irrigated as % of total sown area*	
	Canal		*Tank*		*Well*		*Other*		*Total*	*Total*	*1974*	*When sanctioned projects completed*
1. *Northwest*												
Haryana	950	67	17	1	437	31	4	—	1,408	4.6	47	54
Himachal Pradesh	—	—	—	—	3	3	91	97	94	0.3	18	18
Jammu and Kashmir	272	97	—	—	1	—	6	2	279	0.9	47	47
Punjab	1,306	46	—	—	1,524	54	6	—	2,836	9.3	80	84
Rajasthan	753	37	198	10	1,087	53	21	1	2,059	6.8	18	25
Delhi	14	30	1	2	32	68	—	—	47	0.2	52†	—
2. *North Centre*												
Bihar	815	36	187	8	490	22	787	35	2,279	7.5	29	49
Uttar Pradesh	2,423	36	360	5	3,792	56	244	4	6,819	22.5	45	54
3. *Northeast*												
Assam, etc.‡	362*	63	2*	—	—	—	339*	—	572*	1.9	19	20
West Bengal	941	64	334	23	16	1	187	13	1,478	4.9	33	37
4. *West Centre*												
Gujarat	196	17	28	2	917	80	9	1	1,150	3.8	16	22
Madhya Pradesh	669	47	175	12	518	36	69	5	1,431	4.7	10	13
Maharashtra	312	22	225	16	821	57	73	5	1,431	4.7	10	14
5. *Southeast*												
Andhra Pradesh	1,488	47	1,071	34	502	16	128	4	3,189	10.5	34	41
Kerala	204	48	72	17	5	1	142	34	423	1.4	21	29
Karnataka	398	35	373	33	260	23	113	10	1,144	3.8	17	24
Orissa	235	23	521	51	40	4	231	22	1,027	3.4	25	33
Tamilnadu	906	36	879	35	691	28	31	1	2,507	8.3	46	46
INDIA	12,256	40	4,448	15	11,146	37	2,490	8	30,340	100	27	33

* According to the Irrigation Commission, this is temporary small stream irrigation of low reliability.
† 1971–72 figure.
‡ Manipur, Meghalaya, Nagaland and Tripura.

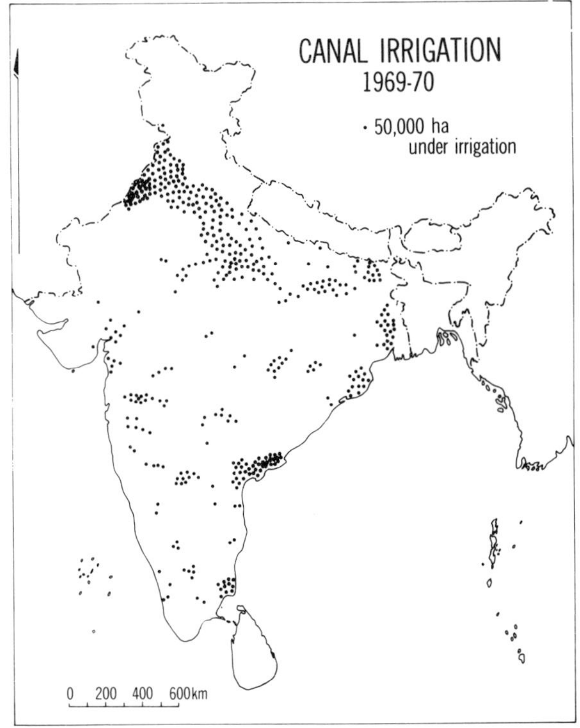

FIG. 4.1

FIG. 4.2

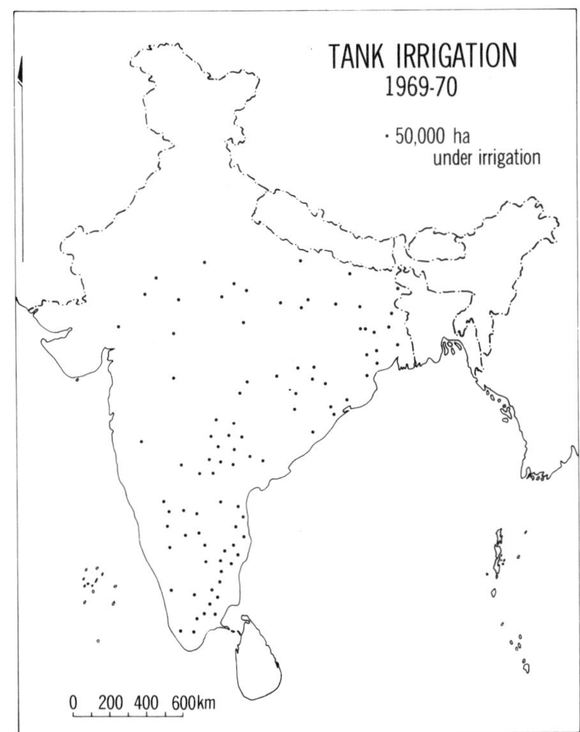

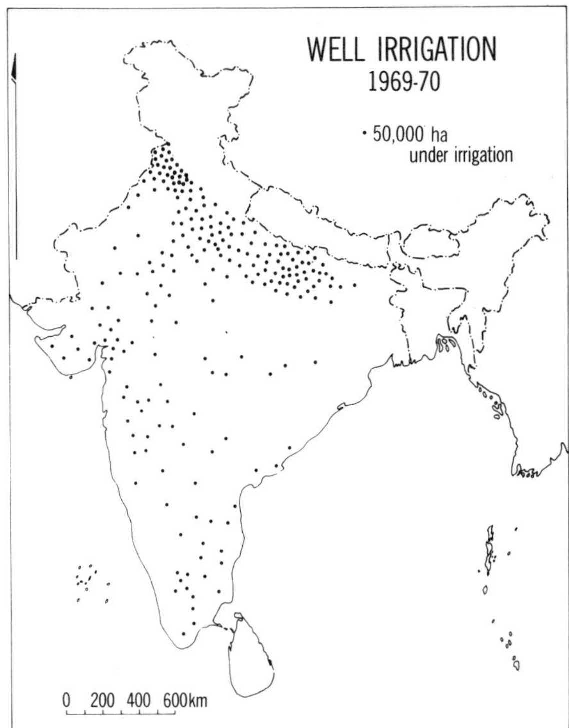

FIG. 4.3

and 4.5a). In many cases the annual surface flow within a basin has had to be estimated by irrigation and power engineers without the benefit of long runs of data from gauging stations, The precipitation characteristics for the basins can be generalized from the climatic maps (Figures 3.8 and 3.9).

Annual flow in the systems is a function of rainfall and the area of the catchment. The Himalayan rivers account for 58 per cent of the total, the Brahmaputra alone yielding 31 per cent (see Figure 4.5b). The regimes of these rivers are less extremely biased to the rainy season of the summer monsoon, as they drain extensive snowfields which catch winter precipitation, particularly in the west, and yield the stored water in the spring melt. The mean run-off of the three Indus tributaries of most value to India is distributed between quarters thus:

River	*Average runoff million (m^3)*	*Seasonal flow (%)*			
		April-June	July-Sept	Oct-Dec	Jan-March
Ravi	7,993	30	51	8	11
Beas	15,961	15	15	10	8
Sutlej	16,072	23	62	9	6

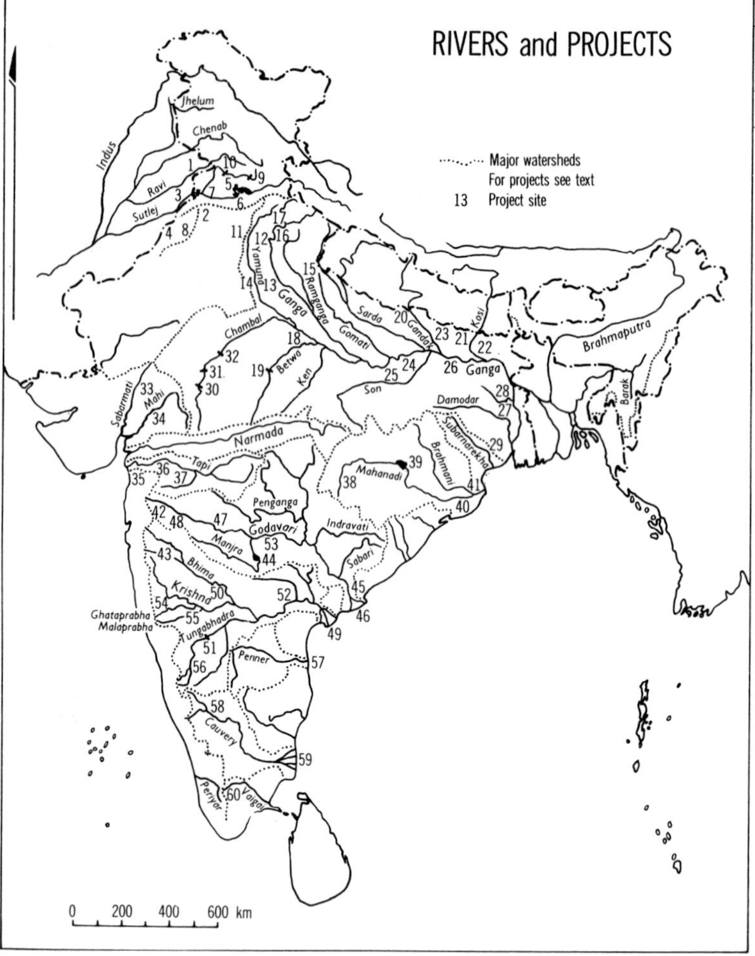

FIG. 4.4 Rivers and projects.

Indus Basin

1 Upper Bari Doab Canal
2 Sirhind Canal
3 Eastern Canal
4 Gang Canal
5 Bhakra Dam
6 Nangal Barrage
7 Harike Barrage
8 Rajasthan Canal
9 Pandoh Dam and link tunnel
10 Pong Dam

Ganga Basin

11 West Yamuna Canal
12 Upper Ganga Canal
13 Lower Ganga Canal
14 Agra Canal
15 Sarda Canal
16 Ramganga Project
17 Tehri Dam
18 Betwa Canal
19 Matatila Dam
20 Western Gandak Canal
21 Kosi Project
22 Rajpur
23 Bagmati Project
24 Son Canal
25 Son High Level Canal
26 Badua
27 Damodar Valley
28 Mayurakshi
29 Kangsabati
30 Gandhi Sagar
31 Ranapratap
32 Kota Barrage

Minor Basins of Gujarat

33 Sabarmati Dam
34 Mahi Canal

Tapi Basin

35 Kakrapar Weir Project
36 Ukai Dam Project
37 Girna Project

Mahanadi Basin

38 Mahanadi Canal
39 Hirakud Dam
40 Mahanadi Delta Scheme
41 Orissa Canal

Godavari Basin

42 Godavari Canal
43 Nira Canals
44 Nizamsagar
45 Godavari Barrage
46 Godavari Delta Canals
47 Jayakwadi Project
48 Mula Scheme
53 Pochampad Project

Krishna Basin

49 Krishna Delta Canals
50 Bhima Project
51 Tungabhadra Dam
52 Nagarjunasagar Dam
54 Ghataprabha Project
55 Malaprabha Project
56 Upper Tungabhadra Project

Penner Basin

57 Penner Scheme

Cauvery Basin

58 Krishnarajasagar Dam
59 Cauvery Delta Canals

Periyar Basin

60 Periyar Dam and Tunnel

TABLE 4.5
Water Resources and Utilization by River Systems
(Thousand million cubic metres and Megawatts Installed Capacity)

River System	Annual surface flow	% total	Storage	% of flow	Water utilization: From surface water	From ground water	Total	% of flow	% From ground water	% India total	Hydro-electric potential: Potential MW at 60% load factor	% India total	Installed capacity MW	% India total
1. Indus tributaries in India	73	3.8	14	35	47	14	60	138	23	10.9	7,750	16	3,027	20.8
1.1 Ravi, Beas, Sutlej	40	2.1	—	—	—	—	55	—	—	10.0	3,500	7	—	—
1.2 Jhelum, Chenab	31	1.6	—	—	—	—	5	—	—	.9	4,250	9	—	—
1.3 Ghaggar	2	—	—	—	—	—	—	—	—	—	—	—	—	—
2. Ganga	557	29.2	31	—	132	42	173	—	—	31.3	6,000*	13	2,512	17.2
2.1 Himalayan rivers	424	22.4	7	2	82	32	113	27	28	20.5	—	—	1,593	10.9
2.2 Right bank tributaries, Chambal-Son	88	4.6	20	23	22	8	30	34	25	5.4	—	—	815	5.6
2.3 Damodar, etc.	45	2.4	4	9	28	2	30	36	5	5.4	—	—	104	0.7
3. Brahmaputra, Barak	591	31.2	—	—	8	1	9	1.5	8	1.6	12,000	25	276	1.9
4. Between Ganga and Mahanadi	44	2.3	4	9	10	0.3	10	23	3	1.8	1,100	2	130	0.9
5. Mahanadi	71	3.7	8	11	25	0.4	26	37	1	4.7	1,000	2	270	1.9
6. Between Mahanadi and Godavari	17	0.9	—	—	10	0.2	10	59	2	1.8			—	—
7. Godavari	118	6.2	15	13	51	8	59	50	13	10.7	6,000	13	1,349	9.3
8. Krishna	63	3.3	30	47	57	9	66	105	13	12.0	1,500	3	1,893	13.0
9. Between Krishna and Cauvery	25	1.3	2	8	27	6	33	132	17	6.0	—		—	—
10. Cauvery and southwards	28	1.5	5	20	32	4	36	130	11	6.5	1,000	2	975	6.7
11. Rivers of Saurashtra and Kutch	12	0.6	—	—	5	13	17	141	73	3.1	—	—	—	—
12. Mahi, Sabarmati, etc.	16	0.8	5	31	9	4	13	81	30	2.4	100	—	—	—
13. Narmada, Tapi	64	3.4	11	17	14	5	19	30	27	3.4	2,000	4	300	2.1
14. West Coast rivers	218	11.5	14	6	18	1	20	9	6	3.6	4,500	9	3,846	26.4
INDIA total	1,897	100	139	7	451	108	551	29	20	100.0	47,950†	100	14,578	100.0

* Includes 2,000 on Nepal border rivers
† Includes 5,000 for minor systems

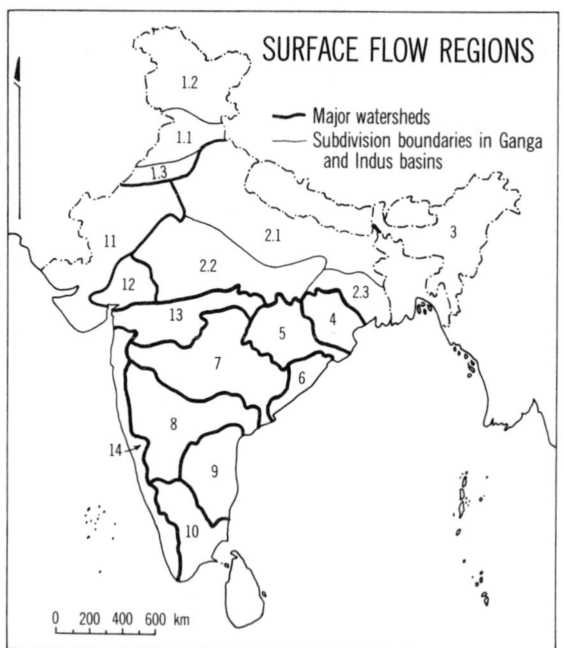

FIG. 4.5(a)

FIG. 4.5(b)

FIG. 4.5(c)

FIG. 4.5(d)

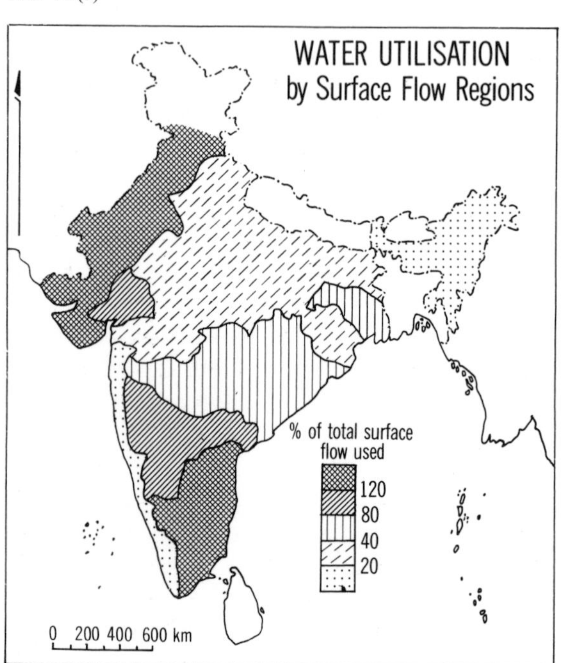

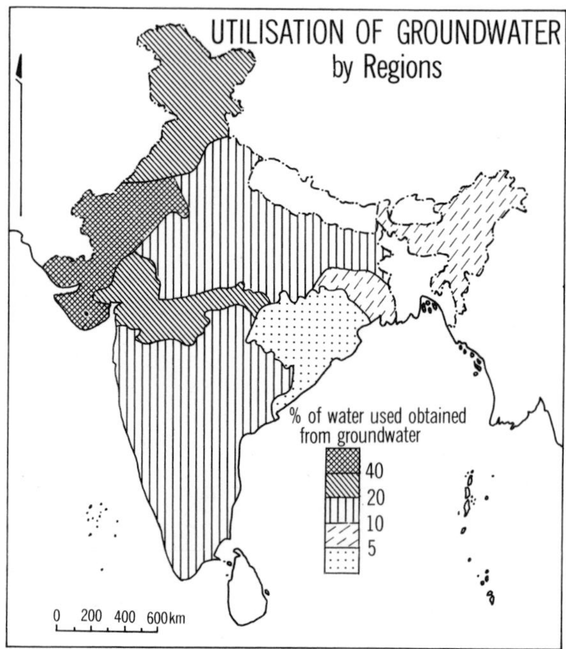

The huge dams on the Sutlej and Beas have a capacity to store 35 per cent of the flow, thus ensuring rabi season irrigation from the surplus from the kharif rains.

It can be seen that the Ganga basin is much more liberally watered by the Himalayan tributaries and main stream Ganga than by those entering from the Peninsula to the south, which contribute but a third of the total. However because of the greater need for irrigation of the drier lands of these southern basins (Chambal and Son, principally) and of flood control and industrial water in the east (Damodar Valley), storages have been constructed to hold 23 and 9 per cent of the flow of these tributary systems respectively. A major drawback to storage on the Himalayan tributaries is that the most suitable sites for dams on several of the important rivers lie over the border in Nepal.

The pattern of river basins in the Peninsula is highly asymmetric. Apart from the Mahandi and the minor catchments adjoining it, the major basins have the remotest part of their watershed close to the coast on the opposite side. This is specially true of the Godavari and Krishna systems, giving them very extensive catchments which tap the heavy rainfall of the Western Ghats. The Mahanadi drains extensive uplands in Orissa and Madhya Pradesh. In all three basins, the Mahanadi, Godavari and Krishna, storages have been built to hold 11, 13, and 47 per cent of flow, respectively. It should be stressed that the data for storages cover only the large ones, and a very considerable additional volume is held in the thousands of tanks that are rarely out of sight on the plateaux of Andhra and Karnataka. The catchments between the Krishna and Cauvery are individually small and do not stretch far enough to the west to collect water from a rainfall regime different from or more prolific than their own. The Cauvery however is better favoured in this respect and 20 per cent of the flow from its Western Ghats headwaters is stored before the river spills onto the Tamilnadu plains. Together the eastward flowing rivers of the Peninsula have 19 per cent of the country's surface water resources. The regimes of the Peninsula rivers follow closely the pattern of rainfall. Allowing a month's delay for overland flow and groundwater movement, Nagpur's seasonal rainfall would convert to river flow thus: 4 per cent comes in April–June, 70 per cent in July–September, 22 per cent in October–December and 3 per cent January–March (cf the Indus tributaries above).

Towards the northwest the Narmada and Tapi with long narrow catchments reaching east on either side of the Satpura Range are the largest rivers flowing to the west coast; the catchments of the southern Aravallis in Gujarat and Rajasthan are very limited both in area and rainfall. The rivers draining the Western Ghats to the Arabian sea are all short, but collectively account for 11.5 per cent of the total. Six per cent of their flow is stored, mainly to provide constant flow to power stations that make effective use of the steep drop of the Western Ghats. Heavy rainfall, with a short dry season in the south, accounts for the high yield of these rivers.

HYDROELECTRIC POWER

The hydroelectric potential and development is shown for the major river basins in Table 4.5 and Figure 4.6. In the case of power, the Indus tributaries, because of the development of the Bhakra-Nangal project, lead the Himalayan rivers of the Ganga basin by a small margin. Together all these Himalayan rivers have 32 per cent of India's installed capacity, almost coinciding with their share of water utilization. The east-flowing rivers account for 34 per cent of installed capacity, the Krishna, Godavari and Cauvery being outstanding. Power sites on these rivers are located in their upper or middle reaches where gradient can be concentrated, but on account of the long gentle slopes that characterize the region, power development lags behind water utilization (49 per cent). Outstanding in the number of sites with abrupt falls on strong perennial rivers, are the west coast rivers, notably those descending the Western Ghats. Including the small development on the Narmada, they account for almost 29 per cent of installed capacity, more than double their share of utilization. If the power development on the westward-diverted eastward flowing rivers like the Koyna is transferred to the west coast's budget their share rises to 36 per cent of the nation's total. At present about 30 per cent of the hydroelectric potential has been harnessed approximately in proportion to the potential of the basins. The

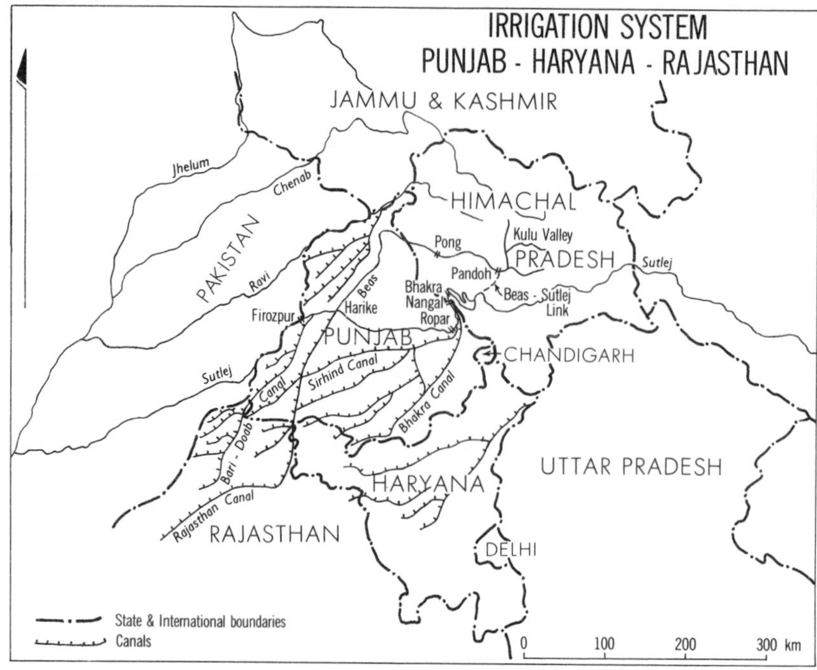

FIG. 4.6

Brahmaputra and smaller river systems of the Northeastern Hills, which have 25 per cent of India's potential, register less than 2 per cent of the installed capacity. The lack of local demand for power or for irrigation water in this very wet corner of the country has delayed development of this valuable reserve. Incidentally the 12 million kW potential excludes one site on the Brahmaputra which must be the hydroelectric engineer's dream; diversion of the river into a 20 km tunnel starting on the Chinese side of the border could deliver 30 million kW of energy at the foot of the drop on the Indian side. Damming the Brahmaputra could enhance this still further, but realization of such a dream belongs to the twentyfirst century. The industrial aspects of hydroelectric development are examined below.

WATER UTILIZATION

When considering the utilization of the water resources of a drainage basin, water should not be conceived of as a commodity which once used is necessarily lost to the ocean until it reappears as rain in a subsequent 'turn' of the hydrological cycle. Some of the rain falling on a catchment immediately enters the groundwater reserve, and more is added by seepage from canals, tanks and drainage downwards from fields. Water within the system may be used and reused several times as it progresses towards the sea. Absolute loss occurs when it is incorporated in the tissues of living matter or passes to the air through evaporation or evapo-transpiration. Thus some of the percentages shown for utilization of annual surface flow exceed 100 per cent. The data for utilization cover canals and tanks as sources of surface water, with wells accounting for the groundwater figure.

In terms of utilization (Figure 4.5c) several basins are outstanding in that the level of utilization is disproportionately high in comparison with the basic flow. Thus the Indus tributaries have 11 per cent of the utilization as against 4 per cent of the flow of India's rivers. Intensive canal and well irrigation raised utilization here to 138 per cent of the surface flow, and the proportion coming from groundwater is correspondingly high at 23 per cent (Figure 4.5d). In the Ganga basin, its share of utilization more nearly matches its share in flow. Groundwater is relatively important in the Ganga system, except in the eastern tributary basins where dry season rabi cropping is as yet not much developed, there being two rain-fed kharif rice crops possible.

The Godavari and Mahanadi basins together with the small basins between show only a modest level of water utilization in relation to total surface flow (Figure 4.5c). Compared to the Krishna to the south where 47 per cent of the flow can be retained, storages account for only 11 and 13 per cent in the Godavari and Mahanadi respectively. In all these systems groundwater plays but a minor role reflecting the scarcity of aquifers except in the deltaic sections of the basins. There is some re-use of water through the 'flights' of small tank irrigation schemes along minor river valleys, the surplus water and drainage from schemes in the upper reaches supplying tanks downstream. That the utilization ratio is very high in basins southwards from the Krishna is probably due largely to tank irrigation.

In the west, the outstanding features are the high levels of utilization in the dry lands of Gujarat, where the modest rainfall available is intensively used and re-used via groundwater. By contrast the narrow west coast lowlands have a poor status in utilization. Alluvial plains are here of limited extent, and much land lies in dissected platform-like interfluves along the base of the Western Ghats. No doubt more use could be made of groundwater here and on the lowlands of the basins in Orissa which show even lower ratios of ground to surface water utilization. The relative ease with which rainfed crops can be grown in these areas, as in the Brahmaputra Valley, must inhibit the investment of energy and capital in well-digging. Population pressure will probably provide the incentive to the next generation to intensify the use of groundwater during the dry season.

WELLS AND TANKS

Wells and tanks, the traditional sources of irrigation water, are still very important. The area commanded by wells has increased by 120 per cent since independence. Rural electrification has made possible the energizing of power pumps, displacing to some degree the great variety of traditional methods used to raise water from hand-excavated wells, sometimes lined with masonry for permanence. The depth to which they are excavated to find a good aquifer is limited by cost and the technology available for lifting the water. The increasingly general availability of electricity and diesel engines for pumping has popularized their use not only in conjunction with the traditional well, but for lifting water from rivers and tanks to higher levels, and most important of all, from tube-lined wells which can be sunk to and operated at much greater depths than the traditional well. Their value in controlling waterlogging is discussed below.

23 From the top of Nandidrugh, near Bangalore, Karnataka, one looks down on a landscape in which bottom lands are irrigated from tanks while upper slopes are rain-fed. One tank in a series strung along the valley is seen in the centre right, another in the right background. The neat rectangular fields in the valley bottom are irrigated, those to the left from a tank outside the picture. The rainfed fields are only roughly levelled and have less regular shape. The hill, just beyond the central tank shows expanses of bare granite, seen also in the larger hill in the left background.

Tanks are widespread in the 'hard rock' terrain of southern India. Since they control only small catchments they are very susceptible to the seasonal variations in rainfall, and merely concentrate for an area below and around the tank (if farmers have pumps) the rainfall from a larger area. The gently rolling landscape provides only shallow valleys for tank construction, by simply raising a low earth dam, sometimes faced with granite blocks, across a river. The tanks are not designed to withstand severe flood waves, and failure of a whole series of tanks in a valley is not unknown. Seldom do tanks store water for the dry season, their principal function being to provide enough water during and immediately after the rainy season, to enable irrigated crops like rice and sugar cane to be taken in a region where these might not otherwise be raised. As they dry out, the floors of the tanks are used for grazing, for cutting fodder grass, and for excavating the accumulated silt for brickmaking in the dry season.

24 An electrically powered pump raises water from a cement lined well to irrigate a wheat crop in Rajasthan.

CONFLICTS OF INTEREST

Rivers are developed and water utilized for other purposes besides irrigation, and the multipurpose development of water resources has long been a desirable aim, though it inevitably spells some conflict of interest among the beneficiaries. Some examples are given here to illustrate how such various conflicts have been resolved.

The Damodar river in eastern Bihar and West Bengal drains an elongated basin narrowing to a bottle-neck before opening out to join the Hooghly below Calcutta. It has a long history of disastrous floods which rise with great rapidity after rain storms in its upper reaches. The range of natural flow used to be from nil to 18400 cumecs (cubic metres per second), a level of discharge which used to disrupt communications between the Hooghlyside conurbation and its heavy industrial hinterland on the coalfield in the valley. In 1948 as the first major river project undertaken after independence, the Damodar Valley Corporation was set up to control the river by dams and barrages, to develop hydroelectric power, to provide an assured water supply for industry, to make water available for irrigation, and to establish a canal link between the Damodar coalfield and Calcutta. As industrial and urban demands for water and power have grown, the needs of agriculture have tended to be given lower priority. Further discussion of the industrial aspects of the DVC appears in Chapter 11.

In the case of the development of the Koyna River, a tributary of the Krishna, a different kind of conflict of interest occurred, and again was resolved in favour of power generation. The Koyna rises close to the edge of the Western Ghats and flows parallel to them for 40 km or more before turning away east, thus presenting the opportunity to divert a well-developed river through a tunnel and thence over the edge of the Ghats in a long drop of about 600 m to give a potential of 860 MW. Excellent as this may be from the standpoint of a public frequently irritated by power shortages, the scheme meant directing water out of a basin where droughts are endemic, into the west coastal belt where rainfall is high and irrigable lands are in any case rare. Commenting on the scheme, the Irrigation Commission of 1972 recommended that further captures of east-flowing rivers for power development should not take place. The much earlier diversion of the Periyar, a *west*-flowing river in Kerala was more generally beneficial. Fortunately here the eastern slope of the Southern Ghats is more abrupt than the west, and leads down onto the dry irrigable lowlands in the rain shadow around Madurai, in Tamilnadu. The water can thus satisfy the needs of both power generation and irrigation in turn.

The largest of all India's schemes, the Bhakra-Nangal on the Sutlej has been the cause of conflict of a different kind. Here the first big storage dam built in the Himalaya is called upon to generate electricity and to provide irrigation water through the rabi season to an extensive canal system watering Punjab, Haryana and northern Rajasthan. In order to conserve water for power, the irrigation supply has sometimes to be curtailed. The farmers' misfortune may be doubled in that in those years when canal water is deficient, so too may be electricity. They are then frustrated in their efforts to make good the shortage of canal water by extracting groundwater using electrically powered pumps. The Bhakra-Nangal scheme is examined in some detail here as an example of the considerable modification man is bringing about in the Sutlej and Beas River systems (see Figure 4.6).

The Bhakra-Nangal scheme is part of a complex of works that harnesses the waters of three Indus tributaries for India's use. The main elements are complete or nearing completion. Before independence the British had built barrages across the Ravi, to supply the Upper Bari Doab Canal (1879), and the Sutlej, for the Sirhind Canal (1887), both at the points of emergence of these rivers onto the plain. Another barrage diverted the Sutlej at Firozpur, below its confluence with the Beas to feed the Gang Canal (1928) and the Eastern Canal (1933). After independence a minor system has been provided for the Bist Doab between the Beas and Sutlej. This is fed from the Sutlej at Ropar with some supplementation from the Beas at Tanda. The major works, however, have been the high dam on the Sutlej at Bhakra, with a 'live' (usable) storage of almost 8,000 million cubic metres, and the Nangal Barrage, 13 km downstream. The latter diverts water into a canal for hydroelectric development, and thence into the Bhakra Canal

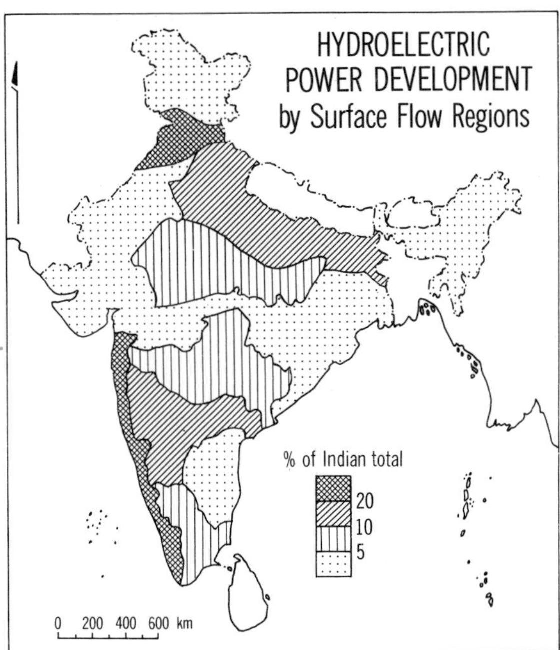

Fig. 4.7

system below Ropar, to irrigate nearly 15 million ha in Punjab, Haryana and Rajasthan. Just below the confluence of the Sutlej and Beas Rivers a barrage at Harike supplies the Rajasthan Feeder Canal which carries water to the Rajasthan Canal system in the arid districts of Ganganagar and Bikaner, though its ultimate extent in this direction is in some doubt. To reinforce these schemes, particularly the storage and power capacity of the Bhakra Dam, a link tunnel is being dug to carry water from a diversion on the River Beas at Pandoh. Bhakra will receive an additional 4,590 million m^3 and 990 megawatt of power will be generated *en route*. Lower down the Beas, the Pong Dam is being constructed to store 6,908 million cubic metres to provide for the canal systems taking off below Harike.

Conflict at the political level bedevilled the development of several projects on rivers forming the boundary between Indian states, and between India and its neighbours. The Tungabhadra scheme on a major tributary of the Krishna had a long history of political frustration dating from pre-independence days, and echoing the division of India into British Provinces and princely states.

25 Cattle driven down an inclined plane raise water from a well on the Deccan Lava Plateau near Bijapur, Karnataka. The cow in the foreground is chewing crushed sugar cane waste.

The Krishna river formed the boundary between the Dominions of the Nizam of Hyderabad, and the British Presidency of Madras. For more than forty years after the scheme was first proposed in 1901, Hyderabad declined to cooperate on the grounds that it would lose 87 km^2 of land beneath the proposed lake. Even after agreement had been reached in 1944, progress was held up by disputes over which side should control the construction of the project, and the dam was finally built to a common design by separate teams working from either side. The redrawing of state boundaries after independence eventually placed the dam in Karnataka, though problems still remained in the areas to be irrigated which lay in both Karnataka and Andhra Pradesh, their new boundary crossing some feeder channels.

The partition of the Indus waters under the treaty of 1960 resolved a conflict at the international level which had been a running sore in Indo-Pakistan relations ever since independence. The new frontier between them cut right across the canal schemes of the former British province of the Punjab, leaving in India the headworks of some schemes that supplied water to Pakistan. Under the treaty, India was allotted the waters of the Ravi, Beas and Sutlej, Pakistan getting those of the Jhelum and Chenab whose upper courses are in India. In the east, a dispute over Ganga water use is a cause of friction with Bangladesh. The Farakka Barrage on the Ganga just before it enters Bangladesh, is designed to divert water into the Hooghly, a Ganga distributary, in order to flush sediment out of the Port of Calcutta, which is threatened with closure by silting. Bangladesh fears this will diminish dry season supplies for rabi crop cultivation particularly in its Ganges-Kovadak scheme which uses irrigation water pumped out of the Ganga 150 km downstream of Farakka. Agreement has been reached to guarantee Bangladesh a reasonable share of the low-water flow.

Within India today the federal system (under a strong central government holding the developmental purse strings) can resolve inter-state disputes in the common interest. Co-operation among the states becomes increasingly necessary as the demand for water for all purposes approaches the limits of availability, and the possibility has been mooted of altering the Constitution to transfer to the centre the control of water resources. The concept of inter-basin transfer of water is extended in the proposals to establish a national water grid to link the Ganga to the Cauvery. The scheme is regarded as technically feasible by United Nations experts, but is unlikely to progress beyond the level of investigations and sketches for another decade. The surplus water from the Ganga system (and maybe the Brahmaputra also) for the use of which little land remains available in the Ganga plains, would be brought south to increase the agricultural intensity and productivity of the Peninsular interior, and to remove one of the limits to urban and industrial growth. For the scheme to have much impact on the region's periodic drought problem very large storages would have to be provided.

WATER-USE PLANNING AND PROBLEM SOLVING

At the practical level of today's activities, new approaches to the planning and operation of canal commands are being taken to improve the level of efficiency in water utilization. The earliest canals built by the British as 'protective' works for the purpose of removing the threat of famine due to climatic vicissitudes were followed by others designed as 'productive' works whose aim was to settle people on the land in canal colonies. In neither case was maximum output per unit of area cultivated, or of water consumed a major consideration. Thus the channel capacities were appropriate to spreading water widely to benefit as many farmers as possible which meant it was usually spread thinly. Channel design ultimately controls how the system will be operated. Modern scientific agriculture requires the farmer to apply the correct amount of water at the right time to the right place. This may mean heavy application to a small proportion of the land growing a high-yielding water-demanding crop, rather than a light application to the whole; or it may mean a change in the frequency of watering without necessarily any change in the total amount applied. Obviously a new approach to system design and to water management is called for. At present water is released to a predetermined schedule to which farmers have to adapt. End of season shortages, and those that

26 Low lift diesel pump set raising water from a creek at Utnur in the Gond country of northern Andhra Pradesh. Such pumps have the advantage of being reasonably easy to move from site to site and so may serve several small commands in the same season.

27 Channelling irrigation water to lava soils growing cotton at Utnur, in the Gond country, northern Andhra Pradesh.

occur at the tail end of canal distributaries are not always foreseen by the engineers, let alone by the farmers. Unless he has the resources and initiative to install a well (assuming groundwater is available and suitable) and so to become master of his own destiny, the farmer has to conform to the general pattern of cropping dictated by the canal system.

A widespread consequence of prolonged canal irrigation is the rise in the level of the water table, the depth at which the groundwater body stabilizes in the sub-soil. In early canal schemes inadequate attention was given to drainage of surplus water accumulating in part due to seepage from unlined channels. Over many years large areas have become waterlogged and in some cases rendered toxic to plants by salinity. River water contains salts in solution usually at such low concentration as to be harmless to plants. The process of irrigation tends to increase the level of salinity. Evaporation and evapo-transpiration return pure water vapour to the air, leaving the saline content to concentrate in the remaining water or to crystallize out in the soil. Furthermore, water draining through the soil takes into solution soluble salts which build up the salinity of the groundwater. Under the conditions of high evaporation that obtain in the subhumid parts of India for most of the year, water is drawn upwards to the surface by capillary action, and on evaporating leaves its salts behind on the surface. Where waterlogging has caused the groundwater itself to reach the surface, stronger concentrations of salt may be brought up. Not all groundwater is toxically saline, but where it is or where it is approaching toxic levels, remedial or preventive measures are necessary. The basic solution is to prevent water surplus to that used to irrigate the crops from reaching the main groundwater body. This can be achieved by adequate drainage at the surface. Waterlogging must be minimized by preventing excessive watering, by lining canals and distributary channels to reduce seepage, and by ensuring the swampy tracts do not develop. The latter commonly form in the borrow-pits alongside roads and railway lines and it requires foresight to prevent otherwise beneficial engineering works from creating areas where flood waters can be ponded back and so given time to infiltrate. The latter problem is widespread due to the construction of canals, roads and railways transverse to the gentle slope of the alluvial plains of the Indus and Ganga basins, and can now only be mitigated by providing adequate culverts beneath these barriers to overland flow.

Where, as in extensive areas of Punjab, Haryana and UP, waterlogging and salinity have taken hold and agricultural land is progressively being put out of production, as if by a kind of wasting disease, remedial measures are necessary. Generally these involve the provision of plenty of surface drains and the sinking of tubewells to pump groundwater to the surface, thus drawing down the level of water in the sub-soil. The water so pumped to the surface may be reused after dilution with canal water provided the resultant mixture is acceptable to plants. Vigorous application of such measures has reclaimed large areas of Punjab and Haryana. Waterlogging is defined as the condition when the water table is less than 1.5 m from the surface and so will saturate the root zone of crops, preventing aeration. Its extent is hard to determine exactly, but is thought to have exceeded one million ha in Punjab before being brought under control. In Haryana 650,000 ha and in UP possibly 810,000 ha are affected.

Over the new Chambal command in Rajasthan and Madhya Pradesh, the water table is rising, and by 1968 groundwater was within 3 m of the surface beneath 405,000 ha. Only a combination of preventive measure and the control of irrigation practices can prevent waterlogging happening here. Elsewhere, notably in *regur* (black lava soil) areas of the Maharashtra and Karanataka Deccan, newly brought under irrigation, it has been found necessary to control what crops the farmers grow, to prevent alkali toxicity developing. The area under sugar cane particularly, a crop demanding plenty of water for a long period of the year, has to be strictly controlled, in favour of crops requiring lighter irrigation. The authorities are faced with the dilemma of having to prevent farmers from chosing what is currently the most profitable crop to grow in monetary terms, in the longer-term interests of the same farmers and of the community at large. In humid regions, while waterlogging does occur quite widely as in Bihar and West Bengal for example, the higher rainfall and lower evaporation rates prevent serious salination.

CHAPTER FIVE

DROUGHT AND SCARCITY

India is so heavily dependent on agriculture both for the immediate subsistence of the rural population and for the economy of the nation as a whole, that fluctuations in rainfall, in the amount received and in the regularity of its incidence can have disastrous effects. Farmers have over many centuries of trial and error built up systems of land use which have long-term stability, even if for one or maybe two years in succession, periods of drought temporarily disrupt those systems. In the past drought caused extreme hardship, and millions of people died as a result of starvation, or more directly from epidemic disease which struck hard at populations weakened by hunger. Some of the most devastating famines that occurred during the nineteenth century were in regions where normally rainfall is adequate to support dense populations, as in Bengal, Orissa and UP. Yet maybe ten million died in Bengal in a famine of 1770, 800,000 in UP in 1836, and one million in Orissa in 1865–66. Extensive areas in the sub-humid belt of the Peninsula suffered in 1876–78, in two successive years of scarcity estimated to have killed $5\frac{1}{2}$ millions in Gujarat, Maharashtra, Andhra Pradesh and Tamilnadu.

Famines at this scale, and the lesser shortages that have occurred more recently, have not been due simply to rainfall deficiency, though that undoubtedly triggered off the process of economic impoverishment that could ultimately lead to the starvation of the poorest in the sight of plenty. The first and hardest hit in any famine are the landless labourers, for whom there is no work in times of extreme drought, and who have no property or possessions against which to borrow. The share-cropper, the tenant farmer, the small marginal owner farmer, and all those in the village community who depend for their livelihood on the fortunes of those with land and resources are soon affected, and even the land-owning farmers, starting with the smallest, may find their resources inadequate to withstand the strain of prolonged drought. Unscrupulous opportunists have ever been ready to take advantage of natural calamity by buying and hoarding food, and by striking hard bargains over loans with all in need. That it is necessary to provide the destitute with the means to purchase food has long been recognized by the authorities, and dating from the Reports of Famine Commissions of 1867, 1898 and 1901, famine relief works have been financed to meet this need. Each state has a Famine Code ready to administer in times of severe scarcity. As K. Suresh Singh puts it in his excellent analysis of the effects of famine in the Palamau District of Bihar, one of the assumptions behind the Code is that 'the Indian famine was a famine of work not a famine of food'.[1] Several factors have combined to reduce the severity of famine in the present century. The interconnection of regions by railways and roads makes possible the speedy transfer of foodstuffs to areas of shortage, and administrators are alert to the need to watch for the first signs of economic distress so that action can be taken early to mitigate the process of economic deterioration. The rural economy itself has improved greatly through the provision by government of canal irrigation in many areas of insecure or low rainfall, and by the more widespread adoption of well irrigation by farmers. However the spectre of scarcity cannot be said to have disappeared entirely from the Indian scene. Population pressure on land resources encourages farmers to grow the most profitable crops and those that will provide most

[1] K. Suresh Singh, *The Indian Famine 1967*, New Delhi, 1975.

food for his family. These are not necessarily the crops that could best survive in a season of drought. Rice tends to be the preferred food crop wherever conditions are normally suitable, yet this crop is probably the most sensitive of all to water shortage during growth. This fact seems to lie behind the paradoxical situation that some of the worst famines and scarcities have occurred at the margin of rice-growing regions, when these have been stricken by drought.

The year 1970–71 was a very good one in terms of rainfall, and obviously of crop production also. The Indian Meteorological Department issue data comparing monthly, seasonal and annual rainfall with normal, or average amounts, for 35 regions. Rainfall within the range 19 per cent above or below average is regarded as 'normal', more than 20 per cent is 'excess', less than 20 per cent is 'deficient' and less than 60 per cent 'scanty'. Figure 5.1 shows the monsoon rainfall for the good year 1970–71 and for two bad years, 1965 and 1966. 1970 was remarkable in that only one region, south interior Karnataka, had deficient rainfall. Yields per hectare for rice, wheat and bajra were 7, 12 and 62 per cent respectively above the average for the preceeding three years, although jowar fell by 11 per cent. The impact on national output was considerable, as Table 2.4 on page 31 shows. In five states rice yields rose by more than 20 per cent. Bajra's success was in part due to the introduction of HYV from 1969, but the good monsoon was undoubtedly mainly responsible and yields fell in subsequent years. Jowar's failure may be attributed to its importance as a rabi crop in those parts of Maharashtra and Madhya Pradesh which suffered poor post-monsoon winter rainfall. The kharif crop in Gujarat and Rajasthan was 32 per cent and 58 per cent above normal respectively.

In 1965 and 1966 poor rainfall was experienced in a belt across Gujarat eastern Rajasthan, Madhya Pradesh, eastern UP, plateau Bihar, and Orissa. Rice yields fell most severely in Rajasthan (by 72 per cent), Gujarat (42), Madya Pradesh (41), UP (25) and Orissa (19); the falls in jowar yields were less dramatic but serious enough, Orissa (28), Maharashtra (26), Gujarat (22), Rajasthan (18), and Madhya (14); bajra showed substantial declines in Bihar (37), Rajasthan (19), and Maharashtra (18), which also had a decline in wheat yield of 24 per cent. In national terms, production fell and imports had to rise to unprecedented levels to compensate (see Table 3.4). The broad regional view these data reveal, obscures much harsher realities in some areas, by generalizing the severity of drought in one part of a region, with the lesser suffering of another. For this reason the famine of the crop years 1966–67 and 1967–68 in Bihar, and the widespread scarcity in Maharashtra in 1965–66 are examined in some detail to demonstrate the impact of drought at district level.

FIG. 5.1

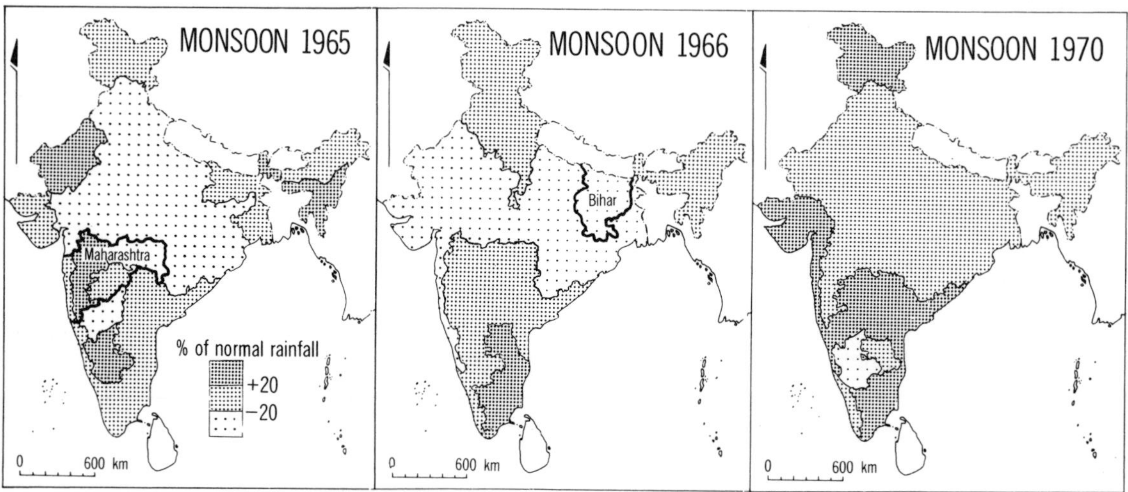

MAHARASHTRA 1965–66

The state of Maharashtra is outlined on the map of 1965 monsoon rainfall in Figure 5.1. It can be seen that at the level of the Meteorological Department's regions, only the eastern third of the state, Vidarbha, showed a rainfall deficiency of 20 per cent or more. Only when the monsoon monthly rainfall is examined at district level together with the pre-monsoon rainfall, does the reason for such widespread scarcity as did occur become clear. Figure 5.2 maps pertinent data by districts. The Konkan coastal region has an average high rainfall, everywhere over 1500 mm, and extensively over 2000 mm. In the rainshadow of the Western Ghats precipitation falls off abruptly to below 750 mm in a belt about 220 km wide, within which are pockets with less than 500 mm. Eastwards again the total increases to reach 1500 mm along the furthermost border. The degree to which districts differ in the provision of irrigation as a protection against drought is indicated. Only in the extreme east, significantly beyond the limit of the black soils area does the proportion of the total sown area (TSA) under irrigation equal or exceed 15 per cent. Here tanks command over 80 per cent of the irrigated area. Elsewhere the rainshadow districts closest to catchments in the Ghats have 10–14 per cent TSA irrigated, and the adjacent belt within the 750 mm isohyet 5–9 per cent, mostly from wells, though canals are important in Pune and Ahmednagar. For the rest irrigation is negligible but the moisture retentive qualities of the black soils of the Deccan lava plateau must not be overlooked in the context of drought survival.

At the time of the drought the population of the state was 45 million, with 65 per cent of the gainfully employed in agriculture, rather more than half as agricultural labourers. The overall drop in production of major crops in 1965–66 was as shown in Table 5.1 compared with the preceding 'normal' year.

The decline in some parts of the state was of course much greater. In the easternmost districts rice constitutes 53 per cent (Bhandara) and 32 per cent (Chandrapur) of the TSA. Yields fell by 59 per cent in unirrigated areas of both districts and by 44 and 56 per cent respectively even in the irrigated tracts. In this area irrigation is mainly by tanks and of all irrigation systems tanks are most likely to fail in drought years. In Konkan districts south of Bombay, less affected by the drought of 1965–66 because of higher total rainfall, the crop was reduced by a quarter. In some districts where kharif jowar accounted for a third or more of TSA, yields fell between 43 and 65 per cent. Rabi jowar, which is sometimes irrigated, makes up two thirds of Sholapur's TSA; the irrigated crop lost 31 per cent in yield, while the rainfed crop lost 67 per cent. In other districts declines of over 30 per cent for rainfed rabi jowar were common. Similarly bajra, a rainfed kharif crop renowned for its capacity to withstand drought, dropped by more than 42 per cent in six out of eight districts where it exceeded a tenth of TSA, and by 22 and 33 per cent in the others. Cotton, the major cash crop of the state, accounted for 42–49 per cent TSA in Akola, Amravati, Yeotmal and Wardha, dropped 33–63 per cent in those areas. Translated into losses of income to farmers, and reduced opportunities to earn wages on the part of the labourers, the drought assumed disaster proportions.

At the worst point of the scarcity half a million people were employed on relief works to provide them with the means to buy food. The cost of

TABLE 5.1
Crop Production: Maharashtra

	Rice	*Wheat*	*Kharif jowar*	*Rabi jowar*	*Bajra*	*Ground -nut*	*Cotton*
Production 1965–66 (1000 tonnes)	885	280	1147	1150	370	464	179
Per cent deficit on 1964–65	39	31	32	27	23	44	21
Per cent drop in yield per ha	37	27	33	25	26	43	17

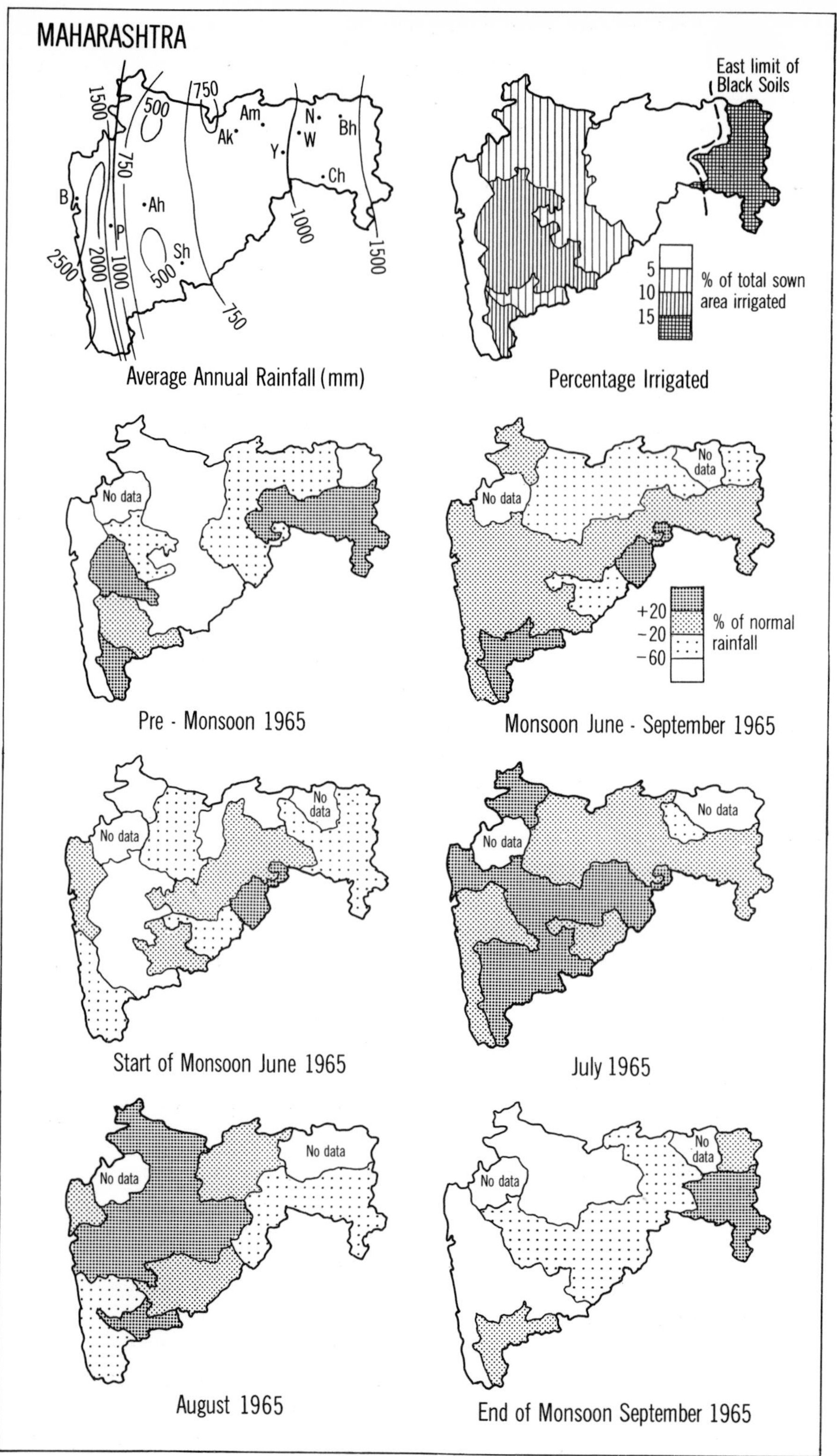

FIG. 5.2 Rainfall 1965 by districts: B Bombay; P Pune; Ah Ahmednagar; Sh Sholapur; Ak Akola; Am Amraoti; Y Yeotmal; W Wardha; N Nagpur; Ch Chandrapur; Bh Bhandara.

providing emergency supplies at fair prices tends to fall on the nation as a whole. Because of its large urban population in Bombay, Maharashtra is normally a deficit state drawing food grains from outside to supplement what is available locally. In the fair years of 1963–64 and 1964–65 the level of deficit was 264,000 and 562,000 tonnes. The drought forced up the level of drawing to 829,000 tonnes in 1965–66 and 954,000 tonnes in 1966–67.

How a deficiency in monsoon rainfall affecting only a third of the state's districts became a disaster hitting 19 out of 26 districts can only be appreciated if the pattern of rainfall is examined for the pre-monsoon period, as well as for each month of the rainy season. Generally over 80 per cent of the annual total rainfall comes in the four monsoon months. (See Figure 3.11 on page 55 for the rainfall regimes of Bombay and Nagpur, and Table 3.2 on page 50). In most districts pre-monsoon rains were negligible or deficient, and preparation of land could be begun in only a few areas. The monsoon arrived on time but produced only light falls (except in Konkan) insufficient or barely sufficient to start sowing. July rains, adequate on the coast were generally short inland, and produced a variety of responses from farmers seeking to alter their cropping strategy before it was too late. Cotton that had failed to germinate had to be resown, and in some areas cotton, groundnuts and bajra were abandoned and replaced by kharif jowar or a rabi crop. Seedling paddy sown late in the east was suffering water shortage as tanks had not refilled and irrigation could not be maintained. August brought better falls in some parts, but too late to be of much value. From Yeotmal eastwards rainfall was deficient to scanty. Something might have been garnered from the parched fields had not the monsoon tailed off in September. Only four districts had normal rainfall or better in September. October and November continued in the same pattern, there being virtually no rain at all in ten districts, and deficiencies of 55 per cent or more in the rest. So the kharif harvest proved very bad, and the rabi crops were only reported good on the heavier soils. Winter rains are never better than palliatives to evapo-transpiration from crops that have to rely on soil moisture, and this year was no exception. The above account is based on the contemporary matter-of-fact record contained in the annual *Season and Crop Report* for Maharashtra, and underlines vividly the importance of the timely occurrence of rainfall in regions where at best it is moderate.

THE BIHAR FAMINE 1967

Unlike Maharashtra, Bihar is a state with a normal expectation of 1000 mm or more of rainfall, except in a small zone running west from Patna District, which has at least 863 mm on average. The state may be located on Figure 5.1. The six southern districts constitute the meteorological region of Plateau Bihar, the remainder form Plains Bihar (Figure 5.3). Irrigation is provided to upwards of 18 per cent of TSA in the southern plains districts, reaching over 38 per cent in Patna, Gaya, Shahabad and Bhagalpur. In the south central plateau and along the Nepal border in the north, centre and east, irrigation (at this time) commanded from 2 to 5 per cent TSA. Canals are the main source but channel diversions, wells and tanks are all used. The cropping pattern is dominated by late kharif (winter) rice, which in every district exceeds 23 per cent TSA, while maize and wheat each exceed ten per cent in six districts and in eleven of them, 40 per cent.

Of the total population of 53 million, 82 per cent of the economically active were engaged in agriculture, a little more than half of these as cultivators, the rest as labourers. In April 1967 more than a quarter of the population, 13.4 million, were in areas severely affected by famine, where the kharif crop was deficient by 25–50 per cent.

In the case of Bihar it would be misleading to look only at the situation caused by the drought of 1966 alone, for the period of scarcity lasted, to some extent, into the following year, despite the apparent recovery of rainfall to within normal limits in most districts. The position may be summarized as in Table 5.2, using 1965–66 as a normal year.

The extent of aid from Central Government is seen in the sharp rise in the rate of drawing from its pool. This had been 444,000 and 436,000 tonnes in the two normal years preceding the drought, and rose to 662,000, 1,288,000 and 1,891,000 tonnes in 1966–67, and the two years following. Suresh

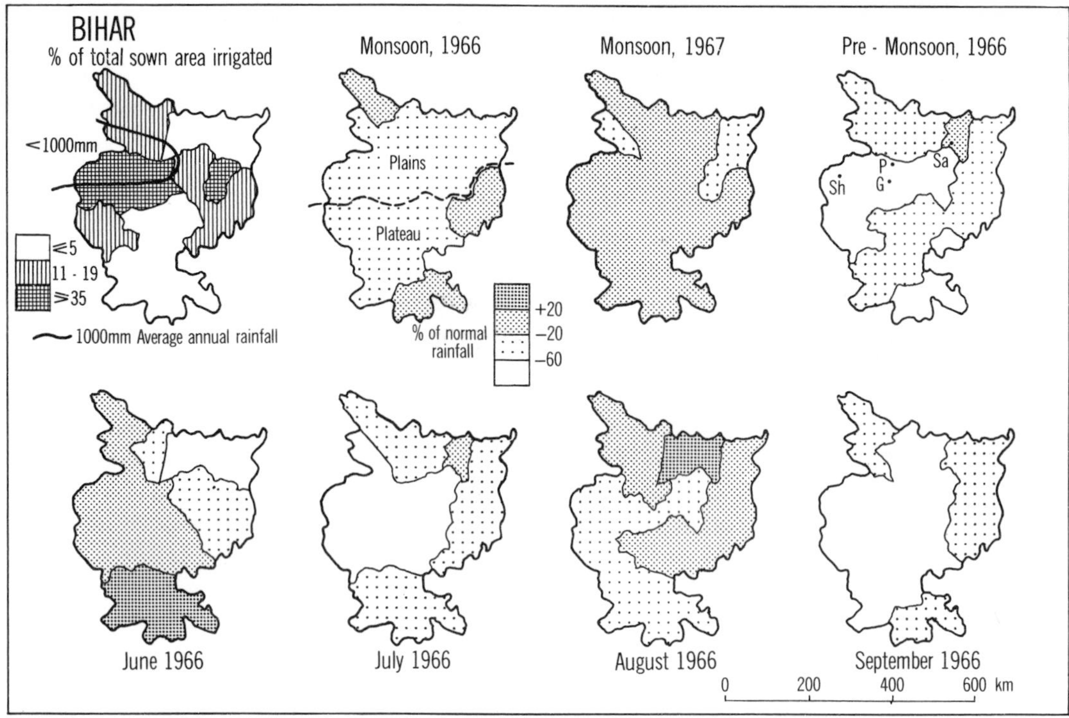

FIG. 5.3 Rainfall 1966–67 by districts: Sh Shahabad; P Patna; G Gaya; Sa Saharsa.

TABLE 5.2
Crop Production: Bihar

	Winter rice	*Wheat*	*Total foodgrains and pulses*
Production 1965–66 (1000 tonnes)	4049	477	7243
1966–67	1284	365	3624
Per cent change	−68	−23	−50
1967–68	3618	914	7369
Per cent change relative to 1965–66	−11	+92	+2

Singh suggests that the overall foodgrain deficit in Bihar was usually of the order of 1.3–1.6 million tonnes, calculated on a per capita ration of 420 grams per day. This in itself is a sorry commentary on the backwardness of the rural economy of Bihar. In 1966–67 the shortfall was 4.6 million tonnes only half of which could be found in the event. Thus, seen at the state level, against a need of over 9 million tonnes, 4.1 million were grown locally and a further 2.6 million brought in from outside to make a total about 25 per cent short of requirements. For many poor people the deficiency was of course much greater than this.

The concentrated efforts to raise productivity, by Central Government agencies, voluntary organizations and the people and administration of Bihar itself had some longer term benefits. Foodgrain production in the years immediately following the famine reached 8.6 and 8.8 million tonnes in 1967–68 and 1968–69 respectively, almost cancelling the state's chronic deficit.

The onset of drought may be traced back to the pre-monsoon season of 1966 when not a single district showed a positive deviation from the normal range, and only one was within that range, with 18 per cent below average. Many of the remainder had but 'scanty' rainfall, and the rest were deficient. The monsoon started early but produced deficient to scanty falls in the northeast quarter of the state; elsewhere conditions were normal to good. The probability of disaster became apparent with the total failure of the July rains, essential for the survival of crops planted at the beginning of the monsoon. As in the pre-monsoon period, only Saharsa, with 19 per cent deficiency just scraped into the 'normal' category, everywhere else there was deficiency or worse. This degree of failure meant that many crops died, and the irrigation resources dried up as the rivers and groundwater were not replenished. August brought some relief, five districts achieving positive deviations within the normal range, or better in the case of two of them. But these rains were too late to be much help, and of the remaining districts five were normal but deficient, and five more had less than 20 per cent of the average rainfall. September clinched the disaster. Ten districts registered scanty falls, and the best of the rest reached only to within 28 per cent of normal. The post-monsoon season was fractionally not quite so bad, but the winter brought practically no rain at all. Hardship forced many farming families to sell their work animals and to consume the grain they had set aside for seed. At the worst phase of the famine in mid 1967, 534,000 were employed on famine relief works and a further 707,000 were in receipt of free hand-outs.

The pre-monsoon rainfall of 1967 was generally very good, but could affect only the kharif crops which could get a good start and be well established by the time the light to moderate monsoon arrived. Again the post-monsoon rains were a near total failure, but the enormous increase in tube wells, rushed in to relieve the calamity, enabled the rabi wheat crop even to exceed that of 1965–66. To quote Suresh Singh: 'In one year of famine relief as many tube wells were sunk as there were before the famine. The area under irrigation in 1967–68 increased by only one per cent over 1965–66, but that served by tube wells rose by 125 per cent, to account for 9.2 per cent of the total.

The failure of the monsoon in the first year of famine was so nearly total as to reduce the yield of winter rice by 74 per cent or more in half of the districts, and by not less than 38 per cent in the remainder. As some land went out of use, production fell even further than yields. In over half the 17 districts output fell by more than three-quarters, and in a quarter of them by 90 per cent or more. The price of winter rice rose 90 per cent in Patna, 81 per cent in Gaya and Shahabad Districts, and by 54 per cent over the state as a whole.

Wheat yields were less severely affected, but fell by not less than 20 per cent overall. The pattern was irregular in that seven districts registered a fall of 40 per cent or more, and another seven showed an increase or no change from the previous year. Recovery from disaster of the magnitude of 1966–67 was not immediate, despite much improved rainfall in the monsoon of 1967–68. The winter rice crop was still 11 per cent down on the pre-famine year. In seven districts where rainfall had recovered to within the 'normal' range, production was 20 to 45 per cent below that of 1965–66; increases above that year's level were achieved in seven districts. Wheat did much better, more time being available for rehabilitation, and every district showed an increase in production over pre-famine years. Maize demonstrated its resilience during the drought and yields showed an increase of from 9 to 48 per cent in five districts, underlining the possibility of designing alternative cropping strategies to enable the farmer to accommodate to drought when it threatens. Crops like jowar and maize, requiring less water than does rice, would at least reduce the risk of severe scarcity. It is easy to be wise after the event, and farmers are all too prone to hope for better times around the corner rather than to take bold action that may in the event prove unnecessary and less profitable.

LIABILITY TO DROUGHT

It will be appreciated from what has been said above, that liability to drought and liability to scarcity are not synonymous. Scarcity has not been confined either to areas of low average rainfall, nor to areas having a high probability of deficient rainfall. Figure 5.4 shows the area where the probability of the annual rainfall being more than 25 per cent below normal is more than 20 per cent, i.e. would occur at least one year in five on average. Most of Bihar and half of Maharashtra lie outside the belt so defined by the Meteorological Department for the Irrigation Commission of 1972. If this map is compared with that of average rainfall

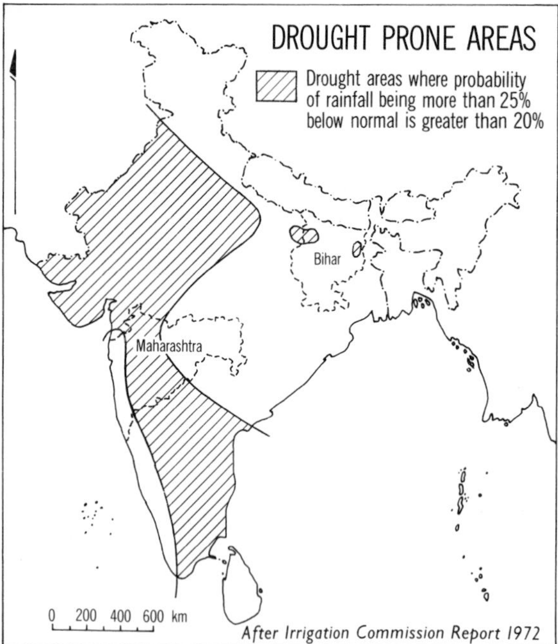

FIG. 5.4

FIG. 5.5

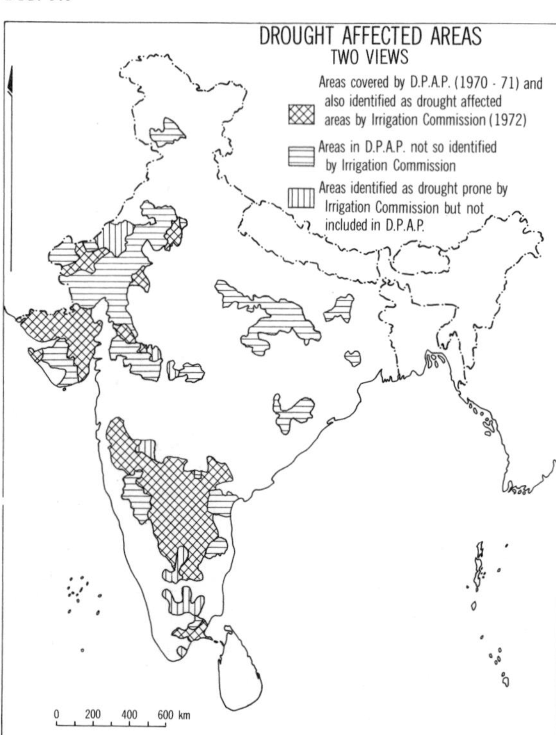

(see Figure 3.8 on page 54 it will be noted that there is an approximate correspondence of the boundary of the drought areas with the 1000 mm isohyet. The only area exceeding 1000 mm that lies within the drought zone is the belt of late season rainfall following early summer drought that lies in Tamilnadu.

Scarcity, as we have seen, is not simply a matter of rainfall amount or even of its incidence. It also reflects to a degree the inflexibility of the land-use system in the face of climatic stress. The Irrigation Commission invited the States to nominate the areas they considered as drought-affected. Their list corresponded closely with the districts covered by the Drought Prone Areas Programme from 1970–71, and extends far beyond what the Commission itself was prepared to admit as drought-affected (see Figure 5.5). That drought and even famine has occurred outside the meteorologists' boundary is undeniable, but the infrequency of their occurrence there is all important in this context.

Notwithstanding, funds made available under the DPAP are being used to improve irrigation facilities and communications in these areas, and the need is realized to pursue energetically research into dry farming techniques. Water resources within the drought affected zone more narrowly defined are understandably limited, and less than 20 per cent of the cropped areas of the zone is likely ever to be brought under irrigation. The problem of how best to use the water available is a matter not only of scientific investigation and experiment, but also of designing appropriate institutions to manage these scarce resources. A major risk is that the arid and semi-arid lands will lag behind the better watered areas in their level of economic and social development. The alternative is to encourage migration from these areas, leaving fewer farmers and pastoralists to manage the dry zones, using extensive methods at a profitable scale.

For the areas subject to occasional scarcity in the higher rainfall regions, avoidance of the recurrence of famine will depend more on the development to the full of water resources and of cropping systems that do not leave farmers exposed to serious risk. That over-dependence on agriculture by the population of such areas can be a compulsion upon farmers to take risks is a difficulty to be overcome by broadening the economic base.

CHAPTER SIX

MODERNIZATION OF AGRICULTURE

SUMMARY

Modernization in the context of agriculture implies change both in the infrastructure and the technology of farming. The traditional system of agriculture while it embodies much common sense built up over centuries of trial and error, also contains some elements of archaic folklore, religious belief, superstition and prejudice which collectively can only be labelled as irrational by modern scientific man. In abstract terms modernization aims to create for the cultivator within a given physical environment a framework of socio-economic conditions which will enable him, acting rationally and using factors and methods of production in a scientifically appropriate way, to achieve an optimum level of efficiency.

The relationship of the farmer to the land he tills is an important factor influencing his willingness to invest money and energy in its productivity. For whom does he labour and risk his wealth? For a landlord who takes half of his crop and makes no contribution to the costs of production other than the land? For the moneylender into whose clutches he has fallen in bad years or to meet social obligations involving ostentatious expenditure? For himself? Reform of the landholding system is proceeding fitfully in the Indian states since it involves probably the strongest challenge to tradition within the whole area of development. It requires that the agricultural revolution that replaced rent capitalism with productive capitalism in Europe a century and a half ago, be engineered rapidly and independently of the industrial revolution.

How much land a farmer, whether owner or tenant, operates is another matter bearing on his efficiency as does also the question of its consolidation from a number of traditionally scattered parcels into a contiguous holding. Ceilings for land ownership are set for each state in a move towards a more equitable distribution of resources, but a proprietary holding is not necessarily an operational holding, and it is the latter which is of more

28 Shepherd's shelter and crossbred sheep (Corriedale X local breed) at breeding station established with Australian assistance near Hissar, Haryana. The scheme is upgrading the wool quality of local flocks. The shepherd spends his nights here with the sheep, visiting his village when the job permits.

fundamental economic importance. A basic problem for government is to balance the political demand for equity against the more pragmatic necessity to maximize agricultural productivity in the national interest; the two are at times in conflict.

After land the farmer's most urgent need is generally for credit to enable him to finance his operations. Modern methods require investment in better seed, in fertilizers, in pesticides, in irrigation equipment, in wells, storehouses, etc. Easier access to credit at a fair rate of interest for farmers with little or nothing to offer by way of collateral has become an important instrument of modernization policy.

The term 'green revolution' can loosely be assigned to the use of modern technology in agriculture. It covers essentially the adoption of high yielding varieties (HYV) of seed, the use of artificial fertilizers in quantity, and the chemical protection of plants against pests and diseases. A prerequisite for the green revolution has been an assured and controllable irrigation supply. Modernization is now spreading to non-irrigated farming, and new HYV are being evolved for semi-arid as well as for flood lands. To achieve the close water control demanded by the dwarf varieties which formed the thrust of the HYV programme initially, farmers, whether or not they live within canal commanded areas, often invest in their own wells and in pumps energized by electricity or oil. They may also apply inanimate forms of energy in tractor ploughing, further to free themselves from the limitations of traditional village labour relationships.

'LAND TO THE TILLER'

The modernization of the socio-economic environment within which the cultivator operates has long been accepted as essential to the achievement of the goals of national self-sufficiency and social justice. The latter may currently be interpreted to mean as wide a distribution as possible throughout the community of the ownership and right to cultivate land. To quote *India 1975* (p. 175): 'The directive principle embodied in . . . the constitution lays down that the ownership and control of the material resources of the community are to be so distributed as best to subserve the common good and prevent concentration of wealth and means of production in a few hands to the detriment of the community'.

Since independence much has been done to further these aims particularly by the Central Government in its planning and investment policies, and by legislation. Much still remains to be done, however, especially at state level, to translate into reality the intentions expressed in laws on the statute books.

The land-holding system has been the subject of much legislation. There is not enough land for those who are or who would be farmers, and the country suffers from intense rural over-population. Operational holdings, the units actually farmed by agricultural households, as distinct from areas owned or rented by individuals, are often too small to provide subsistence for a family. Many families must supplement their income by casual employment when agricultural work is slack, or by having one or more members more or less permanently absent in some urban or non-agricultural occupation. The *average* size of operational holding ranges from less than a hectare in Kerala, the Vale of Kashmir, the UP Himalaya and parts of West Bengal, all areas of intensive rice cultivation, to over six hectares in the dry lands in the centre of Maharashtra, western Gujarat and western Rajasthan. A more appropriate way of presenting the realities of the situation is to try to show the middle position, since the very many quite uneconomic holdings that are included in the total tend to distort the picture. Figure 6.1 is based on data in the *National Sample Survey, 26th Round*, 1971–72, which enable an estimate to be made of the size of operational holding above and below which half the agricultural area is farmed. The map shows the tertile distribution of the sampling regions; the median value is 2.4 ha and the extreme range 0.7 to 11.1 ha. The third of the regions with the central tendency lying below 2 ha are seen to be mainly within the rice dominated areas (see Figure 7.3), where the crop is rainfed or irrigated, as in the case of southern Tamilnadu and parts of UP. Apart from these latter regions all enjoy over 1000 mm of rainfall. With or without the support of irrigation rainfall can be argued as a factor for agricultural intensity in the regions of the middle tertile. In the upper tertile there are areas with holdings around

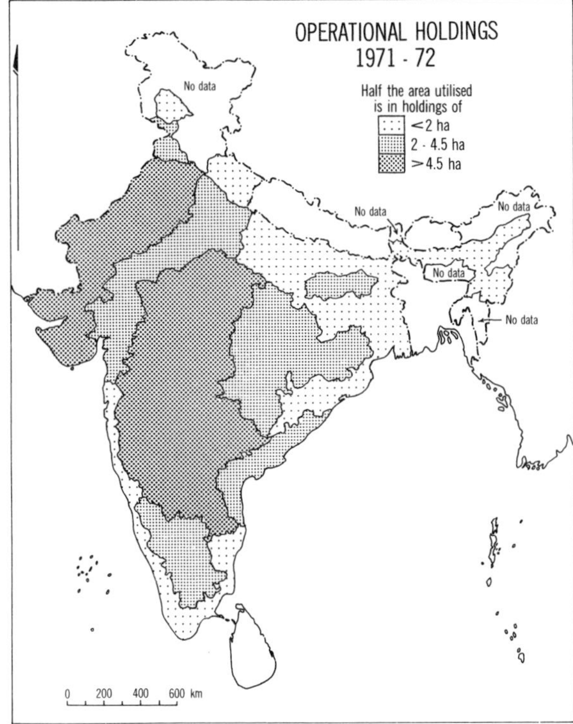

FIG. 6.1

4.5 ha, exclusively in the belt with less than 1000 mm of rain. The Peninsular interior and the arid zone are separated by a belt of middling value along the line of the Aravalli Hills where the terrain encourages smaller farm units based on well irrigation. The relatively large size of holdings in the irrigated south Punjab and Haryana probably reflects the greater measure of commercialization of agriculture in these go-ahead states, which were colonized from semi-desert over the past seventy years.

Efforts have been made to control the upper limit of the size of land holdings by the 'land-ceilings policy'. States are required under a Central Government Act, to introduce legislation to distribute to the landless and to smaller-holders the lands held surplus to the ceiling levels determined in each state or region. Ceilings vary with the quality of land within the state, and lie generally well above the minimum required for subsistence. In the states where rice growing predominates, the lower ceiling ranges from 3.7 ha in Jammu and Kashmir to 5 ha in West Bengal, most states using 4.05 or 4.86 ha. The wheat-millets states have ceilings ranging upwards from 7 ha in Punjab to 7.25 in Haryana, UP, Maharashtra and Rajasthan. The upper limit (applicable to the least productive land) is most commonly 21.85, but wide variations occur: Assam uses 7 ha, Himachal Pradesh 28.33 ha. The Draft Fifth Five Year Plan bemoans the meagre results of all this legislation, suggesting that ceiling levels were set too high, and that landowners have been able, aided and abetted by dilatory and unenergetic implementation on the part of the State authorities, to avoid the intentions of the laws by malafide transfers of land and by dividing a property up among close relatives while continuing to operate it as a single holding. Performance has lagged far behind precept and the optimistic promises held out in the 1950s that 26 million hectares would be found surplus to the ceiling levels have been whittled down to a mere 1.6 million ha now available for redistribution. Since 1972 Karnataka has taken up the challenge and is well on the way to becoming, to use words of its adviser on Land Reforms, 'a State having only small and medium peasant proprietors, each cultivating his holding personally with the labour of his family members and the minimum of hired labour.' Tenancy has been abolished and the occupiers of land can become owners by purchase from Government at far below market value. Lands not cultivated by the owner but to which occupiers cannot prove tenancy title, become vested in Goverment and are added to the pool of surplus land for redistribution to the landless cultivators. Similarly land above the new ceiling limits goes into the pool. A family of ten may own at most 44 ha. The basic ceilings for ownership by a family of five are as follows:

double cropped wet land	4.0–5.3 ha
single cropped wet land	6.1–8.1 ha
rainfed wet land	10.1–12.1 ha
dry land	21.9 ha

These areas represent ten units of land in each category. A family larger than five members may own two additional units per member up to a maximum of 26 units. It is expected that a pool of about 162,000 ha will result, onto which 80,000 families, half of them from Scheduled Castes and Tribes, will be settled.

The land reform legislation seeks to reduce the disparity in holdings; it is not attempting to lay down the optimum size. An attempt to quantify the concept of 'economic holding' has been made by A. M. Khusro[1] writing before the full implications of the Green Revolution had been realized. He used three measures of economic size: the 'plough unit', i.e. the area that a pair of bullocks could on average manage to cultivate; the 'work unit', the area that family labour could cope with; and the 'income unit', the area that would yield an income of Rs 1200. Converted into rounded hectares his minimum values are as shown in Table 6.1.

TABLE 6.1
Size of economic holding (ha)

State	*Plough unit*	*Work unit*	*Income unit*
Andhra Pradesh	4	2	4
Punjab-Haryana	4	3–4	8
Tamilnadu	2	3	—
Uttar Pradesh	4	3	4
West Bengal	3	—	6

Farmers applying the most modern technology can no doubt attain the desired income level with less than the minima given above, and there may also be reductions in the size of work unit now that operations need to be more labour intensive, but the general levels are an indication of scale, much below which a farm is likely to be economically marginal or sub-marginal, compelling the farmer (and his labouring family) to add to their subsistence efforts by finding outside work.

Aggravating the small size of many holdings is their common fragmentation into separate parcels of land often at opposite ends of a village or in a neighbouring village, making the farmer's access to work wasteful in time, and close supervision of all his fields difficult. In several states, holdings have been or are in an advanced state of being consolidated, but the process is terribly laborious and slow, bedevilled with legal niceties and problems of establishing ownership. The northwestern states and Maharashtra have gone furthest in consolidation, but elsewhere little has happened. One major consideration that may have deterred administrators and tenants is that the procedures can become the opportunity to evict legally insecure occupiers from the land.

Tenancy conditions are a more fundamental handicap to modernization than the size of holdings or their fragmentation. Traditional tenancy and crop-sharing arrangements for using land are relics of the rent-capitalist system, the disappearance of which from the western world was part of the agricultural revolution in the eighteenth and nineteenth centuries. The essence of rent-capitalism was that the landowner was content to draw rents from his land while minimizing his investment. In productive capitalism which replaced this system in the west, the landowner saw land as a medium through which he could increase his income by investing in its high productivity irrespective of who managed the enterprise. W. Ladejinsky has pointed to the indirect connection between land reform and modernization as comprehended in the concept of the 'green revolution', the success of which depends on the occupier of land, whether owner or tenant, being able to acquire credit to finance his farming operations.[1] Recent estimates put 20 per cent as the proportion of the land under tenancies, with double this figure in some areas. Dating from the Second Five Year Plan, the call has been to give 'land to the tiller', with the abolition of tenancy as the objective. Many of those who farm lands they do not own do so under various forms of informal verbal agreement with the landlord, which are very difficult to establish in law. Thus much of the legislation to give land to tenants who have cultivated it for a number of years has proved abortive. Laws to limit the rental to not more than one fifth or a quarter of the gross product of the land (figures which are varied to one third in Punjab, Haryana, and parts of Tamilnadu, and to even a half in farms of under 5 ha in Jammu and Kashmir) are difficult to enforce in a semi-literate tradition-bound population. Doreen Warriner's comment to the effect that the relationships between idle landlords, peasant owners, tenants, share-croppers and landless labourers are founded in caste rather than in economic terms is apposite.[2] The socially and economically weak near the bottom of the caste structure are understandably reluctant to assert themselves against their age-old landlords of high caste.

[1] A. M. Khusro, *Economics of Land Reform and Farm Size in India*, 1973.

[2] W. Ladejinsky, 'Ironies of India's Green Revolution', *Foreign Affairs*, 48(4), 1970, pp. 756–768.

[3] D. Warriner, *Land Reform in Principle and Practice*, Oxford, Clarendon Press, 1969.

29 Fishing provides an important supplementary source of protein, and is an important village activity in many coastal areas. This view in Kerala shows fishermen preparing their nets beneath coconut palms. Much cordage used is made from coir fibre obtained from the coconut husk. Behind the nearest boat a crew can be seen pulling their boat ashore. Their village houses shelter among the palms in the background.

An attempt is being made to out-flank the handicap of non-ownership of land, by government agencies becoming more closely involved in the process of providing credit to small and marginal tenant farmers. As was observed in the Godavari delta in Andhra, development officers were empowered to guarantee to the rural bank one fifth of a loan for an approved purpose, such as sinking a well. All in all the feeling is current that the Centre is serious about the land reform policies and intends to press these home to the states with considerable vigour. In the field of supplying credit, as also for providing farmers with material inputs such as fertilizers and ensuring the proper processing and marketing of their produce, the co-operatives have an important part to play, despite their very mixed record in India. Habits die hard, such as continual heavy indebtedness, or giving way to the wishes of members of higher caste and status, but the small man is beginning to realize he has rights under the law.

So far we have been discussing some of the intangible elements in the infrastructure of development and modernization. On the material side progress has been considerable, though one must hasten to say that there are finite limits to the green revolution. At best it must be seen as providing a short breathing space in the unequal race between population demand and food supply, which must be used to bring about changes in the dynamics of demographic growth, and in the degree of the economy's dependence on the land.

THE GREEN REVOLUTION

Too often it is popularly supposed that the essence of the Green Revolution has been the introduction of newly developed high yielding strains of wheat, rice and other crops. While this was an important element, equally important were the provision of irrigation at the place and time required, and the availability of other material inputs such as fertilizers and chemicals for plant protection. The wider provision of credit with which to dig wells, to purchase pumps, and to apply manures and pesticides, has had an impact upon agriculture as a whole and not merely on the cultivation of the specifically HYV crops.

The HYV Programme began in 1966–67 with the introduction of new fertilizer-responsive dwarf wheats developed in Mexico. In that crop year, 4.2 per cent of the area under wheat was HYV. By 1970–71 this all-India figure had risen to 35 per cent, and to 57 per cent in 1973–4. In the more important wheat-growing states the proportion was even higher: virtually 100 per cent in Bihar, 87 per cent in Haryana, 83 per cent in Punjab, and 56 per cent in UP (See Table 6.2). Apart from fertilizer the major constraint on the cultivation of HYV of wheat is water availability, since they require 5–6 shallow waterings as against the 2–4 needed for local varieties. Sufficient water is not always obtainable from the tail end of canal systems, especially if the farmers higher up the system have taken to HYV also but more problematical is the

TABLE 6.2
Statewise Data on Modernization

State by Region	*Villages electrif-ied %*	*Pumps ener-gized (thousands)*	*Fertil-izer used kg/ha cultivated*	*Per cent TSA irrig-ated*	*% Wheat area HYV*		*% Rice area HYV*	
	1975–76	*1975–76*	*1973–74*	*1970–72*	*1970–71*	*1973–74*	*1971–72*	*1973–74*
North								
Jammu -Kashmir	27	0.4	16.2	38	29		67	
Himachal Pradesh	38	1	7.8	18	24		37	
Punjab	71	145	58.7	77	68	83	56	81
Haryana	100	138	23.2	45	54	87	17	
Centre								
Uttar Pradesh	28	253	20.1	35	33	56	16	22
Rajasthan	20	91	4.4	15	25		23	
Madhya Pradesh	16	141	6.9	8	6		7	
West								
Gujarat	34	119	21.1	13	18		19	
Maharashtra	54	402	13.5	9	23		21	29
East								
Bihar	15	112	8.9	26	72	100	9	12
Orissa	22	4	7.5	23			8	8
West Bengal	25	8	14.0	27	88		16	15
Assam	6	1	2.9	3			10	
Meghalaya	4							
Manipur	11		10				9	
Nagaland	18		5				2	
Tripura	3		1				4	
South								
Andhra Pradesh	39	283	21	30			33	56
Karnataka	52	220	17.9	15	15		20	25
Tamilnadu	98	729	46.2	46			59	78
Kerala	94	45	27.9	21			46	31
INDIA	29	2,710	16.9	24	35	57	19	26

30 So-called 'Chinese' fishing nets, Cochin harbour mouth, Kerala. The rocks tied to the ropes act as counter-weights to help raise the nets. Birds share the paltry catch.

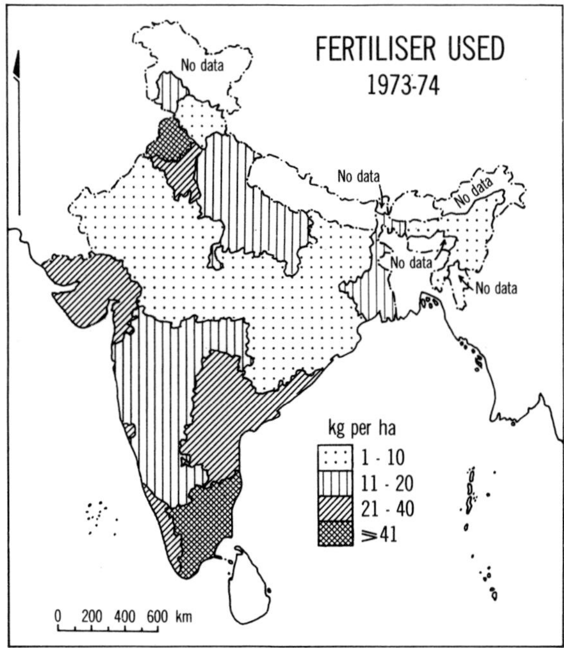

FIG. 6.2

inability of a canal system designed to meet traditional needs to cope with a radically different pattern of demands. The high income to be made from growing the new varieties enabled many farmers to invest in their own independent supply of water from pumped wells or tube-wells. These however, generally depend on electricity which tends to be in short supply in the same season as the canal waters are inadequate, and for the same reason, that is, shortage of storage in the multi-purpose reservoir. The smaller farmers are hardest hit in these circumstances, as they often rely on water purchased from the larger operators who understandably look after themselves first. Undoubtedly HYV have had an impressive affect on wheat productivity, whether measured in increased tonnage or in yields per hectare. Production in Punjab rose from 2,494,000 tonnes in 1966–67, at an average yield of 1544 kg per ha to 5,368,000 tonnes (2233 kg/ha) in 1972–3, an increase in yield of 44 per cent. Other states could not match this performance except Bihar (taking the post-famine year 1967–68 as base) with 44 per cent increase. UP achieved 27 per cent and Haryana 23 per cent. In terms of meeting India's increasing food needs, the HYV was largely responsible for more than doubling wheat production between 1966–67 and 1972–73.

The same degree of success has not yet been achieved with rice for a number of reasons. Several HYV of rice have been available from the late 1960s and have been found suitable to particular areas. All, however, are dwarf varieties, so bred to give them strength of stem to prevent wastage due to lodging, which reduces photosynthesis in the leaves flattened and shaded by those bent above them. Shortness of stem is a handicap in many lower parts of the deltas where rice is the main crop, and where the traditional varieties have been selected over time to cope with flooded conditions. The natural environments in which rice has to grow in much of eastern India are far from ideal for the new varieties so far available, though better adapted HYV are being bred. In the irrigated plains of the upper Ganga and Indus tributaries, close control over the depth of water can more readily be maintained, and the HYV dwarfs have done well. In 1973–74 26 per cent of the all-India area under rice was in HYV, compared with 2.5 per cent in 1966–67, and 19 per cent in 1971–72, Adoption of HYV has been greatest in Punjab (81 per cent of the area), Tamilnadu (78), and Andhra Pradesh (56). Kerala (31), Maharashtra (29), Karnataka (25) and UP (22) follow with reasonably high percentages assisted by the closer water control possible in those states than in Orissa (8) and West Bengal (15). Bihar (12) is also liable to floods in parts, and might have been expected to be a high adopter in view of its record with wheat. Water supplies are less certain and less controlled in the east of India where more reliance is placed on direct rainfall. It is in the dry season wherever irrigation can be assured, that HYV rice has proved most popular, because then the risk of deep flooding is absent, and conditions approach the ideal, the clear skies and low humidity discouraging pests and diseases. Locally, as in the Godavari delta, traditional cropping patterns are being modified using the shorter maturing period of HYV to make possible a rabi rice crop while water is still available. The major constraint in the rabi season is the availability of water. Unless there are wells, water may be uncertain since tanks and canals tend to have diminishing supplies relying on storage from the monsoon rains.

The potential impact of HYV rice in areas where water levels can be controlled is seen in Punjab, where an overall yield of 2289 kg per ha was recorded for 1973–74, an increase of 93 per cent over 1966–67. Hooghly in West Bengal reached 3450 kg per ha for rabi-grown boro rice in 1971–72 in contrast to the autumn aus crop at 893 kg and the winter aman crop at 1342 kg per ha. In the latter seasons HYV are as yet unimportant in West Bengal though HYV aman is rapidly gaining acceptance in neighbouring Bangladesh.

There were some doubts when the HYV programme was first introduced whether the farmers would adopt the new technology. It is now clear that given the right local conditions, farmers need no persuasion to accept innovation. Priority needs to be given to the breeding of HYV for a wider range of growing situations and to improving the systems of water provision and control so that more farmers can grow existing varieties. If the price for the product is right farmers will seek avidly for the necessary inputs. Recent rises in

FIG. 6.3(*a*) TRADITIONAL ECONOMY OF SUBSISTENCE RICE FARMER

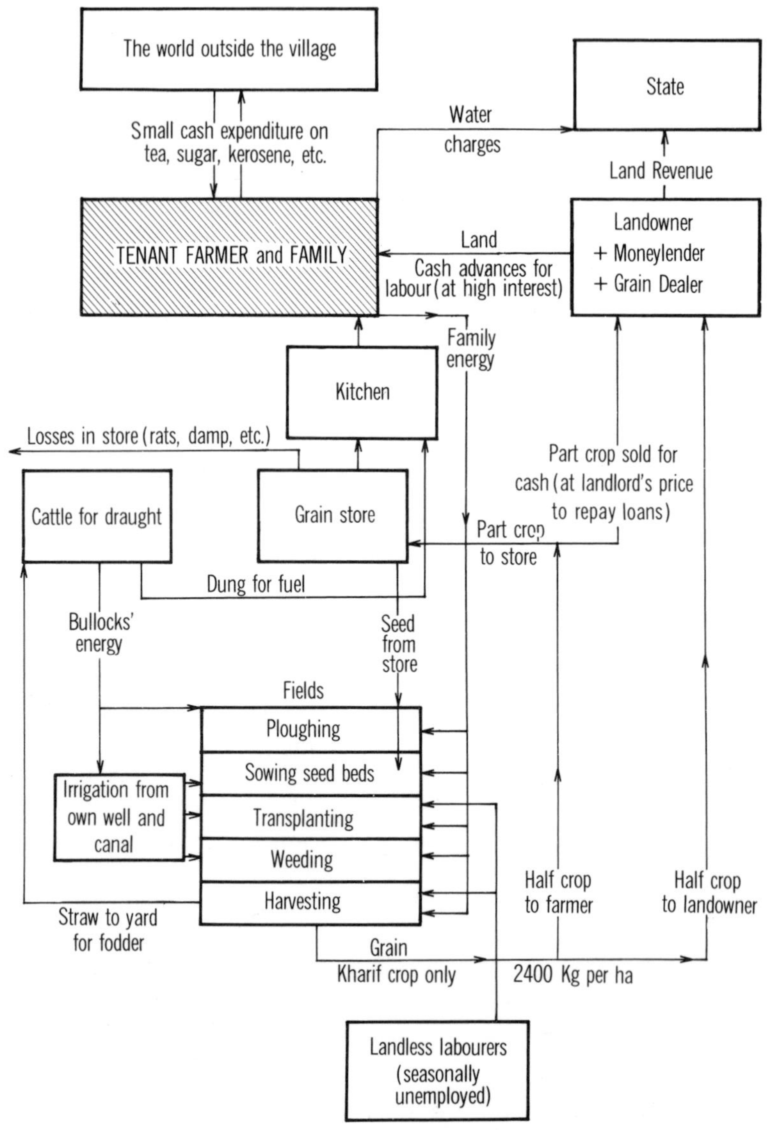

fertilizer costs while rice prices remained stable have tended to deter farmers from using the prescribed applications, with the result that in some areas yields have fallen, for example by 24 per cent in Bihar between 1971–72 and 1974–75.

Other crops for which HYV are becoming increasingly available are maize, jowar, bajra and some of the pulses. In 1973–74, 13 per cent of the maize, 7 per cent of the jowar and 22 per cent of the bajra area were expected to be in HYV. The new varieties of bajra have proved susceptible to disease, but geneticists are likely to be able to breed resistance into a future variety. The International Crops Research Institute for the Semi-Arid Tropics (ICRISAT) established at Hyderabad, is trying to do for the millets and pulses what was done for wheat and rice in research institutes in Mexico and the Philippines respectively.

Ultimately HYV may be found to suit every niche in the agricultural environment, but their introduction into the cropping system will make increasing demands on the farmer, and through him on the industrial sector.

Chief among the agricultural inputs that must be manufactured are fertilizers. The increase in demand is shown in Table 6.3 (overleaf).

FIG. 6.3(*b*)

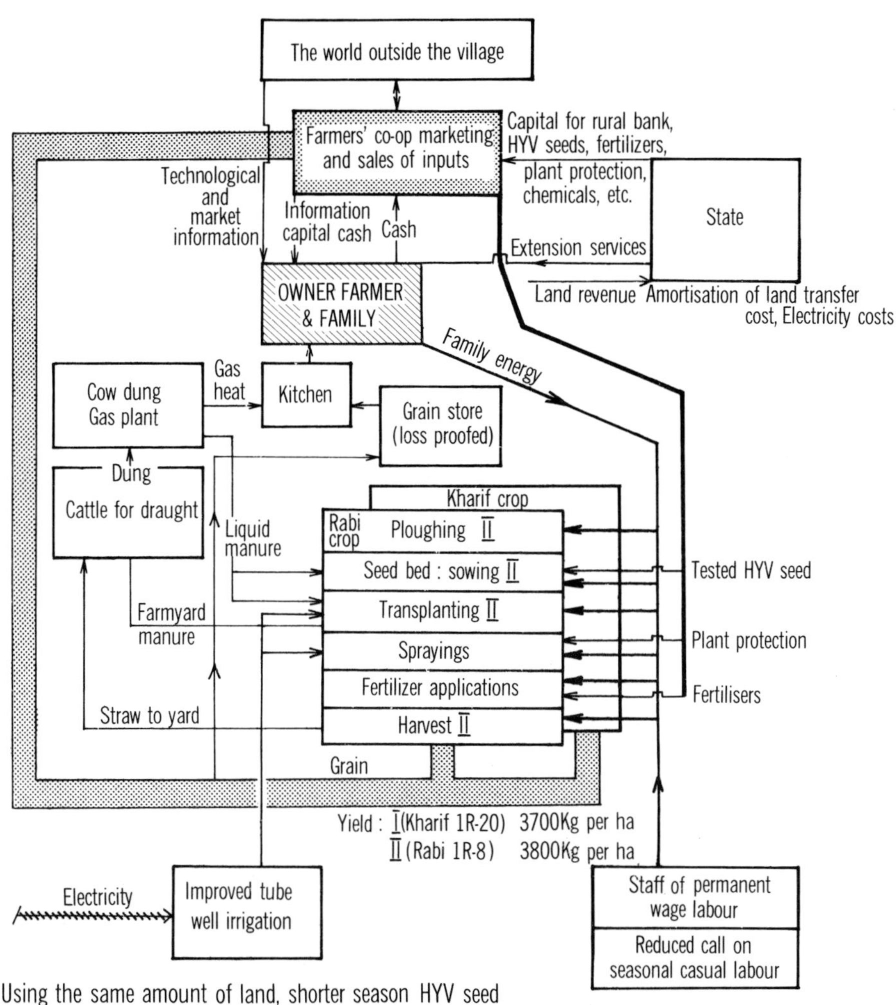

Using the same amount of land, shorter season HYV seed and modernised inputs, much higher yields per hectare are achieved: 6900 Kg. More labour is utilised over a longer period.

TABLE 6.3

Fertilizer Production and Imports (thousand tonnes)

		Production	*Imports*	*Distributed*
1952–53	N	53	44	58
	P_2O_5	7	—	5
	K_2O	—	3	3
		60	47	66
1972–73	N	1,055	691	1,742
	P_2O_5	330	211	535
	K_2O	—	316	312
		1,385	1,218	2,589

In response to the demand a huge new industry has sprung up all over India with a capacity approaching two million tonnes. The Fifth Plan aims to bring production to over four million tonnes. The consumption of fertilizers has increased four-fold since 1964–65 and now exceeds 20 kg per ha of cropped land in eleven states. Rajasthan, Madhya Pradesh, Orissa, Bihar and Assam are the main states failing to reach a level of 10 kg per ha, a fact attributable at least in the case of the first two to their low ranking as irrigated regions. The others are relatively backward states in terms of modernization generally. (See Figure 6.2.)

An aspect of modernization that is making rapid progress is rural electrification, an essential service for powering pumps. It is interesting to note that the areas that appear relatively backward in respect of the percentage of villages electrified, are the same as those at the bottom of the list for fertilizer consumption. In the current five-year plan, a minimum of 40 per cent of villages electrified is the target for each state (see Table 6.2).

While the energizing of pumps with other than muscular energy is encouraged, the extension of mechanization in the sense of using fossil fuelled tractors and other farm machinery to replace human labour does not have universal approval. It is recognized that tractors can be justified on the grounds that they do not consume food when not in use, and because they may in some circumstances so speed the processes of cultivation as to permit a higher intensity of land use. The larger farms of advanced regions like Punjab (which had 47,00 tractors in 1972) are probably the most efficient in the country. UP with 30,000 Haryana with 20,000, and Rajasthan and Gujarat each with 12,000, are well ahead of the other states. The latter can barely muster 35,000 between them. On the small holdings of the rice growing regions four-wheeled tractors, unless they are centrally managed for whole village communities, cannot be conceived as economical. More justification would seem to exist for replacing the fodder-hungry bullocks by small two-wheel tractor ploughs of the type common in Japan, Malaysia, and Sri Lanka. So far modernization of agriculture in India has tended to be labour-consuming rather than labour-replacing. In some regions seasonal labour shortage is being experienced, but between times there is still much under-employed and concealed unemployment.

Table 6.2 summarizes some indices of modernization and enables comparison to be made between states, while Figure 6.3 indicates some of the contrasts between traditional and modernized systems.

CHAPTER SEVEN

PATTERNS OF CROPS AND CROP ASSOCIATIONS

CROPS

The Indian farmer still cultivates to a degree for the direct subsistence of himself and his family. While the larger farmers sell about two thirds of their production, the smaller ones retain a similar proportion for subsistence. What crops the farmer decides to grow within the physical constraints of soil, climate and the availability of irrigation to supplement rainfall, are in part a reflection of these subsistence requirements, in part a response to market opportunities. The crops grown, the methods of tilling the soil and of tending the plants, the nice adjustment of farming activity to the climatic and hydrological calendars, and the manner of adaptation to local variations in site such as floodplains, slopes and upland interfluves, all owe much to tradition, built up over millenia of trial and error. Over the three decades since independence, traditional agriculture has been subjected at an accelerating rate to pressures towards change. Some of these trends will be examined below against the basic patterns of the country's agricultural geography.

The area under the principal field crops in 1974–75, with 1947–48 for comparison, is given in Table 7.1. The percentage change since independence is also shown. Crop areas fluctuate from year to year, the total for 1974–75 being a little below that for 1973–74, 154.8 million, which represented an increase of almost 50 per cent over the 1947–48 level. Figure 7.1 shows the leading cereal or tuber crop used as the basic food, and Figure 7.2 the areas where these crops exceed 15 per cent of the total sown area (TSA). These figures should be referred to as each major crop is discussed below.

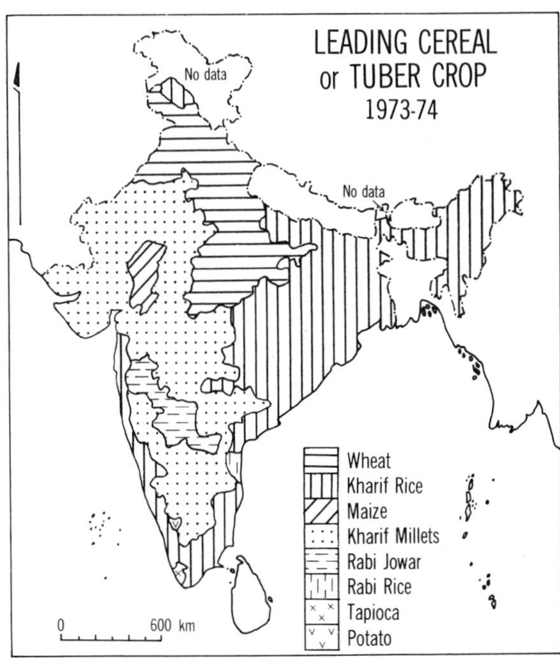

FIG. 7.1

Rice

This is India's premier crop, occupying almost a quarter of the total sown area, a proportion that has barely changed since independence although the total has increased by almost half. As Figure 7.1 shows, the area of rice dominance extends eastwards from the eastern parts of Uttar Pradesh and Madhya Pradesh to include the whole of eastern India, southwards along the Andhra coast into the coastal plain of Tamilnadu, and along the west coast from Valsad (S. Gujarat) to Alleppy (Kerala). The Vale of Kashmir forms a detached outlier. If the areas are added where, although not

TABLE 7.1
Area under Principal Crops: 1947–48 and 1974–75
(thousand ha and per cent of total; per cent change)

Crop	*1947–48*	*%*	*1974–75*		*%*		*% Change*
Rice:	25,585	24.8	37,922		25.4		+48.2
autumn rice			*16,443*		*11.0*		
winter rice			*19,543*		*13.1*		
summer rice			*1,936*		*1.3*		
Millets	22,899	22.2	29,648		19.9		+29.5
kharif jowar rabi jowar	*13,896*	*13.5*	*15,856*	*9,699* *6,158*	*10.6*	*6.5* *4.1*	*+14.1*
bajra	*6,789*	*6.6*	*11,261*		*7.5*		*+65.9*
ragi	*2,214*	*2.1*	*2,530*		*1.7*		*+11.4*
Wheat	7,852	7.6	18,108		12.1		+30.6
Barley	3,013	2.9	2,931		2.0		−2.7
Maize	2,993	3.0	5,921		4.0		+97.8
Other cereals	6,058	5.9	4,510		3.0		−25.6
TOTAL CEREALS	68,400	66.2	99,038		66.3		+44.8
Gram	7,811	7.6	7,150		4.8		−8.5
Arhar	2,019	2.0	2,540		1.7		+25.8
Other pulses, kharif Other pulses, rabi	8,929	8.6	12,889	*7,631* *5,258*	8.6	*5.1* *3.5*	+44.3
TOTAL PULSES	18,759	18.2	22,578		15.1		+20.4
Groundnut	3,905	3.8	7,167		4.8		+83.5
Other oilseeds	5,225	5.1	8,418		5.6		+61.1
TOTAL OILSEEDS	9,130	8.8	15,586		10.4		+70.7
Cotton	3,971	3.8	7,621		5.1		+91.9
Jute	265	0.3	665		0.4		+151.0
Sugar cane	1,722	1.7	2,604		1.7		+51.2
Condiments and spices	1,016	1.0	1,243		0.8		+22.3
TOTAL CROPS	103,263	100	149,335		100		+44.6

31 Drying pepper in the sun on a roadside in inland Kerala. Pepper is a smallholder crop grown on vines supported on tree trunks. Usually it forms only a part of the smallholder's enterprise.

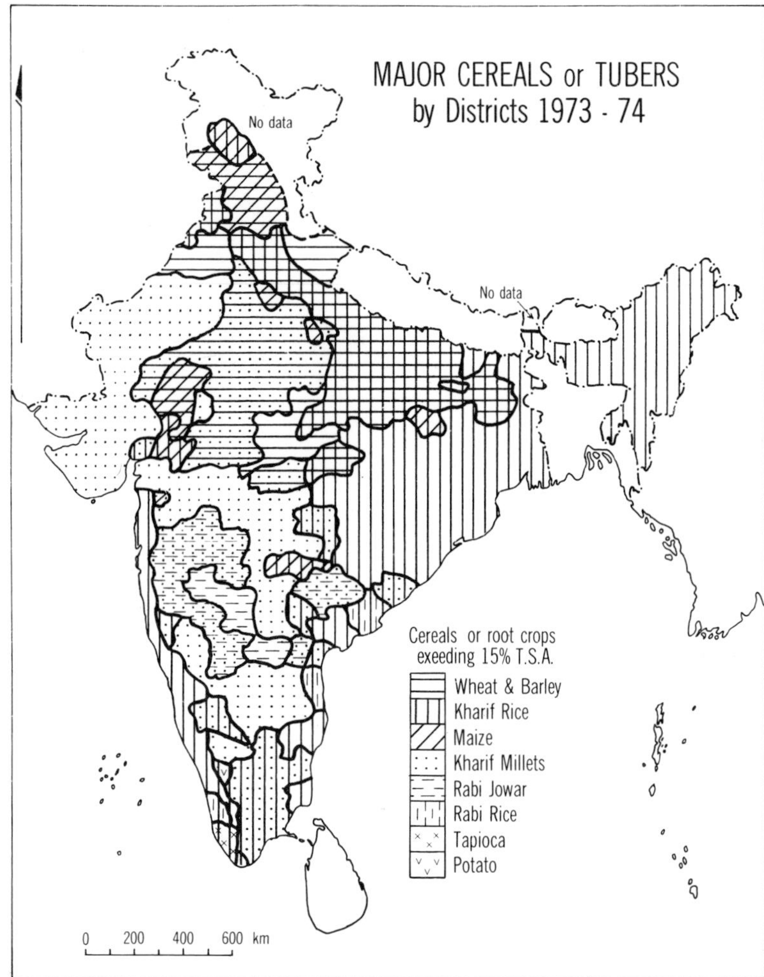

FIG. 7.2

dominant, rice exceeds 15 per cent of the TSA, the region can be extended into the plains of western UP and northern parts of Haryana and Punjab, and into the plateau country of Tamilnadu and central Karnataka (see Figure 7.2). East central Gujarat would also be added. Figure 7.3a presents the distribution of kharif rice growing areas and brings out the significant concentrations in the alluvial plains. Rice is mainly a kharif crop. Modern statistics make a distinction between an autumn crop, sown in the early rains to be harvested as the monsoon rains slacken in August, and a rather larger winter crop, sown in mid-monsoon for harvest during the dry season. The term kharif covers them both. While the kharif crop is mainly rainfed, 37 per cent is irrigated. This is essential wherever the rainfall is less than about 1000 mm (see Figure 3.8 on page 54), i.e. in northwest India, the Deccan and much of Tamilnadu. The small rabi rice crop requires irrigation and is further restricted to regions with a mild winter (see Figure 7.3b). Thus it is not found north and west of a line joining Bombay-Nagpur-Allahabad. Elsewhere the area of rabi rice is expanding under the impetus of the HYV programme.

Millets

Three quite distinct plants are linked under the term millets.[1] Together they rank after rice and wheat in popularity as food grains, but are nonetheless widely cultivated where moisture and temperature con-

[1] Bajra is *Pennisetum typhoideum*, or bullrush millet; jowar is *Sorghum vulgare*, or grain sorghum; ragi is *Eleusine coracana*, buckwheat or finger millet.

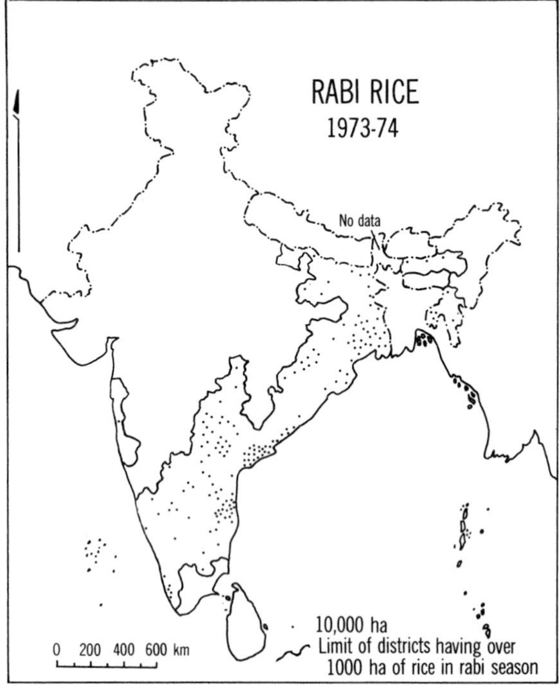

FIG. 7.3(*a*)

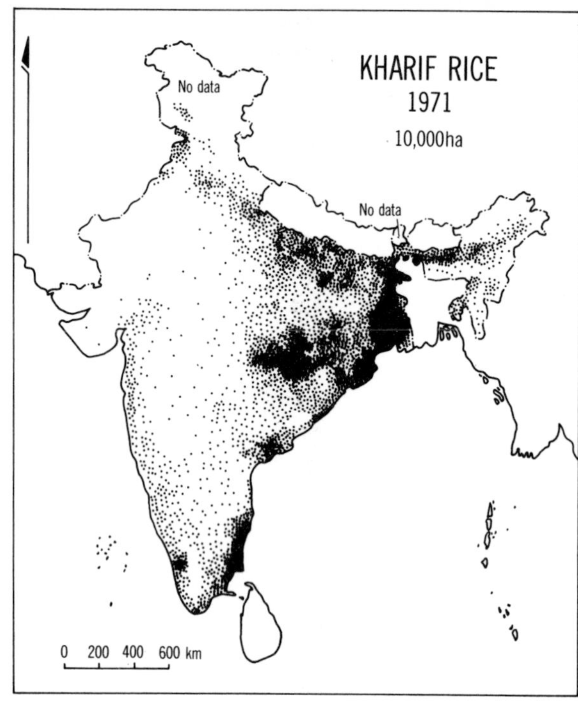

FIG. 7.3(*b*)

ditions inhibit the growth of the preferred cereals. *Jowar*, the most favoured of the millets for food-grain and fodder, is grown both as a kharif crop (63 per cent) and as a rabi crop. Rabi jowar dominates as the leading cereal in a belt running southeast from Pune and Ahmadnagar on the Deccan Lava Plateau behind Bombay, across northern Karnataka into southern Andhra Pradesh (see Figure 7.1). A few districts in which rabi jowar reaches 15 per cent or more of TSA lie adjacent or close to this belt. Figure 7.4 shows its distribution clearly, with the main concentration on the moisture-retentive black soils of the Deccan lavas (see Figure 3.13 on page 58). Rainfall here will support only one crop, either kharif or rabi, the latter on the basis of soil moisture carried over into the dry season.

A much larger area is dominated by kharif millets (Figure 7.1). The relationship to sub-humid conditions is clear (see Figure 3.8 and 3.12). These crops are mainly rainfed, and where they are important though secondary to rice they occupy the drier slopes and interfluves above irrigated strips of tank-fed paddy along the valley floors. Where they overlap with wheat it is as a drought-

FIG. 7.4

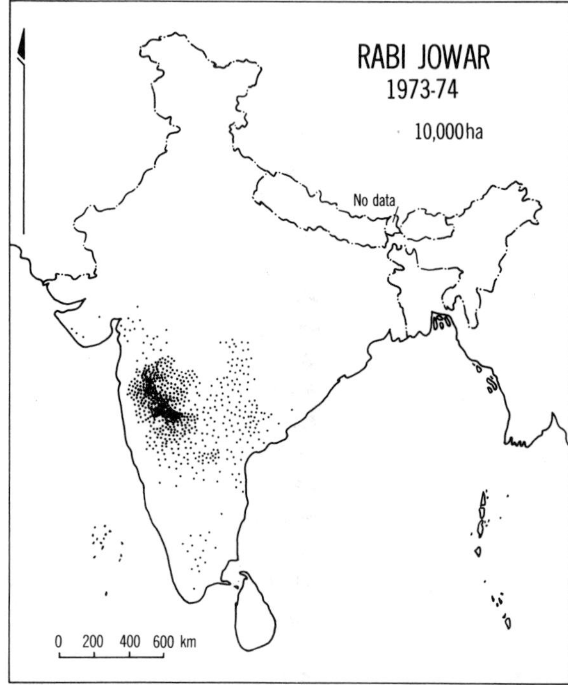

resistant grain on the fringe of the belt of monsoon rainfall whose moisture may alternatively be conserved for the rabi crop.

Bajra is the hardiest of the millets (see Figure 7.5), and can tolerate conditions of low and precarious rainfall and light sandy soils, in which other food and fodder crops would wilt. Thus it dominates the semi-arid lands of Rajasthan and northern Gujarat, and an area spreading east into non-alluvial and so largely non-irrigated parts of southern UP and western Madhya Pradesh. In the Deccan it is particularly popular in the rainshadow of the Western Ghats. The considerable increase of bajra since independence (the 1973–74 area was 101 per cent higher than that for 1947–48) is accounted for by the introduction of HYV bajra from about 1969.

Kharif jowar (see Figure 7.6) is preferred to bajra in the moister parts of the sub-humid zone and on heavier soils. Its limits to the east and southwest almost exactly coincide with the 1000 mm isohyet.

Ragi (see Figure 7.7), although the least prestigious of the major food grains, and of small importance at the national level, is the dominant crop in southern Karnataka where it thrives on

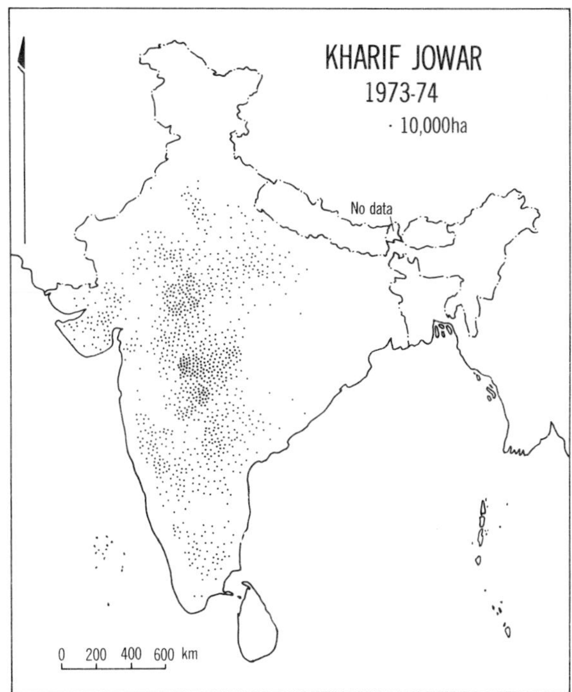

FIG. 7.6

FIG. 7.5

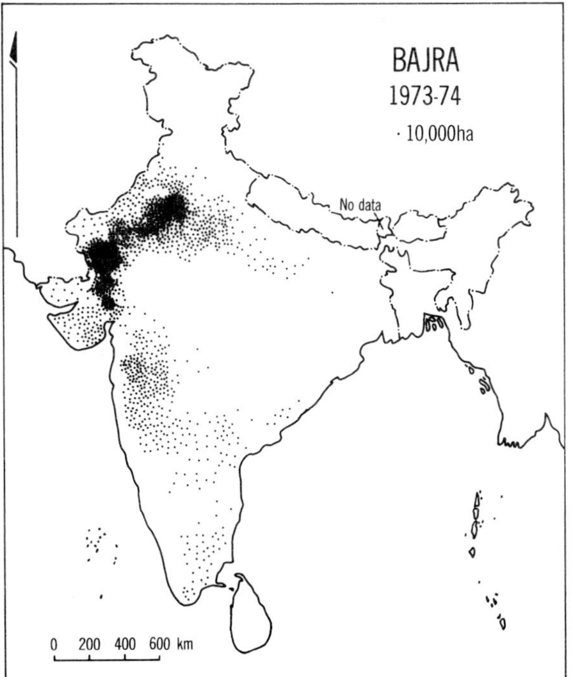

FIG. 7.7

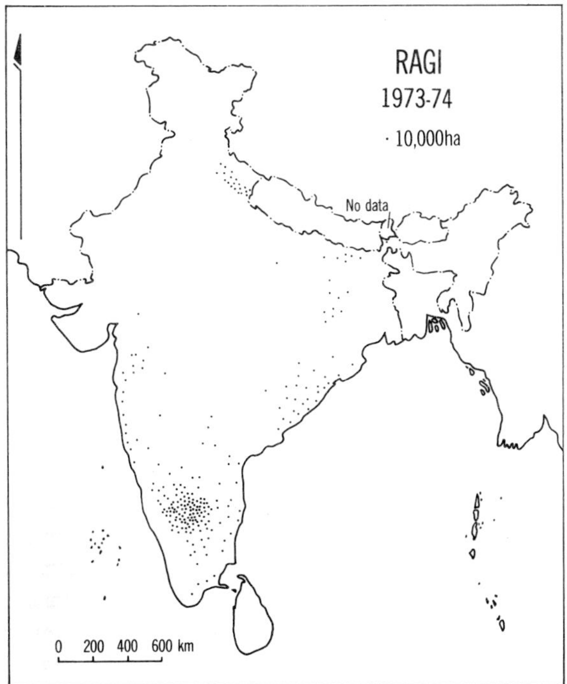

the moderate rainfall and thin soils on extensive interfluves in gently undulating granite-gneiss country with limited tank and canal irrigation. To a limited extent ragi is found as a transplanted irrigated crop in competition with rabi rice. Outside Karnataka it achieves minor importance in the hilly districts of UP and the plateau of Bihar and Orissa.

Wheat

This crop (see Figure 7.8) vies with rice as the preferred grain. It can be baked into less perishable forms of ready-to-eat food and thus is popular with the increasing urban population. The latter even in traditionally rice-eating areas have become familiar with wheat through its import to meet foodgrain deficiencies. As the earliest and most successful of the HYV grains, its area had increased by 143 per cent since independence, up to 1973–74, and 131 per cent to 1974–75. Its share of the total cropped area has increased from 7.6 to 12.3 per cent. It is the leading crop in Punjab, Haryana, western and central UP, and in a broad wedge of northern Madhya Pradesh (see Figure 7.1). From this belt, areas of secondary importance extend west into eastern Rajasthan, and east into eastern UP and Bihar (Figure 7.2). As a minor crop it is found on the lava soils of central Gujarat, and as far south in the Peninsula as Madurai in Tamilnadu. Eastwards it has penetrated West Bengal and the Assam Valley. Everywhere it is a rabi crop. In its traditional Indian home in Punjab–Haryana it is sown in the autumn following the kharif harvest, generally on lightly irrigated land. It is also quite widely grown without irrigation, using residual moisture from the monsoon and any rains that winter may bring.

Fig. 7.8

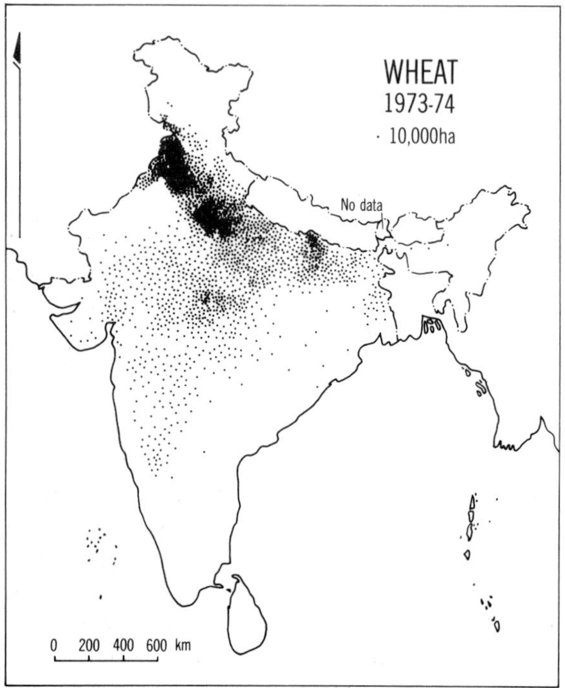

Barley

This is a minor grain as a rule, being regarded as an insurance crop. Often it is sown in a mixture with wheat in areas where lightness of soil means that moisture is likely to diminish rapidly, conditions which barley is better able to tolerate than wheat. In calculating the leading and major cereal crops, barley has been combined with wheat, with which it is frequently blended in use.

Maize

In tolerating droughty soils maize (see Figure 7.9) is somewhat similar to barley, but is almost always a kharif crop. It achieves a leading position in the rocky Aravalli Hills, and plays an important subsidiary role in the western Himalayan foothills. In a few plains districts in UP, Bihar and Andhra it is found on soils unsuited to rice, but its greatest virtue is an ability to thrive on colluvial soils on steep or roughly terraced hill slopes. Starch factory demand is locally an important factor. As with bajra the introduction of HYV maize has stimulated the extension of the crop, though, unlike other HYV, maize requires a longer rather than a shorter growing season than the ordinary varieties.

Tapioca and Potatoes

Figures 7.1 and 7.2 include these two tuber crops, which achieve the status of leading crop in very limited areas. It is unlikely that either tapioca flour or potatoes take precedence over rice in the diet of those who grow these crops. Both enter considerably into commerce, tapioca as the basis for starch and glucose industry, potatoes as a widely used supplementary food.

Tapioca has become important in Kerala,

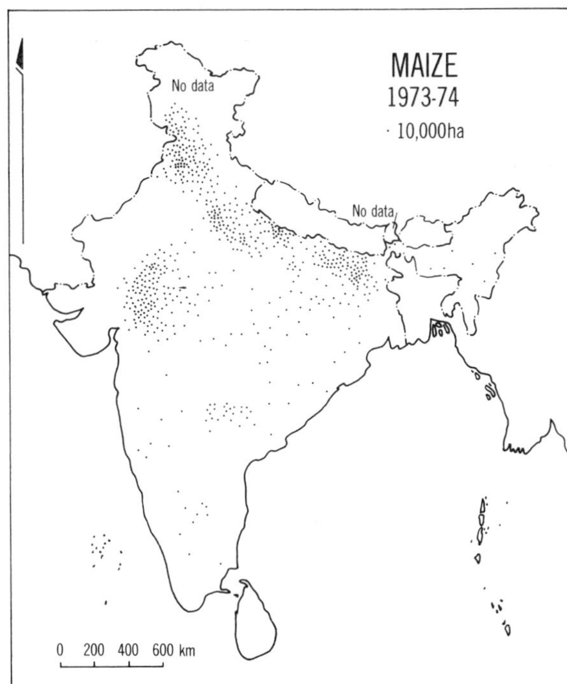

FIG. 7.9

particularly, where it is grown on slopes and interfluves of lateritic soil unsuited to rice. In this, the most densely populated state, it has provided a much needed mode of producing food from otherwise relatively unproductive niches in the environment. In Trivandrum and Quilon tapioca dominates among the field crops, while in Alleppy and Kottayam to the north, it ranks after rice but with over 15 per cent TSA. As a minor crop, accounting for between 5 and 15 per cent TSA it is found throughout the remainder of Kerala, but is as yet of no great importance elsewhere. A number of processing factories have been established in coastal Andhra to make starch from tapioca grown on the poor soils of the low plateau and slopes that adjoin the delta plain. Time will tell whether with increasing population pressure tapioca will spread into the humid hill country of north-eastern India.

Potatoes are widely grown throughout India on a small scale, but reach high percentages of TSA in limited areas only. It is the dominant crop in the Nilgiri Hills, where it is a cash crop exported to the lowland towns. Slight concentrations of potato growing generally seem related to the proximity of industrialized urban markets. Like tapioca, potatoes will probably increase in importance as a heavy-yielding source of starchy food in an ever hungry and populous country.

Pulses and oilseeds

In comparison with the two-thirds of the cropped land under cereals, pulses at 15.1 per cent and oilseeds, 10.4 per cent, have a disproportionate significance in Indian agriculture. For the large mass of the population pulses are the major source of protein. Religious beliefs prohibit some from eating meat, but even for the others meat is a comparatively rare luxury. Oilseeds provide cooking oil, a less expensive substitute for traditional *ghi*, clarified butter. Together with coconut oil, also used in cooking in the south, the oilseeds are in demand as industrial raw materials, notably for soap-making and food industries at home and abroad. These demands for vegetable oils from the tropics are likely to increase with world population. Animal fats, which represent the end product of an expensive food chain, are likely to recede further out of reach of a rising proportion of that population. A further virtue of the pulses and of the principal oilseed groundnuts, is their ability to fix atmospheric nitrogen in the soil.

Pulses are widely grown as rabi and kharif crops. Gram (chick pea) is the main rabi pulse, arhar or tur (pigeon pea) the main kharif pulse. Rabi pulses are often complementary to kharif rice cultivation in which role they are important in the Ganga Plain in UP, Bihar and West Bengal, and in the Mahanadi Delta in Orissa. In a belt through central Rajasthan the crop alternates with kharif bajra, not necessarily in the same year unless rainfall has been abundant. In both cases the fertilizing propensities of pulses seem a significant factor.

Kharif pulses, like their rabi counterparts, tend to be relatively neglected and low-yielding. Some, like arhar, have a long growing season and are harvested in mid-winter. They are of little importance towards the wetter northeast and southwest where land is too valuable to use on such low yielding crops unless they can be taken casually after an early rice harvest. In Rajasthan they are used to make use of feeble monsoon rainfall on

32 Tapioca tubers, peeled and washed are passed up to the grinders at a mill in West Godavari District, Andhra Pradesh.

33 Women sieving crushed tapioca to a fine flour which runs away to settling troughs: West Godavari District.

34 Washing tapioca flour, before drying and packing, West Godavari District.

light soils and to provide both food for man and fodder for his flocks and herds in an inhospitable environment. For the rest, kharif pulses are fairly evenly spread throughout the Peninsula with some tendency to be preferred to rabi pulses in the black soil regions, where they fit in as a fertilizing crop alternating with cotton.

The oilseeds also divide into kharif and rabi groups. Kharif oilseeds which account for about 60 per cent of the total, include the larger part of the groundnut crop, and all castorseed and sesamum. There is a marked concentration of kharif oilseeds, mainly of groundnuts, in Kathiawar and to a lesser extent on light soils in Andhra and Tamilnadu. These crops favour sub-humid conditions and are largely absent where rainfall exceeds 1000 mm. Rabi oilseeds show a more diffuse pattern. A minor concentration occurs in Punjab–Haryana where rape and mustard are popular, and spreads into Rajasthan UP and Madhya Pradesh; mustard is the staple source of cooking oil in Bengal and Assam. They are absent from the west coast, but otherwise are found very widely throughout India. In the humid coastlands the coconut palm provides an alternative source of vegetable oil. Oilseeds, processed into vegetable oils and residual oilcake, contribute to the export trade as do the pulses to a lesser extent. In 1973–74 almost 800,000 tonnes of groundnut oilcake, 825,000 tonnes of cottonseed cake, and 72,000 of linseed cake were exported, mainly to UK, Continental Europe and USSR as cattle fodder. Oilseed production in India, at 12 million tonnes, runs 0.7 million tonnes short of requirements which are made good by imports of soybean oil and tallow, even though groundnuts are exported to win more valuable foreign exchange when opportunity presents. India's exports of vegetable oil are of mainly inedible grades, such as castor oil used in lubricants and soap.

Cotton

Cultivation of cotton is confined to several clearly defined areas (Figure 7.10). The major region is a broad belt extending through the Deccan Lava soils from the northernmost district of Andhra into central Gujarat. Through most of this area cotton exceeds 15 per cent TSA, reaching 47 per cent and more in four districts of Gujarat, and over 40 per cent in four in north Maharashtra. Cotton is a kharif crop as a rule, overlapping to a small extent into the rabi season on heavier moisture-retentive soils. Another cotton region has its core in a belt running across mid-Karnataka from Dharwa to Kurnool in Andhra. This lies on the southern margins of the black lava soils. A smaller area based again on black soils, but not related to lavas, lies in west-central Tamilnadu between Coimbatore and the Tirunelveli coast. In all these areas cotton is mainly a rainfed crop, thriving on relatively dry conditions, and prone to damage in unusually wet years. In the Punjab it is irrigated. The disproportionate increase since independence in the area under cotton is attributable in part to the loss to the manufacturing industry of the product from the Pakistan Punjab and Sind, and in part to the expansion of domestic demand. There has been some recent increase in area following the introduction of HYV. Indian cotton is of medium to short staple, and for fine materials long-stapled lint has to be imported, principally from Egypt. There is some export of raw cotton (346,000 bales of 180 kg in 1973–4) against which has to be set the import of an average 642,500 bales

FIG. 7.10

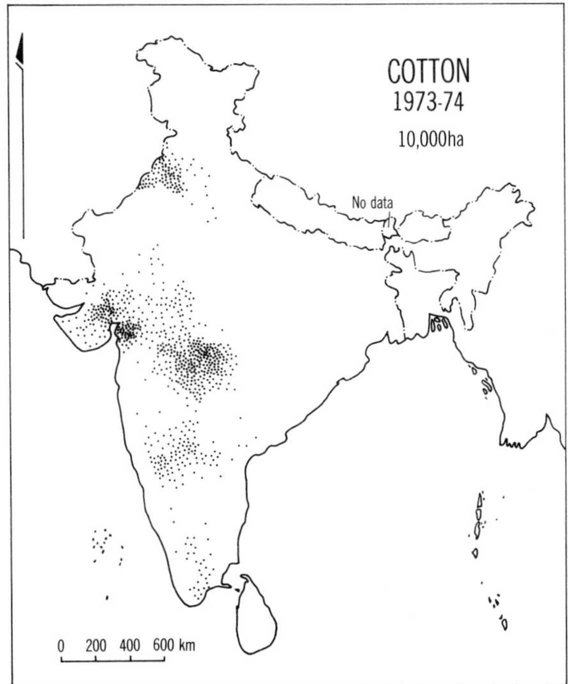

35 Cleaning cotton balls before beginning to remove seeds, at Bijapur in the black soils region in the north of Karntaka.

over the past ten years, reducing to a minimum of 178,000 bales in 1973–4. Consumption runs upwards of 6.5 million bales; in 1973–4 it stood at 6.9 million. Home production was then 6.6 million bales.

Jute and Mesta

In contrast to cotton, these coarser fibre crops are grown under humid conditions, though the latter is less demanding of rich soils and high rainfall. West Bengal (418,500 ha), Assam (149,000 ha) and Bihar (144,000 ha) are the main producing states followed by Orissa (57,300 ha), UP, Tripura and Meghalaya. Only in Nadia (West Bengal) and Purnea (Bihar) does the crop reach over 15 per cent TSA, but in a belt bordering Bangladesh and extending up the Assam Valley to Nowgong, it exceeds 5 per cent and often ten. Expansion by almost 200 per cent was necessary after independence to meet the demands of the jute mills which formerly drew their raw material mainly from the richer deltaic areas of what is now Bangladesh. The hardier mesta or kenaf produces a more brittle fibre, suitable however for manufacturing into sacking. Its total of 371,400 ha is spread mainly among Andhra Pradesh, West Bengal, Maharashtra, Bihar, Orissa, Karnataka and Madhya Pradesh.

Sugar-cane

This crop is increasingly popular under the impetus of high prices for factory-refined sugar for export to earn foreign exchange, and a strong domestic demand. Much of the latter is for the simpler product of the gur or jaggery producing plants, often set up seasonally to crush cane and boil up the juice over fires fuelled with waste cane. Sugar is planted during the dry season to be harvested up to a year or more later, during most of which time an assured supply of water is essential. Manures and fertilizers are liberally applied to achieve high yields, and the Government's problem is to prevent sugar-cane absorbing too much of the inputs of water and fertilizers which are needed for foodgrain production. Cane cultivation is very widespread, often on a small scale for local consumption. Particularly strong concentrations are found in the canal-irrigated tracts of the Indo-Gangetic plain from Punjab to Bihar and the Krishna–Godavari delta, in Kolhapur in southern Maharashtra, where an important jaggery collecting centre has developed, and around refining centres like Mandya in Karnataka and Coimbatore in Tamilnadu. Bagasse, the crushed cane residue, is not all burnt for fuel; where there is an abundant supply it is used to support seven paper mills.

36 Crushing sugar cane (seen growing in the background) using bullock power to turn the rollers. Juice trickles into a drum let into the ground. Crushed waste litters the surface behind: near Hissar, Haryana.

37 After sugar cane juice has been reduced by boiling in a pan over a fire of crushed cane, the gur is poured into a mould to cool. Lumps of gur in the right foreground. Near Hissar, Haryana. Gur is the form in which most rural Indians take sugar. It is whole sugar, unrefined, tasting like fudge with a rich syrupy flavour.

38 Jaggery, raw sugar, in blocks weighing about 12 kg at a wholesale market Kolhapur, Maharashtra. Scales such as these, using standard weights seen on the left, are common throughout India, but are gradually giving place to conventional weighing machines.

39 Drying chillies and on the racks, tobacco, Guntur District, Andhra Pradesh.

Condiments and Spices

The group of crops known collectively as condiments and spices includes annual crops like chillies, ginger, turmeric, coriander seed, cumin seed and several others, as well as perennial plants like pepper and cardamom. The latter two are associated with plantations and small-holders' gardens in Kerala. Insofar as no Indian meal is complete without several of these spices as ingredients, many of them are grown to a small extent in homestead gardens. There is some commercial specialization, however, though this rarely brings the area under spices to over 5 per cent TSA. Andhra Pradesh leads in the production of chillies notably from Guntur District where in February patches of the picked pods drying in the sun form a carpet of brilliant glistening red. Maharashtra and Karnataka are also substantial growers and eaters of chillies. Ginger, very much Kerala's speciality, and turmeric in Andhra, Maharashtra and Orissa, are much less important.

Tobacco

Among the field crops grown commercially for local use and for export, tobacco accounts for 447,000 ha yielding 441,000 tonnes of leaf per year (1973–4). Half of this comes from Andhra, much of it being sun-cured on racks in the dry season. Gujarat and Karnataka are important producers, and it is grown in most of the states where rabi season night temperatures do not approach freezing. The four states in the northwest thus have a negligible production. Much tobacco is consumed as bidis, small 'smokes' of dry tobacco fragments packed in rolls of a forest tree leaf. Some 250,000 million bidis and 63,751 million cigarettes are made each year. The 1973–74 export of 72,200 tonnes of tobacco (16 per cent of production) was a middling figure in a fluctuating trade.

Tree Crops

These are an important element in the pattern of land use in the moister and milder parts of India. In terms of entrepreneural scale, production ranges from the small homestead orchard planted for domestic use, to the large plantation. British capital and managerial personnel established the plantations over the past one hundred years, but increasingly Indian staff and 'Rupee' companies are taking over.

Fruit trees of which mangoes are the most popular, are widely grown, and often cover an area equivalent to one per cent of the area under field crops. There are however some outstanding concentrations. In all the districts running south from Ernakulam in Kerala the equivalent of 13–20 per cent of the TCA is in fruit, while along the Andhra coast from Vishakhaptnam to the Krishna delta and further south at Chittor the figure is 4–5 per cent. Other important areas are found in eastern UP and Bihar where several districts record 2–3 per cent. Except in the case of bananas which become productive after a year, fruit production, and in fact all tree and shrub crop production necessarily requires a long term commitment to a particular land use, and tends to change only slowly.

Coconuts, a major source of vegetable oil and of the fibre which is the basis of the coir industry, occupy 1.1 million ha (1973–4), (586,000

40 Drying coconut to make copra, on a roadside in coastal Kerala. Half coconuts newly laid out in the foregrounds with a later stage of drying beyond. Husks behind, from which coir fibre will be obtained.

41 Plaiting roofing material from coconut palm leaves, Kerala. The leaves form useful prefabricated sheets, shedding rain and insulating against sunshine.

42 Handloom manufacture of coir doormat: trimming surplus fibre. Alleppy, coastal Kerala.

in 1947–8), and are particularly important along the west coast, southwards from Goa to Kanyakumari (Cape Cormorin). In Kerala the area under coconuts exceeds that under field crops in Kozhikode, and exceeds half of it in six of the remaining eight districts. Traditionally the ground beneath the palm trees was used at most for grazing, but now it is common to till and fertilize the plantation, and growers are encouraged to cultivate tapioca, bananas, vegetables, spices, etc. within the groves. The coconut is not exclusively a coastal crop, and grows extensively in the tank-watered valleys of the southern Karnataka plateau, to exceed 10 per cent TCA equivalent in two districts there and in the adjacent Tamilnadu uplands. The coasts of Tamilnadu and Andhra Pradesh are important for coconut and it is also common in Orissa and West Bengal. Overall the pattern reflects tropical conditions with mild winters, moderate to high rainfall or alternative access to moisture.

Frequently found in association with coconuts, but less tolerant of brackish water, is the arecanut palm, the fruit of which is the so-called 'betel nut' much in demand for chewing with lime and the leaf of the *Betel piper* vine. Arecanuts are an important cash crop in Kerala, the moister parts of Karnataka, and in Assam, which together have over 90 per cent of the area of 183,400 ha (1973–4), and 95 per cent of the production. The production of 151,700 tonnes (1972–3) was consumed in India, apart from 221 tonnes (worth nearly Rs.2 million) exported mainly to Indian communities abroad – so firmly is the betel chewing habit a part of Indian life.

A third nut tree, the cashew *(Anacardium occidentale)*, is exotic both in its antecedents and its principal markets. A native of South America, introduced by the Portuguese as a fruit tree, it is of particular interest to the economic geographer in that it occupies two environmental niches otherwise relatively neglected and unproductive. The cashew thrives on the sometimes lateritic dissected platform-like coastal plateaus of the Peninsula, on the west coast from Ratnagiri southwards to its major area of production in Kerala, and on similar country in coastal Andhra and Tamilnadu, as well as on sandy beach ridges in the latter state. While the fresh fruit is used in preserves, the nut has a dual use. It contains an inner kernel which when separated constitutes the 'cashew nut' of commerce. In addition, the oil extracted from the nut-shell has acid-resistant qualities and serves a number of industrial purposes in plastics and paints. Cashew kernels rank high in India's export trade, earning Rs.736 millions in 1973–4 from 52,000 tonnes sent mainly to USA and USSR. The shell liquid earned a further Rs 6 millions, from 5,000 tonnes exported. There is scope for increasing production which cannot satisfy the demands of the processing plants, located chiefly in Kerala. These import East African nuts, from which to re-export the kernels and oil. 70–100,000 tonnes of Indian nuts are processed annually, as against 125,000 tonnes imported, but as East African producers are expanding their own processing industry, India must stimulate domestic production if this valuable export trade is to be maintained. Suitable land is available in plenty on the coastal plateaus of Maharashtra and Karnataka.

Because of the relatively small scale of their individual enterprises, but more important because of the separation of the growing from the processing aspects of the industry, the tree crops discussed above cannot properly be termed plantation crops. By contrast, tea, coffee, rubber and cardamom are produced in varying degree on plantations which also process the product.

Tea

In tea, India leads the world, producing 34 per cent of the total. Tea exports account for 7 per cent of foreign earnings, Rs.1700 m out of a total of Rs.24,560 m (1973–4). About 45 per cent of production is exported, viz. 217 million kg out of 486 million kg (1974). Total output in 1975 is estimated as 478 million kg. With 571 companies employing over three-quarters of a million labourers to pick 360,662 ha organized in some 13,000 gardens, the industry looms large in the Indian economy. Two British plantation firms rank among the top nine companies of all descriptions remitting profits overseas.

Tea produces best in a warm humid climate without too marked a dry season and requires well drained land. Indian production is mainly from Assam which has more than half of the total area in four districts at the head of the Brahmaputra Valley. There is a smaller area in Cachar, adjacent

43 'Cutting' tea with shears, Wallardie Estate, Kerala. The leaves are collected in the plastic bag attached to one blade. This method is used when conventional hand pluck cannot keep pace with rapid growth.

to the tea-garden belt of Sylhet, in Bangladesh; south of the latter are the tea estates of the Indian state of Tripura. All this tea is grown at a relatively low altitude, as is that in the Duar belt which fringes the Himalayan foothills in western Assam and north Bengal. At higher levels are grown the fine teas of Darjiling. Further west there are small areas of tea grown in the Himalayan foothills of Bihar, UP and Himachal Pradesh. In South India the main producing regions are in the Southern Ghats astride the Kerala-Tamilnadu border, and in the Nilgiri Hills north of the Palghat Gap. An area of lesser importance for tea but well known for coffee lies in and northwest of Coorg.

In Table 7.2 tea production for the year 1974–75 has been grouped by regions. The area and production of tea in North and South India is given in Table 7.3 for three years indicating the considerable expansion of the industry. The number of estates registered by the Tea Board is also shown. The increase in numbers in South India is due more to the registration of formally unregistered small estates than to expansion of the tea area there.

It is clear that the industry in the north is organized on a much larger scale than in the south. A recent study shows that in 1970, 82 per cent of North Indian tea was in estates exceeding 200 ha, and 0.02 per cent in holdings of less than 6 ha.

TABLE 7.2

Tea Production July 1974–June 1975 (thousand kg)

INDIA TOTAL	478,955
Assam Valley	232,927
Cachar	26,046
Duars and Terai	99,142
Darjiling	10,429
Others in North India	6,301
Southern Ghats	55,432
Nilgiri Hills	45,738
Karnataka (Coorg etc.)	2,940

(*Source: Agricultural Situation in India*, India, Ministry of Food, Agriculture, Commodity Development and Cooperation, August 1975)

TABLE 7.3

Tea: Area, Production and Number of Estates

	1938	*1961*	*1972*
Area (thousand ha)			
North India	248.6*	256.9	284.7
South India	68.3	74.3	74.0
Total	316.9	331.2	358.7
Production (million kg)			
North India	169.8*	273.3	352.3
South India	34.1	81.1	103.1
Total	203.9	354.4	455.5
Estates registered			
North India	2,264*	2,521	2,520
South India	3,593	6,978	10,479
Total	5,857	9,499	12,999

*Includes 134 estates now in Bangladesh

In South India by contrast, 65 per cent of tea was in estates over 200 ha, and 10 per cent in holdings below 6 ha. The latter were supported by 15 co-operative factories. There is an interesting contrast between North and South India in the rhythm of production through the year, the north showing more marked seasonality due to its more severe dry season from December to March, when low temperatures also inhibit growth. In the south the effect of seasonality, though present, is much less, as Table 7.4 demonstrates.

Tea production fluctuates somewhat, depending on year to year climatic variations, especially important being the duration of the rainy season. As the figures above suggest, the cessation of the monsoon rains is followed quickly by a substantial drop in production, in North India to almost nil.

Population increase and the popularization of tea-drinking as living standards rise, account for the increase in internal consumption from 74.7 million kg in 1953–54 to 231 million kg in 1972–73. Exports have fluctuated but have shown little overall change since independence: 201.9 million kg in 1948–9, 213.5 million kg in 1953–54, 217 and 225 million kg respectively in 1973–74 and 1974–75.

Coffee

This crop is more cultivated on the small estate, and its production is largely confined to the three southern states. Out of a total of 146,458 ha Karnataka has 89,990, Kerala 31,852 and Tamilnadu 23,410. Annual output reaches over 90,000 tonnes in a good year (as in 1974–75; 91,000 in 1972–73). Internal consumption is fairly steady at around 38–39,000 tonnes, but exports are rising. In 1973–74 52,688 tonnes were allocated for export, and the targets for the subsequent two years set at 55,500 and 58,264 tonnes. Arabica and Robusta varieties share the output in ratio 59:41, Arabica dominating in Tamilnadu and Karnataka where the coffee is grown at higher levels than in Kerala, where Robusta is the main variety. While much is grown on small estates, the highest yields per hectare are recorded by the larger units. Estate sizes, production and yields for 1970–71 are given in Table 7.5.

Rubber

Most of the world's natural rubber comes from equatorial regions where seasonal fluctuations in production are minimal. In India, the area most closely approximating to equatorial conditions is Kerala, where 92 per cent of the total area under rubber is located. Tamilnadu and Karnataka account for most of the rest. This area represents an increase of 224 per cent over the pre-independence figure of 1947, and output had correspondingly increased from 15,180 to 107,274 tonnes by 1973. With the help of a factory at Bareilly with a capacity of more than 26,000 tonnes of synthetic rubber (derived from alcohol made from sugar refining by-products) the country achieved self-sufficiency in 1973–4. Holdings are generally small, averaging 2.2 ha in Kerala, though for Trichur District the figure rises to 12.5 ha, and in Coorg (Karnataka) ten estates average 136.7 ha.

TABLE 7.4

Monthly production of Tea in North and South India 1972, (million kg)

Month	*Jan*	*Feb*	*Mar*	*Apr*	*May*	*Jun*	*Jly*	*Aug*	*Sep*	*Oct*	*Nov*	*Dec*	*Total*
N. India	.4	.1	5.6	15.7	23.8	40.8	44.2	59.7	57.5	53.3	32.6	13.6	352.3
S. India	5.0	6.4	6.6	5.9	11.0	15.8	7.2	7.7	9.7	10.3	9.8	7.8	103.2

TABLE 7.5

Coffee Production by size of estate

	less than 2 ha	*2–4 ha*	*5–9 ha*	*10–99 ha*	*more than 100 ha*
Number of estates	32,650	5,646	4,120	1,727	193
Area planted (ha, 1970–1)	22,898	14,010	23,267	42,384	26,880
Average size	0.7	2.5	5.6	24.5	139.3
Production (tonnes)	9,518	9,253	20,234	42,270	27,594
Yield per ha (kg)	415.6	660.5	869.6	997.3	1,026.6

44 Plantation of cardamoms in partly cleared rain forest near the crest of the Cardamom Hills, at about 1500 m on the Kerala-Tamilnadu border.

Cardamoms

The cultivation of this spice occupies a relatively small area, sometimes being planted in lightly opened forest, sometimes as an undercrop to rubber, or in association with coffee. 76,500 ha in Kerala, Karnataka and Tamilnadu produce 2,900 tonnes of which 1,800 tonnes were exported (1973–4). Sikkim contribute a further 200 tonnes. Production is being expanded to meet increased demand from the Arab world, whose purchasing power has risen dramatically in recent years, and where cardamom is an essential ingredient of mutton pillau.

Shifting cultivation

This was estimated by the Indian Council for Agricultural Research in 1958 to involve the cutting of 3.8 million ha of 'forest' annually, mainly by tribal groups in Orissa (3.4 million ha) and the Northeastern Hills (275,000 ha) with lesser areas in Kerala, Karnataka and Tamilnadu in the south, and Madhya Pradesh, Gujarat, Rajasthan and Maharashtra. It was calculated that about 3.7 million people were involved. The practice continues in the Northeastern Hills and Orissa, but certainly to a much reduced extent in the latter and elsewhere in the Peninsula. Anxiety to prevent the silting up of the storage dams of new river development schemes, combined with efforts to introduce backward tribes to permanent agriculture and improved ways of life generally, have enabled the authorities to eradicate the practice in some areas, though the extent of its continuance is not known.

45 Cardamom fruits grow on shoots close to the ground; picking requires much back bending labour, as seen here at Vandiperiyar, Kerala.

CROP ASSOCIATIONS AND CROPPING INTENSITY

India is a country of fascinating agricultural diversity. Its farmers usually grow several crops within their individual enterprises, their choice reflecting a variety of considerations and traditions. Because of natural climatic or edaphic factors, or because irrigation is available, many are able to cultivate a proportion of the land more than once during the year. Seasonality in agriculture is summarized in Figure 7.11 which shows the ratio of kharif to rabi cropping. Since direct rainfall is the main source of moisture for crops it is to be expected that kharif crops dominate the agricultural system. The median of all district values in this regard indicates that about 65 per cent of the TSA is under kharif crops. About a third of all the districts has 80 per cent or more under kharif crops. The area of strong dominance of kharif cropping covers the Assam Valley and the North-eastern Hills, much of the plateau country in South Bihar and Orissa, most of Tamilnadu, Kerala, coastal and southern Karnataka, Gujarat and the coast of Maharashtra. Inland of these is

FIG. 7.11

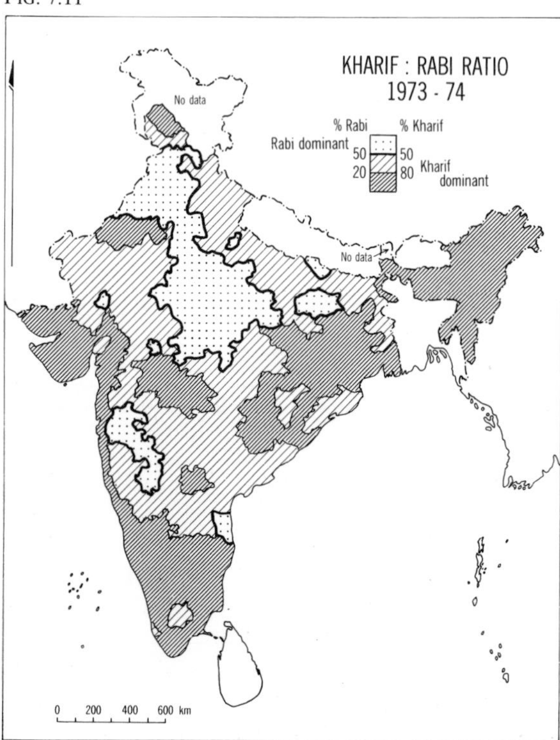

a block of districts in the lava region of Maharashtra–Madhya Pradesh, and northwards two areas in Rajasthan and the Vale of Kashmir. Several reasons may be adduced for this pattern (see also Figures 3.8 of Annual Rainfall and 3.11 Rainfall Dispersion Diagrams on pages 54 and 55.

1. High rainfall supports kharif rice as the major crop in the eastern areas mentioned, along the west coast from Kerala to Maharashtra, and in Kashmir.

2. Late kharif rainfall supplemented by canal and short-term tank irrigation explains the area in lowland Tamilnadu. On the Karnataka Plateau thin soils and a modest rainfall support kharif cropping but allow only a small amount of tank-fed rabi cropping.

3. On the lava soils of Maharashtra–Madhya Pradesh and the adjoining part of Gujarat, non-irrigated cotton, bajra and jowar are profitable rainfed crops, while towards Kutch there is no question of rabi cropping on account of the very low rainfall and sandy soils. The same can be said for much of Rajasthan.

4. In Kashmir winter cold tends to inhibit rabi cropping.

At the other extreme, in another third of the districts more than half the TSA is in rabi crops. These districts are more concentrated in area, in a broad belt dominated by wheat, stretching from Punjab into Madhya Pradesh, and through southern Uttar Pradesh to Patna in Bihar. A much smaller belt where rabi jowar is favoured, runs southeast in the Deccan behind Bombay. These are all areas of relatively low rainfall. The northern plains benefit considerably from irrigation and from the small amount of winter rainfall which may occasionally reach as far east as Patna. Southwards into the plateau country these advantages are largely lacking. The slight predominance of rabi wheat over the alternative kharif jowar probably reflects dietary preference in an area where kharif rainfall is inadequate for rice. On the Deccan between Pune and Bijapur, rabi jowar does well on moisture retained from monsoon rainfall by the black soils. The preference here for a rabi crop shows a nice adaptation by the farmers to the need to conserve the light rainfall in this rain-shadow belt to be used in the cool season when evaporation is at a minimum.

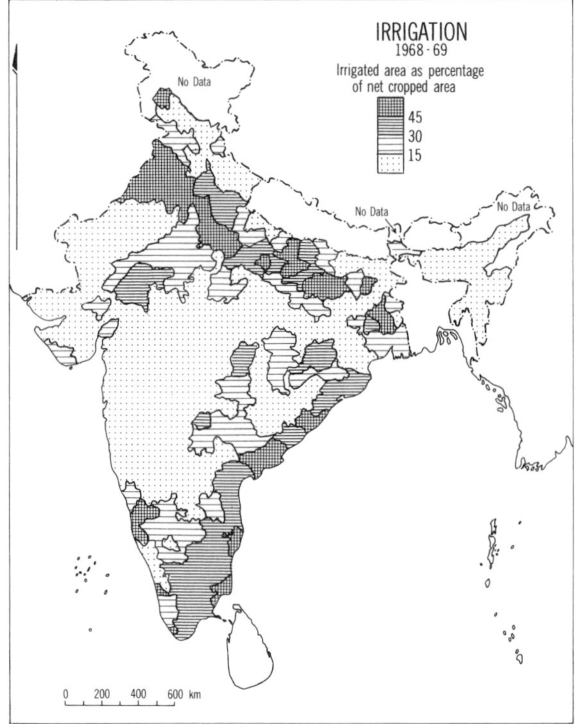

FIG. 7.12

FIG. 7.13

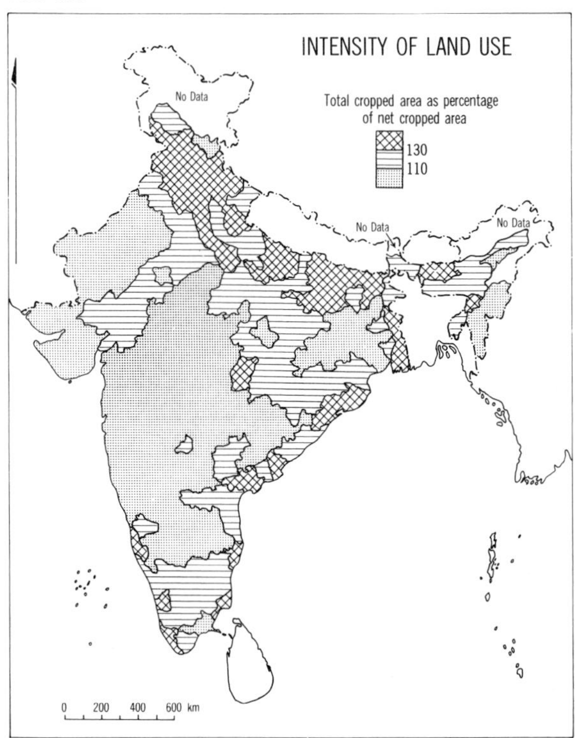

The proportion of land irrigated and the overall intensity of land use are closely related as Figures 7.12 and 7.13 illustrate. Irrigation in general guarantees the farmer a kharif crop by assuring him of water in the periods of uncertain rains perhaps at the commencement and more certainly towards the end of the monsoon, enabling him to maximize the use of this season. He is thus often able to extend his cropping programme into the dry season and may succeed in taking two crops off the same land.

The map of crop associations, Figure 7.14 has been generalized from the available district-wise crop data, chiefly on the basis of those crops achieving a primary level of importance, i.e. exceeding 15 per cent of TSA. A crop occupying 5–15 per cent of TSA is regarded as 'secondary'. It must be remembered that it is only rarely that a regional boundary is other than a zone of transition. There may be a sharp line demarcating irrigated and non-irrigated land in arid areas, or alluvial plain and mountain slope, but gradational changes are more usual. Furthermore a district may exceed 10,000 km^2 in area, and its consolidated agricultural data can obscure variation in cropping pattern. In three major regions the ratio between the two principal elements in the crop association pattern is used to establish a 'break-even' line where an approximate balance is reached. The system of crop association regions is as follows; the numbering refers to Figure 7.14.

CROP ASSOCIATION REGIONS

1. Regions tending to *dominance of rice*, even to its monoculture in places. No other food grain reaches the level of 15 per cent TSA, and rarely do other crops, since very few of them are able to share the agricultural environment created by the farmer to suit the rice crop: bunded fields holding water on the land for weeks at a time. Furthermore, in eastern India the paddy fields are often called upon to carry an autumn (in Bengal the *aus*) crop of rice before the main winter *(aman)* crop, and some may even continue in cultivation under a rabi rice *(boro)* crop. The growing of crops other than rice is thus inhibited at least in some degree by that plant's specialized requirements. To the extent that minor crops lend distinc-

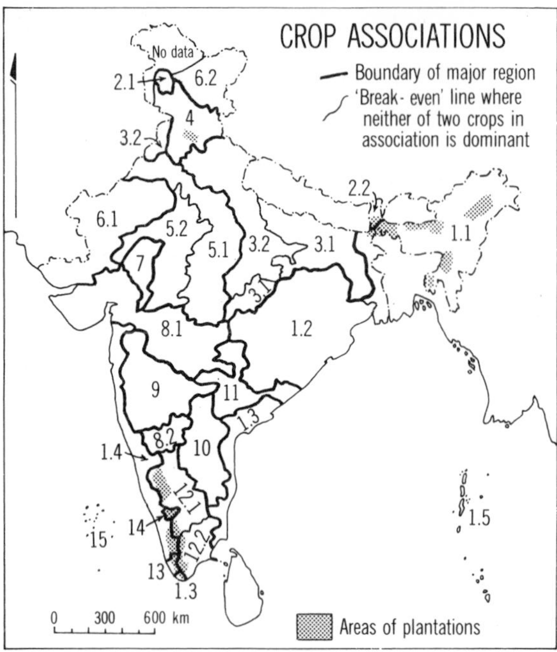

FIG. 7.14

tiveness to parts of the rice-dominated area, they are mentioned below.

1.1 In northeastern India the monotony of the paddy landscape is relieved in winter by rabi oilseeds along the Assam Valley, to which is added kharif jute in a continuous zone from mid-valley west and south around the Bangladesh border. Within West Bengal, a little wheat indicates the eastern limit of a crop combination that extends as far as the Pakistan border in Punjab. Tea plantations are an important element in the economy of the valley but are completely divorced from field cropping. Within the hill country of Arunachal Pradesh, Nagaland, Manipur, Mizoram and to some extent Tripura, the cultivation of rice and maize in permanent fields is supplemented and in places supplanted by shifting agriculture. Data for the latter are not collected however. Usually a mixture of seeds is planted at the beginning of the rains on slopes whose bamboo and scrub jungle of three or more years' growth has been slashed and burned. Typically hill rice, maize, various millets, beans, cotton, cucumbers, and bananas are dibbled in together to be harvested piecemeal through the year. The Meghalaya plateau is rather more developed than the border hill country, producing some jute and potatoes as a speciality.

1.2 The plateau country of south Bihar, Orissa and the eastern districts of Madhya Pradesh remains one of the least developed regions of India. Kharif rice, seldom insured by irrigation, is very dominant and cropping intensity is extremely low. On the northern flank of the region in plateau Bihar, maize is a subsidiary crop, while in the Mahanadi delta and towards Madhya Pradesh rabi pulses rise in places to over 15 per cent TSA.

1.3 The Andhra deltas and the east coast generally south to the Cauvery delta have well developed irrigation to supplement rainfall, which though moderate extends over a longer period due to the effect of the retreating monsoon in the south. The cropping pattern lacks diversity except at a minor level. Rabi rice reaches 15 per cent TSA in the Godavari–Krishna deltas and Nellore. Kanyakumari in the uttermost south is an outlier of this crop association type, having 94 per cent TSA under rice.

1.4. With the exception of the two southernmost districts of Kerala, the whole west coast as far north as Valsad in Gujarat is a region dominated by kharif rice, relieved in Kerala by subsidiary tapioca, and by kharif pulses and jowar northwards, the latter exceeding 15 per cent TSA on sloping lands unsuited to paddy. Tree crops decline in importance northwards: coconuts and areca nuts on the coastlands, and the more tolerant cashew on the coastal platforms. Plantation crops are confined to the southern part of the region, extending little further north than Coorg.

1.5 Rice reaches near monocultural status in the Andaman and Nicobar Islands, strung out in the Bay of Bengal between southeastern Burma and Sumatra. Coconuts and arecanuts are important, and rubber, coffee, oil palm and various spice trees are also grown.

2. *Rice is combination with maize* as a substantial kharif crop in two widely separated and topographically dissimilar areas.

2.1 In the Vale of Kashmir, maize reaches 31 per cent TSA occupying the slopes and gravel terraces, with rice, 49 per cent, on the better alluvium of the Jhelum flood plain. Brilliant yellow rabi mustard and deep green wheat watered by winter rains add colour to this naturally beautiful landscape in the springtime.

2.2 Near the other end of the Himalaya in Darjiling maize, 28 per cent TSA with ragi on the poorer terrain are in association with rice, 53 per cent. The area is more renowned however, for its high level tea. A similar crop association extends into Sikkim.

3. *Rice and wheat* are in combination almost the full length of the plains from the Pakistan border to West Bengal, and there are extensions from this belt into the Himalaya and south onto the Peninsular foreland in Madhya Pradesh. In the western part of the region wheat is more important than rice and the converse is true in the east.

3.1 The western limit of the area of *rice-wheat* association corresponds closely to the 1000 mm isohyet, reaching furthest west on the Nepalese border and in the Bagelkhand region of the plateau in Madhya Pradesh. In a few districts close to the Nepalese border maize is added to the combination, an indication of coarser soils in the *Charbar-terai.*

3.2 The area in central UP and northern Madhya Pradesh where *wheat leads rice* in combination shows a great deal more variety among the minor crops than does the rice-wheat regions. The reason probably lies in the fact that when the land is under wet rice little unflooded space is available for pulses and oilseeds, rabi varieties of which can stand alongside wheat without difficulty. The sub-montane plain in western UP has a higher rainfall (close to 1000 mm) than the more southerly part of the Ganga plain this far west. This together with abundant groundwater for tube-well irrigation allows *sugar cane* to assume a major role in the crop association with wheat-rice in many districts. Further west in northern Haryana, and again in Amritsar and Gurdaspur on the Pakistan border, maize reaches primary level after wheat-rice. The patch in Haryana lies astride the Yamuna–Ghaggar interfluve – the Indo–Gangetic divide, and both areas are relatively close to the gravelly Sivalik foothills, conditions likely to give rise to environmental niches more favourable to maize than to the other crops in the association. On the finer soils of Firozpur canal irrigation supports the intensive cultivation of wheat-rice with kharif cotton and rabi pulses as minor crops. Man's efforts as a traditional engineer have produced in the UP Himalaya remarkable feats of terracing to provide irrigated fields for rice and wheat, with ragi as a hardy kharif millet grown on the marginal land. Locally important, but insignificant in the gross pattern are temperate vegetables and potatoes grown for urban centres in the plains where these are scarce during the hot season.

4. A *wheat-maize* region can be distinguished in the western outer Himalayan foothills of Jammu–Kashmir and Himachal Pradesh. Compared with the Vale of Kashmir to the north, and the UP Himalaya discussed immediately above, rice slips into a secondary and even a negligible position in some areas where the establishment of a paddy soil is too difficult in coarse alluvium and colluvium. Steep hill slopes are roughly levelled into stone-faced terraces to support rainfed crops, but the ground created is too porous for paddy.

5. Merging into the wheat-rice region (3.2) to the east, and into the area of bajra dominance to the west, the *wheat-kharif millets* region forms part of an east-west continuum across northern India.

5.1 In a great arc extending from Ganganagar at the northern tip of Rajasthan, eastwards through southern Haryana and southeast from Delhi in a broad stretch reaching to the Maharashtra border, wheat is the more important crop in association with jowar and bajra. Irrigation compensates for semi-aridity in the northern part, while southwards rainfall becomes *relatively* more reliable. Rabi oilseeds and pulses are commonly found in secondary roles.

5.2 Within and west of the arc just described, kharif millets, increasingly bajra, assume first place as rainfall and its reliability decrease, and as soils become sandier and stonier in the Aravalli belt. The pockets of better agriculture have the support of local irrigation, but for the most part the farmers follow moisture-conserving dry-farming practices involving long fallow periods. (See Chapter 8). Subsidiary crops are similar to those in the preceding area, with kharif oilseeds, pulses and sometimes maize in evidence.

6. *Regions dominated by kharif millets*

6.1 Ultimately with diminishing rainfall, a region is reached where bajra's dominance as the primary food grain is uncontested. Pulses, sown extensively though thinly for food and fodder are associated crops at primary or secondary level, particularly

important in a region where livestock, camels, sheep and cattle, play a vital role in the economy.
6.2 The remote high valleys and plateau of Ladakh in inner Kashmir are a dry land of a different sort, an agricultural environment of even more extreme difficulty than Rajasthan on account of cold winters and very intense insolation during summer. Ragi dominates as the kharif crop with winter wheat, hardy barley, and oilseeds in support, but the economy leans heavily on transhumance of sheep and yaks.

7. *Maize* associated with wheat and barley in the north, or with rice in the south characterizes the agriculture of the south-central Aravalli Hills from southern Rajasthan into western Gujarat. A variety of secondary crops include kharif millets, cotton and oilseeds, and rabi pulses and oilseeds, indicating the diversity of crop environments available within the small compass of this sometimes rugged region.

8. Southwards through the Peninsular interior the millets take the place of wheat as the leading food grain wherever rice cannot be grown. Cotton and kharif oilseeds play important roles.

Cotton and the kharif millets jowar and bajra form a dominant association on the *regur* soils of the Deccan lavas of northern Maharashtra and Kathiawar, and on the intervening alluvial area around the head of the Gulf of Cambay, and again on the southern edge of the lava country in Karnataka.
8.1 The main cotton belt of Maharashtra–Gujarat is a region of low cropping intensity where kharif crops dominate to a high degree. Rabi jowar sometimes reaches primary level, but other rabi crops such as pulses, oilseeds and wheat achieve only secondary level though they are widely grown except in Kathiawar. Here an important, sometimes dominant role is assumed by groundnuts as a kharif crop.
8.2 The 'little' cotton belt of Karnataka is in a region of deep regur. Cotton and kharif jowar, in one district rabi jowar also, stand in primary position in the crop-association, with as many as five crops at secondary level, including kharif pulses and oilseeds, rice and wheat.

9. Separating the two cotton belts on the Maharashtra–Karnataka Deccan lava plateau is the *jowar region* par excellence. Through its centre runs a belt where rabi jowar predominates (see also Figure 7.1) but kharif jowar shares primary status at either end of this belt, and dominates throughout the rest of the region. The role and types of secondary crops vary a good deal. Where water is available for irrigation, rice and sugar cane appear. Normally however, the minor crops depend on rainfall or remanent moisture. Rabi wheat, pulses and oilseeds, kharif cotton, pulses and oilseeds variously join the association with jowar.

10. *Kharif jowar* combines with *kharif oilseeds*, particularly groundnuts, in this region, comprising most of the Andhra Deccan south of Hyderabad. From the Krishna southwards granites and gneisses give place to slates and quartzites making for considerable variety in soil quality. Where irrigation is available rice enters the combination, but this is only important in the south, and for the most part rainfed agriculture prevails. Kharif pulses are widely grown, with chillies and tobacco important.

11. Kharif, sometimes rabi jowar, and rice reach a balance in what may best be described as a *zone of transition* between the last three regions and those to the east dominated by rice alone. The zone follows the Wainganga valley and the middle Godavari to above its delta, and incorporates the low hilly country through Khammam to the sea at Vishakhapatnam, corresponding to a narrow belt with less than 1000 mm rainfall (see Figure 3.8). Appropriately in a transition zone, there are generally three crops exceeding 15 per cent TSA and up to five above 5 per cent.

12. In the remaining large region from central Karnataka to the dry coast of southern Tamilnadu, *kharif millets and rice* are in association, the ratio favouring millets in the north, rice in the south. Ragi is the millet preferred in the north, jowar and bajra in the south. The ability to grow rice depends largely on the availability of tank irrigation, though canals and wells, now operated commonly by electric pumps, are present in some parts. Cotton is an additional ingredient in the south. The accent is on kharif cropping and intensity is at best only moderate, at worst very low. Coconuts and arecanuts are locally quite important, and the numerous toddy palms are reminders of the

times before Tamilnadu introduced prohibition and the brewing of alcoholic beverages for sale was forbidden.

13. Trivandrum and Quilon in southern Kerala have a crop-association of *tapioca with rice*, both at primary level. No other field crop reaches even three per cent TSA. Tree crops are present in abundance: coconuts, arecanuts, and rubber in the lowlands, and at higher levels, coffee, cardamoms and tea.

14. One district, the Nilgiri Hills, constitutes a *potato-rice* region. Potatoes occupying 56 per cent TSA mainly on slopes, are grown for sale in the plains, while rice, on 25 per cent TSA is cultivated on terrace fields for local subsistence. Temperate vegetables do well in this hill country, much of it over 2000 m. Spices, ragi and tapioca add to the variegated pattern of field crops in a landscape interspersed with tea, coffee, cinchona and eucalyptus plantations.

15. For the sake of completeness it may be noted that the economy of Lakshadweep, the group of coral islands in the Arabian Sea, is based on coconuts and tuna fishing. Field cropping is practically non-existent. Marine resources have for centuries attracted the population neatly described by Schwartzberg as 'oceanic Muslim'.

CHAPTER EIGHT

AGRICULTURAL TRANSECTS

For the reader who would like to trace the changing agricultural patterns across the face of India, and so to correlate some of the factors involved, seven line-transects are provided below covering the major regional types of agriculture in their ecological setting. A standard format is used to facilitate comprehension and comparison, but it must be stressed that the diagrams themselves are not drawn to a single scale in either direction. The schema is as follows:

Each transect is divided into convenient sections for the major regional types. Under each section there are eleven sub-heads, thus:

1. Name of the district or districts characteristic of the region.
2. Physiography.
3. Soils.
4. Annual average rainfall.
5. Irrigation: percentage of cropped area irrigated.
6. Percentage of cropped area under kharif crops.
7. Percentage of cropped area under rabi crops.
8. Cropping intensity index: 100 means no double cropping, 150 means half the fields carry a second crop in the year, etc.
9. Perennial/tree crops (where relevant).
10. Comment on field cropping system.
11. Trends in cropping currently visible and anticipated.

Alongside this information for each section of the transect, the crop calendar shows how the land is used during the year, against the pattern of rainy months. A rainy month is one in which rainfall (in mm) is more than twice the average temperature (in degrees Celsius). The key to abbreviations and symbols used is given here, and a map showing the location of the transects appears as Figure 8.1.

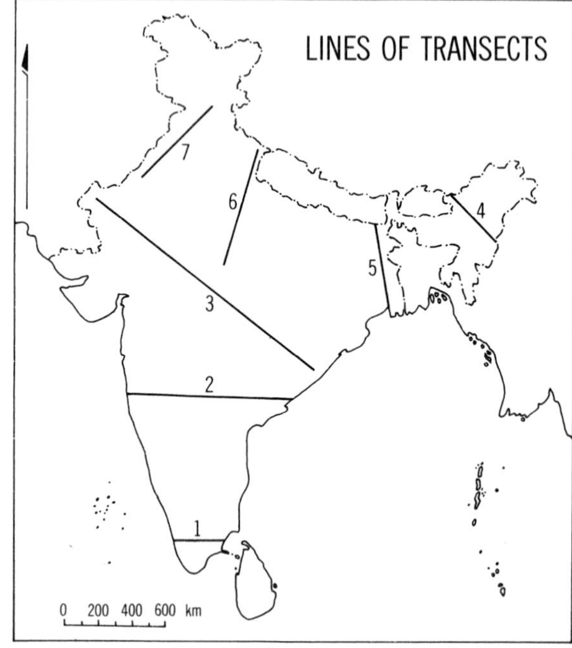

FIG. 8.1

KEY TO TRANSECTS

Rainfed crop

Irrigated crop (or one where irrigation supplements rainfall)

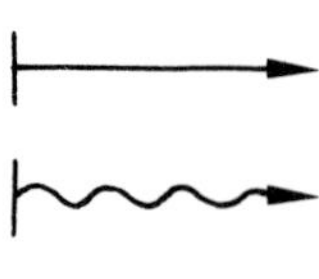

Fallow (shown only to indicate alternating rotations)

The arrowhead indicates when harvest takes place, the vertical stroke is sowing. Crossing of lines indicates a long-term rotation extending beyond a calendar year.

Kh indicates kharif.

R indicates rabi.

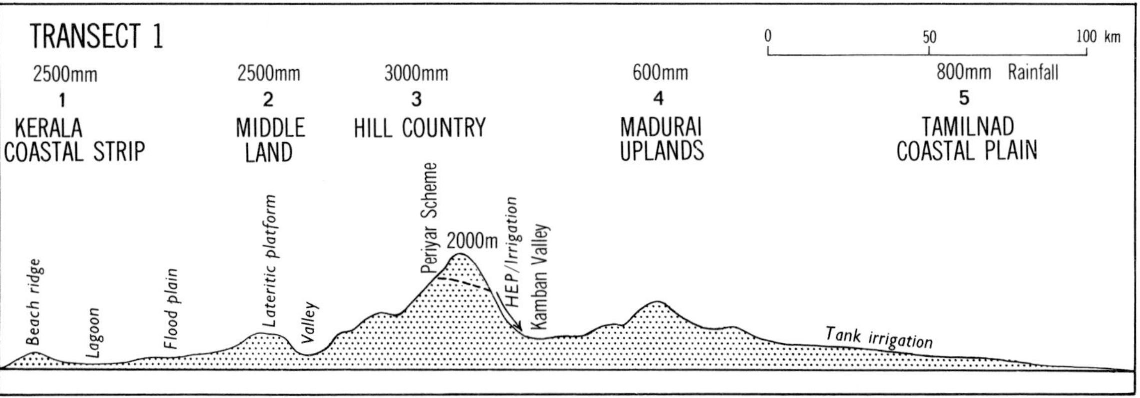

FIG. 8.2

TRANSECT 1: KERALA-TAMILNADU

1. Kerala coastal strip		
1 Kottayam	4 2,500 mm	9 Coconut dominant on sandy soils. Pepper vines, arecanut.
2 Coastal beach ridges backed by lagoons, tending saline in dry season; alluvium on inner flood plains	5 I 25% 6 Kh 85% 7 R 15% 8 150–200	10 Rice in low areas: double cropped where saline water is kept out. Reclamation by poldering on small scale. Tapioca, sometimes as under crop to coconut-arecanut. Some canal irrigation, mostly rainfed.
3 Alluvial & sandy		11 Multicropping under tree crops; fertilizer use to help intensification; increasing control of salt water to maximize double rice cropping. Diversification of dry season cropping to make better use of water available.

J F M A M J J A S O N D
rice 1 — rice 2
oilseed — rice 1 — rice 2

2. Middle land		
1 Kottayam/Iddiki	4 2,500 mm	9 On non-alluvial lands, gardens of arecanut, coconut, banana, pepper, cashew nut. Rubber in estates and small holdings.
2 Lateritic platforms dissected by flat floored valleys	5 I 25% 6 Kh 60% 7 R 40% 8 200–300	10 Rice dominant, double, even triple-cropped on alluvium. Sugar cane. Chillies, pulses in rabi. On slopes and benches tapioca, groundnut, ginger, turmeric (often intercropped with perennials).
3 Lateritic and alluvial		11 Diversification to utilize land more continuously using pulses, oilseeds, tapioca varieties.

J F M A M J J A S O N D
rice 3 — rice 1 — rice 2
sugar cane
Inter crops — ginger/turmeric/linseed — tapioca
tapioca (Late sown)
short season — tapioca

3. Hill country		
1 Iddiki	4 2,500–3,000 mm	9 Tea on estates at middle to high levels, rubber at lower-middle levels. Cardamoms in lightly cleared forest, or under shade trees, on estates and small holdings. Cashew at lower levels & areca nut, pepper, coffee on small holdings.
2 Steep slopes, narrow valleys, hills to 2,000 m, but generally 700–1,500 m	5 — 6 Kh 75% 7 R 25% 8 100–135	10 Rice, mostly single cropped; some pulses on flat land; potato sugar cane, tapioca on slopes. To east, late rains allow rabi rice and late tapioca.
3 Hill soils and alluvium		11 Hybrid maize, potato, temperate vegetables have potential. Tapioca can be intercropped with young tea, coffee, etc.

J F M A M J J A S O N D
pulses — rice 1 — rice 2
pulses — rice
rice
tapioca — late
tapioca maincrop

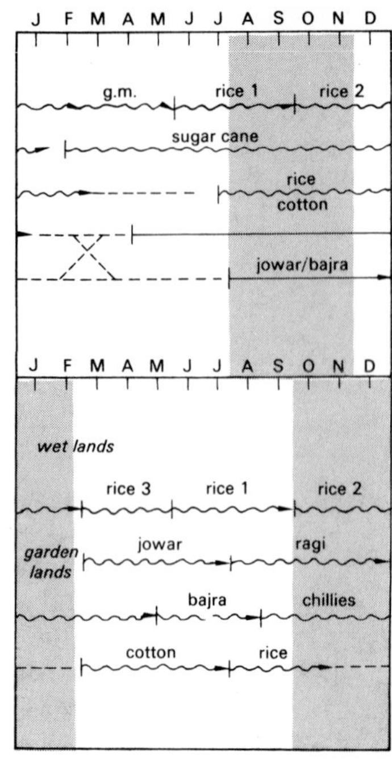

4. Madurai uplands

1 Madurai
2 Kambam valley at foot of S. Ghats; much rolling plateau; rain shadow
3 At best deep red loams and some black soils; much thin red loam
4 600 mm
5 I 37%
6 Kh 78%
7 R 22%
8 150–200
9 Coconuts and mangoes.
10 Availability of perennial irrigation from Periyar Dam (in Kerala) and from wells, crucial to intensive cropping. Wet lands: rice, sugar cane. Dry lands: jowar (Kh & R) bajra, groundnut, cotton.
11 Short season HYV rice could give three crops on perennially irrigated land, R ragi, cotton, bajra or maize, ragi, cotton on dry lands, with some supplementary well irrigation.

5. Tamilnadu coastal plain

1 Ramnathpuram
2 Slightly undulating plain with shallow valleys and numerous tanks and wells; some canal irrigation; late rains may start in Aug–Sept
3 Red and black soils; short late rains
4 750–900 mm
5 I 40%
6 Kh 92%
7 R 8%
8 150–200
9 Coconuts and cashew nuts near coast.
10 Rice dominates wet lands: three crops are possible with perennial irrigation. Garden lands, well-irrigated for bajra, jowar, cotton etc.
11 Double cropping with rice or jowar can be extended with wells. Garden lands already intensively exploited.

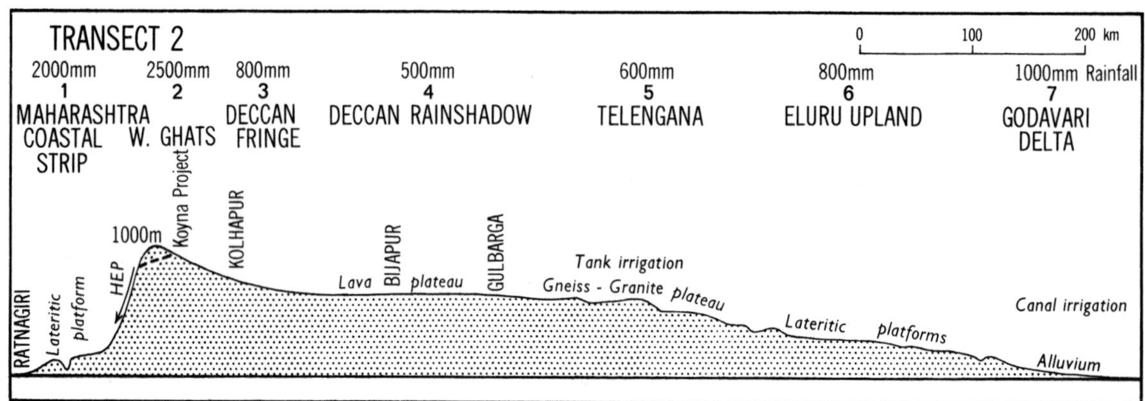

Fig. 8.3

TRANSECT 2: MAHARASHTRA-ANDHRA PRADESH

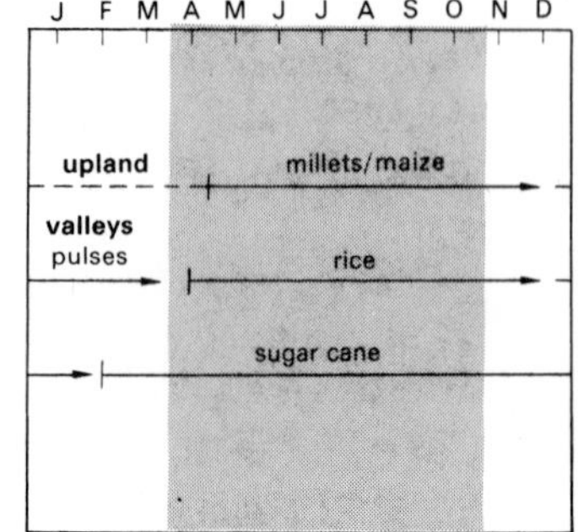

1. Maharashtra coast

1 Ratnagiri
2 Dissected lateritic platforms; narrow valley flood plains
3 Lateritic, droughty and often shallow on platforms: little alluvium; red-brown.
4 2,000–2,500 mm
5 I 5%
6 Kh 93%
7 R 7%
8 110
9 Cashew nuts can survive on slopes and platform surfaces where otherwise little else but grass can. Coconuts in valleys; mango, jak, tamarind, arecanut.
10 Rainfed cropping: rice in valleys; Kh millets, ragi, jowar, groundnut, maize. R gram on upland fields. Sugar cane.
11 Intensification only possible where Koyna Project tail-race water can be used along valley e.g. double crop rice, or rice-wheat vegetables.

2. W. Ghats

1 Ratnagiri/Kolhapur
2 600–1,000 m steep sloping scarp; some valleys on eastern side.
3 Skeletal-colluvial; a little alluvium, red-brown

4 2,500–1,250 mm
5 —
6 —
7 —
8 100

9 Mangoes.
10 Shifting cultivation of hill millets on slopes. Some bajra, ragi maize, arhar, wheat, jowar in permanent fields. Rice and pulses and sugar cane along valleys.
11 Best if slopes allowed to revert to forest.

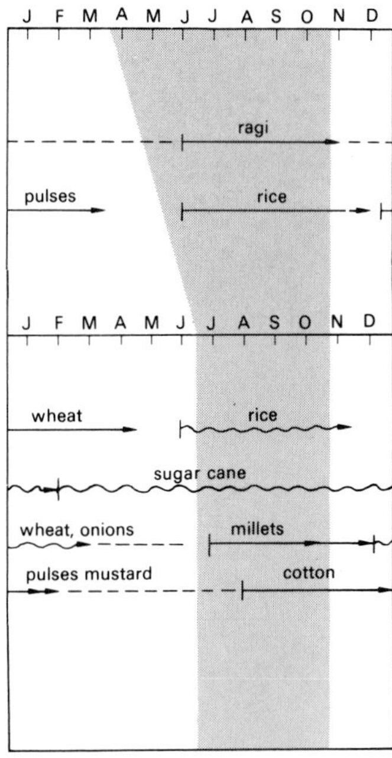

3. Deccan fringe

1 Kolhapur
2 Lava plateau, 600 m wide valleys, flat mesas
3 Grey-black soils, heavy in valleys

4 700–1,250 mm
5 I 12%
6 Kh 90%
7 R 10%+
8 110

9 —
10 Well irrigation in valleys for sugar cane, and rice a localized speciality. Rainfed Kh ragi, bajra, jowar, groundnuts, cotton. Rabi wheat, pulses, onions, mustard, sometimes with some irrigation. Sheep from eastern Deccan graze stubbles on payment for manure.
11 Double cropping of rice-wheat, groundnut-hybrid maize, cotton-wheat can be extended by using irrigation or just HYV short season varieties to utilize soil moisture economically.

4. Deccan rainshadow belt

1 Belgaum/Bijapur/Gulbarga
2 Undulating lava plateau
3 Medium black calcareous, variable thickness – finer and thicker down slope; some red soils in laterite cappings to east

4 500–600 mm
5 I 5%
6 Kh 47%
7 R 53%
8 100

9 —
10 Whether the main crop is taken in Kharif or Rabi depends on soil. Retentive deeper soils grow R jowar, cotton; lighter soils Kh jowar or bajra, pulses. A fallow period is usual.
11 HYV give best hopes for improved yields. Prospects for double cropping are poor unless irrigation can be provided, when cotton-wheat, groundnut-jowar are possible.

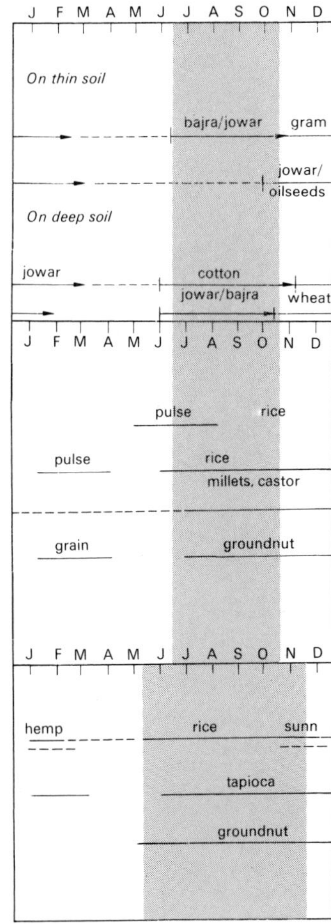

5. Telangana

1 (a) Mahbubnagar/ (b) Guntur
2 Plateau of gneiss-granite with inselberge 300 m
3 Red soils

4 500–700 mm
5 I (a) 8% (b) 40%
6 Kh (a) 82% (b) 60%
7 R (a) 18% (b) 40%
8 100–150

10 Areas commanded by Nagarjunsagar dam (Guntur Dt.) have water June–Dec. or Aug–Feb. Other areas are rainfed or supplement rainfall by seasonal tanks.
(a) Dry or tank areas: jowar, bajra, groundnut, castor, gram – single cropped with fallow.
(b) Irrigated areas: single rice crop or rice-pulse. Tobacco, chillies are a Guntur rabi speciality.
11 Short season HYV rice and jowar permit intensification during periods of water availability.

6. Eluru upland

1 W. Godavari
2 Dissected lateritic plateau edge, 200 m
3 Mixed red and black soils

4 800 mm
5 —
6 Kh 85%
7 R 15%
8 100

9 Oranges, cashew nuts, mango.
10 Remote parts still have shifting cultivation by tribals on 4 year cycle, growing millets, maize, ginger, pulses and oilseeds. Elsewhere, where water accumulates rice, but mostly crops are direct rainfed, kharif, groundnut, tapioca, linseed: rabi fodder sunnhemp, tobacco.
11 —

7. Godavari delta		
1 E. Godavari	4 1,000 mm	9 Coconuts, mangoes important.
2 Delta – salinity affected at coast	5 I 54%	10 Irrigation in rabi allows pulses after 2 crops of rice in kharif. HYV rice cold resistant and insensitive to day length, makes this a possible alternative to former practice of rice-pulse-rice and makes better use of water when abundant, leaving pulse to mop up the soil moisture.
3 Alluvium	6 Kh 68	11 Wells supplementing canals are giving impetus to intensification.
	7 R 32	
	8 100–300	

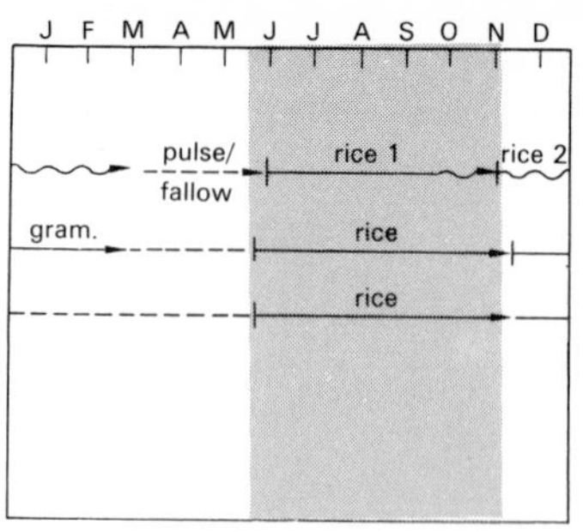

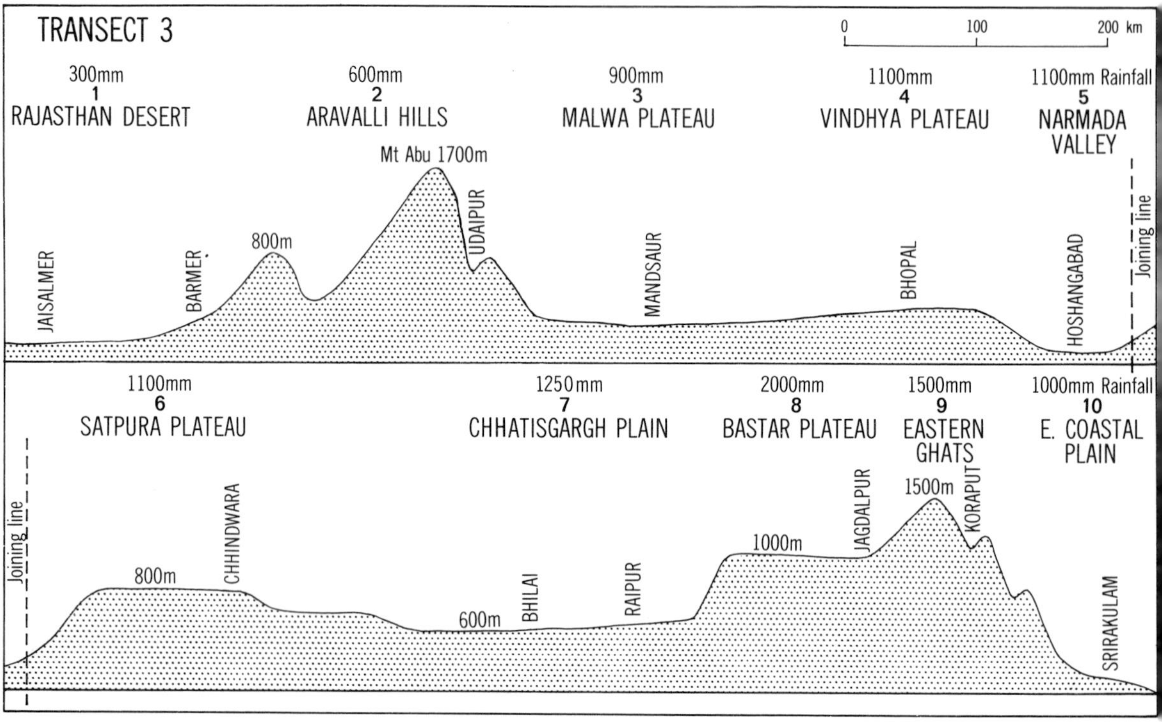

FIG. 8.4

TRANSECT 3: RAJASTHAN – MADHYA PRADESH – ORISSA – BAY OF BENGAL

1. Rajasthan desert		
1 Jaisalmer/Barmer	4 200–400 mm	9 —
2 Desert, part sandy	5 —	10 Dry farming, fallow to conserve moisture Kharif crops use sparse monsoon rains, bajra and guar (pulse) drought resistant. Rabi wheat/mustard in hope of winter rain.
3 Desert soils	6 Kh 70%	11 HYV bajra and jowar helpful, but without water prospects are limited.
	7 R 30%	
	8 100	

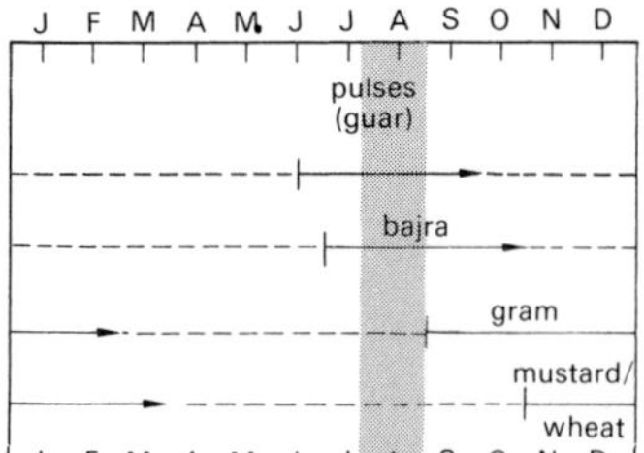

2. Aravalli hills		
1 Udaipur	4 500–700 mm	9 —
2 Semi desert, rocky hills, water concentrates in valleys	5 I 30%	10 Fallow usual and always precedes a demanding crop (wheat). Maize on hills tolerates rocky soil.
3 Skeletal, yellow-brown, in patches	6 Kh 60%	11 Irrigation increasing through wells and pumps, allowing some double cropping.
	7 R 40%	
	8 100	

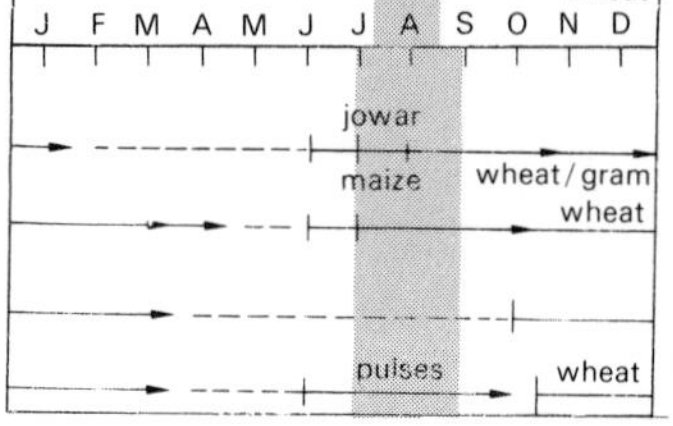

3. Malwa plateau

1 Mandsaur/Rajgarh
2 Lava plateau
3 Medium black

4 800–1,000 mm
5 —
6 Kh 60%
7 R 40%
8 100–150

9 —
10 Fallow still important to retain water. Options are for one crop, Kh or R. A pulse crop may precede wheat, or groundnut follow jowar.
11 Little change in prospect beyond use of HYV short duration crops for efficient water use and so raising intensity somewhat.

4. Vindhya plateau

1 Sehore
2 More accidented relief on meta-morphic sediment-ary rocks.
3 Black; some mixed red

4 1,000–1,200 mm
5 I 4%
6 Kh 25%
7 R 75%
8 100

9 —
10 Soils less moisture retentitive than in (3) so continuing need to fallow. Kharif jowar or rabi wheat main alternative.
11 Careful nursing of moisture can give both Kh and rabi short-term crops.

5. Narmada valley

1 Hoshangabad
2 Structural trough in Deccan lavas
3 Deep black soils

4 1,000–1,200 mm
5 —
6 Kh 30%
7 R 70%
8 100

9 —
10 Moisture retentiveness makes cool season R cropping better than Kh. Wheat dominant Kh jowar, cotton, groundnut. Rice with irrigation.
11 Irrigation possibilities of Narmada can be exploited to extend double cropping.

6. Satpura plateau

1 Chhindwara
2 Raised N. edge of Deccan lava plateau
3 Shallow black soils

4 1,000–1,200 mm
5 I 4%
6 Kh 65%
7 R 35%
8 100

9 —
10 Soil dictates Kharif dominance – jowar pulses, maize. With irrigation, rice – wheat on small area.
11 Limited prospects for change.

7. Chhatisgarh plain

1 Raipur
2 Alluvial basin
3 Red and yellow

4 1,000–1,500 mm
5 I 24%
6 Kh 82%
7 R 18%
8 100

9 —
10 Irrigation not secure – bolsters Kh rainfall only. Low intensity. Rice dominant, rotated with rabi pulses and oilseeds.
11 Irrigated cropping could be rejuvenated to promote higher intensity.

8. Bastar plateau

1 Bastar
2 Plateau on archaeon rocks at 720 m
3 Red shallow soils

4 2,000 mm
5 I 2%
6 Kh 3%
7 R 97%
8 100

9 —
10 Extremely poor region. Rainfed rice or 80% TSA, maize and Kh pulses.
11 Much cleared recently should be returned to sal forest.

9. Eastern ghats

1 Koraput
2 Dissected plateau steep slopes
3 Mixed soils; much degraded forest soil due to clearing

4 1,000–1,500 mm
5 I 1%
6 Kh 90%
7 R 10%
8 100

9 —
10 Shifting cultivation still in evidence towards east. Much cleared land on steep slopes suffering soil erosion. A backward area. Kh rice (70%) ragi maize and pulses.
11 The problem of producing a crop from these hills while conserving soil is being tackled by planting sisal, cashew nut, cardamom, pepper.

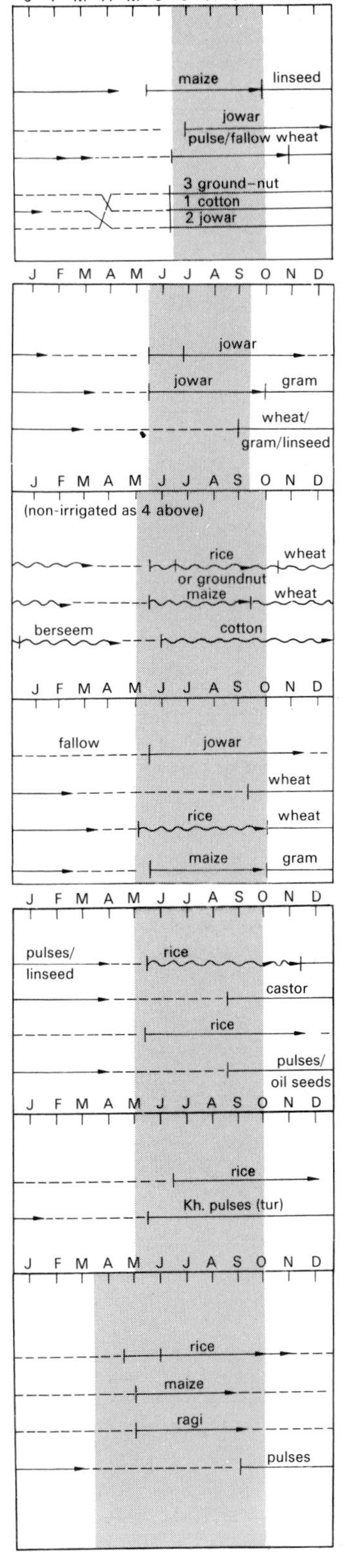

10. East coastal plain

1 Srikakulam 2 Alluvial lowland 3 Alluvium	4 900–1,100 mm 5 I 47% 6 Kh 90% 7 R 10% 8 100–150	9 — 10 Tank irrigation needed for rice; ragi, Kh oilseeds and jute; rabi pulses. 11 Short season rice makes possible a ragi crop before rice.

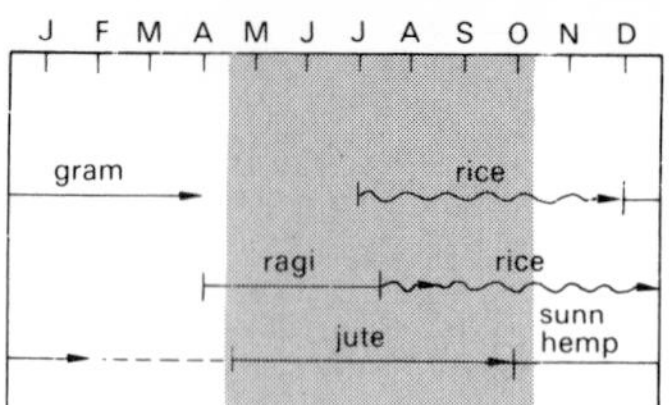

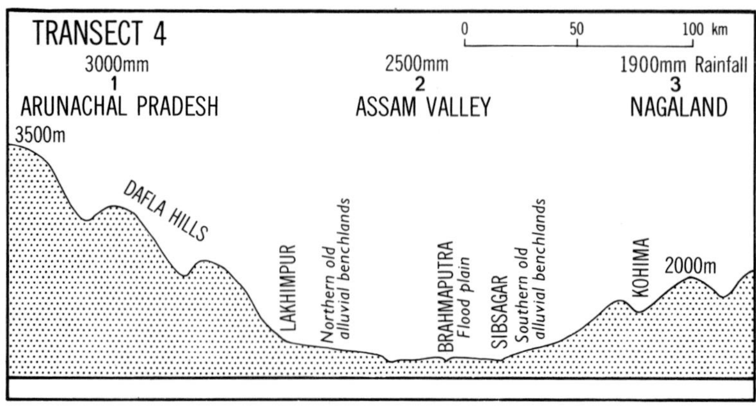

FIG. 8.5

TRANSECT 4: ASSAM VALLEY

1. Arunachal hills

1 Arunchal Pradesh 2 Himalayan spurs, heavily forested 3 Hill soils	4 4,000 mm 5 — 6 — 7 — 8 —	9 — 10 Shifting cultivation of maize and millets. 11 —

2. Assam valley

1 Lakhimpur/ Sibsagar 2 Brahmaputra flood plain and terraces 3 Alluvium/old alluvium	4 2,500 mm 5 I 8% 6 Kh 90% 7 R 10% 8 100	9 Tea plantations extensive above flood plains. 10 Deep flooding lands have boro rice only (rabi season). Remainder has winter rice. Rabi, oil seeds, mustard and pulses. 11 Intensification to double rice, and diversification with soya, maize is possible.

3. Naga hills

1 Nagaland 2 Tertiary sedimentary dissected hills 1,000 m 3 Hill soils, acid	4 2,000–2,500 mm 5 I 14% 6 Kh 95% 7 R 5% 8 103	9 Oranges. 10 Shifting cultivation (jhuming) on slopes for maize, millets, dry rice, potatoes, cotton, in 5 to 10 year cycle. Valley floors and lower slopes terraced for wet rice, potatoes, vegetables. 11 —

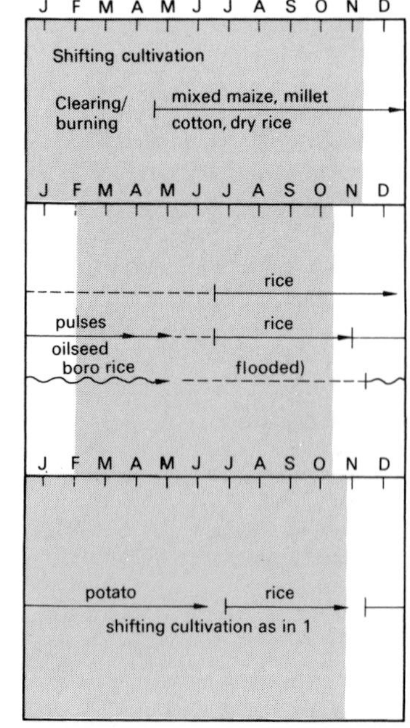

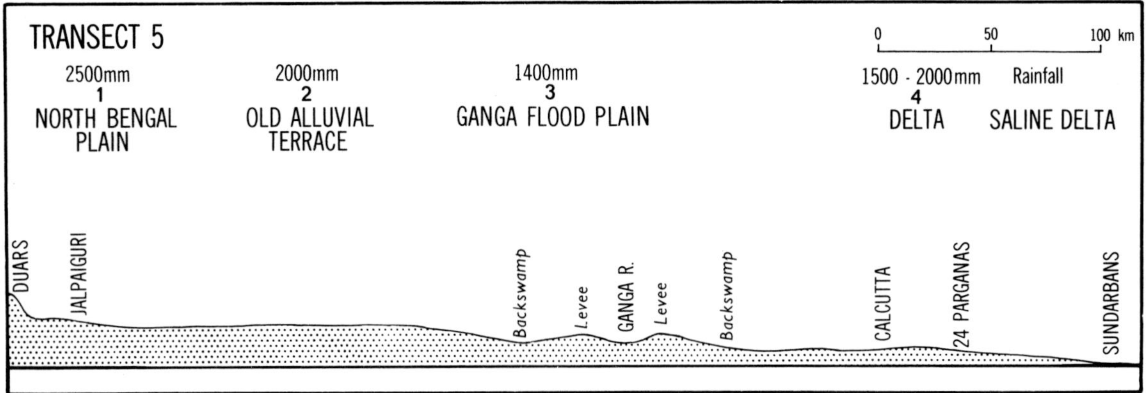

FIG. 8.6

TRANSECT 5: NORTH BENGAL

1. North Bengal plain

1 Jalpaiguri	4 2,500 mm	9 Tea estates on well drained bench lands.
2 Alluvial fans of Himalayan rivers with patches of old alluvial terrace	5 I 22%	10 Kharif broadcast autumn (aus) and transplanted winter (aman) rice dominate; jute.
3 Recent sandy alluvium, acid, old alluvial red earth	6 Kh 93%	11 Utilization of rabi season by well irrigation of wheat. Too cool for boro rice unless planted late as an early 'boro aus'.
	7 R 7%	
	8 120	

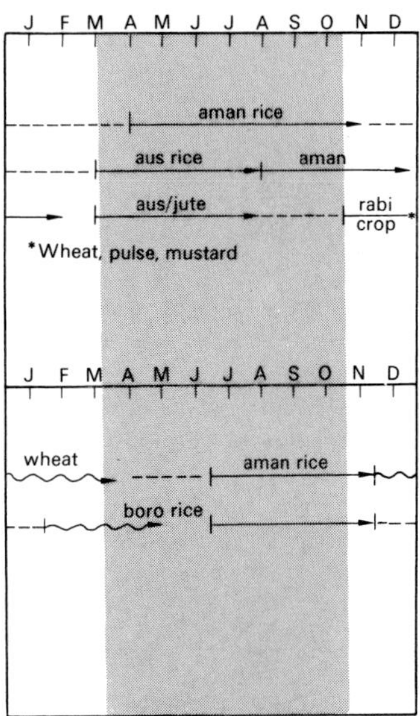

2. Old alluvial terrace

1 West Dinajpur	4 2,000 mm	9 —
2 Old alluvial terrace above present flood levels	5 I 4%	10 Soil intractable until moist, traditionally monocultural in aman. On light soil tracts jute.
3 Laterite red earths, hard baking in dry season	6 Kh 80%	11 Tube well irrigation makes rabi wheat possible on high ground, late boro rice on low areas.
	7 R 20%	
	8 130	

3. Ganga alluvial plain

1 Nadia	4 1,400 mm	9 Mangoes.
2 Flood plain with levees and back swamps	5 I 3%	10 Low lands flood, upper light soils do not make good wet paddies, so rainfed aus rice or jute common, with rabi mustard/grain.
3 Young alluvium, loamy lighter on levees, heavier in backswamps	6 Kh 65%	11 With pump irrigation from rivers or tube wells, lightly irrigated rabi crops (wheat, potato) or boro rice can be grown.
	7 R 35%	
	8 150	

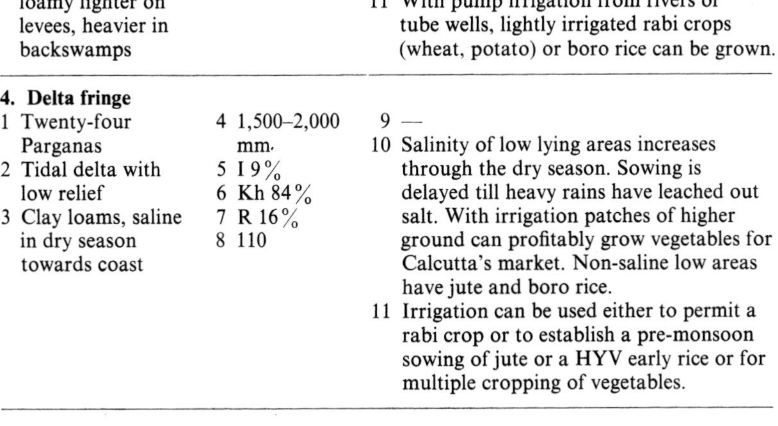

4. Delta fringe

1 Twenty-four Parganas	4 1,500–2,000 mm.	9 —
2 Tidal delta with low relief	5 I 9%	10 Salinity of low lying areas increases through the dry season. Sowing is delayed till heavy rains have leached out salt. With irrigation patches of higher ground can profitably grow vegetables for Calcutta's market. Non-saline low areas have jute and boro rice.
3 Clay loams, saline in dry season towards coast	6 Kh 84%	11 Irrigation can be used either to permit a rabi crop or to establish a pre-monsoon sowing of jute or a HYV early rice or for multiple cropping of vegetables.
	7 R 16%	
	8 110	

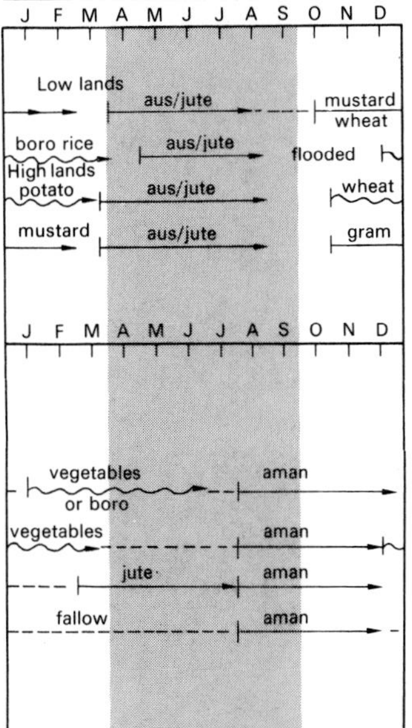

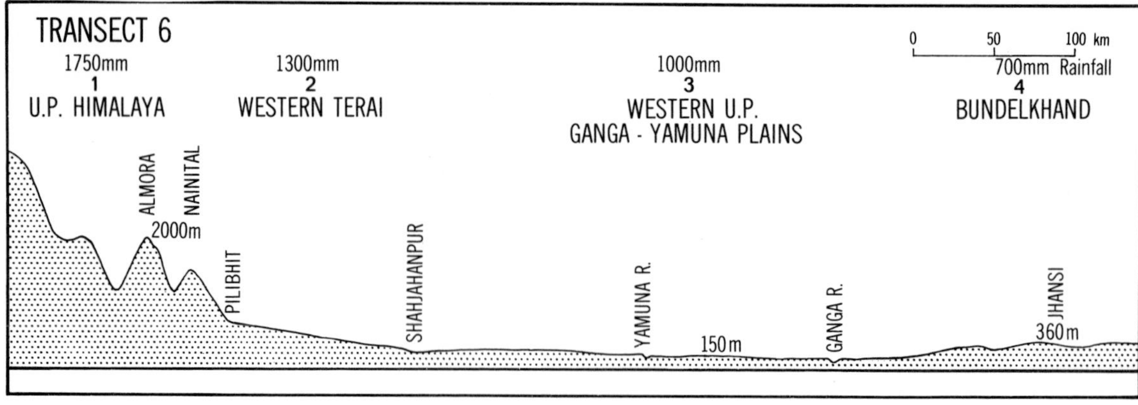

FIG. 8.7

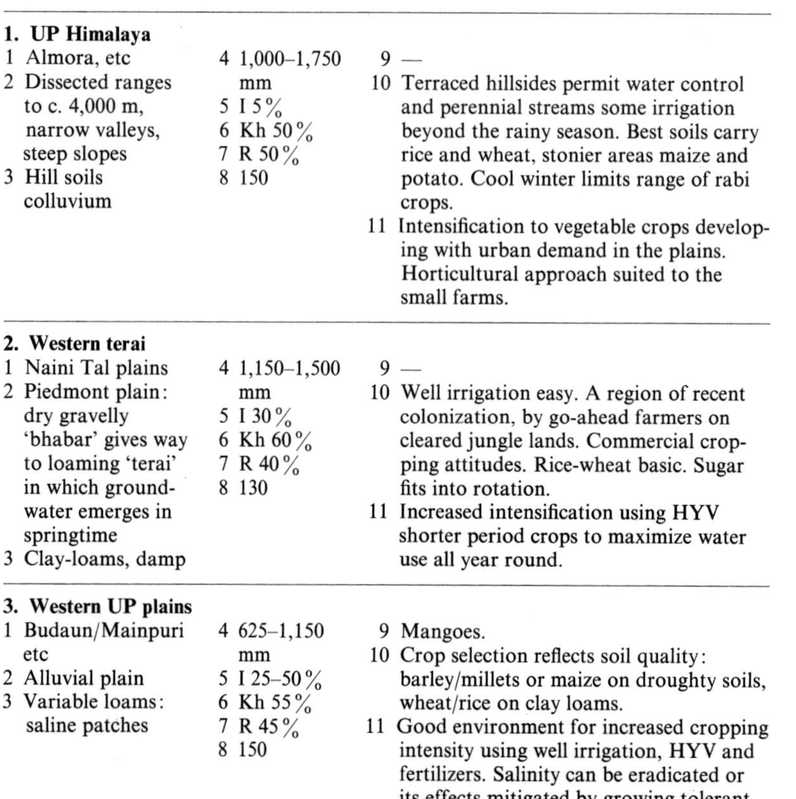

TRANSECT 6: UP HIMALAYA – GANGA PLAIN – BUNDELKHAND

1. UP Himalaya 1 Almora, etc 2 Dissected ranges to c. 4,000 m, narrow valleys, steep slopes 3 Hill soils colluvium	4 1,000–1,750 mm 5 I 5% 6 Kh 50% 7 R 50% 8 150	9 — 10 Terraced hillsides permit water control and perennial streams some irrigation beyond the rainy season. Best soils carry rice and wheat, stonier areas maize and potato. Cool winter limits range of rabi crops. 11 Intensification to vegetable crops developing with urban demand in the plains. Horticultural approach suited to the small farms.
2. Western terai 1 Naini Tal plains 2 Piedmont plain: dry gravelly 'bhabar' gives way to loaming 'terai' in which groundwater emerges in springtime 3 Clay-loams, damp	4 1,150–1,500 mm 5 I 30% 6 Kh 60% 7 R 40% 8 130	9 — 10 Well irrigation easy. A region of recent colonization, by go-ahead farmers on cleared jungle lands. Commercial cropping attitudes. Rice-wheat basic. Sugar fits into rotation. 11 Increased intensification using HYV shorter period crops to maximize water use all year round.
3. Western UP plains 1 Budaun/Mainpuri etc 2 Alluvial plain 3 Variable loams: saline patches	4 625–1,150 mm 5 I 25–50% 6 Kh 55% 7 R 45% 8 150	9 Mangoes. 10 Crop selection reflects soil quality: barley/millets or maize on droughty soils, wheat/rice on clay loams. 11 Good environment for increased cropping intensity using well irrigation, HYV and fertilizers. Salinity can be eradicated or its effects mitigated by growing tolerant crops. Short duration legumes can fill gap between rabi/kharif.

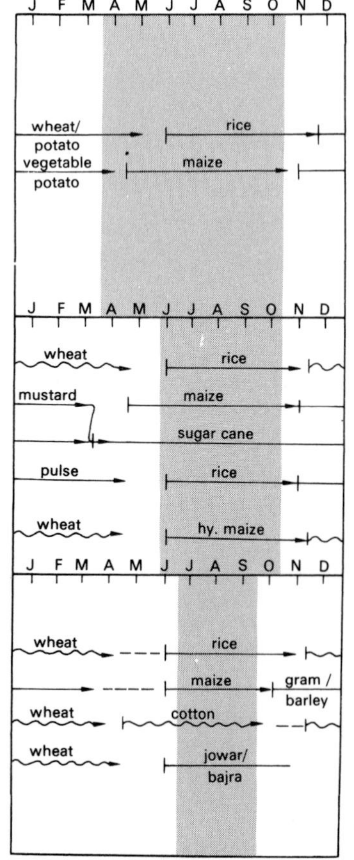

4. Bundelkhand

1 Jhansi/Jaluan 2 Plateau on metamorphic rocks 3 Mixed red-black soils sometimes shallow and skeletal	4 600–750 mm 5 I 15% 6 Kh 25–35% 7 R 65–75% 8 100	9 — 10 Water shortage becomes a problem off the alluvial plain, and subsistence millets/wheat cultivation tends to rule with little cash cropping. Fallowing much practised. Two year rotations used to prepare for wheat by a Kh jowar mixed with arhar pulse followed by Kh fallow before wheat in the second rabi. 11 Improvement will probably be limited to replanting traditional with HYV strains wherever water conditions allow.

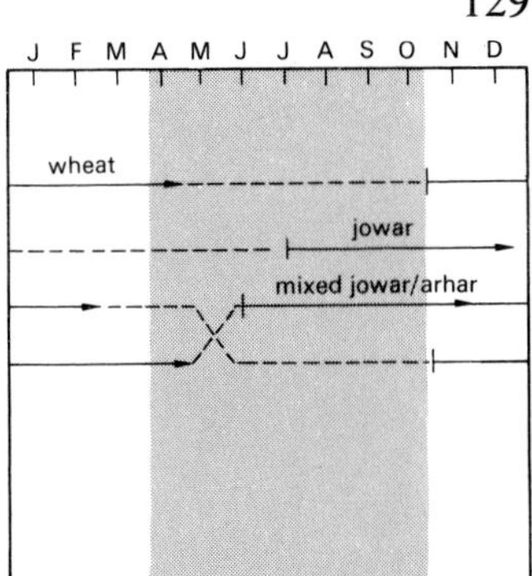

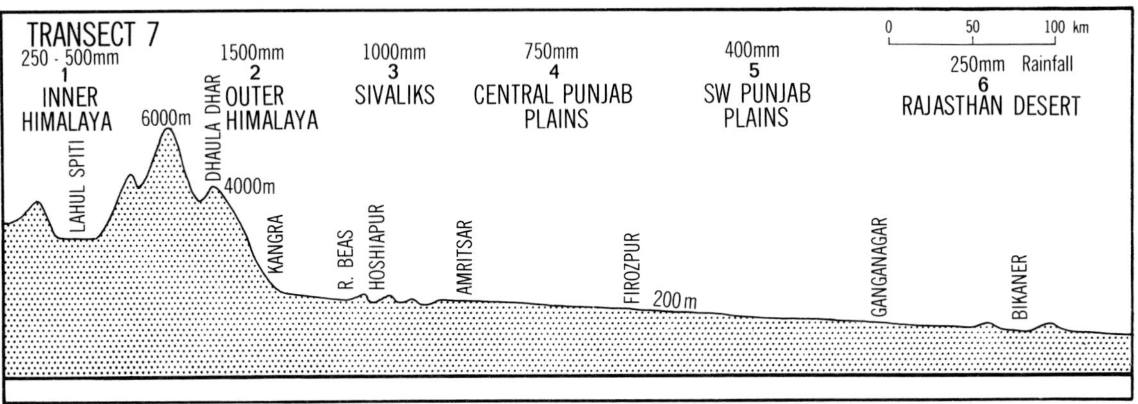

FIG. 8.8

TRANSECT 7: HIMACHAL PRADESH – PUNJAB – RAJASTHAN

1. Inner Himalaya

1 Lahul & Spiti 2 High mountains and intermontane plateaux 3 Skeletal	4 250–500 mm 5 I 100% 6 Kh 30% 7 R 70% 8 100	9 — 10 Cold winters but some precipitation then allows winter wheat/barley to lie dormant. Irrigation essential: crops mature slowly so single cropping. 11 Without improved communications the region will remain basically subsistent. Eventually potatoes could find markets outside.

2. Outer Himalaya

1 Kangra 2 Gravelly piedmont plain below Dhaula Dhar Range 3 Coarse alluvial/colluvial	4 1,500 mm 5 I 20% 6 Kh 50% 7 R 50% 8 150–200	9 Tea, apples: fruits have potential. 10 Climate and water resources are good but soils mediocre and 'hungry'. Maize on stoney terraced slopes, rice where more water retentive. Wheat/mustard in rabi. 11 Hybrid maize introduced: other HYV pose problems of fertilizer cost on coarse soils.

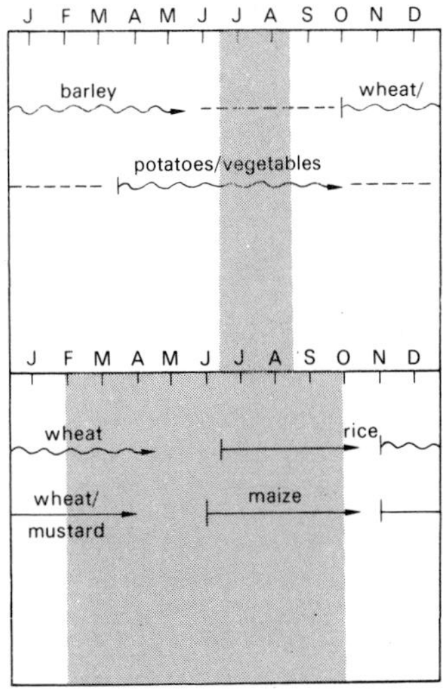

3. Sivaliks

1 Hoshiapur/Jullundur	4 750–1,500 mm	9 —
2 Dissected Sivalik formations; much gullied	5 I 25–50%	10 Best lands capable of intensive production with irrigation to supplement reasonably well distributed rainfall. Winter rains helpful but too small to classify months as 'wet'. But land much broken up by soil erosion.
3 Coarse alluvial & loams reddish-chestnut	6 Kh 34%	11 Three crops possible using short duration HYV. Maize, – rice – wheat succession.
	7 R 66%	
	8 100–150	

4. Central Punjab plains

1 Amritsar	4 500–1,000 mm	9 Fruits.
2 Alluvial plain	5 I 90%	10 Canals and tube wells. Most advanced and efficient agricultural technology in India: highly commercialized. Water resources the main constraint, and need to rehabilitate salinity-affected water-logged zones. Light winter rainfall helpful in rabi.
3 Alluvial, some saline patches	6 Kh 40%	11 —
	7 R 60%	
	8 150	

5. S. W. plains

1 Firozpur/Ganganagar	4 < 500 mm	9 —
2 Flat alluvial plain	5 I 50–75%	10 Single cropping with fallow the rule. Water short at tail end of irrigation system and rainfall minimal and unreliable. Drought resistant rainfed crops favoured (bajra, guar pulse) as insurance.
3 Semi-arid serozem-desert soils; some salinity	6 Kh 35%	11 As Rajasthan Canal comes into full flow conditions should improve and cropping intensity rise with perennial irrigation.
	7 R 65%	
	8 100	

6. Desert

1 Bikaner/Ganganagar	4 200–300 mm	9 —
2 Desert plain with some dunes & nalas (dry creek bed)	5 —	10 Unirrigated desert tract excepting a few wells. Cropping depends on monsoon and erratic winter showers. Agriculture often subsidiary to grazing of cattle, sheep, goats and camels. Fallowing practised over long terms, e.g. Kh bajra may be followed by a rabi pulse after a rabi and kharif fallow: guar and jowar alternate as kharif crops with rabi fallow, wheat and gram as rabi crops with kh fallow.
3 Sandy-desert soils, some salinity	6 Kh 92%	
	7 R 8%	
	8 100	

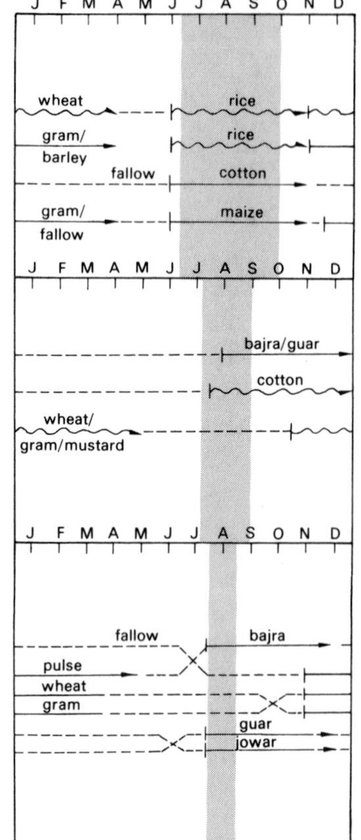

PART III

Industry and Urbanization

CHAPTER NINE

INTRODUCTION TO INDUSTRY

High among the priorities in the struggle to reduce the rate of population increase and to improve living standards demographers place the related objectives of industrialization and urbanization. It is clear that India cannot afford to wait for industrialization and urbanization to bring about a change in demographic trends, but they are none the less essential elements in the total development that must be held out as an incentive to people to change their attitudes to family limitation. India, ever since independence has been progressing along the path of transition from an economy dominated by traditional semi-subsistence agriculture and industry, to one in which modernized forms of enterprise in both these areas are the rule. In both cases progress is inevitably slow and the range of activity spans what has taken 200 years of technological, social and economic evolution to achieve in the developed world.

In the short run India's problem is to preserve existing jobs and to create new employment opportunities for the ever-burgeoning population. Consequently, labour-intensive industries are favoured at the expense of economically more attrac-

46 Shipbuilding, Vishakhapatnam. These shipyards have an annual capacity of up to three ships of 12,500 d.w. each, and are expanding to produce six totalling 80,000 d.w. Other shipyards are in Calcutta, Bombay and Cochin.

47 Human haulage in Cochin underlines the cheapness of labour.

tive capital intensive ones, and traditional craft industries are protected against the competition of efficient modern industry. A mixed system such as this is difficult for planners to control in the national interest. Efficient exporting industries seek maximum modernization in order to compete with overseas competition, and they need a share of the home market from which to make their merchant ventures. The reservation of a part of the domestic market for village industries can run counter to the interests of the former group. India, as has been said before, must work out Indian solutions to her problems.

Modernization must go on, but as was pointed out by Gunnar Myrdal in his famous analysis of South Asian economies, too much must not be expected of industrialization in too short a time particularly in respect of providing jobs. Several decades will be needed for the effects of industrial development to make an impact on employment. Meanwhile there will be two distinct economic sectors: a small but gradually growing, fully modernised sector of large-scale and small-scale manufacturing enterprises and a vastly larger sector that will use labour-intensive techniques not too different from the traditional ones and continue to give work to most of the rapidly increasing labour force.[1]

A measure of the strength of the various sectors is given in Tables 2.10 and 2.11 on page 37. In brief, 'organized' manufacturing industry registered as such, employed 5.2 million in 1974; there were 4.14 million in enterprises registered with the Small Industries Development Organization; these together make up most of the total of 10.7 millions recorded by the 1971 census as employed in 'other

[1] Myrdal, G *Asian Drama*, 1968 chap. 24.

48 Motorcycle assembly line, Faridabad, Haryana. India manufactures the parts for this and the motor vehicle industry generally.

than household manufacturing, processing servicing and repairing'. Household manufacturing accounted for 6.4 million. In addition, nearly a million are employed in mines and quarries (three quarters of these in the organized sector) and over a million on plantations, both primary economic activities with important manufacturing implications.

Despite the problems that face industry as it develops, the range of manufacturing and the record of achievement since independence are impressive, as may be gauged from Table 9.1 which shows for 37 items the scale of production in 1950–51 and 1974 and the projected targets to be reached by the end of the Fifth Plan in 1978–79. India has the capacity to manufacture almost all the kinds of goods and machines needed for a modern nation; she is however at the stage when not all the quantity required can be produced. In this respect India differs from the majority of developing countries which with limited resources cannot hope to reach a comparable level of self-reliance.

TABLE 9.1
Industrial Production

Item		*1950–51*	*1974–75*	*1978–79 target*
Coal	million tonnes	32.8	83.3/95.3†	135
Petroleum crude	million tonnes	0.4	7.5/8.3†	15
Petroleum products	million tonnes	0.3	19.5	35
Electricity, installed capacity	million kW	1.8	18.5*	35
Electricity, generated	thousand million kWh	5.9	69.4	130
Iron ore	million tonnes	3.6	35.5	58
Steel ingots	million tonnes	1.5	6.8/7.5†	12.8
Aluminium	thousand tonnes	3.9	150 †	370
Copper	thousand tonnes	7.2	22 †	45
Lead	thousand tonnes	0.9	5 †	20
Zinc	thousand tonnes	—	27 †	100
Manganese ore	thousand tonnes	1.3	1.5	
Motor vehicles	thousand	16.5	103*/82	170
Tractors	thousand	—	29	80
Motor cycles, etc.	thousand	—	149	570
Bicycles	thousand	99	2,490	3,500
Diesel engines (stationary)	thousand	5.5	138*/114	NA
Electric motors	thousand h.p.	144	3,108	6,000
Power pumps	thousand	41	339*/282	NA
Radio receivers	thousand	54	2,000	5,400
Sewing machines	thousand	33	335	670
Nitrogenous fertilizer	thousand tonnes N	11	1,182	4,000
Phosphatic fertilizer	thousand tonnes P_2O_5	11	323	1,250
Sulphuric acid	thousand tonnes	101	1,434	3,200
Caustic soda	thousand tonnes	14	426	785
Paper, paper board	thousand tonnes	134	825	1,200
Newsprint	thousand tonnes	—	55	151
Cement	thousand tonnes	2,730	14,700	25,000
Cotton yarn	million tonnes	265	1,025	1,270
Cotton textiles, cloth	million m	4,736	8,288	10,000
mill made	million m	(3,728)	(4,316)	
hand-loom, etc.	million m	(1,008)	(3,972)	
Jute textiles	million tonnes	889	1,049	1,500
Rayon yarn	million tonnes	2.1	116	180
Sugar	million tonnes	1.1	4.8	5.7
Tea	million kg	277	493	560
Coffee	million kg	21	86	114
Vanspati cooking oil	million kg	170	581*/352	740

* 1973 data where this gives a better measure of capacity
† Latest estimate
Sources: Monthly Abstract of Statistics; Fifth Five Year Plan – Draft Outline: India – A Reference Annual, 1975; Times of India *Directory and Year Book 1976.*

CHAPTER TEN

RESOURCES FOR INDUSTRY

It must be stressed at the outset that an entrepreneur, be he the Chairman of a State undertaking, a Tata or a Birla with access to vast capital resources, or a humble villager seeking to better his family income, undertakes manufacturing in order to satisfy the needs of the market. Perceiving a need, and possessing or having access to technical ability to meet that need, material resources may well be the least of his problems. Seen however at the national level, resources are important, as they may spell the difference between self-sufficiency and economic dependence on imports to support essential industries, and they may, if abundant, be developed in excess of domestic needs, to be exported to earn foreign exchange with which to purchase food, raw materials, and capital goods currently beyond the country's capacity to produce in sufficient quantity or at desired quality.

POWER RESOURCES

India is at a stage when one can see, side by side, industries persisting at the same craft level as they were for many centuries before the industrial revolution, and the large-scale technically very advanced industries which are the outcome of that technological and entrepreneural revolution. One of the hallmarks of the industrial revolution as it occurs in any country, is the substitution of inanimate power for muscle. In western Europe, and subsequently in America, which were the areas first to experience the industrial revolution, steam power raised from coal brought to the factory was the basis for industrialization. For economic reasons industrialization developed mainly on the coalfields, or where coal could easily be transported. Later the development of electricity as a form of

49 Instant shirt makers, Utnur, Andhra Pradesh. Sewing machines are made in Ludiana, Punjab. These treadle models are independent of power supplies other than the seamsters' feet.

50 Coal-fired thermal electric power station, Durgapur, Damodar Valley, West Bengal. The British-built Durgapur Steel Works are visible on the right horizon.

energy which could be transmitted readily over a grid system covering hundreds of kilometres from the source of power, and the invention of the internal combustion engine using liquid petroleum products which could conveniently be stored and transported in bulk, freed many industries from the economic necessity of locating close to the origin of the energy. India's industrial revolution starts with electricity as the main form of industrial energy, obtained from coal and water power for the most part, with nuclear energy an important alternative in areas far from the coalfields. Petroleum is still the major basis for energizing transport, and its use is being discouraged for static power raising in view of domestic scarcity and recently escalated import costs. It represents almost half the energy used, with electricity and coal (excluding that used in power generation) accounting for about a quarter each. From being somewhat in the economic doldrums in the early 1970s, coal is now looked to by the planners as the cornerstone of industrial development in the current decade. Remaining hydroelectric potential becomes increasingly costly to exploit as it is the more remote and technically difficult sites that have yet to be harnessed. Petroleum production is now on the brink of a major expansion as the off-shore Bombay High wells in the Gulf of Cambay come 'on stream', but it would be rash indeed to forecast self-sufficiency, let alone a surplus of oil, within the decade, though the reserves of this structure alone are well in excess of known reserves ashore.

Coal

The coal mining industry (see Figure 10.1) has been called upon to raise production from about 95 million tonnes in 1975 to 135 or even 145 million tonnes by the end of the Fifth Plan in 1978–79. Most production comes from the Lower Gondwana formations in the Damodar Valley extending westwards from the Raniganj field in West Bengal to the Jharia, Bokaro, Karanpura and Ramgarh fields in Bihar (see Figure 11.6). These account for about two thirds of India's Gondwana coal production, but future expansion is likely to come from the hitherto minor fields of central India and their extensions into the Mahanadi and Godavari valleys. The structural extension of the Damodar Valley trough embraces the Sangrauli field in Madhya Pradesh, south of which a number of extensive fields include the important Korba coal, exploited for power for aluminium reduction

FIG. 10.1

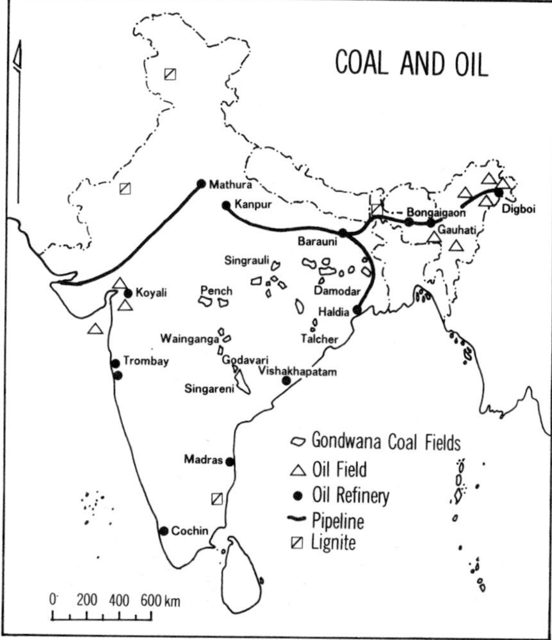

51 Some passenger and many goods trains are still hauled by coal burning locomotives like this one, near Rohtak, Haryana.

52 Modern coal mine headgear, Chinasuri No. 4, Damodar Valley, West Bengal. The engineer on the right is a Sikh.

and for coal to blend with Damodar coking coal at the Bhilai steel works. Several outcrops of Gondwana coal lie to the southeast parallel to the Mahanadi and Brahmani Rivers, the principal being at Talcher in Orissa, developed for power. Further west four groups of small fields may be noted roughly aligned with the Pench-Wainganga and lower Godavari valleys. They include a group in the Pench valley in Madhya Pradesh, 150 km northwest of Nagpur, the Kamthi field in Maharashtra close to that city, and another group centering on Chandrapur 150 km to the south. Further south again, in Andhra Pradesh and 200 km east of Hyderabad, Singareni is the centre of several productive structures.

Beyond these regions, coal and lignite are mined from Tertiary formations in Assam, Meghalaya and Arunachal Pradesh, Darjiling, Jammu and Kashmir, and the lignite deposits of Rajasthan and Tamilnadu. On the whole these fuels are of inferior quality. Tamilnadu's lignite at Neyveli, is used to generate power, for making briquettes and as a basis for the manufacture of urea fertilizer; that at Bikaner in Rajasthan is used for briquettes for railway locomotives.

Qualitatively the Gondwana coals are by far the best and include valuable coking coals which are still being wastefully consumed for steam raising. Their importánce as a diminishing resource of metallurgical significance is recognized, and the railways are progressively adapting locomotives to use less efficient but more abundant non-coking grades or are electrifying their lines, with similar

TABLE 10.1
Coal Reserves: (million tonnes)

	Gondwana coals	*Tertiary coals*	*Total*
Category A (13–15% ash)			
1 To depths 300 m			
Coking	2,294	—	2,294
Non-coking	3,446	1,250	4,696
2 300–600 m			
Coking	935		935
Non-coking	2,079	800	2,879
			10,804
Category B: inferior coals			
1 To depths 300 m			
Coking	7,932	—	7,932
Non-coking	13,970	2,483	16,453
2 300–600 m			
Coking	3,985	—	3,985
Non-coking	3,475	—	3,475
			31,845

results. Indian production is about 23 per cent in coking coals, 74 per cent in non-coking and 3 per cent lignite. Reserves proved by the Geological Survey in seams upwards of 1.2 m thick total 42,649 million tonnes. Their distribution by quality is shown in Table 10.1.

By 1978–79 electricity generation will be the major consumer of coal (34 per cent) followed by the steel industry (24), general industry (15) and transport (10). Some further aspects of coal-mining are examined in relation to electricity below, and in their locational and industrial context in Chapter 12.

Petroleum

(See Figure 10.1.) India is now able to supply 35 per cent of her petroleum needs from domestic production, a proportion that is likely to rise when the Bombay High structure comes 'on stream' during 1976. Output is at present 8.8 million tonnes, to which Bombay High is expected to

53 Off-shore oil drilling rig, Bombay High structure off the Maharashtra coast, now contributing a valuable resource. Development is under the Oil and Natural Gas Commission, a government agency.

add 2.5 million tonnes by the end of 1977–78. Demand is also rising however, and the search for oil-bearing structures is being vigorously pursued, especially in off-shore areas. The Tamilnadu coast is considered particularly promising. The oldest oilfield in the country is in Assam, and is still in production. Since independence the Gujarat fields around the head of the Gulf of Cambay have been developed at Kalol, Anklesvar, Ahmadabad, Mahesna and other structures. Refineries for domestic crude have been established in the Assam Valley at Digboi (.53 million tonnes capacity), Gauhati (.75) and Bongaigaon (1.0), connected by a pipeline which also carries crude further west to Barauni (3 million) in Bihar. The latter is connected to the deep-water port and refinery at Haldia (2.5) which uses imported crude, and to Kanpur for distributing products in UP. The Gujarat crude is refined at Koyali (3 million tonnes) which is linked by pipes to its several tributary fields. The line from Sataya, a new deep-water off-shore terminal in the Gulf of Kutch, to Mathura (6 million) will feed imported crude to the largest Indian refinery. Other refinery capacity is located at major ports, two at Trombay (5.5 and 3.5), in Bombay harbour, and the rest at Cochin (3.5), Madras (2.5) and Vishakhapatnam (1.6).

Electric Power

(See Figure 10.2.) Since independence India's capacity to generate electricity has increased tenfold, yet demand continues to outstrip supply, and power cuts in areas of heavy load, particularly during periods of drought have been a serious embarrassment to industrial and agricultural production alike. In 1974–75 cuts of 25 per cent were common. In Tamilnadu, Punjab, Haryana, and Delhi cuts up to 60 per cent were experienced, all areas with high demand from cultivators using pump irrigation. In total India's power output was 68,200 million kW hours in 1974, giving over 100 kWh per head of population, a huge increase compared to 15 kWh in 1950–51 and 38 kWh per head in 1960–61. Economic and social modernization uses a great deal of energy in this most readily deliverable form. The greatest demand is from industry which uses 67.3 per cent of the total; domestic and public lighting takes 14.7 per cent, agricultural pumps 12.5 per cent, railways 3 per cent and public water and sewage undertakings 2.3 per cent. The rural electrification programme being undertaken to raise the quality of life in the villages, along with the multiplication of electric pumpsets for irrigation will quickly expand demand. The Fifth Plan calls for near doubling of capacity (Table 10.2).

TABLE 10.2
Electricity Generation
(millions of kW installed capacity)

	1950–51	*1960–61*	*1965–66*	*1974–75*	*1978–79*
Steam	1.1	2.4	4.5	11.0	20.7 (Steam and Diesel)
Diesel	0.1	0.3	0.4	0.3	
Hydro	0.6	1.9	4.1	7.0	13.4
Nuclear	—	—	—	0.6	1.3
Total	1.8	4.6	9.0	18.9	35.4

Supply through the 1960s was fairly evenly balanced between hydro and thermal sources, but inevitably the bias is changing towards coal and nuclear energy, as Table 10.2 demonstrates.

The hydroelectric potential of India's rivers is estimated at 48 million kW of which some 30 per cent has been harnessed. (See Table 4.5). The seasonal irregularity of flow in a monsoon climate makes it difficult and expensive to exploit this potential fully. Where water storage for irrigation and to check flood surges is an urgent need, multipurpose river developments are politically and economically attractive. Fortunately hydel potential and coalfields where thermal power can most cheaply be generated do not generally overlap, and the only substantial areas where local energy resources must be augmented with materials brought in from elsewhere are northwestwards from Bombay to Delhi. The location of nuclear power stations at Bombay and in Rajasthan is entirely justifiable at such a distance from coal. Others are being constructed at Kalpakkam near Madras, and Narora, UP. With the extension of high tension grid lines during the Fifth Plan period, it is hoped to facilitate the transfer of power throughout the main regional systems which are at present dominated by State electricity authorities. The efficient use of available power requires a flexible system of inter-state flow. The four southern states are likely to have the first Regional Authority capable of controlling power flow within the area.

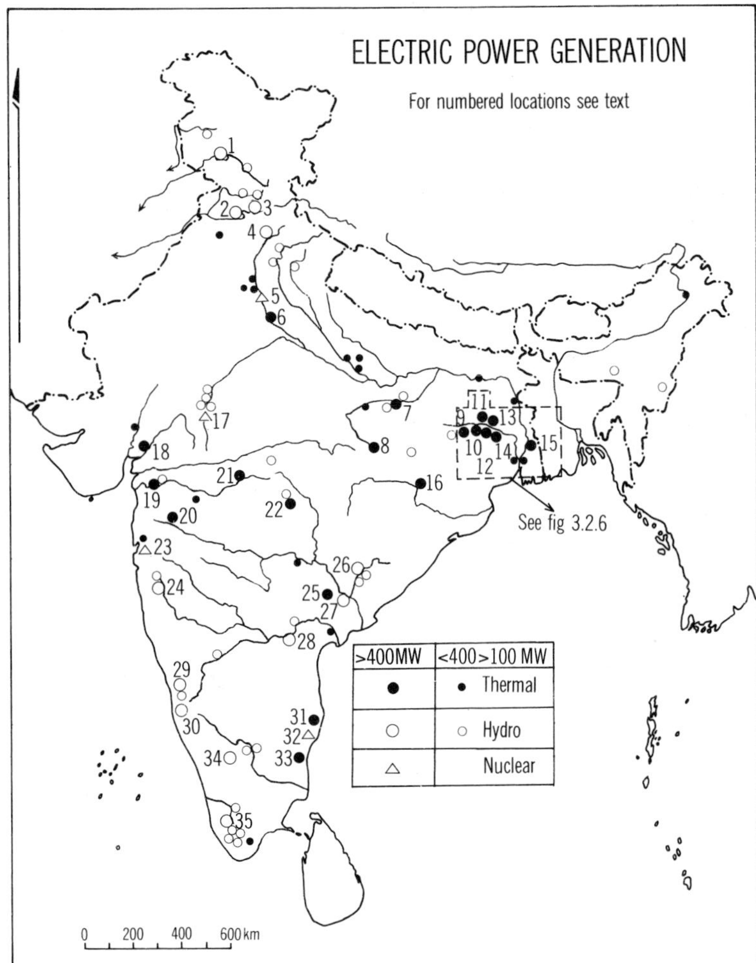

FIG. 10.2 The numbered stations have an installed capacity exceeding 400 MW. All are expected to be in operation or in an advanced stage by 1978–79.

1 Salal (R. Chenab)
2 Bhakra-Nangal
3 Beas Link (Pandoh)
4 Yamuna
5 Narora (nuclear)
6 Harduaganj
7 Obra-Rihand
8 Korba
9 Pathratu
10 Bokaro
11 Chandrapura
12 Santaldih
13 Durgapur (DVC)
14 Durgapur (W. Bengal)
15 Bandel
16 Talcher
17 Ranapratap Sagar (nuclear)
18 Dhuvaran
19 Ukai
20 Nasik
21 Satpura
22 Nagpur
23 Tarapur (nuclear)
24 Koyna
25 Kothagudam
26 Balimela
27 Lower Sileru
28 Srisailam
29 Kalinadi
30 Sharavati
31 Ennore
32 Kalapakkam (nuclear)
33 Neyveli
34 Kundah
35 Idikki

Kerala has surplus capacity which will grow still further, while Karnataka and Tamilnadu are now chronically short of power. A certain amount of inter-state flow already takes place along fixed lines, such as that from Bhakra-Nangal to Punjab, Haryana, Rajasthan and Delhi, and within the integrated Damodar Valley system. Power supply may well become a field in which the Central Government has to insist on national needs taking precedence over a state's assumed rights to the power generated within its borders.

Table 10.3 below shows the state-wise availability of power in 1970–71, and its per capita consumption in industry and irrigation pumping. To the extent that electric power generation attracts industry to its vicinity it is only those power-hungry industries seeking large quanta of power at minimal cost that are found cheek by jowl to the hydel or thermal station which has in several instances been built with the industry's needs in view. Thus one finds aluminium reduction plants at Alwye in Kerala, Mettur in Tamilnadu and Korba in Madhya Pradesh. Electricity is now becoming so widely available that most industries will locate for reasons other than power.

The low levels of available energy and per capita consumption in Assam and Jammu and Kashmir cannot be attributed to any lack of natural resources since both have hydroelectric potential and coalfields, and Assam is India's chief and oldest oil producer. Industrial demand has not yet stimulated local supply nor is agriculture likely to become a major user in these regions of generally well-distributed rainfall. A very different picture is found in Punjab-Haryana and Tamilnadu where the per capita consumption of electricity for irrigation pumping is more than three times greater than in the next highest states of Andhra Pradesh and Uttar Pradesh.

TABLE 10.3

Energy available and consumed in industry and agricultural pumping

States and Union Territories	*Energy available million kWh*	*Per capita consumption in industry*	*Per capita consumption in irrigation pumping*
Andhra Pradesh	2,943	32	9
Assam	362	13	0.02
Bihar (excl. DVC)	2,446	42	1
Gujarat	3,890	95	5
Haryana	1,303	49	30
Himachal Pradesh	188	25	0.2
Jammu & Kashmir	217	17	2
Karnataka	4,746	83	6
Kerala	2,140	60	2
Madhya Pradesh	2,729	38	2
Maharashtra	8.873	120	7
Manipur	7	1	—
Nagaland	5	3	—
Orissa	1,724	69	0.5
Punjab	2,824	105	35
Rajasthan	1,129	27	4
Tamilnadu	6,390	75	31
Tripura	9	1	—
Uttar Pradesh	5,970	35	8
West Bengal (excl. DVC)	4,707	87	0.5
Damodar Valley Corp.	3,745		
Delhi	1,301	124	2
Andaman & Nicobar	4	8	—
Chandigarh	90	157	2
Goa, Daman, Diu	94	78	0.1
Lakshadweep	0.3	0.7	—
Pondicherry	96	100	54
INDIA	57,932.3	59.9	8.3

OTHER LOCALIZED RESOURCES

India is fortunate in possessing or being able to produce a wide range of industrial resources, mineral, vegetable and animal. The principal industrial minerals in which India is deficient are lead and zinc, nickel, tin, silver, mercury, and cobalt. In several minerals there is a surplus available for export (see Figure 10.3).

Iron ores of high quality are worked in several parts of the Peninsula and have been a major factor in the establishment of the iron and steel industries in West Bengal, Bihar, Orissa, Madhya Pradesh and Karnataka. The most productive region extends from Singhbhum in southern Bihar through Orissa into Madhya Pradesh. Its surplus ore is exported through Paradip in Orissa and Vishakhapatnam and Kakinada in Andhra Pradesh (see Figure 11.5). Karnataka's ores are at present used locally, but with the completion of the railway down the Western Ghats from Hassan to Mangalore, export will be facilitated. Goa already exports huge quantities from its immediate hinterland, through Marmagao which thereby heads the list of ports for shipping tonnage cleared. Goa led in iron ore production with 12.1 million tonnes in 1973; the other major producers were

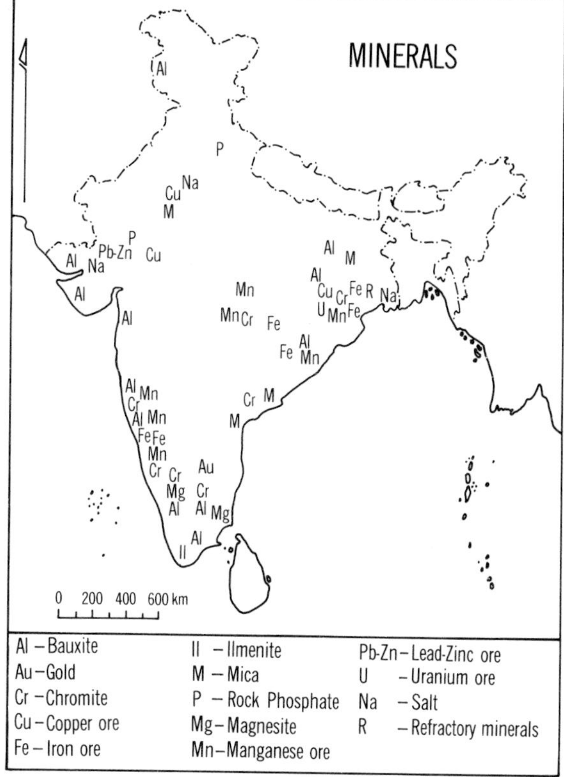

FIG. 10.3

54 Quarrying high grade iron ore in Goa for export, mainly to Japan.

55 Ferrying iron ore on a backwater in Goa. Many of the ocean going carriers stand well out to sea. Local craft in the foreground.

Madhya Pradesh 8.1 million, Orissa 5.9 million and Bihar 4.7 million tonnes in a total of 35.4 million tonnes, of which 21.3 million were exported.

Manganese ore production runs at 1.5 million tons annually, almost half of which is exported. The Nagpur-Bhandara region in northeast Maharashtra is the principal source, but the ore is also found in Karnataka, Goa, Andhra Pradesh and Orissa, Gujarat and Rajasthan. Production of another ferro-alloy, chromite, is on a less important scale. Deposits are found in Bihar, Orissa, Maharashtra, Andhra, Tamilnadu and Karnataka. Figure 10.1 shows the importance of the peninsular shield as the principal mineralized region of India, a characteristic it shares with the world's other Archaean shields, such as those in Western Australia, southern Africa, and Brazil, all presumed fragments of a former single continental mass, Gondwanaland.

India's endowment of non-ferrous metals is less lavish. Reserves of bauxite are more than adequate and allow for increasing exports beyond domestic needs for the aluminium industry. The relative paucity of copper, lead and zinc has encouraged their substitution by aluminium in many uses where electrical conductivity or non-rusting qualities are essential. Bauxite is found in laterite formations in many parts of the country, but particularly around the coastal margins of the Peninsula (Gujarat, Maharashtra, Tamilnadu and Orissa), and in its more humid eastern interior (Madhya Pradesh and Bihar). There are also reserves in the other states of the Peninsula, and in UP and Jammu and Kashmir. Copper is mined in the multi-mineral belt of Singhbhum in Bihar (see Figure 11.5) and in the newly developed Khetri belt in Rajasthan. Output at c. 12,000 tonnes in 1974 met 15 per cent of needs but this should increase to over 40 per cent as the Khetri operation comes into full production. The metal is also found in southern Rajasthan but it is the lead-zinc complex of that area, in Udaipur district, that has attracted exploitation. This is India's only present source of these metals. The ore belt is known to extend into Gujarat, and there are other occurences in Andhra Pradesh and Orissa. Nickel is known in the latter area but is not yet worked. Gold has been produced in a steady small amount from very deep veins in the Kolar field near Bangalore.

With the coming of nuclear power India is fortunate in having source of uranium ore in Bihar – again in Singhbhum – and in the Himalaya in Himachal Pradesh and UP. Reserves are thought to be capable of sustaining power stations with an output of between 5 and 10 million kW. Other minerals for atomic use include monazite, a source of the element thorium, which with ilmenite, for titanium oxide, is extracted from the beach sands of Kerala.

Non-metallic minerals of importance include mica, for which India has long been famous, not only as the major world producer, but also as the home of the most efficient (and probably the lowest paid) 'splitters' of mica, the women of Bihar to whom mica from overseas producers is sent for processing into microscopically thin sheets. Production is from primitive shaft mines in central Bihar, Andhra Pradesh and Rajasthan. Common salt occurs in rock form in the sub-Himalayan belt, but most production is from evaporating sea water notably in the Little Rann of Kutch in Gujarat, and around the Bay of Bengal in Calcutta, Tamilnadu and Andhra Pradesh. Naturally concentrated evaporites are worked in the Sambhar Lake in Rajasthan. With the increasing demand for fertilizers, the search for rock phosphate has been intensified, though the output of 135,532 tonnes (1973) from Udaipur (Rajasthan) and Dehra Dun (UP) falls well short of need, and it is necessary to import 875,000 tonnes. Another essential in the fertilizer industry is sulphuric acid, obtained from pyrites in Bihar, 42,000 tonnes being mined in 1973. Rajasthan and Karnataka have economically viable deposits, but the country still relies heavily on imports which approached 560,000 tonnes.

CONCLUSION

The industrial revolution in the western world began on the coalfields, steam power being its fundamental innovation. Industry consequently was for a long time heavily concentrated close to coal. By contrast India's industrial revolution gets into its stride in a different technological era. Most inanimate energy other than that used in vehicles is transformed into electricity which becomes readily diffusable through a grid of transmission lines. Localized sources of energy can now be made available to distant users. Coal and lignite are the main bases for power generation, and account for 58 per cent of the total. They are likely to increase in relative importance as with time fewer sites with hydroelectric potential remain to be exploited. On current showing resources of petroleum and natural gas seem unlikely to dominate energy supply, though new oil reserves about to come into production off the coast near Bombay will provide a welcome relief from part of the crushing cost of imports.

With its principal coalfields in the northeast of the Peninsula, hydroelectric stations around the steep fringe of the Peninsula and in the Western Himalaya, oils fields in Assam and Gujarat and lignite in Rajasthan and Tamilnadu, the regions most likely to be pressed for energy supplies are Uttar Pradesh and Madhya Pradesh. Nuclear power has been developed in the Chambal Basin to help fill this gap, and other stations are being located to supplement conventional generating stations in areas of particular need such as Bombay and Madras.

In respect of several minerals India is well favoured. High grade iron ores essential for her modern steel industry are available in superabundance and make an important contribution to exports. Similarly manganese and bauxite are plentiful. Other minerals including copper are exploited in increasing volume for use in Indian industry. While these minerals are found in a number of places throughout Peninsular India there is a remarkable concentration of mineral finds and development of both iron and non-ferrous metalliferous ores in a belt lying in the border country between Bihar and Orissa. Their utilization is facilitated by the proximity of the Damodar Valley coalfields and the hydroelectric power of the Hirakud scheme on the Mahanadi.

56 Open cut mining of thick seam of coal, Damodar Valley, West Bengal. Note women carrying head baskets of coal. The coal is loaded into lorries to be taken for use in local factories or to be transhipped by basket loads into railway wagons to be sent all over India. The shelter by the pool covers a pump for keeping the workings dry.

CHAPTER ELEVEN

INDUSTRIES GREAT AND SMALL

There are three fairly distinct levels of manufacturing enterprise in India. At the simplest level of organization and the lowest level of capitalization, is village or household industry employing essentially family labour. This merges with small-scale industry, in which wage labour and a modest degree of capitalization exist. Another distinction is in their measure of modernization. Household manufacturing tends to be confined to traditional crafts little affected by modernization, whereas the small-scale industries are essentially modern technologically speaking, and as advanced in this respect as the third category of industry, the 'organized' sector, registered and regulated under various acts. To a considerable extent the three levels correspond to three types of location: household industry is found obviously in the villages and small towns; small-scale industry is most common in towns and non-metropolitan cities; organized industry in the larger cities and in settlements created specifically for them. This gradation is paralled in the market served by the three levels, which indicates the present lack of integration within manufacturing industry, a feature which seriously handicaps overall economic development.

VILLAGE INDUSTRY

One can only guess at the number of people engaged in village industry since one of its characteristics is part time seasonal employment of members of a family otherwise self-employed or wage labouring in agriculture. The 1971 Census recorded 6.4 million as engaged in household manufacturing, (presumably more or less full-time since the statistics do not provide for dual employment), to which must be added untold millions of part time craftsmen. Many work at hand-looms in their homes, some using home-spun cotton, but the majority weaving mill-made yarn. The hand-loom industry typifies the problems of this sector of Indian economic life. The approach of planners – and more importantly of the politicians whose servants they are – to village industry in general and to the hand-loom industry in particular, has been coloured not a little since independence by sentiment and idealism attaching to the dignity of creative craftsmanship instilled into the newly independent nation by the inspiration of one of its architects, Mahatma Gandhi. He saw in the spinning wheel a symbol as much as an instrument for eradicating rural poverty. The *khadi* movement propagating the making and wearing of hand-loom cloth made from home-spun yarn contained something of nostalgia for long-past glories of Indian hand-made textiles, and a good measure of antipathy to the 'satanic mills' whether in Lancashire, or imposed upon India under the British who were rightly blamed for the decay of rural industry.

However the translation of these notions into economic practice has proved difficult. It is hard to put the economic clock back, and the problem is to provide for the coexistence for some time of the village sector with the modernized sectors of industry. Village industries are kept alive by indirect subsidies through the provision of cheap machine-made yarn, and by the reservation of a sizeable part of the textile market – the making of saris which almost every woman wears – for the village and small-scale sectors. In an incisive study, *Poverty in India* (1970), V. M. Dandekar and N. Rath, investigating the capacity of village industry to create work for the poor, concluded that protection from 'aggressive' modern industry, by limiting the latter's expansion while attempt-

57 Cow dung cakes plastered on the wall, Agra, Uttar Pradesh. The women of the household collect cow dung in baskets and make the dung cakes by mixing in straw as a binding agent. When dry they are stacked near the kitchen to be used as a slow burning fuel. Photograph 86 shows a stack of dung cakes used for firing a kiln. The partly ruined relics of a Moghul style brick house stands behind.

58 A modest Hindu housewife shades her face as she brings drinking water from the well, her drawing rope coiled on her head. She is in 'purdah', that is, she will normally go about veiled, except in the company of her immediate family. Purdah is a Muslim practice adopted by some Hindus particularly in regions of former Muslim dominance, as here in Uttar Pradesh.

ing to expand the former, was of little value wherever it was necessary to protect an inferior technology. They suggested that government should be concerned rather to protect industries in the course of transition from traditional to modern technology and not to try to maintain an old order unchanged, far less to try to re-establish traditional industry where it had vanished. Attempts to re-tool traditional spinning with improved *charkas* (spinning wheels) were shown to be quite uneconomic as measured by the cost in man-hours of the finished product. The Fifth Plan perpetuates these efforts, it presumably being decided that it is better for people to be active than not, even if their work is of no profit to them. Herein lies the crux of the problem: how to mobilize for productive employment the enormous seasonal surplus of man-power available among a population many of them living in extreme poverty, who lack the means to provide their own capital, and the skills to compete in the modernized sector.

Village industry is generally carried on in the home by members of the family using muscle as the sole source of energy. In a few areas of enterprise like silk-spinning from home-bred cocoons, coir production from domestic coconuts, making jaggery (crude sugar) from the farmer's own cane, and the manufacture of simple pottery, metal utensils and carpentry articles for the immediate local market, village industry continues to hold a viable position, but inevitably it must give way to the processes of modernization, and is doing so through the expansion of the small-scale industrial sector. Attempts to link them to larger markets expose them to exploitation by middlemen from outside. A few trades of high craftsmanship following traditional designs capable of commanding markets in the tourist industry and overseas will no doubt survive, but probably as outworking extensions of the small-scale sector which has far greater capacity to organize the marketing end of production.

As one would expect, the distribution of workers in household industry as enumerated by the Census of 1971 (see Figure 11.1) faithfully reflects the distribution of rural population. All-India data are not yet available to enable a study to be made of regional differences in the craft composition of these workers.

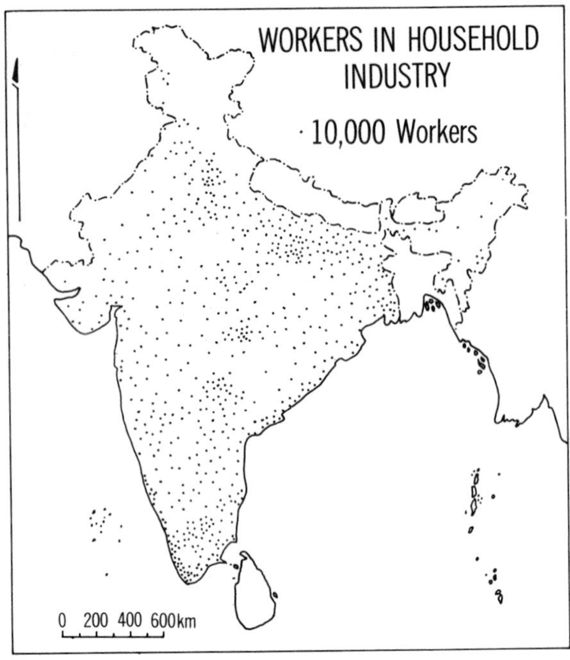

FIG. 11.1

SMALL-SCALE MANUFACTURING INDUSTRY

As now defined, small industries are those having a capital investment of not more than Rs 1 million, or Rs 1.5 million in the case of industries ancillary to an industry in the 'organized' sector. They are usually proprietary or small partnerships a fact that limits their ability to raise credit and to expand the scale of their operations. Their entrepreneurs' lack of technological qualifications places limits on the range of processes they can undertake, though government agencies are trying to bridge the 'information gap' for them. In general they are not industries on the way to developing into larger scale concerns in the organized sector, though it would be a natural evolution for some to become absorbed into that sector through the 'take-over' process.

Under the Small Industries Development Organization these enterprises are able to minimize their disadvantages by calling on the expertise of specialists in all aspects of technology, management, marketing, etc. The SDIO has marked out many fields of activity appropriate for them to enter and assists entrepreneurs to get started in

59 Silk worm cocoons on trays standing in the sun with a basket of cocoons on the left and a field crop drying on the roof: near Mysore, Karnataka.

60 Silk worms on trays: near Mysore, Karnataka where silk making is a traditional craft. After several weeks of feeding on mulberry leaves specially grown for the purpose, the silkworm is moved to a woven tray on which it spins its cocoon (see Photograph 59).

61 The Agra-Fatepur Sikri road, Uttar Pradesh: an old roadside shelter now carries family planning propaganda. The tractor is now a common sight.

62 Bangles and trinkets for sale at a Gond village fair near Utnur northern Andhra Pradesh. Such ornaments are generally made of 'German silver' or other alloys less costly than 'rupee silver' which is used for high grade articles.

them. One important incentive is the establishment of industrial estates provided with the services essential to small industry, but which in the Indian urban area may be difficult for a manufacturer to arrange at a site of his own choosing. In many respects small industries are complementary to those in the large-scale sector, indeed some are so closely linked as to be defined as ancillary. Many process the raw materials (cotton ginning is an example) that large scale industry requires, others utilize the products of heavy industry, fabricating goods for local markets, like spun cast concrete pipes for irrigation, metal furniture, etc. They exist because of enterprise, and are located because of the personal preference of the entrepreneur, finding their raw materials at hand or bringing them from afar, using ubiquitous road transport.

By and large the small-scale industrial sector is performing a vital role as an area in which training and managerial experience can be had in units of optimum scale in terms of the capital available, the size of the market, and the limited technological knowledge of the participants. C. C. Pattanshetti[1] comments that they supply a demand at the medium town level of the market which for many categories of product is beyond the reach of large-scale centralized industry. They function up to the level of the district town, and even to that of the state capital, but seldom at the inter-state or national market level. In economic terms they are frequently quite efficient. The range of the processes and products of the small industrial sector is very great. It is easier to say that they are not in general concerned with traditional products, except where their production can profitably be organized at a level above that of the household, as in the Kashmir woodworking and embroidery crafts, where households may operate as out-working units, with the marketing done entirely by the firm. In competition with centralized industry the small scale sector cannot survive in areas where economies to scale are significant, as in the case of the basic heavy industries and those involved in assembly lines. There remains however a vast field in which small industry can not only compete but may in fact monopolize a part of the market. The ability of small industry to create jobs (unskilled, semi-skilled and experience-giving), and to raise the level of economic activity in the small towns, thereby interacting with the village agricultural economy, makes it a most essential element in the process of Indian modernization.

[1] C. C. Pattanshetti, *Dimensions of India's Industrial Economy*, Bombay, 1968.

63 Sweet meats, soap and bidi smokes for sale at Utnur market, northern Andhra Pradesh. As this display represents his day's stock his profit margin provides a bare living.

64 Ashok Leyland truck chassis ready for export from Madras, Tamilnadu.

65 Sindri fertilizer plant, West Bengal. The spheres are for storing ammonia for use in making ammonium sulphate.

MANUFACTURING IN THE ORGANIZED SECTOR

From the outset at independence India has pursued a policy of industrialization in which public ownership and private enterprise have well defined fields of interest. From 1956 government reserved to itself exclusive responsibility in certain basic industries listed as Schedule A industries, while sharing others with private enterprise, the Schedule B industries, and leaving the remainder for the private sector to develop within the general system of licensing under Government control. The State reserves the power to acquire control of economically 'sick' or mismanaged units in the private sector, and has exercised those rights in a number of cases in the textile industry for example.

Schedule A industries include the mining of coal, iron, petroleum, and the major non-ferrous metalliferous ores; the basic iron and steel, and non-ferrous metal industries; heavy engineering and machine tool manufacture, air and rail transport, nuclear energy and electric power. Schedule B covers aluminium, chemicals, fertilizers, road and sea transport and pharmaceuticals. It will be noted that textiles and food processing industries are not scheduled.

Through its industrial licensing system the Government closely controls industrial development to prevent the over-concentration of power in a few hands and to ensure that industries of a strategic nature are kept within the public sector. Private ownership of some companies in industries in Schedule A persists at least on a sharing basis, notably Tata Iron and Steel, (62 per cent private), Indian Iron and Steel (48 per cent private), and Tata Engineering and Locomotive Co., all being long established firms whose freedom in operation is fairly restricted under Government regulation. Large-scale private enterprises (defined as having capital assets of Rs 200 million or more) are not allowed to engage in production of items reserved for the public sector or for the Small-Scale Industries sector, but they are left a wide range of activities in a schedule of nineteen groups including the following: ferro-alloys, steel castings, boilers, industrial turbines, electric motors, small ships (below 1000 dwt), commercial vehicles, machine tools, tractors, scientific instruments, fertilizers, chemicals, cement. Outside these, large-scale private industry may be allowed to engage in important export industries, but as a rule the excluded fields are reserved for medium- and small-scale enterprises.

Direct Government involvement in industry has grown to be very considerable. Among the 20 companies with assets exceeding Rs 1000 million (1973–74) fifteen are in the public sector, in steel, food, heavy electrical machinery and engineering, petroleum, fertilizers, aircraft, shipping, coal and lignite, air transport and copper. Of the five private firms three are in steel and heavy engineering, and the others in shipping and cement. The top hundred companies include 38 in the public sector.

Government investment in large enterprises like Bharat Heavy Electricals, Hindusthan Machine Tools, etc., enables it to locate plants in order to spread the benefits of central government expenditure over the states hungry for employment opportunities. Through its spread effects such investment stimulates industrialization at growth points around which further diversified development may take place. Bangalore, Hyderabad, Bhopal, Madras, Ranchi and Lucknow are examples of locations where various state-owned engineering industries have been established without specific material or market advantages in their location, but with significant advantages of nodality in most cases.

DISTRIBUTION OF MANUFACTURING INDUSTRY

Figure 11.2 based on the 1971 Census shows the distribution of the population engaged in manufacturing industry (other than household industry), 10.7 million, and that in mining, 0.9 million. At the present stage of India's industrial development which as has been pointed out is far from being fully integrated, it is dangerous to see in the clustering of the industrial population in particular areas the kinds of closely knit industrial regions one associates with a highly developed country. Hooghlyside, the Damodar Valley and Greater Bombay–Thana most nearly correspond to the conventional idea of industrial regions, but the other areas of concentrations are more loosely structured. Pune might be bracketed with Bombay but it is 130 km away; one must consider the sheer

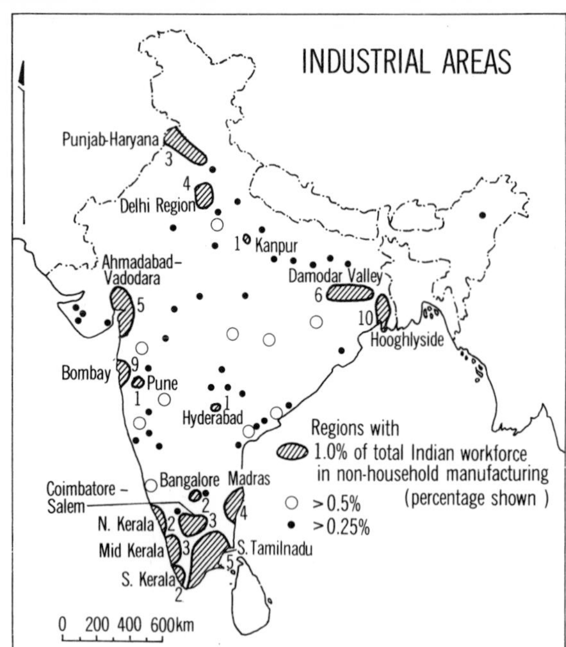

Fig. 11.2

TABLE 11.1

Labour force in Industry and Mining (In regions as per cent of India total)

Bombay-Thana	9.2	
(with Pune	**10.5**)	
Hooghlyside	9.7	
Damodar Valley (incl. Singhbhum)	6.2	
Ahmadabad group	5.1	
N. Tamilnadu group	4.0	
Coimbatore-Salem	3.1	7.6
S. Tamilnadu	4.5	
N. Kerala	1.7	
Mid-Kerala	2.9	6.4
S. Kerala	1.8	
Delhi group	3.8	
Punjab-Haryana	2.6	
Bangalore	1.7	
Hyderabad	1.1	
Kanpur	1.1	

TABLE 11.2

Employment by Industrial Categories, Number of Factories and Value Added

Region and State	*Number employed (thousand)*	*Per cent Indian total*	*Percentage of State total by classes* Food	Textiles	Chemicals	Minerals & metals	Machinery transport equipment	Others	*Factories Per cent Indian* total*	*Value Added Per cent† Indian total*
Northern										
Punjab	105	2.2	8	30	3	13	30	16	3	2
Haryana	77	1.6	6	17	1	18	36	22	2	2
Delhi	87	1.8	3	24	3	12	25	33	2	2
Central										
Uttar Pradesh	384	8.1	19	19	3	16	18	25	7	7
Rajasthan	81	1.7	6	25	3	18	23	25	1	2
Madhya Pradesh	224	4.7	9	23	7	18	17	26	5	4
Eastern										
Bihar	258	5.4	19	3	4	35	24	15	3	6
West Bengal	850	17.9	6	34	3	21	20	16	14	16
Orissa	75	1.6	12	11	3	41	7	26	2	2
Assam	79	1.7	67	3	2	2	11	15	4	1
Western										
Gujarat	405	8.5	7	46	5	11	12	29	9	8
Maharashtra	938	19.7	6	33	8	11	20	22	21	27
Southern										
Andhra Pradesh	282	5.9	23	10	2	8	13	44	6	3
Karnataka	252	5.3	10	19	2	12	41	16	4	5
Tamilnadu	411	8.6	11	27	7	7	28	20	10	9
Kerala	206	4.3	54	11	5	10	7	13	5	4
INDIA	4,758	99.0	13	28	5	15	21	18	—	—

*Total number of factories 12,769
† Value added Rs 20,614 million
Sources: Ministry of Labour and Rehabilitation, *Statistics of Factories, Indian Statistical Abstract 1972.*

size of the country before too readily assuming that the industrial towns of Kerala or of Tamilnadu (with or without Bangalore) constitute functional regions. The strength of the clusters mapped in Figure 11.2, in terms of the percentage of the industrial population located there, is given in Table 11.1.

If the Bombay and Ahmadabad groups are amalgamated, and also the Hooghlyside with the Damodar Valley, 31.5 per cent of the total labour force is covered, divided almost equally between the two regions. Recent data are not available to show the precise breakdown of all the regional totals into industrial categories, but Table 11.2 gives state-wise data for the major classes for 1968. Greater detail where available is listed for 1971 in Table 11.1.

The Annual Survey of Industries published in the *Indian Statistical Abstract (1972)* lists for each state the man-hours worked, the number of factories and the value added by manufacturing. These data have been mapped as percentages of the Indian total in Figure 11.3 from which it is clear how dominant a position Maharashtra (mainly Bombay) and West Bengal have on all counts. Tamilnadu ranks third on each criterion, followed by Gujarat and Uttar Pradesh. The value added by the latter, the largest of the states, is only a quarter of that by Maharashtra.

Food industries processing local products for mainly local markets are fairly ubiquitous, tending to dominate in those states which are industrially rather backward, like Assam and Kerala. The large percentage of employment unclassified against Andhra Pradesh is accounted for in the main by tobacco, a regional agricultural speciality employing 30 per cent of the state's total. The major employer of labour, the textile industry, has wide distribution, but is responsible in large measure for the concentration of industrial employment in the regions listed in Table 11.1, with the exception of the Damodar Valley. There were 689 cotton mills in 1974. Many are mapped in Figure 11.4. The jute mills are highly localized, 62 of the 74

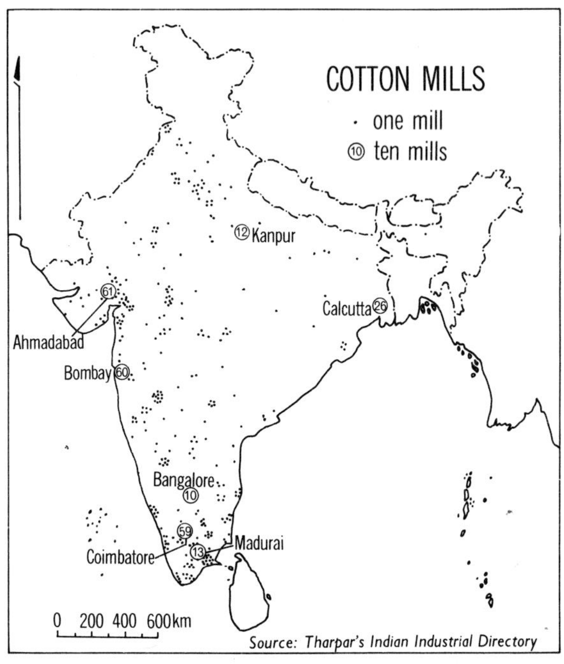

FIG. 11.4

FIG. 11.3

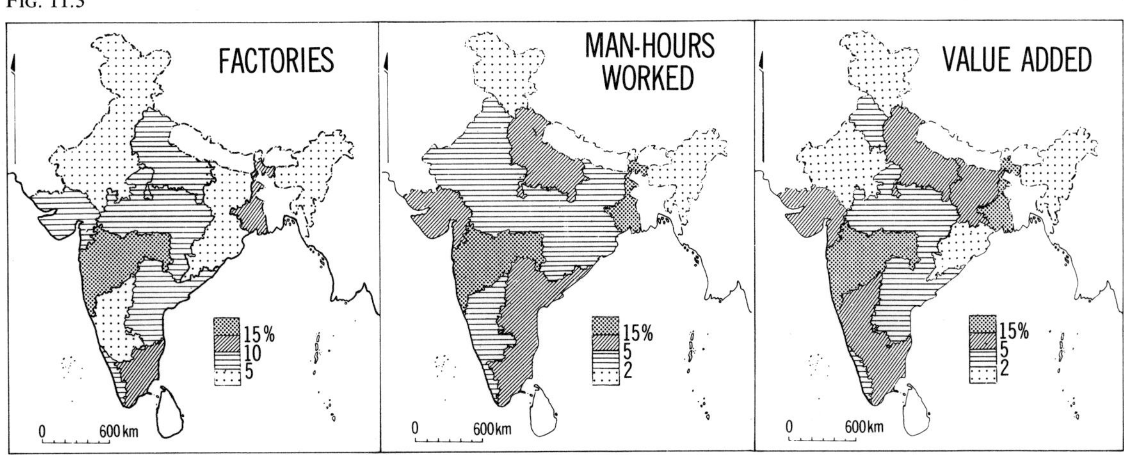

recorded being in the Hooghlyside conurbation where they employ 250,000 workers. The reason in this case is clearly the proximity of East Bengal raw jute in the early days of the industry, which now has to find domestically grown fibre in West Bengal, Assam and Bihar, and imports some from Bangladesh, its major rival as a jute manufacturer.

The widespread distribution of the cotton textile industry is not altogether surprising in view of the use by most Indians of cotton clothing. It does not however reflect faithfully the distribution of population. Bihar and Eastern UP are relatively deficient in mills despite their dense population. The local availability of raw cotton has had some influence, particularly in the past when transport was less well developed. Thus the industry of Gujarat, Maharashtra, Madhya Pradesh and the Coimbatore region of Tamilnadu may be explained. Punjab, Haryana, Delhi and Western UP may be well provided with mills for the same reason, though the industry here is of more recent origin, mostly dating from the introduction of irrigation in the late nineteenth and early twentieth centuries. Elsewhere, in areas like Kerala, and parts of Tamilnadu not growing cotton, and on Hooghlyside, explanation must be sought in entrepreneural and market factors.

The iron and steel industry is the most important component of the minerals and metal working group. It is now to all intents a nationalized industry, since Government has a large share in the two privately established firms. The whole industry is co-ordinated by the Steel Authority of India (SAIL) set up in 1973 to restructure the management in its several plants, and to direct future development. The major steel works in production (1974–75 data) are shown in Table 11.3.

TABLE 11.3
Steel ingot production
1974–75: thousand tonnes

Bhilai	2,001
TISCO, Jamshedpur	1,722
Rourkhela	1,065
Durgapur	820
IISCO, Burnpur	532
Bokaro (under development)	125
Bhadravati	131
Others	959
Total	7,355

In a general sense all these plants are oriented towards materials, iron ore and or coal, but 'proximity to materials' may mean distances of 100 km for the nearest ingredient. Jamshedpur is the oldest of the steel plants, established by the famous Tata family of Bombay industrialists in 1907–11. High grade iron ore is mined in the hills to the south, and west (see Figures 11.5 and 11.6) but although manganese and chromite for alloy steels are available in the same Singhbhum district, better quality materials are brought in from Madhya Pradesh and Orissa. Coking coal is railed in from the Damodar Valley about 120 km distant. Output includes mainly structural steel, plates and sheets, present capacity being about 2 million tonnes. Expansion to 5 million tonnes is contemplated.

Next in order of age is the Indian Iron and Steel Company's plant at Burnpur with a capacity of one million tonnes. Originally based on ironstone shales in the Damodar coal measure series at Kulti (est. 1919) from which good cast iron could be made, the firm set up plant at Burnpur 16 km to the east, near Asansol, to make steel using non-phosphoric Singhbhum ores (up to 70 per cent iron content) brought from over 300 km to the south. The smaller but more specialized Bhadravati plant in Karnataka dates from the same era. Until 1974 it held the unique distinction of being a modern survival of smelting iron ore with charcoal. Rich silica-iron ore from the Bababudan Hills (55–64 per cent iron) is brought to the site on the Bhadra River by rope-way. Coke has now to be railed in from the Damodar Valley, but fuel transport costs are minimized by making pig iron in electric smelters. Although a small producer in terms of ingot tonnage, Bhadravati is an important plant for alloy and special steels made in electric furnaces, such as stainless, spring and tool steel, ferro-silicon and ferro-manganese.

The steel plants established since independence, including the Bokaro works just coming into production, have been set up with foreign participation, Bhilai and Bokaro with Russian assistance, Durgapur with British and Rourkhela with West German aid. Bhilai to date is India's biggest steel plant, laid out on many hectares of level terrain alongside the electrified railway line linking it to the Damodar Valley (whence its coking coal must come 745 km)

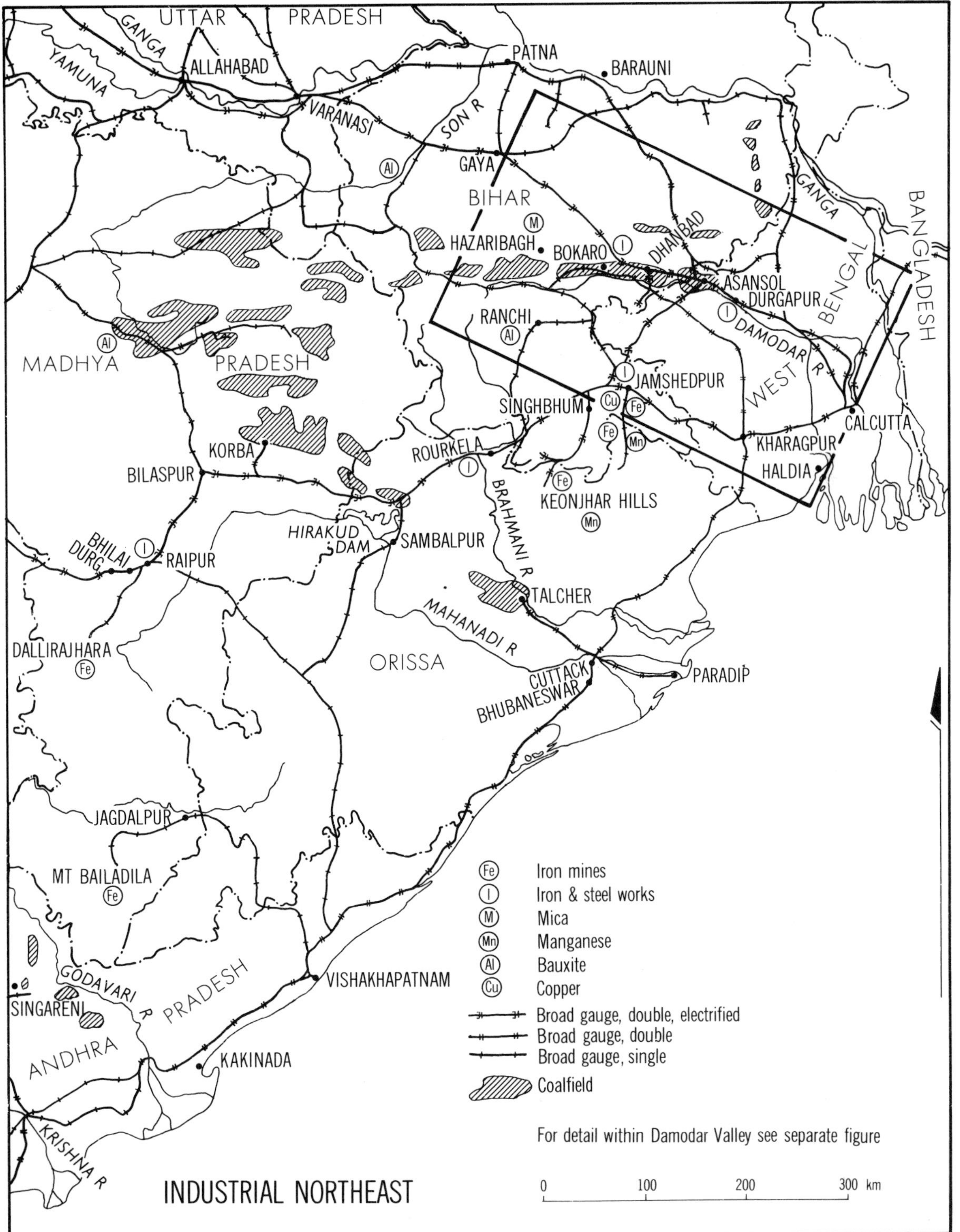
UTTAR PRADESH
GANGA
YAMUNA
ALLAHABAD
VARANASI
PATNA
BARAUNI
SON R
GAYA
BIHAR
HAZARIBAGH
BOKARO
DHANBAD
ASANSOL
DURGAPUR
DAMODAR R
WEST BENGAL
BANGLADESH
RANCHI
JAMSHEDPUR
SINGHBHUM
CALCUTTA
KHARAGPUR
HALDIA
MADHYA PRADESH
KORBA
BILASPUR
ROURKELA
BRAHMANI R
KEONJHAR HILLS
BHILAI
DURG
RAIPUR
HIRAKUD DAM
SAMBALPUR
TALCHER
MAHANADI R
ORISSA
DALLIRAJHARA
CUTTACK
BHUBANESWAR
PARADIP
JAGDALPUR
MT BAILADILA
GODAVARI R
SINGARENI
ANDHRA PRADESH
VISHAKHAPATNAM
KAKINADA
KRISHNA R
Iron mines
Iron & steel works
Mica
Manganese
Bauxite
Copper
Broad gauge, double, electrified
Broad gauge, double
Broad gauge, single
Coalfield
For detail within Damodar Valley see separate figure
0 100 200 300 km
INDUSTRIAL NORTHEAST

FIG. 11.5

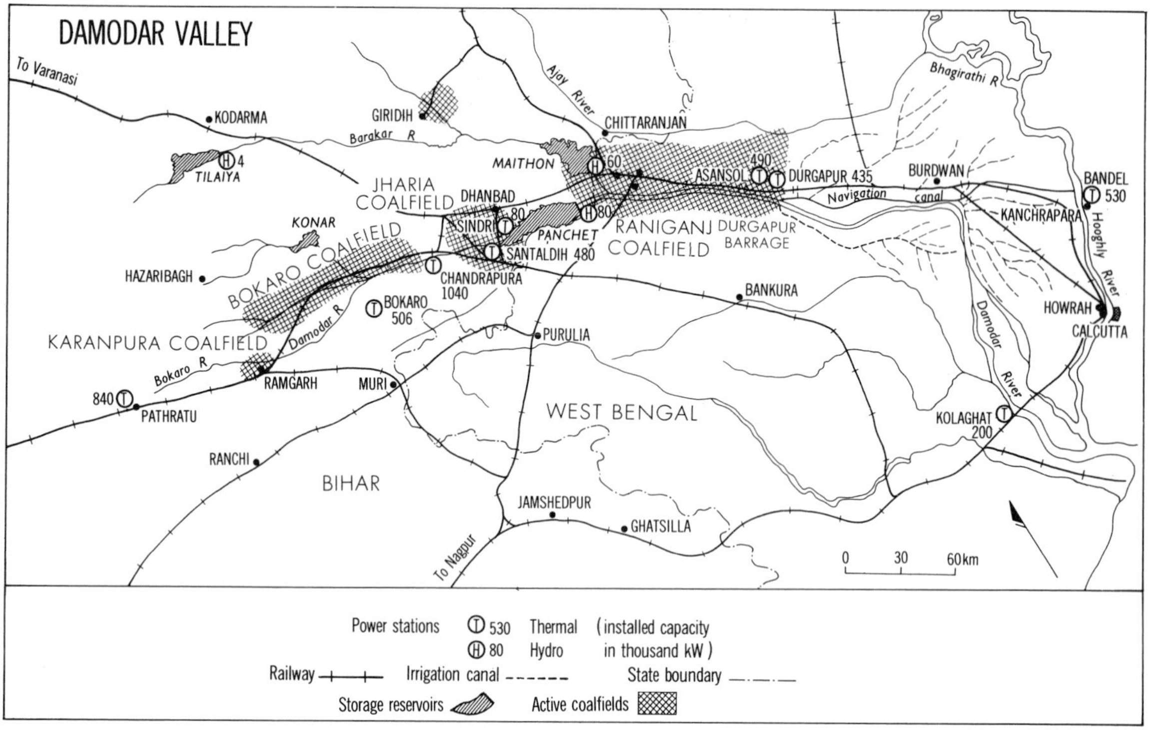

FIG. 11.6

66 Blast furnaces at the Russian-built Bhilai Iron & Steel Works in Madhya Pradesh.

and to Calcutta, and other lines to ports at Vishakhapatnam and Kakinada on the Andhra coast, and to western central and northern India. Iron ore (67 per cent *Fe*) is brought from Dalli Rajhara 97 km to the south. Originally it was intended to use coal from Korba, only 225 km distant to the northeast, but this proved unsuitable for coking unless blended with stronger Jharia coal from the Damodar, in a 30:70 ratio. Manganese can be obtained from Balaghat about 200 km to the west. Bhilai's production is mainly structural steel and rails. Capacity is to be expanded to 5 million tonnes in the Fifth Plan. Durgapur, on the banks of the Damodar River, brings its ore from Naumundi in Singhbhum 329 km away, but is close to coking coal and to lower quality fuel for power generation. Plant capacity is 1.6 million ingot tonnes, but the concern has suffered long teething troubles. The prospect is for achieving 72 per cent capacity and an output of one million tonnes in 1975–76. Alloy steels are made in an adjoining works. Rourkhela near to the Brahmani River just over the border in Orissa on the electrified line from Calcutta and the Damodar Valley, has a capacity of 1.8 million tonnes and a high rate of efficiency. The iron ores of the Orissa–Bihar border hills are close at hand, and the plant brings in coking coal from the Damodar, back-loading in the wagons that carry ore to the Damodar works. Hydro-electric power from Hirakud Dam on the Mahanadi is available. Sheet steel is a speciality.

Bokaro promises to dwarf these earlier plants of the post-independence period. Its locational advantages are similar to those of Durgapur. From a first stage capacity of 1.7 million tonnes of ingot steel, it is expected to develop to 4.75 million tonnes, and the feasibility of further increasing this to 10 million is under study. A major feature of the plants is a hot strip mill of more than 3 million tonnes capacity.

Meanwhile plans are going ahead to establish new steel plants still further from coal than any of those discussed above. The Salem steel plant is under construction in Tamilnadu, to utilize long-known low grade magnitite ores for making alloy and special steels in particular, including electrical steel. Vijayanagar close to Tungabhadra Dam in Karnataka will produce billets and strip products within a capacity of 3 million ingot tonnes, while at Vishakhapatnam a plant of similar size will make sectional steel. As a major exporter of Orissan iron ore through its modernized port, Vishakhapatnam will have no problem in respect of that raw material, but it is not particularly well located for coal or power supplies. However the Hindustan Shipyard building bulk carriers of up to 25,000 tonnes dwt should be an important local market for its output.

After twenty years of development and on-the-job experience, the new Indian steel industry has reached the point where it has become a net earner of foreign exchange from its products which are among the cheapest in the world.

Other industries will be discussed in their regional context, taking as a framework the clusters of manufacturing employment listed in Tables 11.1 and 11.4.

Bombay–Pune

These two cities constitute a functional economic region despite the distance separating their centres. A fast electrified line connects them, and Pune is inevitably drawn within Bombay's dominance. The region is much involved in the textile industry, which in 1971 occupied 30 per cent of the factory workers. Textiles have lost ground relatively (from 41 per cent of workers in 1960) as more forward-looking electrical and mechanical trades have been developing while modernization and expansion of the textile industry have been held back in the interests of the household and small-scale industrial sectors. Tata makes buses and heavy trucks (on licence from Mercedes), International make tractors, Premier Automobiles make cars, trucks and buses, and Mahindra monopolize the manufacture of jeeps, all of them in Bombay. Pune has two factories making motor scooters and mopeds. These plants provide a market for numerous manufacturers of parts and accessories. Almost everything modern in the way of 'consumer durables' (in the sense of being non-traditional) is made in Bombay. Chemicals, pharmaceuticals and film-making are further evidence of the city's technologically advanced status. A combination of factors account for Bombay's industrial pre-eminence, shared by Pune as a satellite. As the major port nearest to Europe (especially when the Suez canal is open) Bombay was the principal point

TABLE 11.4

Workers in major industrial regions (by percentage categories of manufacturing)

Region	Total (thousand)	Food, drink, tobacco	Cotton, wool, synthetic textiles	Jute textiles	Clothing	Wood, paper printing etc	Leather etc	Chemical, oil etc	Non metal	Base metals, etc	Machinery, transport & equipment	Others & repairs
Bombay-Pune	857	5	30	—	5	7	1	12	3	10	18	9
Bombay	*662*	*5*	*30*	—	*5*	*7*	*1*	*12*	*2*	*11*	*17*	*9*
Ahmadabad-Vadodara*	450	14	32	—	7	5	2	5	6	5	6	14
Ahmadabad	*126*	*7*	*45*	—	*7*	*4*	*1*	*3*	*4*	*6*	*9*	*9*
Hooghlyside	921	10	8	13	6	7	3	8	7	10	20	8
Calcutta	*319*	*34*	*1*	*2*	*7*	*14*	*4*	*11*	*4*	*8*	*24*	*13*
Damodar etc†	267	24	3	.1	4	12	.2	7	18	20	8	10
N. Tamilnadu‡	238	16	14	—	6	9	4	7	6	8	12	17
Madras	*93*	*4*	*10*	—	*8*	*14*	*1*	*6*	*1*	*10*	*21*	*18*
Coimbatore-Salem	243	15	45	—	9	4	.4	2	3	4	5	13
S. Tamilnadu§	290	20	23	—	9	8	.4	15	3	6	1	18
Kerala	480	39	10	—	16	8	.3	7	6	4	3	7
Cochin-Ernakulam	*65*	*26*	*7*	—	*12*	*9*	*.5*	*12*	*5*	*7*	*9*	*11*
Bangalore	173	6	21	—	5	5	.5	5	4	4	45	6
Hyderabad	70	13	2	—	7	11	1	17	5	7	21	16
Kanpur	112	10	41	3	6	4	7	4	1	6	12	6

Source: Census of India, 1971: Establishment Tables Part III B (for each state). These figures differ from those in the General Population Tables used for Table 11.1. The latter are derived from the replies of individuals to the enumerators' questions. The Establishment Tables analyse the more or less full-time workforce. A very large number of casual workers are excluded from the tables.

* Includes the seven districts Mehesna, Ahmadabad, Kheda, Vadodara, Baruch, Surat and Valsad.

† Includes ten districts: Hazaribagh, Ranchi, Dhanbad, and Singhbhum (Bihar), Purulia, Burdwan, Bankura, Midnapore and Birbhum (West Bengal), and Sundargarh (Orissa).

‡ Includes four districts: Madras, Chingleput, North and South Arcot.

§ Includes six districts: Madurai, Tiruchirapalli, Thanjavur, Ramanathapuram Tirunelveli, and Kanyakumari.

of entry for the ruling British, and naturally became early the focus of India-based textile manufacture, in which Pune had a share. Fuel and power have always been a problem so far from the coalfields but the foresight, energy and capital of the Parsee family of Tata promoted development of hydro-electricity, exploiting the steep Western Ghats slope. It was a shrewd locational decision that put India's first nuclear power station at Tarapur, near Bombay to serve this concentrated demand for power. As the port most accessible from the Middle East, Bombay has two petroleum refineries, providing the materials for the petro-chemical and plastics industries as a by-product. Many branches of the rubber industry are represented in both Bombay and Pune, as are paper-making, precision instrument and radio-manufacture (e.g. Phillips India in Pune and Murphy India in Bombay).

Ahmadabad–Vadodara (Baroda)

This is a more nearly mono-industrial textile region around the head of the Gulf of Cambay. The smoke stacks on Ahmadabad's skyline are reminiscent of prints of nineteenth century industrial Lancashire. The region as a whole had 32 per cent of its full-time workers in textiles in 1971, and Ahmadabad 45 per cent (see Table 11.4). There has been considerable diversification since 1960, when three quarters of the workforce were in textiles. The initiation of petroleum refining at Koyali (using local oil) has stimulated the petro-chemical industry, while at Vadodara textile-related chemicals, including chlorine and caustic soda, are made, as well as more traditional fine pottery.

Hooghlyside Conurbation

This, with Calcutta as its focus, is separated by barely 110 km of paddy fields from the coalmines of the Damodar Valley (see Figure 11.6). Together they may be considered an economic entity, Calcutta depending a good deal on the power resources and semi-manufactured raw materials of the Damodar, which however has links to industrial foci throughout the country on account of its dominance in coal-mining. The map shows the salient features of the Damodar basin which debouches below Durgapur onto the low flood-plains west of the Hooghly. The Damodar River and its principal tributaries the Bokaro, Konar and Barakar have been brought under control since independence to reduce flooding, produce power, and provide irrigation for the floodplains, and water for industry. The hydroelectric stations are now overshadowed by production in the thermal stations along the coalfield, and now can most effectively be used to provide additional power to meet peak loads four hours daily, the base load being maintained by the thermal stations. The hydroelectric stations are at Tilaiya (4 MW) in the headwaters of the Barakar, Maithon (60 MW) near this river's confluence with the Damodar, and Panchet (40 MW) downstream. The Konar Dam is a flood-regulator and reservoir for industry. The rapid industrial development of this and the Hooghlyside regions has kept the demand for power ahead of capacity to supply, and has led to the siting of several large thermal stations along the valley, utilizing local coal as fuel and the river waters for cooling purposes; similarly the iron and steel plants. The power stations and their installed capacity are shown in Figure 11.6. The Durgapur stations were designed to utilize waste gases from the coke-ovens at the steel works; that at Chandrapura supplies power for the electrified line from Calcutta to Bhilai. A pipeline carries surplus gas from the steel works to Calcutta.

Understandably, industrial demands take precedence over irrigation in the disposal of available water, and the farmers wishing to cultivate rabi crops in the area theoretically commanded by the Durgapur Barrage would do well to investigate groundwater resources, and not expect any appreciable and reliable surplus to industrial needs to be forthcoming during the dry season. The Durgapur Barrage and its canals were designed to irrigate 405,000 ha, three-quarters through the left bank canal, the rest on the right bank. In addition it has to maintain the water level in the navigation canal that links it with Calcutta, at Kanchrapara at the northern end of the conurbation. It is designed to carry two million tonnes of coal annually in 200-tonne barges. Twenty-three locks each capable of taking a tug with two barges are needed to control the descent from Durgapur to the Hooghly, but it is claimed that the journey can be done in forty hours.

The major features of the iron and steel industry in the Damodar and adjacent areas have already been described. An important ancillary industry is making refractory bricks for furnaces, found at Dhanbad and Burdwan, using local clays from the Gondwana series. The fertilizer industry has developed at Sindhri using naptha, a by-product of the coke-ovens, as feed-stock, with coal-based electricity. Super-phosphate manufacture is also located here. Purulia and Muri, south of Bokaro, process bauxite from Lohardaga west of Ranchi, sending the alumina to Sambalpur at the Hirakud Dam in Orissa and the Alwaye in Kerala for electrolytic reduction using hydel power. Dhanbad refines lead and zinc and is a centre for toolmaking and radio industries. Heavy engineering is strongly represented in the railway locomotive works at Chittaranjan, at Jamshedpur where rolling stock are made, the Durgapur plants for constructional steel and mining machinery, and the heavy cable works at Rupnaraianpur, a list far from exclusive. The overall industrial mix may be gauged from Table 11.4.

To the visitor to India from an industrialized country, the visual impression of the Damodar Valley is at once familiar yet bizarre. Pit-head gear rises from the paddy fields; aerial ropeways sweep across the countryside to bring sand from the Damodar's bed for stowing in the mines to minimize subsidence and fire due to spontaneous combustion; sari-clad women are seen at work around the pit-head, pushing trolleys of pit-props, or at sidings head-loading baskets of coal into railway trucks; in open-cast coal workings grass-thatched bamboo huts serve as offices and workmen's shelters, only explosives meriting brick stores in such a transient landscape. Modernization progresses, and efficient mechanical loading is seen at some mines, and neat rows of miners' cottages and houses for the executives, some flat-roofed and maybe topped with a stack of rice straw to feed the family cow. Casual labourers, especially common in the open-cast section of the coal mining industry, fare less well as squatter settlers in simple shacks of matting, mud, wood, bamboo and straw erected on some patch of as yet unclaimed land, the familiar home of the newcomer in search of work in each and every urbanizing centre in India.

As far as industry is concerned, Calcutta and Hooghlyside is a huge sprawling mass of well over one million workers, and untold numbers of seekers after even part-time menial jobs for whatever pittance may postpone starvation for another day. Industrially Calcutta owes its origins to being the port accessible to sea-going vessels on the Hooghly, which gave access to the Ganga. Early Calcutta could tap the wealth of the whole Ganga valley as far as Delhi, the Moghul capital, when European traders were seeking to exploit the possibilities of India. The French established their 'factories' at Chandernagore, the English at Calcutta, thus laying the foundations for India's mercantile capital. When the British became rulers of India, Calcutta was their capital, until in 1912 this was moved to Delhi. Commerce bred industry, for long dominated by the manufacture of jute goods, using raw material brought in by country boats and dumb barges from areas in East Bengal now in Bangladesh. The industry survived partition from its material base by turning to domestic sources and remains strung out along both banks of the Hooghly and in sites a little back from the river. Its viability is at present seriously in doubt through the strong competition from Bangladesh and from synthetic substitutes. The engineering trades are important also, more important in fact nowadays, though their preeminence in India is being challenged by Calcutta's rival, Bombay. Machinery for factories, air-conditioners, typewriters and radios are specialities.

It is pointless to catalogue every industry, even if statistics were available to make this possible. If one extends the concept of the Hooghlyside region to include its new out-port of Haldia with its petroleum refinery, the industrial mix contains as many ingredients as Bombay's, with the addition of jute, and a lesser concentration on cotton textiles. It will be seen from Table 11.4 that Calcutta itself accounts for about a third of the conurbation's workforce. It is more strongly oriented to engineering and less towards textiles than in Hooghlyside as a whole. Its reputation for labour troubles (in 1969, 10 million man-days were lost, out of India's total of 18 million) had greatly diminished by 1972 (4.4 million out of 14 million total), However, it is recognized that West Bengal's political instability in the past, together with its proximity to the international border, not always with a friendly neighbour, have been factors influencing private investment and public sector industry to prefer Bombay, or to locate in the developing cities of the Peninsula. The urban character of the conurbation is considered further below.

Coimbatore–Salem and Southern Tamilnadu

The industrial clusters of India southwards from Bangalore contain almost one fifth of the industrial population. There are some important nodes of sophisticated modern industry as at Bangalore, Madras and Cochin where various branches of engineering prosper, but in general the familiar dominance of the cotton textile mills persists. This is particularly true of the Coimbatore-Salem and Southern Tamilnadu regions, industrial amalgams of several distinct and well-separated towns. The characteristic industrial mix is that of Coimbatore which has steel re-rolling, boiler-making, paper, batteries, electrical heat exchangers, compressors, printing, tool-forging, paints, instrument-making and so on, strung out along its approach roads, seemingly inaccessible to labour. Madras with its immediate hinterland has lagged somewhat in comparison with its port rivals, Bombay and Calcutta, largely on account of its lesser importance in British India. The development of the Neyveli lignite as a source of power, the establishment of an oil refinery and of a nuclear power station, and its selection as the location of several vehicle industries, and the making of film and of films for the Tamil speakers augurs well for Madras's future, though its somewhat eccentric position in a fairly urbanized state suggests that it is unlikely ever to eclipse the totality of its subordinate cities. The printing trades account for the high percentage in the wood, paper and printing category (Table 11.4).

Kerala

Apart from Cochin and its twin town Ernakulam, Kerala is employed industrially in processing its plantation and agricultural products: tea, coconuts for oil and coir fibre, cashew nuts from home and abroad, coffee, rubber, tapioca and rice. Fishing provides another resource for freezing prawns and canning sardines and tuna for export. Timber-working for veneers and plywood, and timber-based rayon and paper-pulp industries draw heavily on forests, which are in danger of being over-cut. Cochin, one of India's finest harbours and a major port, has a new ship-building yard, petroleum refinery, chemical and soap manufacturing, and is likely to provide industrial leadership in a state that badly needs to develop factory employment to absorb its excess population. With the completion of the Idikki hydel scheme, Kerala will have power in abundance. Conversion of metre gauge sections of rail to broad gauge, with an extension into Southern Tamilnadu, should reduce the region's sense of isolation from the mainstream of Indian development.

Bangalore

In part because of its equable climate at 900 m, this has become a centre of specialized engineering. The aircraft industry has its main plant here, and other public sector enterprises include telephones, watches, radios and television sets, transformer equipment, machine tools and soap. There are several textile mills, but their former predominance is giving way to more highly skilled occupations.

Hyderabad

Industrial development at this, the most isolated of India's millionaire cities, has been encouraged by locating key public sector plants there to make cables and heavy electrical equipment, precision bearings, machine tools and electronic equipment, a mixture not unlike Bangalore's.

Delhi

As the nation's capital, the city has attracted considerable industrialization. Its region as here defined includes the neighbouring districts of Meerut and Gurdaspur, the former an industrial city in its own right. Engineering has overtaken the textile trades as the main employer but the total picture is one of diversification (Table 11.2).

Kanpur

Set in the middle of UP, this is still very much a mill town making cotton and woollen goods. It has the highest proportion of workers in leather of any large centre, a relic from its past as a provider of military equipment for the British. Although it has plants dealing in chemicals, rubber, paint,

67 Hyderabad street scene looking down from the Charminar: open fronted shops and street vendors. A Hindu temple tops the roof to the left of the Muslim style arch-way.

68 Young wool carpet weaver under instruction, Eluru, Andhra Pradesh. The wools are natural colours.

metal castings etc., it appears relatively weak in the kinds of industry that go with modernity, a fact of concern to the economic planners (Table 11.4).

Punjab-Haryana

By contrast the group of towns in the piedmont of Punjab-Haryana have more than their proportionate share of light engineering industries. The concentration of sewing-machine and bicycle manufacture at Ludhiana is an interesting case of human 'transplantation' stimulating enterprise, the entrepreneurs being refugees from the Pakistan Punjab. Amritsar is an old textile city in wool as well as cotton, befitting this northern latitude. Engineering trades to serve the advanced agricultural technology of the region are in evidence, including tractor manufacture (see Table 11.2).

CONCLUSION

India can thus be seen as an awakening industrial giant of great potential. Actual development is of no small order. As in agriculture much inefficient traditional manufacturing persists, but however hard the political sentimentalists strive to save and even to recreate the village crafts, most of these are inevitably going to be replaced by modern economically competitive industry. If household industry is to survive it will probably be in a reorganized system of domestic outworking integrated with small-scale modern industry. For the latter there is a promising future as the huge market represented by India's 600 million consumers improves its purchasing power, at present at a dismally low level. While much household industry is anachronistic, small-scale modern industry can hold its own against larger scale enterprise in many fields, as is exemplified widely in the most highly developed countries in the western world.

To a large degree the smaller-scale industries exist to serve local demand at village and district town level, and show no strong regional specialization. The case of large-scale organized industry is quite different, with localized raw materials often exerting a strong influence on factory location while markets tend to be of national scale. However some strong regional patterns of industrialization are already apparent, with the multi-millionaire cities of Bombay and the Calcutta-Hooghlyside conurbation sharing leadership through sheer concentration of the industrial workforce. Some sixteen industrial nodes distributed widely throughout India can be identified each with more than one per cent of the country's 11.6 million workers in manufacturing and mining.

CHAPTER TWELVE

POPULATION DISTRIBUTION, URBANIZATION AND URBAN GROWTH

SUMMARY

India's population is predominantly rural. The proportion living in towns has increased slowly to 20 per cent, but the absolute growth in urban population is substantial, over 30 million between 1961–71, a percentage increase of 3.8 per cent per year compared with 2.5 per cent for the nation as a whole. High density of population is related to agriculturally productive or highly urbanized areas. High levels of population growth occur where developments have taken place in irrigation, industrialization and refugee resettlement; less than average growth is an indicator of economic stagnation, over-population and under-urbanization.

The major cities are seen to be distributed along growth corridors linking the four long-established metropolitan centres of Bombay, Calcutta, Delhi and Madras, three of them being leading ports. Railways have been the main mode of internal communication, but roads and air services increasingly strengthen the basic network.

POPULATION DISTRIBUTION

India is still a land of villages; the expectation that the arrival of the industrial revolution might herald a period of rapid urbanization has yet to be realized. Urbanization is the process of change towards an urban bias in the rural: urban population ratio; it is at once a dynamic term and a static term meaning the percentage living in towns. The level of urbanization has crept upwards only slowly. It took twenty years, from 1911 to 1931, to increase from 10 to 12 per cent of the total population, and another 20 years to reach 17.6 per cent at the 1951 census immediately following independence. The level of urbanization has moved to 19.9 per cent (a far cry from the 86 per cent of Australia for example, another country with an economy strongly rooted in the land). Behind the modest percentage increase in urbanization lies the addition of nearly 46 million people to the urban total since 1951, much of it clearly due to the natural increase of the urban population. Urban growth has certainly been happening on a grand scale, but urbanization in the dynamic sense is only partly responsible. Of nearly 100 cities with over 100,000 population in 1971 one third grew at the same or lower rate than the population of India as a whole in each intercensal decade (1951–61 and 1961–71).

The patterns of overall population density (see Figure 12.1) and of urbanization (see Figure 12.2) are inter-related in an interesting way. Granted that agriculture is the mainstay of the rural population and the predominance of that population in the total, high densities of the latter reflect productive alluvial soils and humid climate (over 1000 mm rainfall), with or without supplementary irrigation. Thus one can explain the high densities in a belt extending from eastern Uttar Pradesh, through Bihar, rural West Bengal, the Assam Valley and the Kerala coast. Urbanization is rarely at above average throughout this area. The upper Ganga plain in western UP and the Indus plains in Punjab-Haryana have similarly high to very high densities in part based on rich irrigated agriculture, in part by above average urbanizm. The remainder of the Peninsula coastlands, extending inland in the south to cover all Tamilnadu, are less well watered by rainfall than the northeastern portion, but intensive irrigation

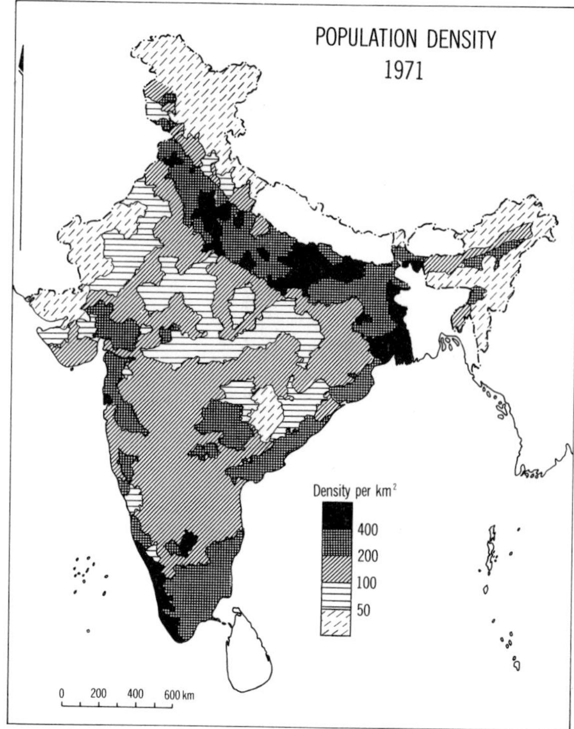

FIG. 12.1

in places, and in some a high degree of industrial urbanizm or a combination of both, results in high population densities overall, from Vishakhapatnam port through the Andhra deltas, Tamilnadu and the coastal belt from Bombay north into Gujarat. (For crop associations, cropping and irrigation intensity see Figures 7.12, 7.13 and 7.14 on pages 115 and 116.) In the interior large urban centres at Indore, Hyderabad and Bangalore account for the high densities of their districts which could otherwise support only modest populations.

At the other extreme, low over-all densities correlate with low levels of urbanization in the hilly and inaccessible areas of the Himalaya, the North-eastern Hills, the Bastar Plateau and the hills of Orissa, where conditions favour neither agricultural nor urban concentration. Figure 12.3 showing the areas more than ten kilometres from a road indicates the inaccessibility of the mountain and hilly regions. Through central India into Rajasthan and Kutch low population density usually coincides with poor plateaux, rocky ranges or desert, all inimical to productive agriculture. The pattern of

FIG. 12.2

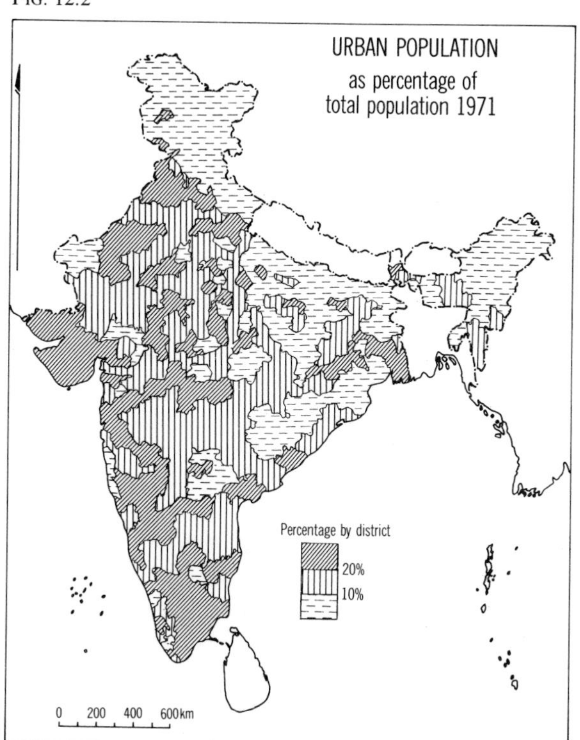

FIG. 12.3

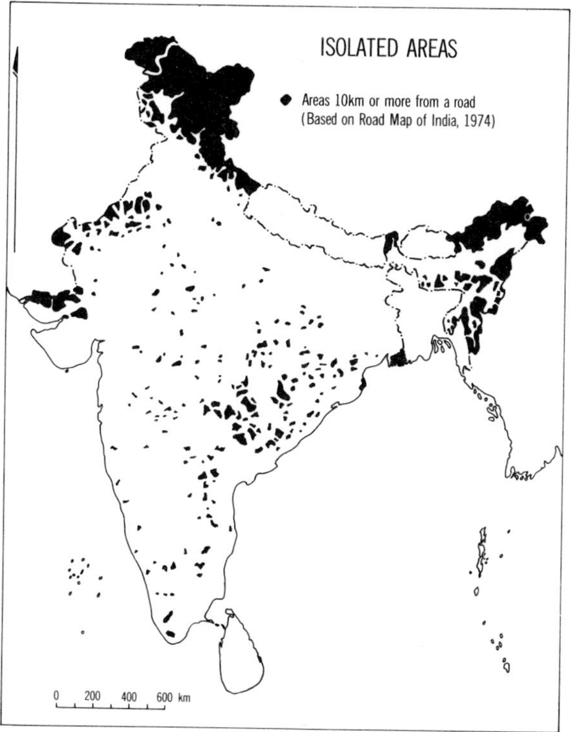

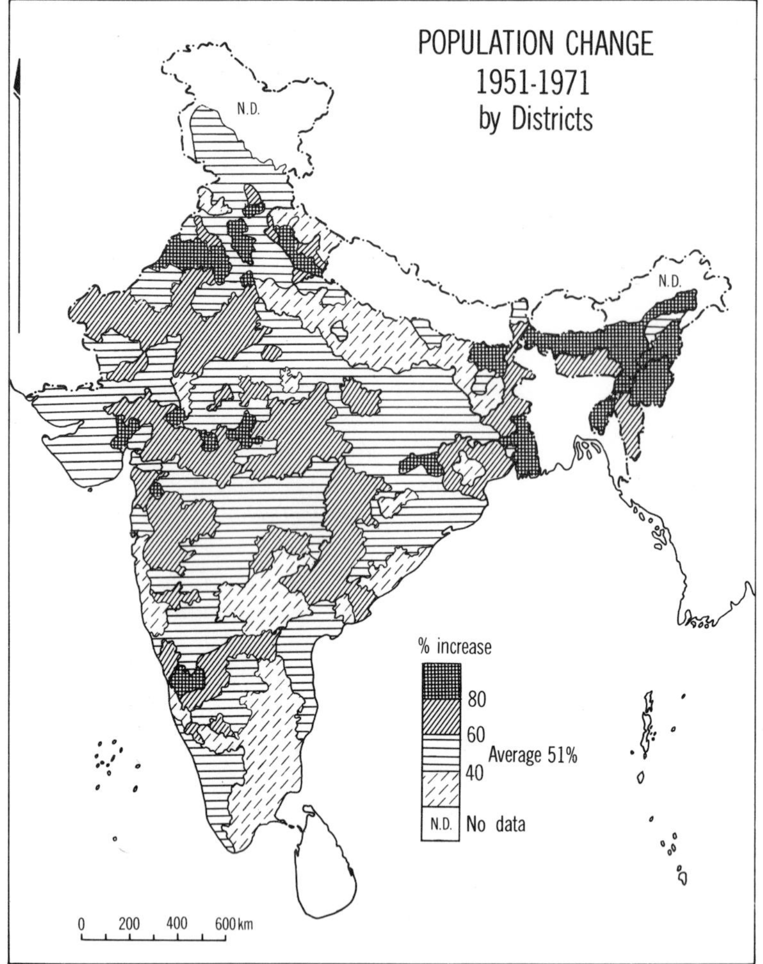

Fig. 12.4

urbanization is less consistent with these physically based criteria. In the case of many districts there is a correspondence of low over-all density with low percentages of urban population, but several instances of high urbanization also occur. The latter is an outstanding characteristic of Gujarat at all levels of population density, and the explanation of this phenomenon probably holds for most of central India also. Before independence these areas were broken up among a large number of princely states of varying size, each with its own capital where the raja held court and centralized his administration and much of whatever development took place in industry, commerce, and education. Once established, centres like this tend to be self-perpetuating despite the changing administrative structure and the loss of princely patronage. Urbanization in the desert areas of Rajasthan and Kutch may be explained similarly, but an additional factor here is the mode of life, part nomadic and pastoral, part extensive and very seasonal dry farming. A lower premium is placed on close permanent rural settlement, which encourages urban clustering for mutual protection from marauders in the past and from the unfriendly elements, and for commerce and the generation of supplementary or alternative means of livelihood to those available in the dry zone.

Between the extremes may be noted the large tracts of the Peninsula whether on the Deccan Lavas or on the ancient rocks of the Shield, which support around average densities, high as they may well be in relation to the resource base. Urbanization here tends also to range within the middle tertile of values (10–19 per cent) which lies below the nation average. Notable exceptions occur in the highly urbanized zone along the Bombay-Calcutta corridor, of which more is said below.

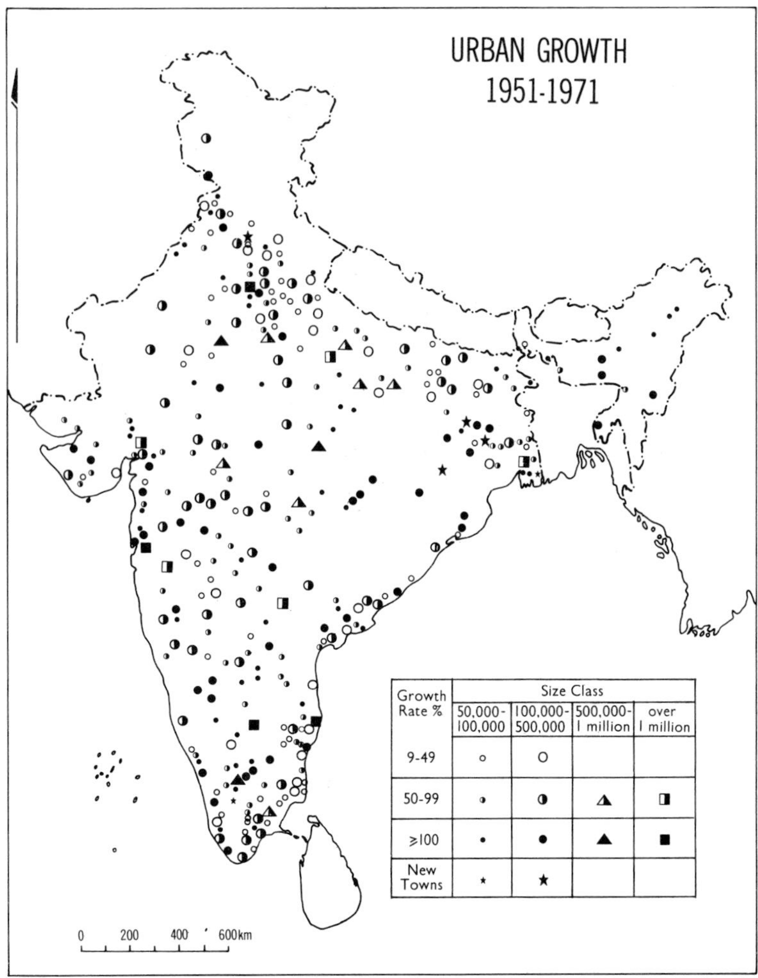

FIG. 12.5

POPULATION CHANGE

The three decennial censuses held since independence allow one to take a twenty-year perspective of population change. The pattern of overall change by districts is mapped in Figure 12.4 and that of the growth of individual urban centres in Figure 12.5. Between 1951 and 1971 the population increased by 51 per cent, and the urban total by 73 per cent. Areas of very high rates of total population increase (over 80 per cent) occur in several regions and for quite different reasons. In Haryana-Rajasthan formerly sparsely inhabited semi-desert has been opened up to agricultural settlement by the introduction of irrigation schemes commanded by the Bhakra-Nangal and related projects. Other areas of very high increase in the northwest, including parts of Haryana and the Nainital-Rampur districts in the UP *terai* have received as colonists refugees from Pakistan, and this explanation holds good also for much of the increase in the Assam Valley and the mainly rural districts of central and north West Bengal. The extension of similarly high rates into the Northeastern Hill states is due rather to deliberate efforts by Central Government to develop the economic and administrative infrastructure of this strategically sensitive area. Elsewhere very high increases are related in the main to urban-industrial growth: thus Delhi, the Hooghlyside conurbation, the steel-based complexes of Rourkhela in northern Orissa and Bhadravati in central Karnataka, Ahmadabad, Indore and Bhopal. Growth in Banswara in the extreme south of Rajasthan may be linked to irrigation developments on the Mahi River, but that in The Dangs, a tribal hill district on the Gujarat-Maharashtra border defies specific explanation.

69 Migrating Rajasthanis in the north of Andhra Pradesh far from home. Beds, babies and cooking pots atop the camel with grandfather in charge. The younger men were herding their flocks of sheep miles along the road, earning their income from manuring farmers' fields. The family's main resource is their flock, though they may be able to get casual carrying work using their camels.

Many of the more general areas of high increase merely extend from the cores already discussed. In many other cases industrial urbanization with its spread effects into urban services and the agriculture of the surrounding district is a clear cause of differential growth. Dehra Dun (UP), Bhatinda (Punjab), Vadodara and Surat (Gujarat), Sagar, Jabalpur and Khandwa (Madhya Pradesh), Nasik and Pune (Maharashtra) and Singhbhum (Bihar) are cases in point. Often, however, it can only be assumed that a happy combination of factors favourable to population growth is present. Extremes are always easier to explain than the nearer-to-average situations.

When one examines the areas of lower-than-average increase it must be remembered that most districts at this level have increased more than 30 per cent in 20 years. In predominantly agricultural communities outside of South Asia such a rate of population increase might be considered a major challenge to the absorptive capacity of the economy. In India such areas are over-shadowed. Some problem regions are pointed up by the low categories in Figure 12.4, notably a great deal of the Ganga Plain in Uttar Pradesh and Bihar. Reference to the maps of population density and urbanization will show that this region is under-urbanized and over-saturated with people. No doubt some of the surplus migrates to seek a livelihood in Calcutta and elsewhere. Tamilnadu and the extension northwards into the drought-prone areas of Kolar, Chittor and central Andhra, are in similar straits, unable to absorb their full share of population increase. For some of these tracts irrigation and power developments now in progress may reverse the trend in the current decade, but the 1981 census will demonstrate how far the 'saturation' effect will spread to areas lacking modern development and devoid of potential, forcing their unemployed to move to the distant centres and corridors of economic growth.

It should be noted that in a study taking the 20-year period as a whole, the impact of development in the later decade may well not have made itself apparent. The population change in the decade 1961–71 may be used to check this to some extent. In that decade increase ran at almost 25 per cent, and districts with over 35 per cent may be taken as in the very high category. Only four districts would have to be added to those already mapped as having an increase of over 60 per cent in the double decade (Figure 12.4). These are Jammu, of great strategic importance on the western frontier and on one of the gateways to the Vale of Kashmir; Kota, the rapidly industrializing district in the Chambal Valley of Rajasthan with hydel and nuclear power stations in the vicinity; Thana well within commuting distance of Greater Bombay; and Hyderabad which in this second decade has been reaping the benefits of industrialization.[1]

[1] For studies of change in the separate decades see G. S. Gosal's two papers: 'Regional Aspects of Population Growth in India', 1951–61', *Pacific Viewpoint*, 3, 1962 pp. 87–99, and 'Population Growth in India, 1961–1971: a Spatial Perspective', *Asian Profile*, 2, 1974, pp. 193–212.

URBAN GROWTH

Figure 12.5 shows the growth characteristics and present size of each urban centre of over 50,000 population in 1971 and covers two thirds of the total urban population. With this increasing at 73 per cent in the double decade, the three categories of growth rate used correspond to low, average and high levels of growth.

From the Census of 1961 the definition of what constituted an urban settlement was clarified as the previous practice of leaving it to the discretion of local authorities led to considerable divergence between states. Now all places that are incorporated as municipalities, corporations, cantonments or town areas are automatically urban, together with all other places satisfying the following three conditions: over 5,000 population, at least 75 per cent of the male working population in non-agricultural occupations, and a density of at least 400 per km^2. This sharpening of the definition 'de-urbanized' a great number of the smaller places regarded as urban in 1951, with the result that there was an apparent fall of 30 per cent in the population in towns in the range 5–10,000 and of 62 per cent in that of towns of less than 5,000 between 1951 and 1961.

In the inter-censal decade from 1961, the overall growth rate for the urban population was 38 per cent, but this was exceeded only in the town classes of over 50,000 population (see Table 12.1).

Growth in the millionaire section of Class I was at the national urban average of 38 per cent, but this obscures the fact that only two of the nine cities, Calcutta and Kanpur were below this level, Bangalore equalled it, and the remaining six bettered it, Delhi and Madras quite substantially, as Table 12.2 shows.

TABLE 12.2

Millionaire Cities: 1971 population and growth rate (%)

Delhi	3,647,023 (55)
Calcutta	7,031,000 (20)
Bombay	5.971,000 (44)
Madras	3,170,000 (63)
Hyderabad	1,796,000 (44)
Ahmadabad	1,742,000 (44)
Bangalore	1,654,000 (38)
Kanpur	1,275,000 (31)
Pune	1,135,000 (44)

In the middle group of Class I, the ten semi-millionaire cities have as a body a slower growth rate, 31 per cent, than the national average: Nagpur (35), Indore (45), Jabalpur (46) and Jaipur (52) exceed the mean for the group, while Varanasi and Allahabad, with 19 per cent are at the bottom of the table; Coimbatore (23), Agra (25), Lucknow (26), and Madurai (29) are strung out in between. The vitality of the smaller cities in this class, with 100,000–499,999 inhabitants, is remarkable by contrast. As a group they have increased their population by 69 per cent, but growth has been strongest among those in the upper half of the size range. Thus among towns between 250,000 and 499,999, 65 per cent had a growth rate of over the national average of 38 per cent, while in the lower half only 36 per cent exceeded that figure.

TABLE 12.1

Growth of Urban Population 1961–71

Class	*No. of towns*	*Urban popn. 1971 (million)*	*Per cent of total urban*	*Growth 1961–1971 (million)*	*Growth 1961–1971 (%)*
Total	**2641**	**109.10**	**100**	**30.16**	**38**
Class I	147	61.09	56	20.10	49
Over 1 M.	*9*	*27.42*	*25*	*7.54*	*38*
500,000–999,999	*10*	*6.43*	*6*	*1.52*	*31*
100,000–499,999	*128*	*27.24*	*25*	*11.14*	*69*
Class II, 50,000–99,999	185	12.00	11	3.95	41
Class III, 20,000–49,999	583	17.46	16	3.93	29
Class IV, 10,000–19,999	874	12,000	11	2.55	27
Classes V and VI, less than 10,000	852	6.56	6	0.15	2.3

Sources: Census of India, Census Centenary 1972: Population Statistics; and Paper I of 1971 Supplement.

70 Orissan tribal folk at a periodic market near Potthangi Korapet.

The Class II towns more than held their own but those in Classes III to VI could not maintain the national level. This supports a subjective impression that urbanization involving the attraction of population towards modern style development is a negligible process in towns below 50,000, and becomes really effective in the Class I towns. The latter account for two thirds of the urban growth, more than half of it in the section below 500,000, and most of the rest among the millionaires. The relative stagnation of most of the cities in the middle range of Class I is significant. The most vigorous expansion here is in a new state capital, Jaipur, and the other two cities exceeding the average, Indore and Jabalpur, are centres of engineering. The laggard five are mostly ancient cities dominated by the textile industry and traditional trades; three of them are in Uttar Pradesh.

The distribution of urban centres can be resolved into a basic pattern of corridors following trunk broad gauge railway routes, with a number of clusters reflecting regional resource development or past political factors. The system of corridors is presented diagramatically in Figure 12.6. The concept of growth corridors as applied to India is derived from a Russian interpretation of the structure of the Indian economy based on 1951–61 developments. The fundamental soundness of the concept is borne out in the decade that followed,[1] though its value is more as a mental construct for organizing data than for anything more profound.

India now has at least nine 'millionaire cities'. Four of the nine millionaire metropolitan centres form the basic pivots to the urban network: Delhi, Bombay, Calcutta and Madras. Two others, Kanpur and Pune, lie within corridors linking the main pivots. Ahmadabad lies at the hub of a cluster of towns that itself overlaps the Bombay-Delhi corridor. Only Hyderabad and Bangalore are outside the primary network.

In terms of developmental growth the Bombay-Calcutta corridor appears to show the most vigour. East of Nagpur (930,459) which by now has almost certainly joined the millionaires, and which with a medium growth rate lies close to mid-point in the corridor, very strong growth is associated with the outer bastions of India's metallurgical industrial complex in Durg-Bhilai-Raipur and Bilaspur. Further east Sambalpur, which is based on Hirakud hydel power, lies a little off the main corridor on a branch line carrying iron ore and surplus pig-iron and steel to the port city of Visakhapatnam. The main line continues through the steel towns of Rourkhela and Jamshedpur-Tatanagar

[1] Galina V. Sdasyuk, Urbanization and the Spatial Structure of Indian Economy, in A. Chandra Sekhar, Gen. Ed. *Economic and Socio-Cultural Dimensions of Regionalisation: an Indo-USSR Collaborative Study*, New Delhi, 1972.

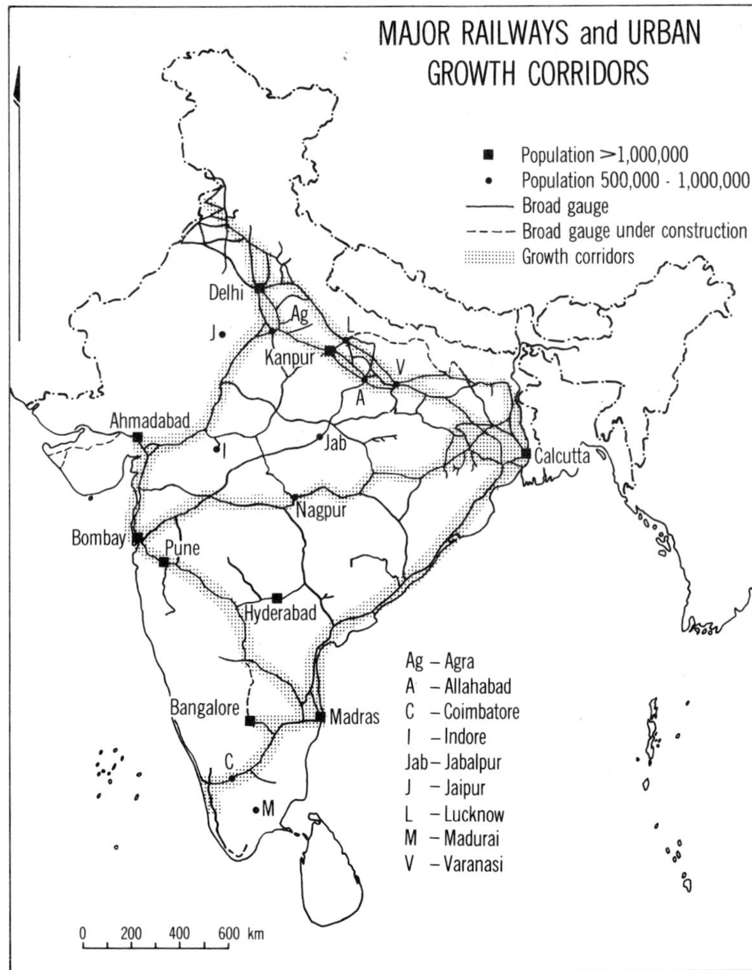

FIG. 12.6

into the Hooghlyside conurbation via Khargpur. Alternative routes form a web that ties the Damodar Valley towns, mostly showing fast growth, both to their ironfields south of Jamshedpur, and to the Calcutta region, thus broadening the corridor at this eastern end, so dominated by heavy industry of importance to the whole of India.

Nagpur, at the centre of the corridor joining the rivals for industrial and commercial primacy, provides a minor pivot at which lesser corridors tie in to Delhi, Hyderabad and Madras. As an important node in the road network also, Nagpur is likely to develop very strongly in future. To its west, five towns of third rank (100,000–500,000, Class I in the Census definition) are strung along the line to Bombay as it crosses the Kandesh Deccan, and three others with more purely local functions lie a little off the corridor. Most have average growth rates, while at the approaches to Bombay, as around Calcutta, fast-growing commuter satellites are typical.

By far the oldest urban corridor in the whole sub-continent follows the Grand Trunk Road the length of the Indo-Gangetic Plain, a line now paralleled closely by railways. The route is studded with historic cities: Varanasi (606,721) the most holy city of the Hindus; Allahabad (513,036) a centre of pilgrimage for Muslim and Hindu; Agra (634,622) and Delhi, both great Moghul alternative capitals; Amritsar (458,029) sacred to the Sikhs. Lucknow (or Lakhnau, 813,982) on a branch of the Grand Trunk Road and an alternative railway route between Varanasi and Delhi, continues its traditional role as capital of the middle Ganga Plain, now covered by the state of Uttar Pradesh. On the more direct line from Allahabad to Agra,

Kanpur, brash and horribly industrial, has insinuated itself into this string of nobler beads. Between Calcutta and Delhi there is no city of first or second rank that has grown at better than middling rate, and outside Delhi's ring of satellites, only Aligarh in the third rank reaches the category of strong growth. This is true generally of the whole broad belt of the Ganga Plain through UP and Bihar, in which there are almost as many centres stagnating in the lowest bracket as there are in the middle growth bracket, yet another indicator of this region's economic backwardness and probably its senility.

North of Delhi the picture is more promising. Chandigarh as a new capital city for the Punjabis, Sikh and Hindu, has been the focus of a remarkable growth from nothing to 232,940 by 1971, no doubt diverting potential that might otherwise have gone into Ambala (102,493 and stagnating). Amritsar with sluggish growth suffers from its exposed position on the Pakistan border, though it is well placed on the Grand Trunk Road to exploit the flow of trade with India's neighbour. Indian films transmitted by Amritsar television are avidly picked up by the citizens of Lahore! By contrast with Amritsar, Jammu (164,253) displays strong population increase, compensating for its flank position on the border by commanding one of the gateways into the Vale of Kashmir, and controlling the Indian side of the cease-fire line in the sector south of the Pir Panjal Range. Towns a little back from the frontier have good records of growth. Ludhiana (401,176) grew by 59 per cent between 1951 and 1961, and again by 64 per cent in the following decade, to give an overall expansion of 160 per cent, largely attributable to refugee settlement and their subsequent vitality as entrepreneurs and parents. Jullundur (296,106) and Patiala (151,041) are in the middle range of growth. In so far as these cities lie on a corridor, it is partly an historic one pointing through Lahore to Peshawar and the Khyber Pass (and still well worn by international travellers entering India by land), but partly a strategic one directed through the piedmont belt towards Srinagar (423,253 and growing moderately). Within India, the Grand Trunk Road and its parallel railway remain major arteries of commerce and communication.

71 Traditional Gond musicians at a fair near Utnur, northern Andhra Pradesh.

The Delhi-Bombay corridor, bifurcating from the Delhi-Calcutta axis at Agra, is less clearly defined by urban development in the section traversing the Chambal Basin much of it semi-arid and rocky. However both Kota (212,991) which has experienced phenomenal growth at 227 per cent in the double decade, and Ratlam (119,247) in the middle growth range, demonstrate as railway junction towns, the value of nodality. Ratlam links westwards to Ahmadabad and the ports on the Rann of Kutch. At Vadodara (Baroda, 467,487) the corridor is reinforced by doubling, with the Ahmadabad-Bombay link through Surat (493,001) and the Bombay satellites.

A fourth corridor linking Bombay to Madras is clearly marked at its northern end by the satellite Thana (207,352) and by Pune, almost within the commuting range of wealthy businessmen. Pune, like Gulbarga (145,588) in northeastern Karnataka and several smaller towns along the line through the dry zone of southern Andhra, evidences average growth at best. The large city of Sholapur (398,361) is an example of the stultifying effect of over-dependence on the cotton mill textile industry which has held it to low level growth. When the metre-gauge line from Guntakal to Bangalore is converted to broad gauge, as planned, the latter city will be brought directly into the orbit of Bombay. At present its broad gauge link is with Madras, though it has a direct metre gauge line to Hyderabad through Guntakal, a relic of princely inter-communication. However the semi-arid rainshadow tracts between Pune and Madras are unlikely to stimulate much urbanization.

The last inter-metropolitan corridor runs along the east coast from Calcutta to Madras, fortuitously stringing together groups of cities and towns of quite independent development (in contrast to the historic interdependence of the cities along the Grand Trunk Road). Several of these were seaward-looking exporting towns in colonial times. The modern railway links the fast-growing twin towns of the Mahanadi delta, Cuttack (205,759) and Bhubaneshwar (105,491) through Berhampur (117,662 medium growth) to the fast-growing port of Vishakhapatnam (363,467), and to Vijayawada (344,607) and Guntur (269,991). Rajamundry (118,805) and Kakinada Port (164,200) on a short spur line with other centres of moderate growth in the Godavari-Krishna delta, are clearly within the influence of the corridor whose ties to the main network are further strengthened in this area by the line northwards through Warangal to Nagpur (and ultimately to Delhi) and westwards to Hyderabad-Secunderabad (and ultimately to Bombay). Southwards the route to Madras passes through the economically rather limited districts of Ongole and Nellore. That the line is now double-tracked or provided with alternative loop routes throughout its length from Calcutta to Madras is an indication of the growing importance of this eastern side of the Bombay-Calcutta-Madras triangle.

From Madras to the southwest, a major corridor, again a cul-de-sac like that northwards from Delhi, ties into the main network the vigorously growing chain of Tamilnad towns extending from Salem (416,440), through Erode (169,613) to Coimbatore (736,203) and beyond to Cochin-Ernakulam (439,066) on the Kerala coast. Northwards along the coast, a branch of the broad gauge runs through Calicut (333,979) to Karnataka's port Mangalore (215,122), soon to be more directly linked to plateau Karnataka through the spectacular metre gauge line up the escarpment of the Western Ghats to Hassan, and designed to carry iron ore exports. South of Cochin the broad gauge is being extended to replace the metre gauge up to Trivandrum and serve hitherto rail-less areas in the far south of Kerala and the Arabian Sea coast districts of Tamilnadu. Kerala's well-founded complaint of isolation will be met to some extent. It is significant, perhaps, that the clusters of cities in southern Tamilnadu centering on the temple city of Madurai (711,501) are served by a metre gauge system, their sole link to the broad gauge network being a spur line from Erode to Tiruchirapalli (464,624). Only one of the cluster of some 25 towns south of Pondicherry shows better than middle range growth, and several of the smaller rank appear to be more or less stagnating.

One corridor of towns characterized by medium to high growth rates runs south from Pune to Bangalore through Sangli (201,597), Kolhapur (267,513), Belgaum (213,872), Hubli-Dharwar (379,166), Davangere (121,110), with a branch to the steel town of Bhadravati (101,358). The broad gauge line terminates at Kolhapur, from which a metre gauge track continues the corridor south to Bangalore, but a fine highway provides an alternative and door-to-door service by heavy trucks, an increasing trend for all but the bulkiest commodities and the longest hauls. The group of Karnataka towns in the 'semi-Malnad' have all grown rapidly to create their own economic identity.

Within the Peninsula two minor corridors elaborate the network to link Hyderabad and Bombay. A short branch brings broadgauge traffic from Hyderabad to the Madras-Bombay main line at Wadi close to Gulbarga, while a longer metre gauge route to Manmad near Nasik on the Calcutta-Bombay line, is beaded with low ranking towns with strong to average growth rates.

72 Packing watches at a factory in Bangalore, Karnataka.

72 All the fun of the fair, near Utnur, northern Andhra Pradesh. Man power turns the wheel.

Break of gauge is a serious defect in the Indian railway system and appears to inhibit growth in towns on the subordinate network. The intergauge transfer of goods involves delays and expense, not to mention high rates of pilferage and spoilage. The stultifying effect on southern Tamilnadu has been mentioned. Part of the explanation of the backwardness of north Bihar and the Uttar Pradesh piedmont along the Nepal border is that these areas are served only by metre gauge lines. The broad gauge track has, no doubt for strategic reasons, been extended to Gauhati in the western end of the Assam Valley. From this terminus the old metre-gauge line wends its way up the valley to serve tea gardens and oil wells and refineries, though a pipeline has been laid to carry products westwards to Bihar. In this region rapid urban growth has occurred, despite the railway gauge, in response to colonization and an awareness of the need to strengthen the infrastructure of this strategic corner of the country.

Madhya Pradesh is a region traversed by railway routes as much constructed to link the major corridors and metropolitan centres as to carry the relatively small traffic generated locally. The inheritance of former princely state capitals and of some embryonic industrial centres of British military inception like Jabalpur (534,845) provides nodal cities such as Bhopal (384,859), Jhansi (198,135) and Ujjain (208,561) on broad gauge junctions, and Indore (560,936) and Gwalior (406,140) at a confluence of such lines with metre or narrower gauge tracks laid down by economically minded princes to serve their domains. Jabalpur and Bhopal, the latter selected to be the capital of Madhya Pradesh, have grown rapidly; Gwalior, Indore and Ujjain at medium pace.

A high level of urbanization has long been typical of desert Rajasthan and semi-arid western Gujarat. Jaipur (636,768) like most state capitals has enjoyed the brisk growth that comes with local primacy, and its attraction for tourists guarantees it a better place in the roadway and airline networks than it has on its metre gauge railway system. Further west, Bikaner (208,984) and Jodhpur (317,612), cities of medium growth, have nodal positions in the same system, which no doubt follows more ancient camel tracks searching out these urban oases. Growth at Udaipur in the south of Rajasthan has been boosted by the development of mineral wealth. Southwest of this, in the seemingly unpromising region of Kathiawar and Kutch, all towns but one show moderate growth or better, indicating economic vitality. The Rann of Kutch provides a deep water port closer to Delhi and the north than increasingly congested Bombay. The new free port at Kandla and the oil terminal at Satiya are served by broad gauge extension from Ahmadabad, and a pipe line under construction from the latter to Mathura, thus linking the region via Ratlam to the mainstream of the Bombay-Delhi corridor, which can be expected to develop even more strongly as a result.

Some idea of the relative strength of the links between the major cities forming the pivots of the corridors may be gauged from the air services that are provided. Indian Airlines operate planes with seating capacities ranging from 36 to 278, and the number of passengers journeys available per week is mapped in Figure 12.7. While Bombay and Delhi have the strongest link, and those between Bombay and Calcutta, and in the triangle Bombay-Hyderabad-Bangalore exceed 3000 seats per week, the ties joining Bombay-Madras, Delhi-Madras, and and Delhi-Calcutta are of a lower order, and that between Calcutta and Madras still weak. Pune

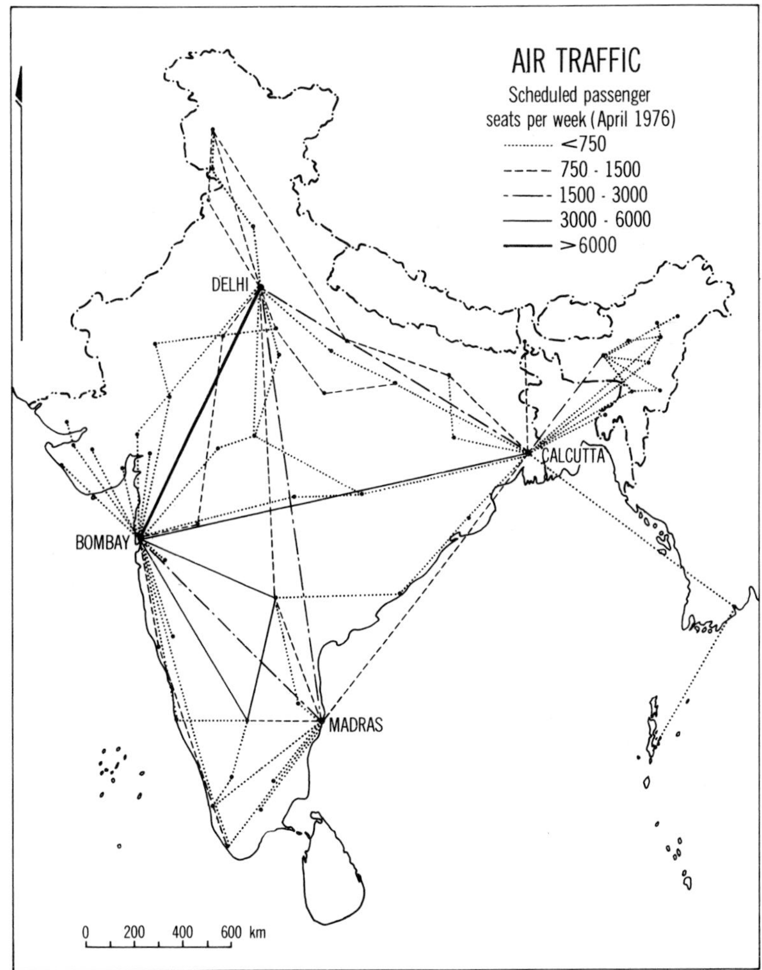

FIG. 12.7

and Ahmadabad look mainly to Bombay, while the millionaire city Kanpur rates a very lowly service to Delhi and indirectly to Calcutta. Some services are mainly for tourist traffic, hence the number into Agra and Jaipur, and the inclusion of Khajuraho, Aurangabad and Udaipur in the system. Airlines are clearly of great administrative and strategic value in the northeast and the northwest, in the latter case also serving the tourist trade into Srinagar. The more heavily patronized routes, however, are basically commerical and administrative, the line of division being difficult to draw in a country with so large a proportion of investment in the public sector.

The port function plays an important role in the development of several cities, old and new. Overseas trade is no less significant to the economy of independent India than it was to the Empire that preceded it. More than 45 per cent of India's total port traffic of 73.4 million tonnes (1974–75) passes through the ports of Bombay (24.5 per cent), Madras (10.9 per cent) and Calcutta (10.2 per cent), the three main outlets for British Indian trade. The former Portuguese port of Marmagao in Goa has 19.2 per cent of the traffic, a figure almost entirely due to the iron ore trade. This it shares with Vishakhapatam (9.8 per cent of total tonnage) and the new Orissan port of Paradip (3.5 per cent). Cochin, an expanding port city with historic links to Vasco da Gama, carrying 6.5 per cent and the new free port of Kandla on the Rann of Kutch (4.8 per cent) complete the tally of major ports which together account for 89 per cent of the total tonnage handled.

CHAPTER THIRTEEN

TOWNS AND CITIES

A SPATIAL MODEL OF THE STRUCTURE OF THE INDIAN CITY[1]

The model city (Figure 13.1) had its origins in the distant past, in its defensive site on a rocky prominence on the high bank of a perennially flowing river which assured its water supply. A mediaeval citadel crowned the highest point within one corner of the fortifications, wall and moat, that protected the city. Gates through the wall gave entry to roads converging on the city from the villages that dotted the surrounding countryside, at intervals of three kilometres or more. The hereditary ruler lived in the citadel palace surrounded by the homes of his kinsmen and other wealthy high caste landowners, rent-capitalists content to enjoy the income from their properties with little concern to invest in productive enterprise, other than the acquisition of more land. Close to this cluster of the élite, and just inside one of the gates was the market, part open space in which the villagers from outside would display their commodities for sale, part built-up with small shops around, in an area honeycombed with narrow alleys where craftsmen, merchants and shopkeepers lived and worked in quarters each characterized by its trade: weavers and tinsmiths, carpenters and tailors, money-lenders and grain sellers. Nearby was the Hindu temple with its ceremonial tank for ritual bathing. Separated from these caste-segregated Hindus and their temple were the Muslims, with their mosque nearby, engaged in their own crafts, with their own servicing trades and shops. Outside the gate lay the main settlement of the Harijans, the outcastes who performed all the menial and filthy tasks for the citizens: the sweepers, watercarriers, washermen. Again beyond the moat would be the temporary camps of migrant workers, assembled seasonally to harvest the crops, or perhaps to work as building labourers or load carriers in the town. It was a pedestrian city; only the wealthy would ride horseback or be drawn in a coach. The bullock carts that serviced the market would be unloaded outside the

FIG. 13.1

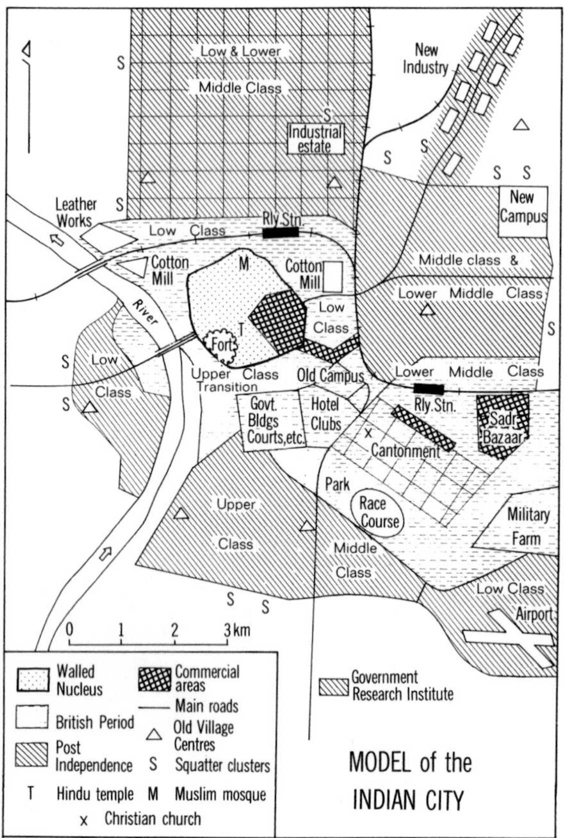

[1] An interesting fuller treatment of this topic is by Andrew Learmonth, 'Towards a spatial model of the South Asian City', in *The Process of Urbanization*, Open University, 1973. Figure 13.1. has its inspiration in a simpler version on the same theme by A. E. Smailes in 'The Indian City', *Geographische Zeitschrift*, 57, 1969, p. 180.

walls and the supplies head-loaded into the town. Human labour of this sort was cheaper than animal labour.

This Indian variant of the pre-industrial city of western Asia and Europe was what the British found when they arrived to establish their administration over the region, in the early nineteenth century. At a healthy distance and upstream from the city they built their permanent camp, the cantonment, laying it out in a grid pattern, with barrack blocks for the troops, bungalows for the officers, hospitals and parade grounds, and a military farm to provide fresh milk. The civilian administrators might be slightly segregated to the side of the cantonment nearest the city, with the courts, revenue offices and jail intervening. A circuit house for visiting officials, a hotel or two and maybe a racecourse provided some amenities, to which over time, English language schools and colleges were added. Here were trained the lower ranks of the administration selected from the youth of the better class indigenous citizens.

The cantonment had its own market in a more densely settled quarter, with a bazaar and clusters of tradesman, and its segregated areas in which lived the servants and menials for the community. The arrival of the railway set another feature in the townscape, skirting the cantonment and the city, with separate stations to serve each, and sidings for goods wagons to be unloaded into bullock carts for transfer to the wholesalers' godowns. Often the railway engineers and administrative staff were Anglo-Indians, the progeny of mixed marriages between British soldiers or junior clerks in business houses with Indian women. They constituted yet another segregated group on the railway side of the cantonment, in quarters provided for them by the railway company.

Towards the end of the nineteenth century factory industry appeared, first the cotton textile mill, located on the flank of the old Indian city now spreading its low class housing beyond the line of the walls, which have largely disappeared, to provide building materials, and giving way to much needed roads following the line of the moat around the city core. Other industries, like leather tanning near the river, and saw-milling near the railway began to process local products for domestic and overseas markets. Merchants built

74 Baskets for storing grain in the home for sale at a tribal periodic market, Potthangi near Korapet, Orissa.

75 Weighing sacks of oilseeds brought in to the tribal periodic market, Potthangi near Korapet, Orissa.

godowns as collecting and storage centres for cotton and oilseeds en route to Bombay or Madras for export.

As population grew the settlement gradually expanded, over-running and absorbing rural villages. The poor found sites in the flood plain across the bridge or out on the fringe of the city away from the cantonment sector. Among the upper class, the more westernized favoured the spacious sector nearest the cantonment, with its better urban amenities and services.

With independence the city perhaps receives a boost in an enhanced administrative role within a new state. Modernization and industrial expansion have been agents for rapid development. An airport has grown up on the site of a military landing ground beyond the cantonment; industrialists have bought up cheap land along the highways on the periphery, creating ribbons of factories, particularly on roads leading to metropolitan centres. The government has laid out an industrial estate on the periphery. Institutions like the University have been forced to relocate or to expand into a more extensive campus. All these moves cause the periphery constantly to expand. While the British have disappeared from the cantonment, their place has been taken by an Indian military élite hardly distinguishable in its life style from its predecessors. The civilian élite, many of them now thoroughly westernized, are no longer inhibited in their everyday life by caste or creed, and concentrate mainly in one sector. They have largely evacuated their ancestral home sites in the old city. These, and the older upper class residential areas outside the city core, near to the civil lines, have become a zone of transition to business houses. As in developed western countries, the upper middle class tends to be drawn into proximity with the élite, but among them, and to an even greater extent among the lower middle and lower classes generally, traditional ideas of segregation persist to some extent.

Government planning has determined suburban layouts in the extensive housing 'colonies' for the middle classes. The poorer groups of established workers and shopkeepers occupy densely populated quarters, some of them provided by government for their low ranking servants. The poorest of all, the latest arrivals in the city, in search of better employment than they can find in their overcrowded villages as landless labourers, camp on the fringe as squatters, constructing similar light frame shelters of grass thatch to those they customarily occupy as migrant agricultural workers. At every stage of the city's growth such squatter settlement has been found on the periphery and alongside any large construction site where they toil for daily wages. Occasionally the squatter settlement proves to be a transient feature, but often it consolidates its buildings into huts of mud or stone and becomes a permanent slum, poorly serviced, cheek by jowl with better class development, contributing to the patchiness of the residential pattern.

76 Cotton mills belching smoke over Bombay: workers walk to work.

In large measure the inner part of the city remains a pedestrian precinct within which a considerable number still live beside their work as craftsmen and petty shopkeepers and tradesmen, while others walk a short distance to work, few moving more than two kilometres. With greater affluence the journey to work becomes longer and the mode more motorized and increasingly individual. Buses carry the middle income groups distances generally in the 2–3 km range, while at higher salaries of Rs 750 per month, motor scooters and motor cycles take a share of the traffic. Cars are the preserve of the wealthy few who can choose where they like to live. Data based on a study of Bangalore is given below.

Thus modernization has altered the complexion of the city, patterning the new suburbs and industries more closely to their western counterparts as individual mobility increases, and as the traditional attitudes of caste give place to a socio-economic stratification of the community based on income. Yet many relict features of the old city remain in its form, and among the poor the limitations on their mobility and on the quality of their shelter are very real. In terms of classic urban theory, the élite live in sectors and select pockets, and the mass of the population show some zonal arrangement in relation to the old core, which is now as tightly settled as ever, but from which the élite have moved away. The very poor squatters tend to be in a peripheral zone, their former sites becoming,

77 Squatters hovels on the fringe of a new suburb of Agra, Uttar Pradesh; hand-made bricks and reed thatch. The ubiquitous charpoy serves as daytime settee and bed.

78 Goats and sheep for market, and a line of squatters' 'homes' in a Bombay street.

like former strand lines on the shores of a retreating sea, fossilized in permanent slums. Here and there throughout the modern city are found rural villages engulfed in its expansion, some even maintaining a semblance of their agricultural antecedents in their milking herds of cows and buffaloes, and in retaining some of the social mores of a village life style.

This model cannot match every Indian city by any means, though most of its elements are present in the larger urban centres. Not every city, particularly the smaller ones, had a military cantonment, though the layout of the areas of the civil administration under British rule was similar if less extensive. Even today government is a very important factor in the urban structure of most towns of over 100,000 population. Apart from its direct presence in administrative buildings government permeates many parts of the city, in the state owned railways, state road transport, state industrial undertakings, police, universities, etc., and in government housing for the associated staff.

An alternative model could have a coastal location with its port function as its initial *raison d'être*, though such cities date generally from the period of European contact. A modern city type not covered by such models is the predominantly mono-industrial town, of which Jamshedpur is the prime example, dating from before World War I.

EIGHT TOWNS AND CITIES

Eight towns and cities have been selected to portray the principal characteristics of the Indian city. Pilibhit and Kolhapur are typical of many small uncomplicated mono-nuclear towns, similar in many respects to the earlier stages of the model described above. Madurai is a rare example of a moderately large city in which the temple, as the focus of regional cultural associations, attracted urban growth, with defence and administration seemingly playing only minor roles. Four very different 'millionaire' cities are included. Bangalore is fairly representative of the smaller millionaire cities, an inland state capital with an impressive industrial development since independence. The others are the three largest multimillionaire metropolitan urban agglomerations: Delhi the historic and present capital, Bombay and Calcutta the twin primate port cities with contrasting situations, sites and functions. Chandigarh is added by way of postscript and pointer: an entirely new city built since independence and now joint capital of Punjab and Haryana.

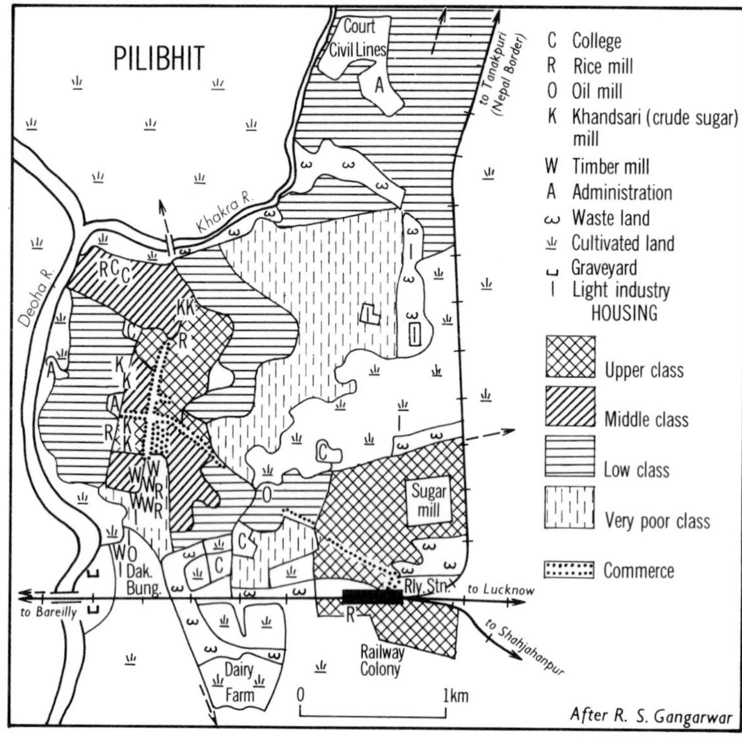

FIG. 13.2

Pilibhit

Pilibhit (see Figure 13.2) is a small district town in Uttar Pradesh, with a population of 63,273 in 1971, serving a district of three-quarters of a million people.[1] But for its railway junction and its role as administrative headquarters of a district Pilibhit would be little more than a local market town. Headquarter status ensures it a court and civil lines (living quarters), which lie still somewhat remote from the main town, though less so now than in 1910 when two kilometres of open cultivated land separated the two. Several colleges at tertiary level reinforce this status. The sugar mill close to the railway station is the modern competitor with the several *khandsari* factories making crude granulated sugar in the older part of the town, where also rice and oil mills and timber yards indicate the town's essential function as a centre of industries processing the products of local agriculture and of the nearby Himalayan foothills at the railhead near the Nepalese frontier.

[1] This section is based, with up-dated statistics, on R. S. Gangarwar, 'Urban Geography of Pilibhit', an unpublished Ph. D. thesis of the University of Delhi.

Commerce clings to the bifurcating main streets which link the two river bridges and branch to the railway station. It is interesting that even in so small a town, expansion has led to the growth of a new upper class suburb near the station, since the older area of élite residences is hemmed in by middle and low class settlement. The very poor occupy a peripheral position on the lowest occasionally flood-prone land beyond the better low class housing. Thus the classic pattern of the pre-industrial city is only disrupted by the development in the southeast corner.

About a third of the houses are of mud-brick or clay with flat roofs; rather more are of burned brick construction, often with tiled roofs. In the late 1960s, 22 per cent of homes had no latrines of any kind and people used roadsides or the nearest fields. Only 3 per cent of homes had flush systems.

Typical of its class Pilibhit has 7 per cent of its work force in agriculture. Manufacturing accounts for 25 per cent (17 per cent in non-household manufacturing), 21 per cent in trade and commerce, 16 per cent in transport and communications, and 26 per cent in other services.

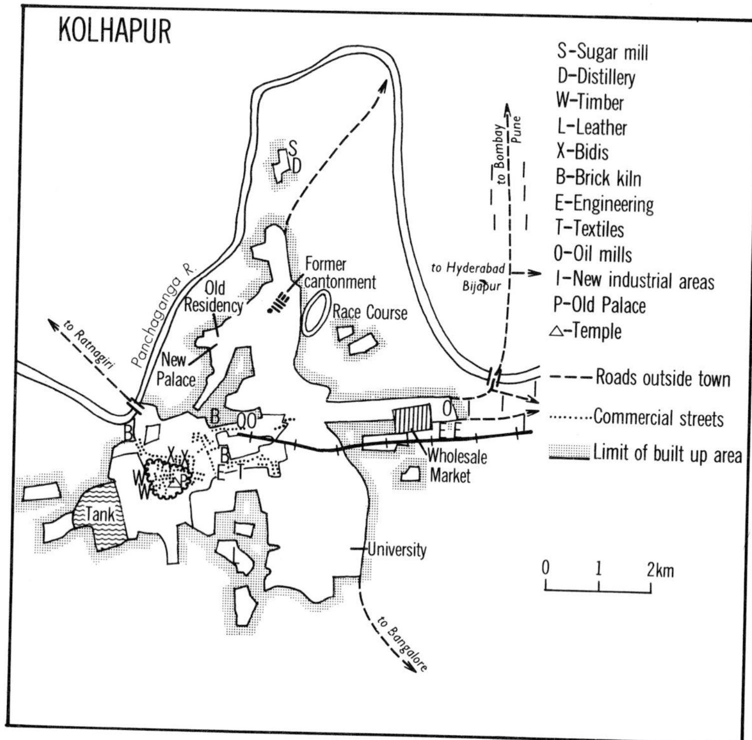

FIG. 13.3 After P. T. Malshe.

79 A street in Kolhapur, Maharashtra. Shuttered shops beneath dwelling houses, cycles, pedestrians and auto-rickshaws predominate.

Kolhapur

Kolhapur (see Figure 13.3) with a population of 259,050 in 1971, is like Pilibhit a district town, but is also the regional capital of the south Maratha country, and so a place of some historic distinction. During the Muslim period Kolhapur was tributary to the Sultanate of Bijapur, 160 km to the east, but was ruled by Hindu princes, thus becoming involved in Shivaji's struggle against the Moghuls during the latter half of the seventeenth century. The old town bears in the alignment of its streets the pattern of the walls of the Maharatha fortifications which occupied the high ground commanding the best bridge point on the Panchganga leading west to the hill fortress of Panhala, 21 km distant.

Following the Maratha wars the British established a garrison at Kolhapur to control the several local princedoms. Characteristically their cantonment was set up away from the Indian city to provide barracks for the troops, bungalows for the officers and civil administration, a residency for the senior British official, and a racecourse for recreation. The ruling prince, for Kolhapur was the chief of the 'native' Deccan States, built his new palace nearby, and the colonial development of the town proceeded. The railway, a spur from the Bombay–Madras line, arrived in 1890, and the first cotton mill was established in 1906. With Indian independence the state was incorporated ultimately into the State of Maharashtra. To its railway connection has been added good road links to Bombay, Bangalore and Hyderabad, enhancing its importance as a collecting centre for *jaggery* (crude sugar) from a wide area. The growth of engineering industries and the founding here of Shivaji University place Kolhapur above the run of towns of comparable size.[1] Figure 13.3 brings out the more congested parts of the old town from which extension has been northwards to the former cantonment, eastwards along the main access road past the wholesale jaggery market to the industrial area on the Pune road, and southeastwards along the Bangalore road past the university. Towards the Western Ghats, westwards, development has been minimal reflecting the small amount of trade and traffic in this direction.

[1] Topographic detail from P. T. Malshe, *Kolhapur*, Poona (1974), to whom the author is greatly indebted for his unstinted help and for personally demonstrating the city and its region.

Kolhapur's occupational structure is closely comparable to that of Pilibhit. Just over 8 per cent of the workforce are engaged in agriculture, almost 30 per cent in manufacturing (24 per cent in the non-household category), 20 per cent in trade and commerce and 10 per cent in transport and communications. A steady growth rate of 38–39 per cent has been maintained over two decades and the city is likely to continue to prosper as the regional centre for a comparatively rich corner of Maharashtra.

Madurai

Madurai, population 549,114 in 1971 (711,501 if 14 outlying urban centres are included to form the Madurai Urban Agglomeration) exemplifies the power of a religious institution to act as the nucleus for urban development in both abstract and concrete terms. The city's origins date back to the sixth century BC, but its present basic physical structure is of the sixteenth to seventeenth centuries AD. Madurai was the capital of the Pandyan kings who in the fifth century held the throne of Ceylon. More importantly it was the religious and cultural capital of the Tamil people.

80 Detail of cloth and dress shop, Kolhapur, Maharashtra. There is a similar shop opposite and a street vendor operating from the roadside.

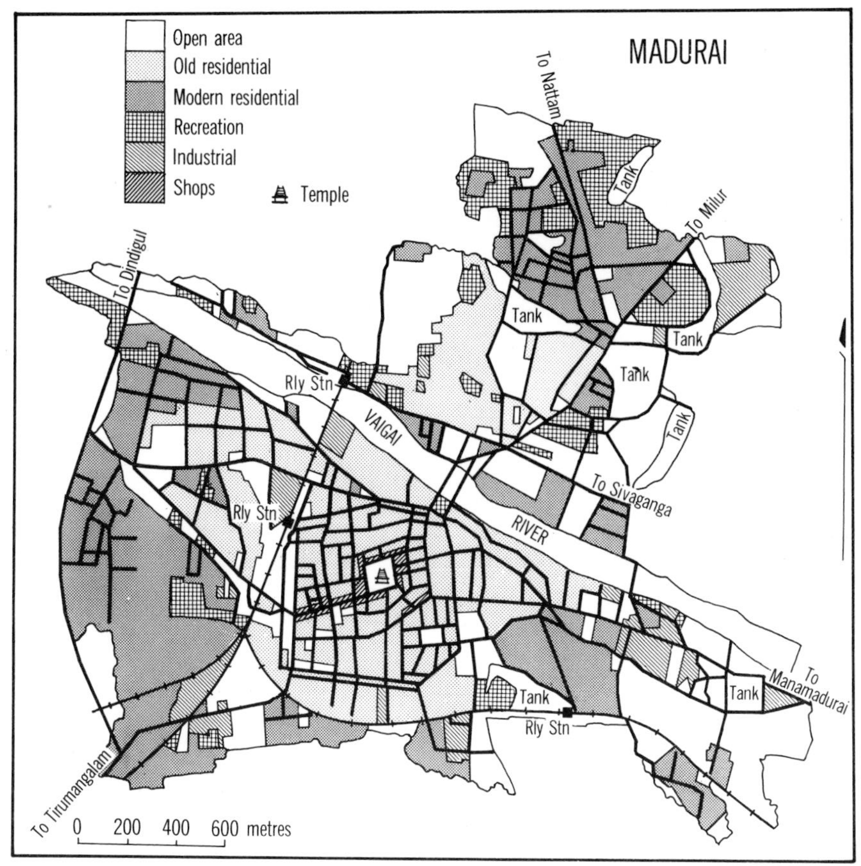

FIG. 13.4 After *Census of India 1971*.

The form of the urban core (Figure 13.4) is a system of concretic squares around the huge Meenakshi Ammam Temple, a pattern which persists for almost a kilometre until contained by the Vagai River and two railway lines. The main expansion of the city has been northwards across the river and west of the railway. The élite suburbs are found along the river bank or further north in association with recreational open space such as the old racecourse. The city core contains older housing and the main commercial streets leading to the temple gates. Extensions of relative congestion parallel the river on the south bank, and are intersperced on lower ground among the tanks on the north bank.

Industry occupies 36 per cent of the workforce, almost 30 per cent being in non-household manufacturing, dominated by cotton textiles. 1754 textile plants range in size from the 1020 with 4 workers or less, mainly in the household sector, to the 14 plants with over 100 workers which employ 23 per cent of those in textiles. While craft industries are located within the city core, there is no room there for 'organized' industry which is found generally along the railways, in the south-eastern extremity and in an industrial estate in the northeast. As befits a cultural centre there are at least eleven colleges and polytechnics, which help to account for the 22 per cent of workers enumerated as in 'other services'; 29 per cent are in trade and commerce and 9 per cent in transport and communications.

Bangalore

Bangalore with a population of 1,540,741 (1,653,779 for its Urban Agglomeration including the adjacent planned industrial townships), ranks seventh among the nine 'millionaire' cities, close behind Ahmadabad and Hyderabad neither of which exceed 1.8 million. The larger cities are well ahead of this group, Madras in fourth place having nearly 3.2 million. Bangalore's development and form approximate closely to the model. The city straddles a minor watershed between streams flowing southwest to join the Cauvery and southeast to the Ponnaiyar. No river here provided a natural defensive site. The mud fort built in 1537 by the Vijayanagar chieftain and the city's founder, Kempe Gowda, stood close to a small water course where now the remnants of a later stone fort face the city market across the busy hub of urban transport routes. As Figure 13.5a indicates, the terrain lends itself to the construction of tanks for storing water. Many have been filled in to provide land for development. Like Kolhapur Bangalore came under the rule of the Sultan of Bijapur in the seventeenth century and subsequently under the Marathas, and then Haider Ali and Tipu Sultan his son, the last to resist the British in South India. It was, despite an extremely eccentric position, the capital of Mysore State, which became the core of a new state of the Indian Union, recently renamed Karnataka. Extension of the state to the Arabian Sea coast and northwards has rendered Bangalore even more distant from its furthest district but its primacy is unchallenged.

While the Maharaja of Mysore resided in Mysore City and conducted most state ceremonials there, he had a secondary palace in Bangalore where his efficient government was located. Here too was the British Resident and the very substantial British military cantonment so situated to benefit from the station's equable climate at 900 m rather than as visible reminder to the generally pacific population. The dual nature of the city remains, each part with its market, bazar and railway station, and clearly differentiated in terms of population density and

FIG. 13.5(*a*)

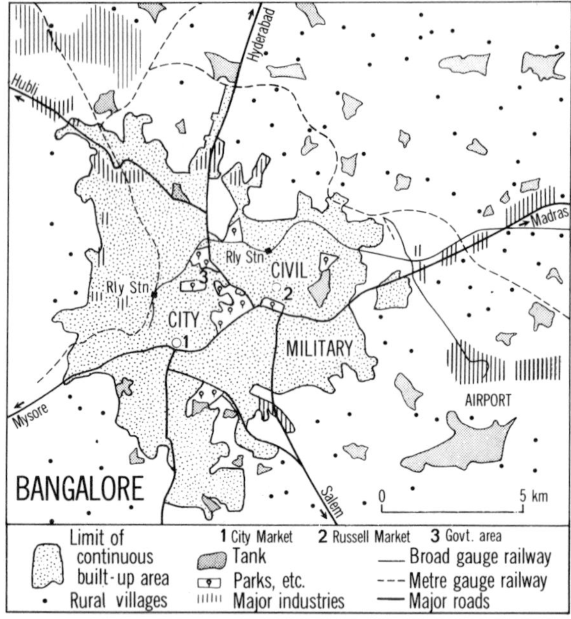

81 Quarrying slabs of gneiss, Bangalore, Karnataka: an industry notorious till recently for exploiting its labour force in conditions of bonded servitude.

occupational structure. The larger and more concentrated focus of population and commerce is around the City Market close to the Fort (see Figures 13.5b and c). Russell Market with its associated congested residential area and nucleus of manufacturing now serves a much wider sector of the northeast of Bangalore than simply the nineteenth-century cantonment. To over-emphasize the city's duality would however ignore the fact that Bangalore is at present a city with several foci. Within the cantonment there are two commercial areas almost a kilometre apart: a more 'traditional' one close to Russell Market and another with a more 'modern' aspect facing the other side of the *maidan* from along Mahatma Gandhi Road. The modern commercial core of the old city has spread from the City Market northwest towards the railway station and northeast in the direction of the government quarter. Here stands probably the most magnificent of India's new generation of state houses of parliament, the great granite block of the Vidhan Soudha, its white domes topped by the three golden lions of Sarnath, the national symbol. This building dominates the older structures of the Maharajas' period, the wine-red High Court and other well-kept pieces of Victoriana, all set in an extensive park. Bangalore's parks, gardens and streets lined with colourful trees have earned it a reputation as India's 'garden city'. They also encourage polycentric development by separating developing nodes in the urban system by stretches of open space. It is to be hoped that these will be jealously preserved from encroachment, and that Bangalore's development will avoid over-centralization and the consequent traffic congestion.

The modernity of Bangalore's industrial structure has been referred to in Chapter Eleven (see Table 11.4 on page 158). Of the third of the workforce in non-household manufacturing, 45 per cent are in engineering. The proportion of the working population engaged in manufacturing is high in two quite different kinds of area (see Figure 13.5d). The twin commercial centres of the two markets attract a great number of small workshops and household-level craftsmen engaged in traditional trades, while on the periphery, especially to the north and west, the concentration reflects the predominance of manufacturing as an occupation of suburban dwellers. The newest industrial townships in the extreme north score upwards of 83 per cent of their resident workers in manufacturing, hardly surprising since government industrial undertakings provide housing for their workforce.

Fig. 13.5(*b*)

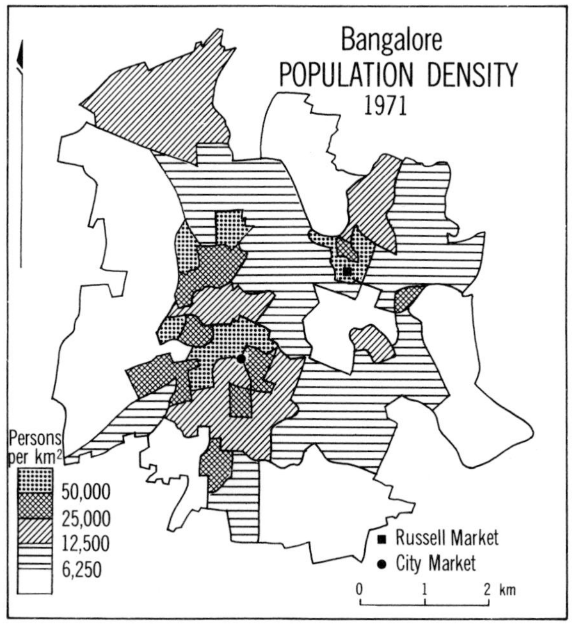

Fig. 13.5(*c*)

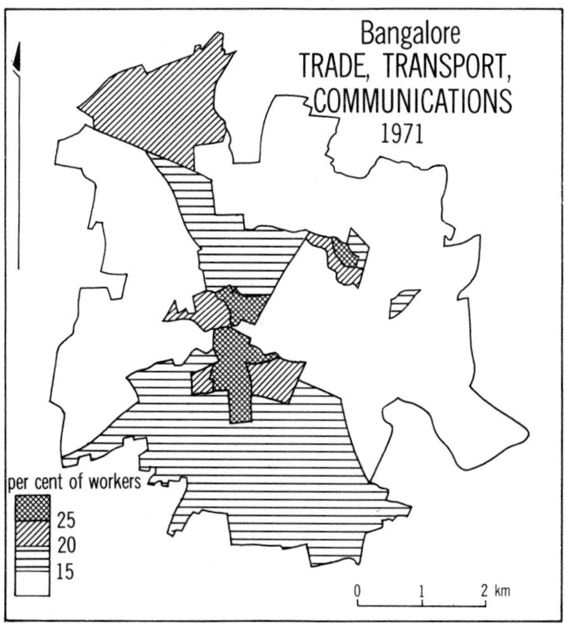

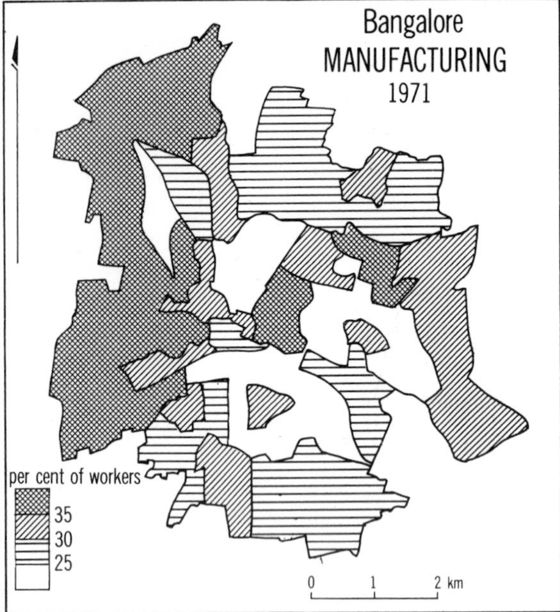

FIG. 13.5(*d*)

In area, Bangalore demonstrates some common tendencies in large modern Indian cities. The residences of the élite which used to lie close to the government area and between city and cantonment, now spread northwards in a generally sectoral fashion. The state is today a substantial landlord and effectively controls housing development directly or indirectly. Enthusiastic replication of principles learned in the West seems to account for the spread of residential suburbs in the south with little regard being paid to the fact that this tends to increase the journey to work for those employed in the industries expanding to the other three cardinal points of the city's periphery. Much modern industrial development post-dated independence, but the tone was set by Hindustan Aeronautics Limited which has grown from an aircraft assembly plant established in the British period, east of the cantonment. Other industries of 'high technology' have followed around the northern margins of the city: Indian Telephone Industries, Bharat Electronics, Hindustan Machine Tools, etc. The decision makers may well have been influenced by the proximity of communications by rail and road to Madras and by road to Bombay. Certainly industrial development has been more vigorous in these directions than southwards towards Mysore. Close to the core of the city the Binney and Minerva Cotton Mills are reminders of an earlier phase of industrialization, which included the mill extension of the Karnataka craft speciality of silk spinning and weaving.

In the case of Bangalore some information is available on the workers' journey to work, based on a sample survey conducted by the Department of Human Geography at the Institute for Social and Economic Change. Almost half (46 per cent) of the workers walk to work over an average distance of 1.16 km. This is typical of the congested inner areas of small industrial units, some of which operate at the level of household crafts. Among the poorest in the sample, with at most Rs 150 per month, 60 per cent walk to work. Bicycles carry 12 per cent an average distance of 3.44 km. A push bike is a luxury for the very poor who would take a bus if they cannot walk, since the capital outlay for their own vehicle is beyond them. Bicycle transport appears significant among those with Rs 150–500 per month. Bus travel is used by 22 per cent of the sample, for journeys averaging 4.21 km. Even in the middle income range of Rs. 300–750 about half use buses, though between a third and a fifth walk to work. Motor cycles or scooters appear as vehicles for increasing proportions of workers with over Rs 500, but carry only 7 per cent of the total. The scooter is the middle class Indian's first venture into motorization, very popular now that petrol prices have risen steeply. It is common to see a crash-helmeted father driving his sari-clad wife side-saddled in billowing silks and their two children astride the tank, to visit relatives on Sunday. Cars are restricted to the wealthy, carrying to work only 15 per cent of those with Rs 1000–2000 and 63 per cent of those with over Rs 2000. The distances travelled by those with private motorized vehicles are less in fact than the average bus journey: 3.67 km by motor cycle and 4.0 km by car. It can only be surmised that travel conditions are likely to be comparable in the five smaller millionaire cities. In the larger metropolitan areas, rail travel is important in Madras, Bombay and Calcutta, while in Delhi bicycles and private motor scooters and cars are likely to be comparatively more widely used on account of the extensive lay-out and functional structure of the capital.

82 Truck transport brings bananas to Bangalore City Market.

Delhi

Delhi (see Figure 13.6a) consists of the Delhi Municipal Corporation (including Old Delhi), Delhi Cantonment and New Delhi. It is India's third urban agglomeration with 3,647,023 citizens in 1971. Such is the spread in area of the city today that it has reached out to incorporate many of the ancient monuments and structures that remind the visitor of Delhi's long history as the major power base of the country's rulers during the Muslim period. The location has been occupied for much longer however; witness the pillars on the Ridge and on rocky outcrops in Kalkaji, inscribed for the great ruler Asoka in the third century BC.

FIG. 13.6(*a*)

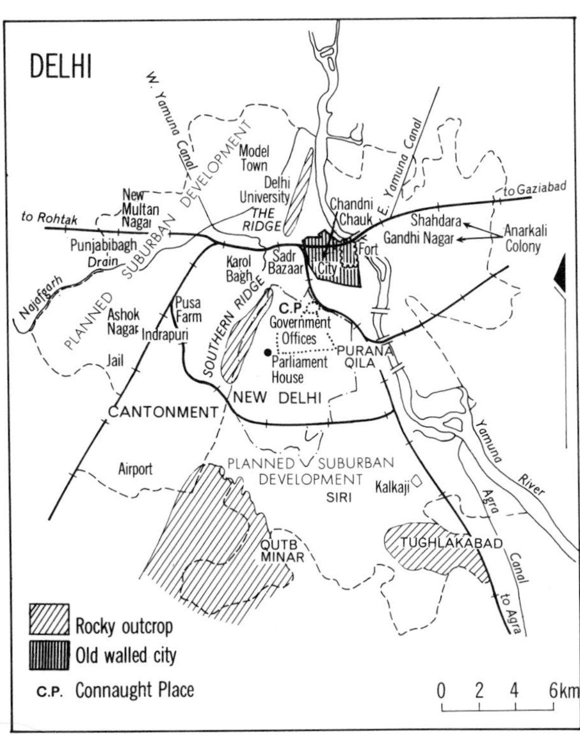

The terrain provides a number of attractive sites for settlement by leaders seized with the strategic importance of the situation at the narrowest point in the Indo-Gangetic Plain. Here the quartzite spine of the Aravalli Hills project above the alluvium to form a barrier to the southward swing of the Yamuna. At Qutb Minar on the city's southern outskirts, Muslims in the Pathan period (twelth to fourteenth centuries) occupied what may have been the original site of a Hindu settlement named after Raja Dhilu in the first century BC. Thereafter Muslims developed several sites as administrative and defensive headquarters: Siri (fourteenth century), Tughlakabad (fourteenth to fifteenth centuries) with structures both on the southeast corner of modern Delhi and on the Ridge in the north, Purana Qila, the 'old' fort (fifteenth to sixteenth centuries), the Red Fort of the Moghuls and the walled city of Shahjahan (sixteenth to seventeenth centuries) with its magnificent mosque, the Jama Masjid. At Agra and Fatepur Sikri there were rival locations for the Moghul capital, and Delhi was not always supreme. With the crumbling of the Moghul empire it suffered at the hands of Maratha and Persian armies and did not regain its prestigious position as an imperial capital until the British moved their administration from Calcutta in 1912. The British developed a planned site at New Delhi south of congested Old Delhi. New

Delhi is now a city of considerable grandeur both in the scale of its lay-out and in the splendour of its government buildings set symmetrically along the broad avenues of Raj Path, and at a greater density along Parliament Street between the Lok Sabha (Parliament House) and the shopping centre around Connaught Place.

Since independence growth has been vigorous. The Delhi Municipal Corporation's area of control has leap-frogged the New Delhi enclave southwards to the edge of the Aravalli rocks, and has expanded east beyond the Yamuna and west in a number of 'colonies' beyond the Ridge. Immediately after independence the influx of refugees, particularly from the Pakistan Punjab, forced the rapid development of suburbs to accomodate them. Several of these are recognizable in names that recall the origins of their inhabitants: Shadara, Anarkali (both reminiscent of Lahore), New Multan Nagar, Punjabibagh, etc.

The dualism of the model outlined above is reinforced in the case of Delhi in the disparity in economic levels between on the one hand New Delhi and the Cantonment with parts of the south-eastern sector of Delhi proper which may be seen as their natural extension, and on the other Old Delhi and the refugee and industrial suburbs that have developed in the north. Population density reflects this dualism clearly. One third (31 per cent) of the population is concentrated in the Old City and its immediate vicinity as far west as Karol Bagh and the closely settled areas immediately south of Delhi University. Because of the relatively low structures of the Old City, rarely more than three storeys high, and the cool winters that militate against the street dwelling communities that can survive throughout the year in Calcutta or Bombay, crude densities do not reach the levels of those cities. One fifth of the 88 census enumeration circles mapped in Figure 13.6b have densities of upwards of 50,000 per km² and six of these exceed 100,000 per km². All are located within the core, which has many of the attributes of the pre-industrial Asian city. At the other extreme the spacious suburbs of New Delhi's diplomatic sector are barely distinguishable from their counterparts the world over.

Most of Delhi's craftsmen in household manufacturing are concentrated in Old Delhi and Karol Bagh. Manufacturing in the modern sense distinguishes an industrial northern Delhi from a south Delhi almost devoid of industry (see Figure 13.6c). From the Old City recent industrial settlements have spread east of the Yamuna and west along railway and roads. The areas shown in the upper quintile of non-household manufacturing contain 32 per cent of all workers, and those in the second quintile 29 per cent. Employment in trade and commerce repeats this pattern rather closely except that there is a greater concentration towards the north centre and less towards the periphery. Only one circle in New Delhi and Cantonment reaches the median value in this regard. Complementary to the pattern of manufacturing and commerce is that of workers in 'other services'. New Delhi, the Cantonment and the southern extensions of Delhi proper are understandably strong in employment in government offices and as servants and functionaries of those in associated employment (see Figure 13.6d). Almost half

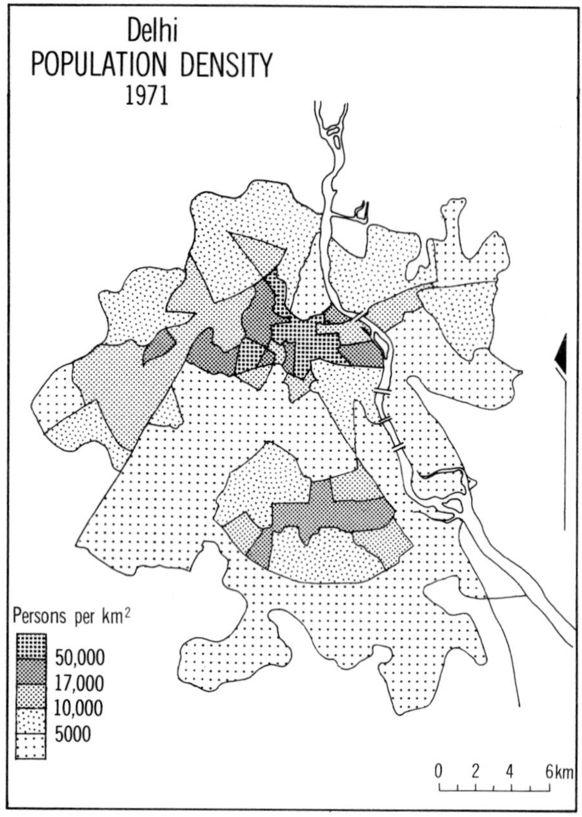

FIG. 13.6(*b*)

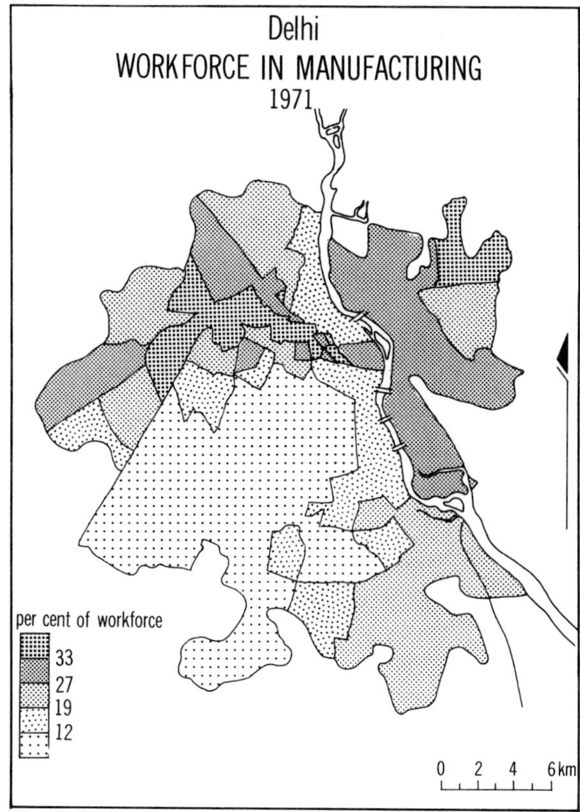

FIG. 13.6(*c*)

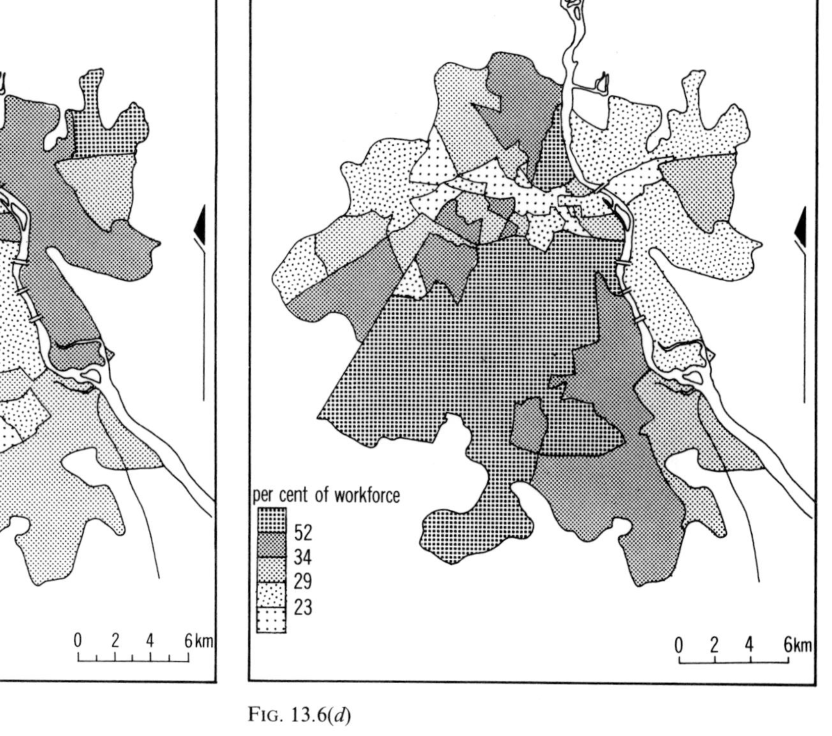

FIG. 13.6(*d*)

(49 per cent) of the workers in this category live in the areas forming the two upper quintiles. A secondary area important for 'other services' lies north of Old Delhi and is associated with the University and some administrative functions like the police lines.

Bombay

Bombay and Calcutta are in several important respects very different. As a single urban unit Greater Bombay is the larger, having 5,970,575 inhabitants against 3,148,746 for the Municipal Corporation of Calcutta, but while Bombay has the character of a huge city with suburbs, the urban agglomeration that contains Calcutta is a straggling conurbation in the proper meaning of the term, with a total population of 7,031,382, contained in some 74 constituent urban units.

The setting of Bombay is shown in Figure 13.7. Its site is constrained by the sea, expansion now being possible only eastwards onto the mainland towards the foot of the Western Ghats. The sunken coastline accounts for the numerous indentations one of which made Bombay harbour so attractive to British traders seeking shelter from the southwest monsoon. The coast itself is sometimes rocky where outliers and spurs of the Deccan lavas occur, but in sheltered sections mangrove swamps and mud-flats are typical. Urban development concentrated first at the southern tip of Bombay Island, a narrow promontory 14 km long and at most 4 km wide, itself comprising three linked islets, separated from the larger Salsette Island to the north by Mahim Bay and the mangrove estuaries and flats of the Mahim and Sion Rivers. Docks were excavated the length of the eastern side of the island. The railway lines from Delhi and Gujarat along the coast, and from Peninsular India, down off the Deccan Plateau, converged to run along the spine of the island to termini in the south. Urban expansion, particularly after independence could only take place outside Bombay Island, on Salsette.

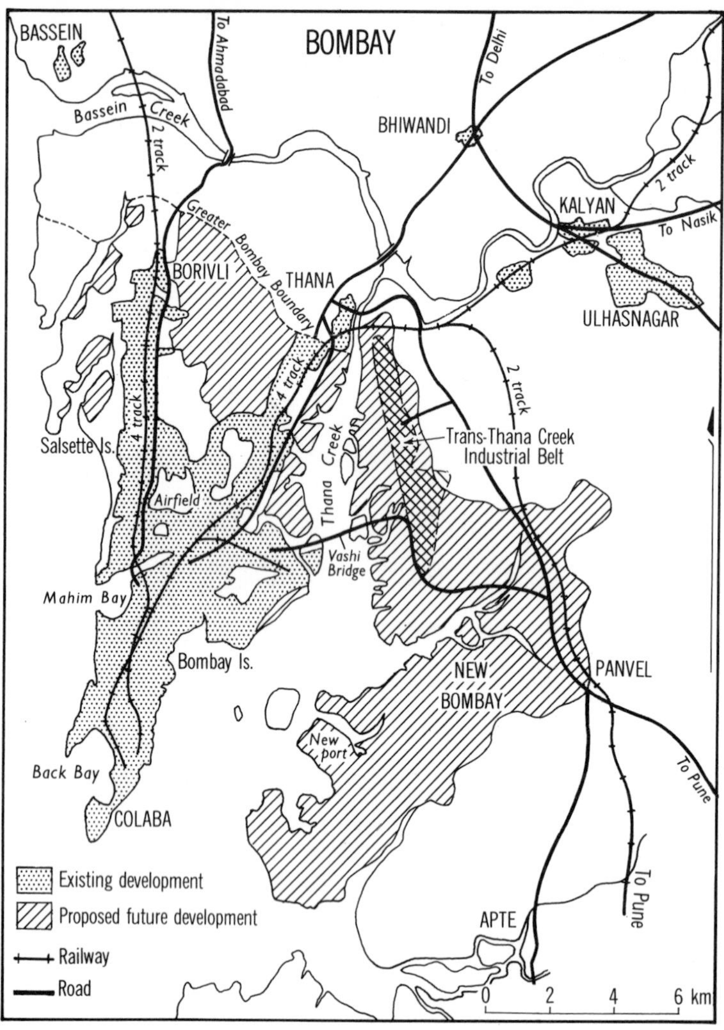

FIG. 13.7

In the intercensal decade 1961–71 the population of Salsette's suburbs grew by 110 per cent while Bombay Island increased by only 11 per cent.[1] At present 53 per cent of Greater Bombay's population live on Bombay Island, 27 per cent in the western half of Salsette and 20 per cent in the eastern half.

Twenty-two kilometres north of the southern extremity of Bombay Salsette Island is separated from the mainland by Bassein Creek in the west and its continuation as Thana Creek on the east. Until 1973 all landward communication with Bombay had to cross these creeks at the northern end of Salsette, but recently the Vashi Bridge across the lower end of Thana Creek has shortened by 12 km the distance from central Bombay to Pune. It has also given impetus to modern industrial development in the Trans Thana Creek Industrial Belt which provides the first substantial element of what will in time become New Bombay, a twin city of two million people facing Bombay across the harbour. Like the older satellite towns of Thana, Kalyan and Ulhasnagar, the TTC Industrial Belt lies in Thana district, outside Greater Bombay but under the unified planning control of the Maharashtra Government. Its industries are strongly oriented towards petro-chemicals. Of 72 plants present in 1974, 25 were manufacturing basic petrochemicals and petrochemical products, while 18 made other chemicals. The 21,000

[1] John E. Brush, 'Elite Residential Colonies', (mimeographed paper, publication pending).

83 Workers tenements, Bombay. Extremely high population densities are reached in such areas. They are reminiscent of the homes of the working class in Britain at the turn of the century. Saris and dhotis (loin cloths) dry in the sun. Each section of balcony indicates a separate home behind. Shops occupy the flats at street level.

84 A wealthy suburb in Bombay, with a Parsee lady going shopping.

employees were less concentrated, 36 per cent being in the chemicals sector and the rest distributed among electricity generation (17 per cent) machinery (20 per cent), metals, textiles and paper.[1] The industrial make-up of Greater Bombay has been discussed in an earlier chapter.

Population density in Bombay is shown in Figure 13.8. The core of concentration is clearly focussed in the wedge fronting onto Back Bay where densities exceeding 70,000 per km^2 occur in an area almost 4 km from north to south and 1.5 km wide. Within this area three wards have densities over 250,000 per km^2, the peak reaching 371,176 for a population of 63,100 occupying 0.17 km^2, giving each human being 2.7 square metres of land surface, including roads. A second area of extremely high density lies just south of Dadar in the city's main textile factory belt. Most of the wards with over 40,000 per km^2 are contiguous to those in the top quintile just described. Outside Bombay Island densities remain high for some distance along the northern and northeastern communication corridors, where suburban railway suburbs are strung like beads along the line.[2] Outliers of concentration occur in Kanhari ward, served by Borival Station in the north, and at Mulund where Greater Bombay merges with Thana Municipality in the northeast, but in general population density decreases with distance from Bombay's CBD and away from the elongated arteries of communication. Colaba, Fort and Esplanade wards at the southern extremity of the island are notable for their lower densities adjacent to some of the highest densities at the centre. Colaba and Fort were the areas of British administration and military barracks, and the Esplanade ward contains many business houses, railway and port terminal facilities, leaving little space for residential habitation. At the other end of Back Bay, Malabar Hill has a moderate density by Bombay standards, 29,153 per km^2, in this the most sought after address for the city's elite. Its low proportion of manufacturing workers (see Figure 13.9) is indicative of its high socio-economic status.

[1] N. A. Ismail, *Growth of Industries in the Trans Thana-Belapur Road Area*, unpublished Honours Thesis, Department of Geography, University of Bombay.

[2] C. D. Deshpande, *Suburbs of Greater Bombay*, Centre for Urban Research, Department of Geography, Osmania University, 1973.

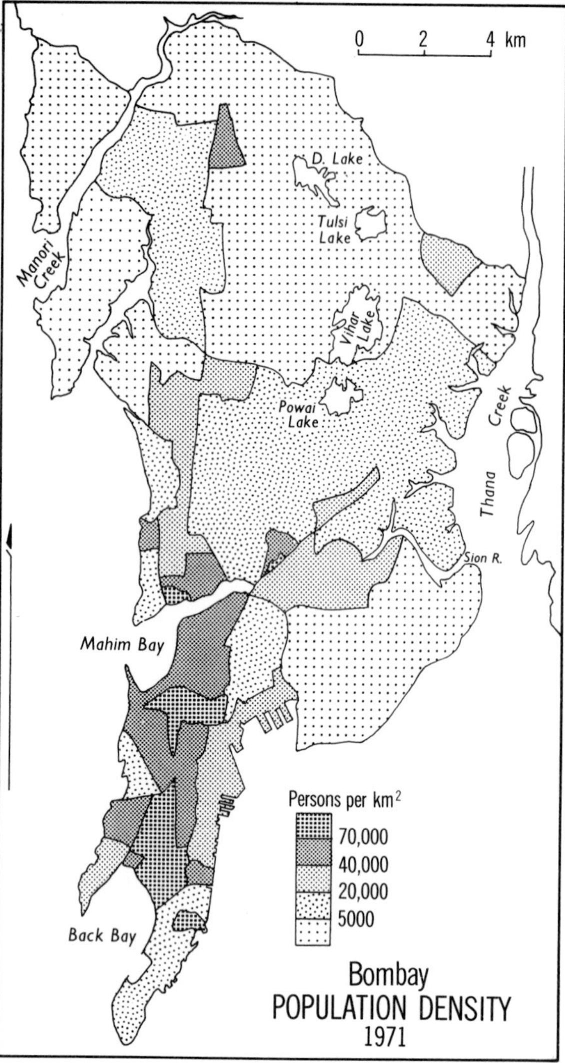

FIG. 13.8

The occupational structure of Bombay's workforce is mapped in Figures 13.8, 13.9 and 13.10. Manufacturing engages over 47 per cent of the workers, over half (53 per cent) of them on Bombay Island, mainly in the northern half where the wards with over 40 per cent of their workers in manufacturing account for 29 per cent of Bombay's total. On Salsette Island, manufacturing is tightly concentrated along the northwest communications corridor towards Thana. Between Kurla and Mulund are 21 per cent of such workers, while another 10 per cent are found along the northern railway in wards in the upper two quintiles.

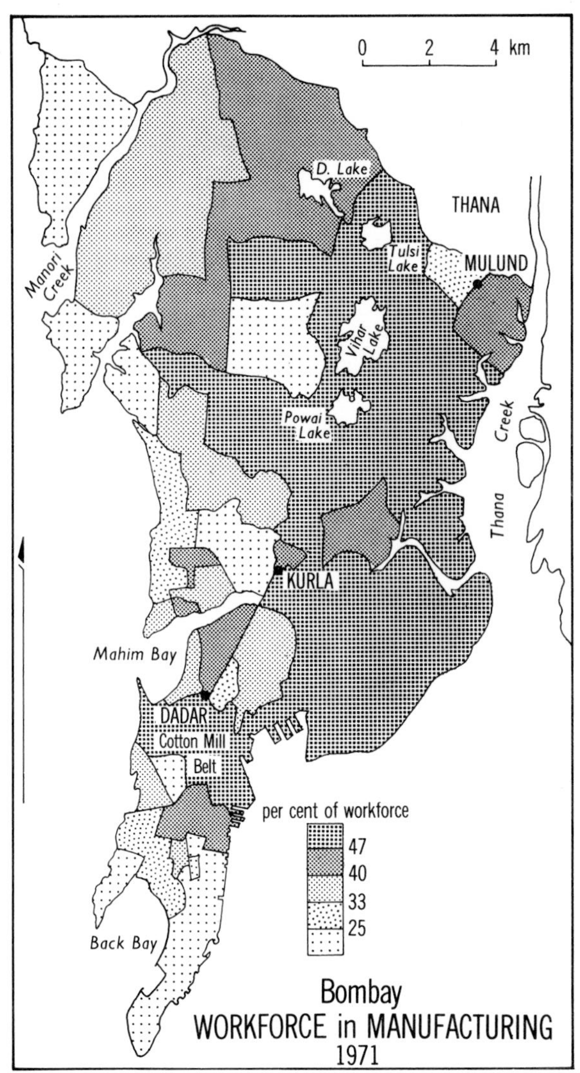

FIG. 13.9

FIG. 13.10

Trade and commerce are specially important in the vicinity of the docks and the two railway termini, near which is the central business district. Outlying concentrations of workers in commerce are found in the high class suburbs at Mahim at the northern end of Bombay Island, and at Santcruz, Kandivil and Borival in Salsette.

Bombay's population grew at the rate of 44 per cent in the decade 1961–71. Migration figures for the 1971 census are not yet available, but there is no reason to suppose that the contribution of newcomers to the total has changed much since 1961. At the latter census, 64 per cent of the population was recorded as migrant, and as is characteristic of such groups the vast majority were males – 64 per cent in this case. What Spate says of Calcutta and Howrah is equally true of Bombay, 'Truly these cities are eaters of men'.[1] The masculinity is reflected in the sex ratio of 667 females per 1000 males in the total population. Only in the age group 0–9 do the sexes nearly balance. The age-sex pyramid (Figure 13.11) shows an excess of population in the age groups 25–39, mainly due to the in-migration of working males, leaving their wives

[1] Spate, O. H. K. and Learmonth, A. T. A. *India and Pakistan*, 1967, p. 596.

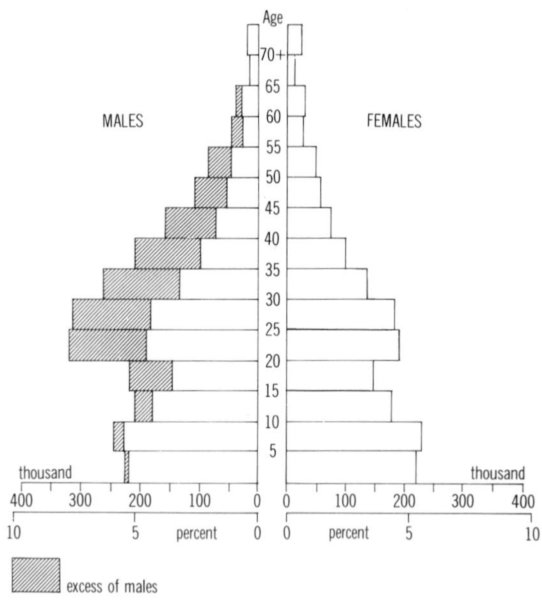

FIG. 13.11 Bombay 1961.

(if any) behind in their villages or country towns. Throughout the age range 20–54 the sex ratio is never better than 587 and falls to 471 between 35–44 years. As would be expected the sex ratio among the migrant group is even more unbalanced: 514 in the age groups 15–34 and 452 between 35–54.

Calcutta

The Hooghlyside conurbation, or in the words of the Census, the Calcutta Urban Agglomeration, corresponding approximately with the area within the jurisdiction of the Calcutta Metropolitan Planning Board is strung out for more than 65 km along both banks of the River Hooghly (see Figure 13.12). Bansberia and Kalyani mark the northern limits well upstream of the twin cities of Calcutta and Howrah, linked by Howrah Bridge. Downstream the conurbation continues for another

85 Dhobi ghats, Bombay: cotton mills beyond. Professional washermen bring their loads here to launder.

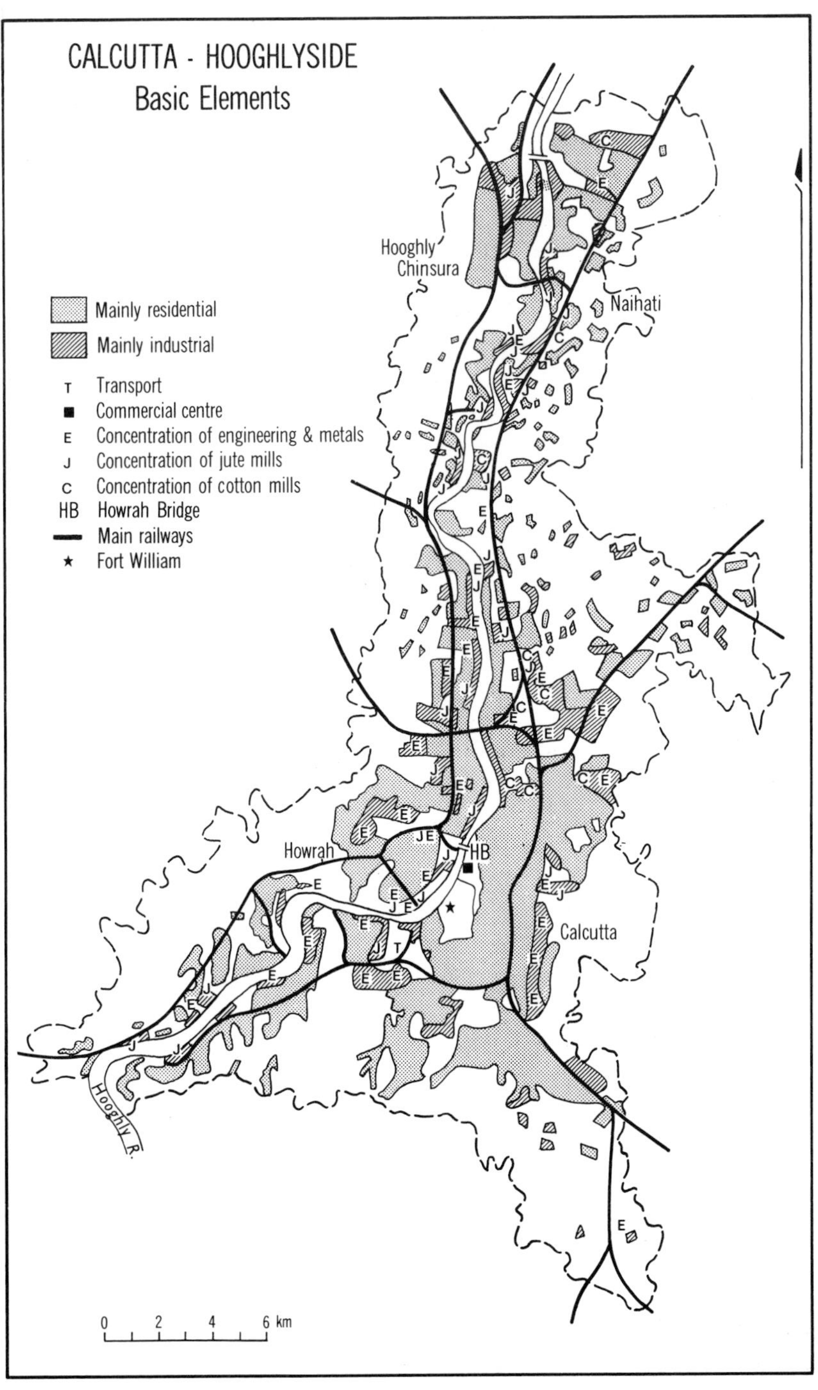
CALCUTTA - HOOGHLYSIDE
Basic Elements
Mainly residential
Mainly industrial
T Transport
■ Commercial centre
E Concentration of engineering & metals
J Concentration of jute mills
C Concentration of cotton mills
HB Howrah Bridge
Main railways
★ Fort William
Hooghly Chinsura
Naihati
Howrah
HB
Calcutta
Hooghly R.
0 2 4 6 km

FIG. 13.12

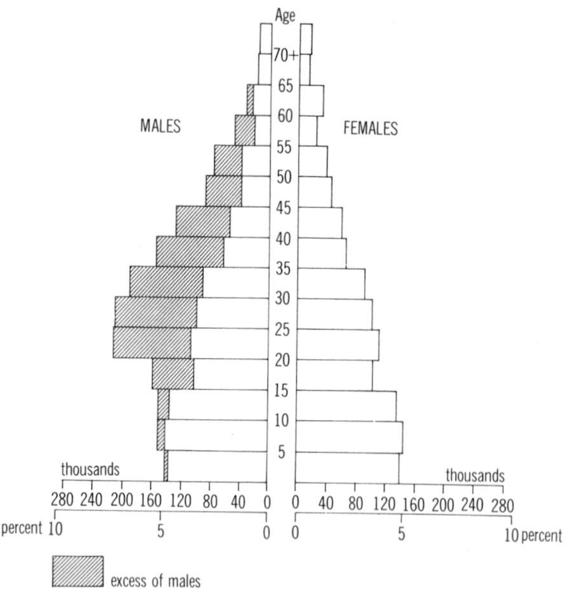

FIG. 13.13 Calcutta 1961.

30 km. In its general form the conurbation is most unusual. For considerable distances it extends back from the river as a built-up zone barely 2 km wide perched on the natural levee of the Hooghly as a narrow dry-point site for settlement between the river and its backswamp depression, low-lying and flood prone as is characteristic of a deltaic environment. Situation rather than site has been responsible for Calcutta's development however. English and French merchants found this reach of the Hooghly navigable by their merchant ships, which could here take on cargoes brought down river from the great cities of the Ganga Plain, the centres of administration and craftsmanship like Delhi, Agra, Allahabad, and Banaras (Varanasi). The English established factories at Fort William, Calcutta, (1691) following the Dutch lead at Chinsura (1653) and in competition with the French at Chandanagore (Chandanagar, 1690–92). Thus were laid the foundations of India's mercantile capital. With the eclipse of the French the British East India Company's base at Calcutta became locally dominant, and here the British built their capital when the Empire of India replaced the administration of the Company. This function was lost to Delhi in 1912 but Calcutta continued as capital of Bengal, and for long as the principal mercantile and industrial metropolis. Railways had replaced river boats and roads as the chief means of transport down the Ganga valley, though to the east river steamers carried cargoes of tea and jute from Assam and the more distant parts of the Ganga-Brahmaputra delta, now in Bangladesh. The railways had their termini on either side of the Hooghly, Howrah in particular owing its growth in large part to its location at the

FIG. 13.14

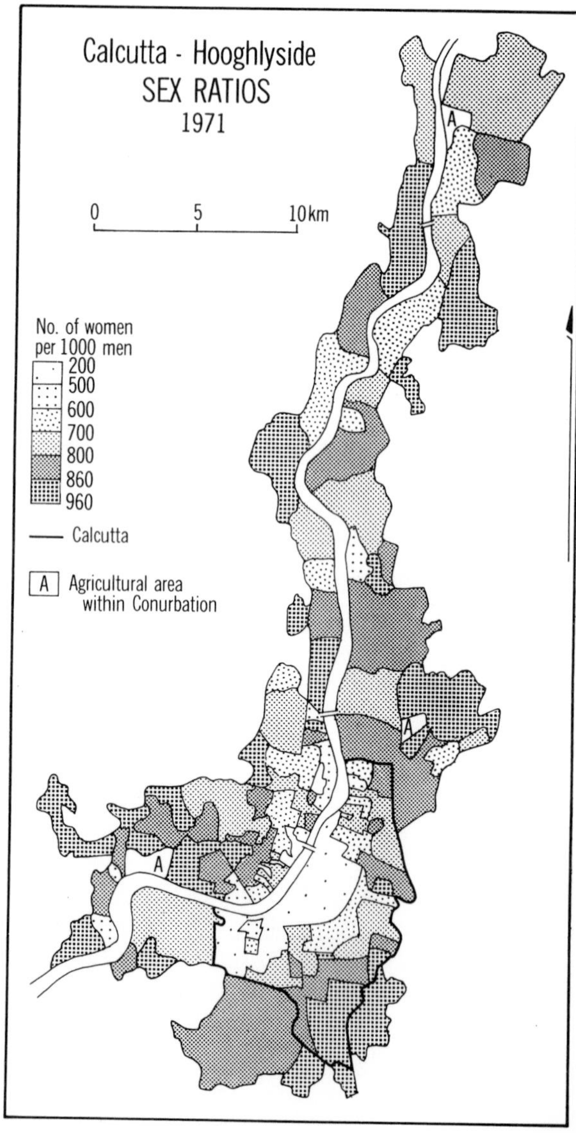

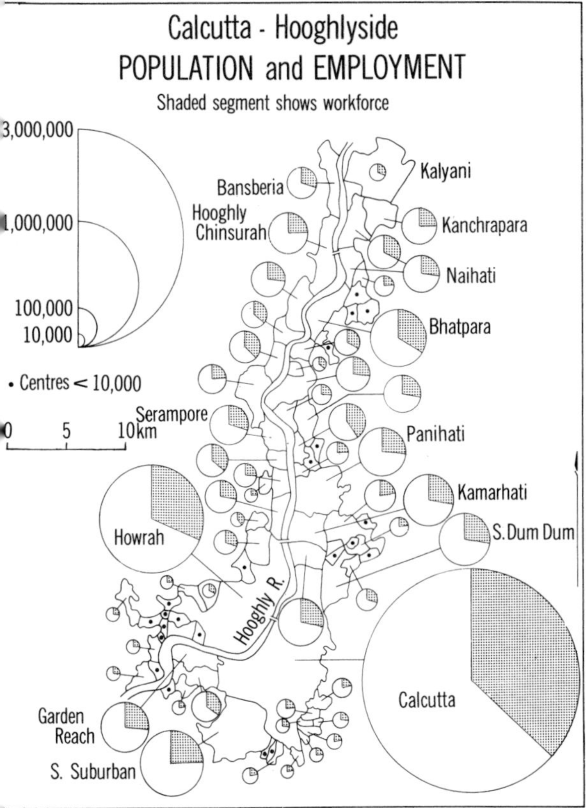

FIG. 13.15

end of lines converging from northwest and central India on the river bank opposite Calcutta. Railways and the opening of the Suez Canal in 1869 gave Calcutta's chief rival Bombay advantages of proximity to Britain from north-western India, and reduced Calcutta's hinterland in this direction. On the other hand railways tied to Hooghlyside the development of the Damodar as an industrial region and source of coal, to their mutual benefit. On the east bank of the Hooghly railways connected Calcutta with north Bengal and Darjiling. Partition severed East and parts of North Bengal from their traditional market for jute, and from the centre of Bengali culture in Calcutta, leaving the latter in a somewhat exposed position close to the East Pakistan border. Despite these accumulated disadvantages, Calcutta and the conurbation have managed to hold their own commercially and industrially. At the time of independence Calcutta became the destination of many thousands of Hindu refugees from East Pakistan. Such movement recurred periodically as friction increased between India and Pakistan. The war of independence in Bangladesh again released a flood of homeless refugees who pressed on the outskirts of Calcutta. Quite apart from these victims of specific political disturbance, great numbers of workless poor have drifted to Hooghlyside in search of livelihood. The condition of the urban poor in Calcutta beggars description. Perhaps half the population has come from outside, many to settle in 'bustees', slums of make-shift

FIG. 13.16(*a*)

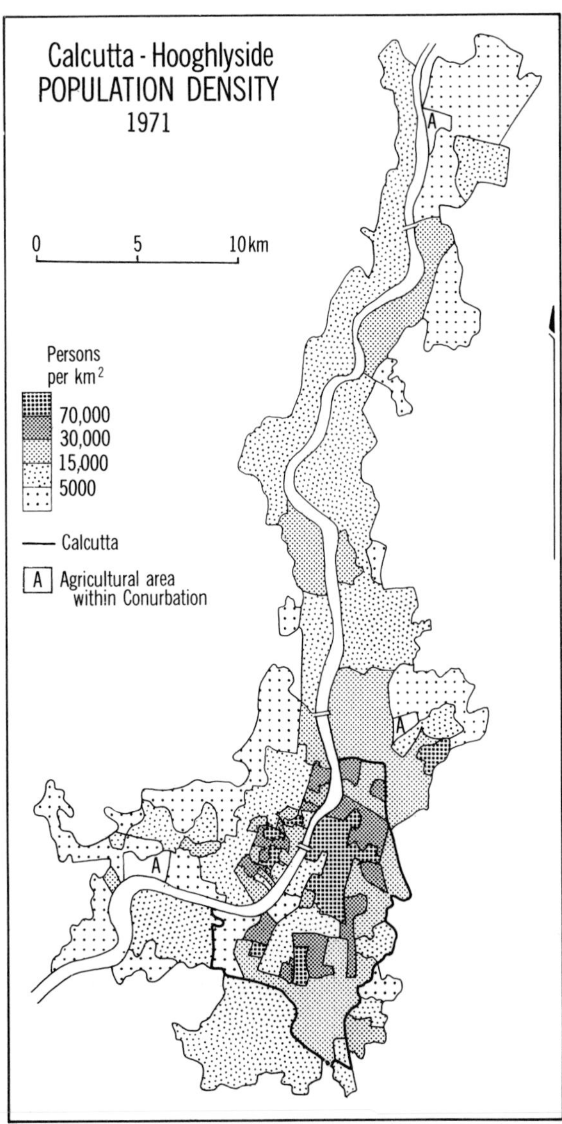

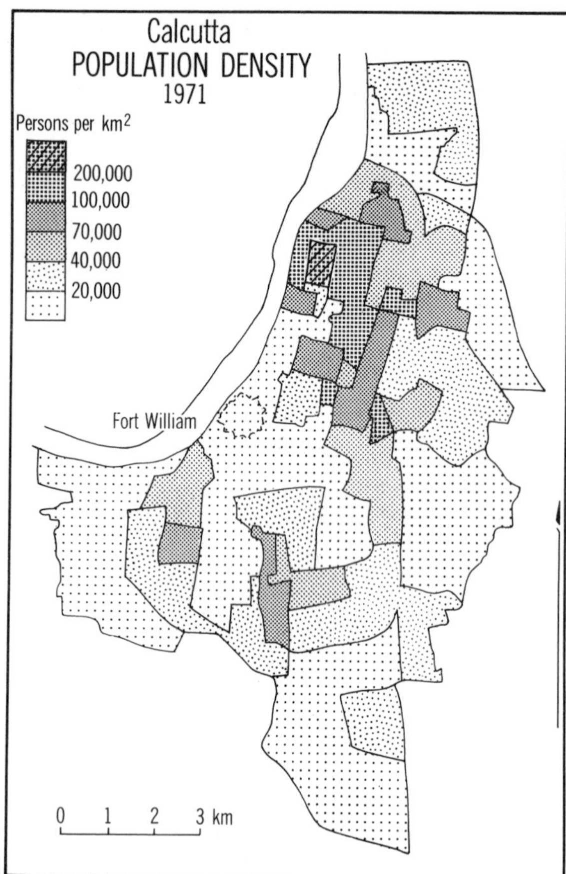

FIG. 13.16(*b*)

shelters in which they cluster in groups with similar language, dialect, caste or birthplace. Just over half (53 per cent) of the population of Calcutta Municipality was migrant in 1961. Although this figure is lower than that for Bombay, Calcutta's sex ratio of 612 is a shade lower, suggesting that the latter attracts a greater number of those who fail to find work enough to support a family in the city, or that the migrants are less permanent residents coming in from densely crowded rural areas at no great distance. As in Bombay there is an abnormal weighting of the population pyramid in the 25–39 age range (see Figure 13.13). Sex ratios between 20 and 59 are never better than 515 and fall to 408 in the 35–39 group. The sex ratio of migrants is only available in broader age groups. Between 15–34 it is 408, falling to 370 between 35–59. It is a sad commentary on the importance of children as breadwinners in the families of the poor that an unbalanced sex ratio of 694 girls to 1000 boys appears even in the age group 0–14, suggesting that the young boys come to town with father, leaving mother and the girls at home. The corresponding figure for Bombay is 886, which again reflects on the more dismal state of Calcutta's poor.

Figure 13.14 maps sex ratios for the whole conurbation. The lowest ratios are found in the core areas of Calcutta and just across the Howrah Bridge, districts close to the rail and river-shipping termini where incoming migrants first set foot in the

FIG. 13.17(*a*)

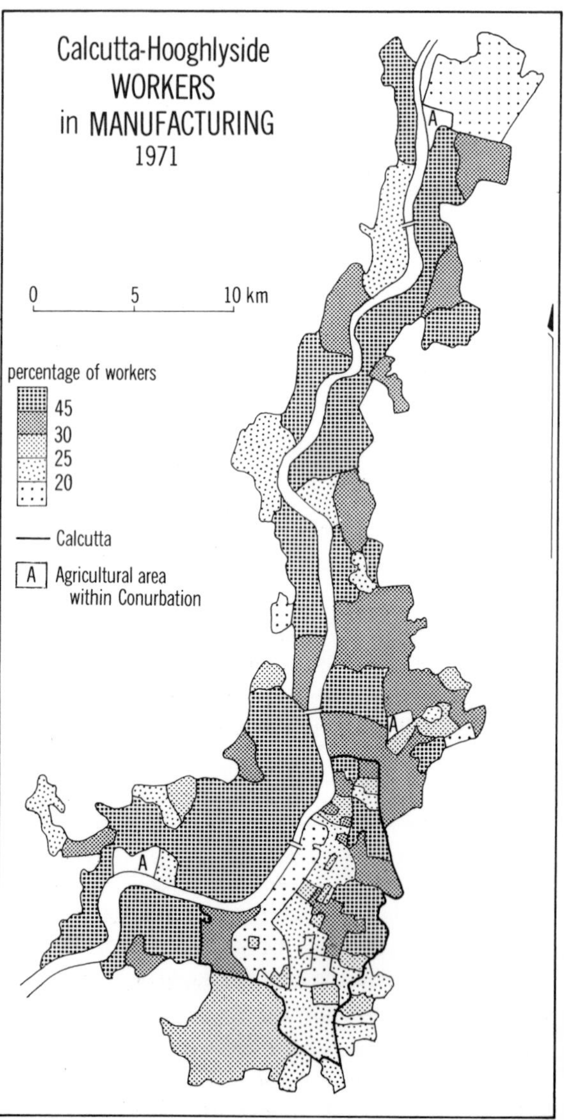

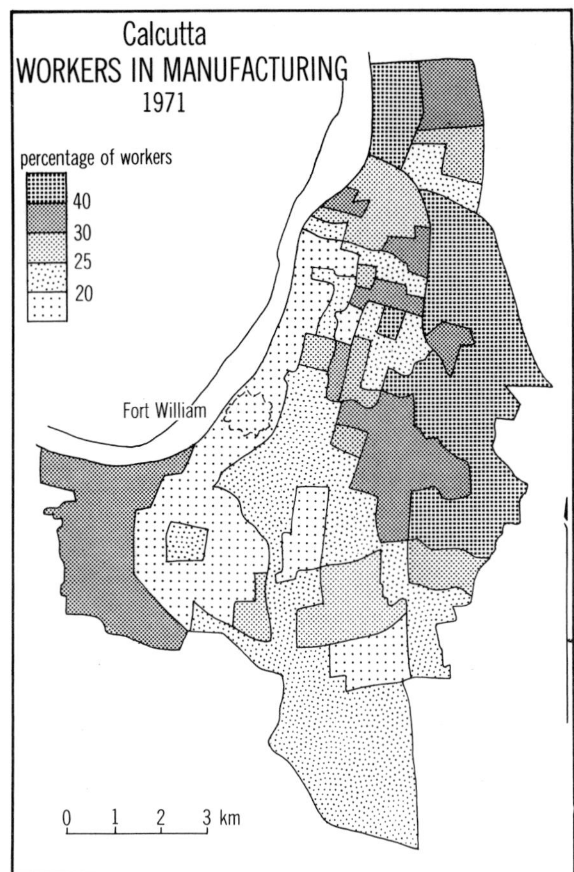

FIG. 13.17(*b*)

conurbation. Areas in which the ratio approaches a normal balance include the better class suburbs of southeastern Calcutta and the smaller settlements which retain closer links with rural life.

Calcutta has been described as an 'immature city'. People have poured in, and the local inhabitants have multiplied fast, but few of the necessities of life have been created to serve them. Employment opportunities increase too slowly to absorb them. Many of the conurbation's difficulties are common to other big Indian cities – water supply, drainage, sanitation, housing – but Calcutta's physiographic site, the 'city in the swamp' aggravates its problems of social hygiene and economic development. The efforts by the authorities to provide permanent shelter seem quite incapable of keeping pace with the inflow and increase of population, and policy today is first to provide the most rudimentary needs to those who live in the bustees: a protected water supply, drainage to prevent domestic waste, faeces and heavy rainfall from forming a seasonal morass, and latrines to control endemic enteric disease. The population of the Calcutta region has grown less rapidly than that of either Bombay or Delhi during the past intercensal decade; 22.6 per cent, compared with 43.8 per cent in Greater Bombay and 54.6 per cent in Delhi. Its problems however seem no nearer solution.

Some characteristics of the urban geography of

FIG. 13.18

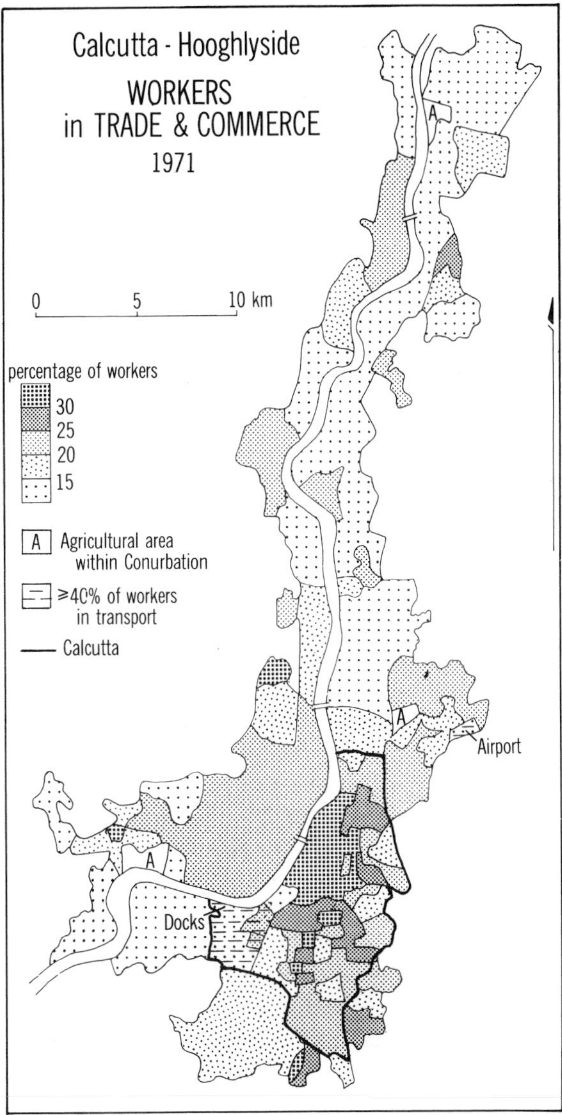

Hooghlyside are mapped in the accompanying figures. About 5 million of the conurbation's 7 million people are in Calcutta (3.15 million), Howrah (0.74 million) and the administrative areas immediately adjoining them (see Figure 13.15). Many of the smaller units are little more than swollen residential rural suburbs with relatively low densities ranging up to 15,000 per km^2 but often less than 5,000 per km^2 because of the non-urban land included within them. Howrah's relatively low overall density of 12,000 per km^2 is deceptive since the Municipal Committee area contains considerable areas of swamp. Figure 13.16a maps densities by quintiles. Outside Calcutta proper there are few areas even within the middle quintile (15,000–30,000 per km^2): Naihati, Bhatpara, Titagarh, Kamarhati, Baranagar and South Dum Dum on the Calcutta bank, Serampore and tiny Banupur on the right bank. Dum Dum alone, with a density of 157,000 per km^2 exceeds this level.

Calcutta's is a different story, requiring a larger scale map to depict the range of its population density (see Figure 13.16b). More than one fifth of its 101 wards have densities exceeding 100,000 per km^2. Indeed two reach the incredible densities of 276,467 per km^2 for a total of 41,500 people, and 228,000 for 22,800 people, a little less than in Bombay's peak ward, but extremely high in the context of Calcutta's more horizontal bustee development. The areas of highest density, in the upper two quintiles, are concentrated close to the Howrah Bridge in north central Calcutta which contains the CBD. There are two lesser nuclei in the south.

In occupational structure Calcutta differs somewhat from the rest of its conurbation. It has the major share of trade and commerce, in which it serves the remainder of the region, while the lesser centres are more strongly industrial (see Figures 13.17 a and b, and 13.18). The eastern wards of Calcutta have a high percentage of industrial workers, but over the rest of the city levels are generally in the two lower quintiles. Extensively in the riverside towns over 45 per cent of the workers are in manufacturing. Transport engages over 40 per cent of the workforce living close to Kidderpore docks and the Dum Dum airport. The industrial character of Hooghlyside has been discussed in Chapter Eleven.

Chandigarh

At the time of independence, where Chandigarh now stands was an undistinguished corner of rural Punjab. Since then the population of the area which is now the Union Territory of Chandigarh has increased ten-fold, to reach 257,251 at the 1971 census. Ninety per cent of these are in the urban agglomeration which ultimately is planned to hold 500,000.

Chandigarh (see Figure 13.19) was started as the capital of the new Punjab State, but partition of that state into Punjab and Haryana led to its becoming a Union Territory, common capital for the two states upon whose borders it stands. Its occupational structure reflects its administrative function. Out of a total of 85,645 workers, one third of the population, 58 per cent are engaged in 'other service occupations', excluding trade and commerce (14 per cent), and transport and communications (4.3 per cent). Only 12 per cent are in manufacturing, with printing and publishing dominating.

In its design and layout Chandigarh embodies in large measure the concepts of the French town-planner Le Corbusier who was closely associated with its development. The city has become a showpiece for architects and planners. It is laid out on a gently sloping plain at the foot of the Himalaya, with intermittent torrents providing limiting features to east and west. A grid of fast traffic roads divides the city into sectors each measuring 800 by 1200 metres. Each sector contains its own schools, health centre and community centre, and an east-west shopping street which crosses a north-south belt of open space. More specialized functions are the government Capitol in the north, towards the hills, the university campus to the west, an industrial sector to the east near the railway, and a wholesale market in the south, all four of these functions being located outside the residential frame. A cluster of central functions – museums, art gallery, hotels etc., link the university area to the central business district at the core of the city.

Chandigarh is said to have succeeded as a new city for Indians to live an Indian life, in contrast to the many new suburbs in expanding cities which seem to be transplants of western patterns too often ill-adapted to an Indian way of life. Chandigarh is valuable as an experiment which other Indian cities can study and emulate, and at the same time is a remarkably fine place in which to live.

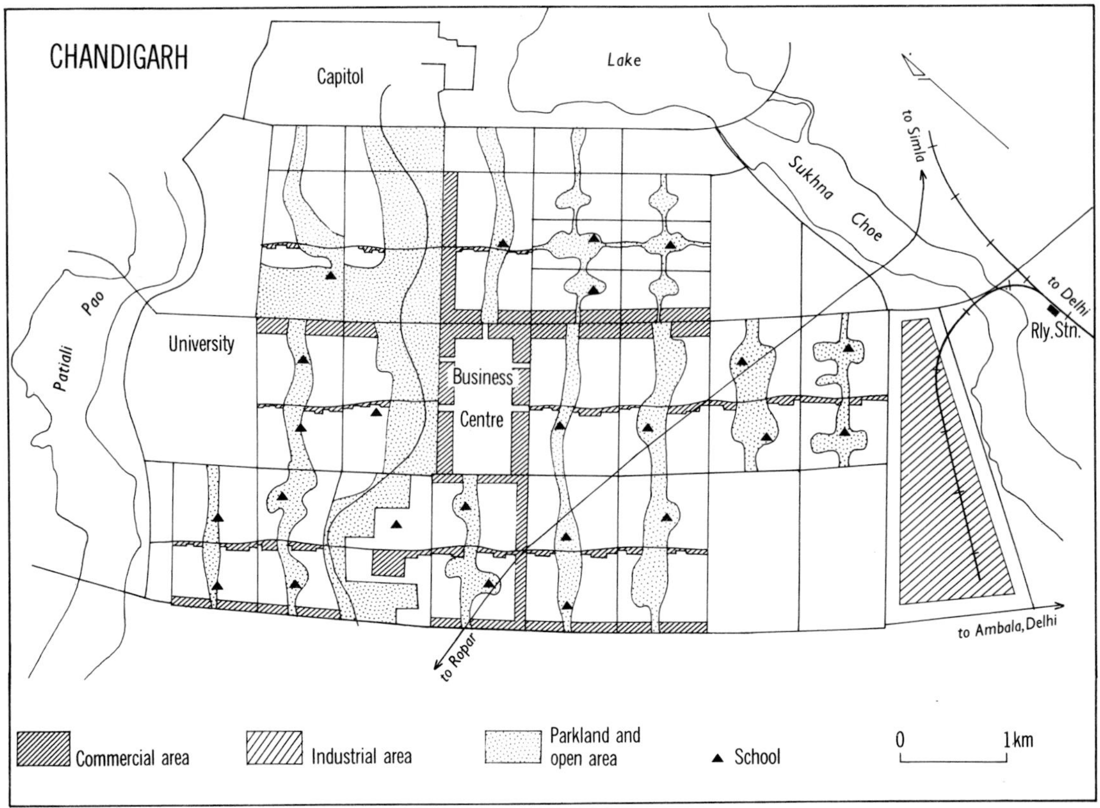
CHANDIGARH
Capitol
Lake
to Simla
Sukhna Choe
Patiali Pao
University
Business Centre
to Delhi
Rly. Stn.
to Ambala, Delhi
to Ropar
Commercial area
Industrial area
Parkland and open area
School
0 1 km

FIG. 13.19

PART IV

India Since Independence: Development in Retrospect and Prospect

India has achieved much in material terms since becoming master of its own political destiny. The preceding chapters have attempted to convey the extent of the progress made in developing its varied physical and human resources. There is no question that the country has resource potential in abundance: sunshine and rainfall, fields and forests, minerals for metals and energy, and a population with skills in cultivation and manufacturing. All these are elements of India's tradition; all were developed to a considerable degree before India's economy was forced into a position of subservience to the industrial economy of the British Empire, becoming distorted, stunted and deformed in the process. From the pursuit of traditional arts and crafts to satisfy the needs and tastes of a pre-industrial self-sufficient Indian society the energies of the people and the riches of their soil were directed by economic policies imposed from abroad, to produce the raw materials for the British industrial revolution. Most crippling of all to the indigenous economy, the Indian consumer was compelled through the law of comparative costs to purchase cheap imported factory goods in preference to the craft products of his own society. Colonial rule meant that India's resources were harnessed to the creation of British wealth in which Indians could have little share. In the terms of Gunnar Myrdal's concept of the development process, Britain enjoyed the benefits of the 'spread effects' of imperial economic growth, British industry breeding more industry in Britain. Meanwhile India suffered the 'back-wash' effects, losing its own traditional industry and experiencing exploitation of its agricultural capacity to feed British mills. The rich became richer, and the poor had taken away even that which they had!

At independence India inherited a colonially oriented economy developed to serve the needs and tastes of a western society and to some extent of a westernized Indian élite. What has been achieved over the quarter century of independence has been in large measure to dismantle the colonial structure of the internal economy while converting external trade from its former bi-lateral channel into multi-lateral (and incidentally multi-ideological) paths. At home industry has grown to manufacture substitutes for formally imported goods, but India's role as a producer of raw or partly processed commodities for markets in developed industrial countries has changed less. Only the pattern of trade has altered to reflect the country's efforts to remain politically non-aligned and to avoid becoming economically dominated by any great power.

Because of its considerable wealth in material resources India is in a stronger position than are many of the less developed countries to preserve its political and economic independence of outside powers. This should help India to find Indian solutions to its problems.

The citizen of the highly developed western country has tended to assume that the kind of development that brought his forebears to affluence is capable of achievement by every country in the world, given time, capital and know-how. Increasingly this view is being challenged, not only as to its validity but also as to the desirability of the whole world accelerating its consumption of irreplaceable resources.

86 Village potter near Agra throwing pots on a wheel turned by stick. Mother looks on, daughter holds the baby. Cow dung cakes behind on the left for fuelling the kiln. Two goat kids are playing in the sun in the background.

India seems to have arrived at a cross-roads towards which it has been moving for two decades. Which road now to take involves a fundamental political decision it has so far been loath to make. The Congress Party that ruled India from independence to 1977 managed to steer a middle way between the extremes of the politically right and left, a course unlikely to change under the ruling Janata party. The property-owning élite have been allowed to continue to emulate the affluent in the west or to persist in non-productive investment in ostentatious expenditure, all the while increasing the gap between their way of life and that of the peasant cultivator and craftsman. At the bottom of the system the lot of the poor has probably deteriorated as their number has certainly increased. In theory India may have the choice of three roads to follow. Those to right and left imply the acceptance of one or other of the world's doctrinaire route maps, both equally alien to Indian tradition. A middle way may yet be charted if India's rulers can inspire in the people a determination to find Indian answers to their problems compatible with the nation's egalitarian goals: Indian aspirations for the community at large, a traditional Indian deprecation of extravagant living and the acceptance of 'moderation in all things' in tune with (but perhaps not at the over-modest material level of) Gandhi's precepts; an Indian adaptation of the modernization theme; a non-violent socio-economic revolution that works with the tolerance characteristic of Hinduism to make all men equal in this most-stratified of societies.

Substantial material progress at the national level has been demonstrated above. Whether the economic lot for the common man has changed for the better is far from certain. Some authorities would hold that development in India has yet to begin. Dudley Seers defines development as the 'realization of the potential of human personality'.[1] In his view three main needs have to be satisfied. The first comprehends man's basic needs for food, clothing and shelter, to provide which man in a commercial economy requires a source of income. Secondly man needs a job not only to yield income, but as an activity conducive to his self-respect. Thirdly he needs a sense of equality and social justice if he is to respond to the demands and admonitions to exertion that come to him from his rulers. If one asks about development in India in Seers's three questions – what has been happening to poverty, to unemployment, and to inequality? the answer to each question can as yet only be 'at best, very little'.

[1] Dudley Seers, 'The meaning of development', *International Development Review*, XI, 4, 1969, pp. 2–6. Also in C. K. Wilbur, (ed.) *The Political Economy of Development and Underdevelopment*, Random House, 1973.

The crucial question must be whether India can achieve development in such terms without very radical change to its body politic understood in its widest sense. This is at the core of Myrdal's analysis in *'Asian Drama'* and as another authority, Keith Griffin, writes, 'the essence of development is institutional reform'.[1] The policies of the later years of Congress Party rule, suggest that the 'soft' approach to development characteristic hitherto may give way to a more determined approach to institutional problems. To date, serious conflcit between the traditional 'haves' – the high castes, the property owners, the socio-economic-political élites – and the vast mass of the 'have-nots', has been averted. A small segment of the political leadership demonstrates its conscience in reasserting with increasing insistence in Plan after Plan, that India is committed to creating an egalitarian society. At the other end of the scale the under-privileged are being assured through education and improved systems of communication by radio reaching into the villages and slums, that they not only *have* rights but that government intends to make those rights real. A reduction in political freedom may be the unavoidable price of greater equality, but in the context of the entrenched conservatism of traditional Indian society it is hard to see any alternative constitutional path to that particular goal. Solutions very much more drastic (as measured in the loss of political liberty and the destruction of traditional society) have been applied elsewhere, for example in China, but these are unlikely to gain acceptance in India where physically and psychologically non-violent methods are so fundamental a part of the culture.

[1] Keith Griffin, 'Underdevelopment in theory', in *Underdevelopment in Spanish America*, G. Allan and Unwin, 1969, pp. 19–31. Also in C. K. Wilbur, *op.cit.* pp. 15–25.

87 Shaping a pounding pestle in granite, Bangalore, Karnataka.

To raise the level of living of the depressed classes that make up 40 per cent of the population involves more than merely reducing that of the wealthiest five per cent. A first essential is that the agricultural sector should prosper. The rural population is 80 per cent of the total, and a real improvement in its purchasing power would have a stimulating effect on the whole economy, providing incentives for small scale industry to meet the simple low-cost needs of this collectively huge potential market. So far agricultural development has merely kept pace with population growth. It must outstrip the latter if poverty and unemployment are to be reduced. Population control is important as much to prevent excess labour supply perpetually depressing wages to a minimum subsistence level, as to enable the provision by government of educational, health and other social services to get ahead of demand and so to improve in quality.

The geographical consequences of pursuing policies having as first priority the reduction in poverty, could mean a significant change from trends apparent hitherto. Emphasis on the manufacture of low-cost goods to meet the modest needs of villagers would replace the laissez-faire policy that allows entrepreneurs to strive to produce in the sector of import-substitution highly profitable luxury goods for a small protected market. The result could be to stimulate greatly small-scale modern industry in widely dispersed centres close to their markets. The heavy industries linked to raw materials, and others committed by technology to large-scale operation would persist in their present and similar locations. However the attraction of foot-loose consumer-goods industries to the big cities might conceivably be reduced, and with it the tendency for these settlements to grow excessively large. Such an industrial policy would require tight and detailed governmental control. Mahbub ul Haq doubts whether the mixture of private and public sectors that characterizes Indian industrial planning is compatible with the pursuit of egalitarian goals.[1] While this may be a sound view of the prospects for industry at the 'organized' level, it is difficult to imagine the kind of bureaucratic organization that would be needed to run a fully state-owned small industrial sector operating efficiently. At this level individual initiative and owner-management is more likely to respond to local demand and to create jobs. One can also hope that demand would be reflected in the supply of goods meeting regional cultural preferences, and not become standardized to the dictates of manufacturers as happens in advanced economies.

India's economy cannot exist in complete independence of the outside world. Imports of some essential commodities and goods that the country cannot produce will be needed. There will have to be exports of commodities and manufactured goods to pay for the imports. In the three decades since independence it has become clear that the pattern of external trade has to change. The populations of the more developed countries are not increasing as rapidly as that of India, and their technological advantage enables them to substitute new materials for the commodities traditionally imported from India. The demand for India's exports is therefore relatively inelastic and their value tends to be depressed. Under these adverse conditions and with the developed countries decreasingly dependent on the less developed, the latter have to strive hard to keep in balance the terms of trade. While the export of manufactured articles from factory and household workshop is expanding, there is still need for fundamental changes in the relationship between the developed and less developed countries. UNCTAD (United Nations Conference on Trade and Development) has come into existence to study these relationships and to promote solutions to the problems of trade imbalance. The dice are loaded heavily in favour of the technically and economically sophisticated countries. They are so far ahead of the less developed countries that it is impossible for the latter to catch up. Yet it is clear that world peace and international harmony depend on co-operation to reduce these gross economic disparities. Under UNCTAD the developed countries are encouraged to increase aid (to the level of 1 per cent of gross national product), agreements are promoted to ensure a fair price is paid to the less developed countries for their products so that they can afford to purchase essential imports, efforts are being made to protect them against fluctuations in commodity markets, and assistance is given to lesser developed countries selling manufactured goods to the more developed. Too much cannot be expected of UNCTAD in the short run, but at least it represents recognition of the problems of the less developed countries and an attempt to counteract the relentless operation of economic forces that had their origin in the colonial era and the industrial revolution.

If an author may be permitted to express a personal view based on thirty-five years of contact with India and with Indians of many levels, it is an optimistic one, despite much apparently contradictory evidence. It is not inconceivable that the traditional tolerance of Hindu culture can be interwoven with the aspirations of India's brand of socialism to produce a unique and satisfactory solution of the problem of adjustment between men and their environments. To the success of such adjustments Indian geographers have much to offer, trained as they are to understand the variety and variability of the elements of the physical environment, and to appreciate with sympathy both the nicety of man's relationship with the environment, worked out in each region over centuries, and the improvements in those relationships and in their productivity made possible by advances in our understanding.

One may fervently hope that within a generation a new India may emerge not as a soulless replica of some alien economist's model of a developed society, but rather as a modern version of an India deeply rooted in the past, and carrying forward a continuity of tradition adapted to the challenges and knowledge of the present.

[1] Mahbub ul Haq, The crisis in development strategies, in C. K. Wilber, (ed.) *op.cit.* pp. 367–72.

IMPORTANT REFERENCES

OFFICIAL PUBLICATIONS

India, Office of Registrar General and Census Commissioner, Ministry of Home Affairs New Delhi, *Census of India 1971*. (For some purposes the 1961 Census is the latest source).

There are many collected writings and monographs produced under the auspices of the Census of India and ranging widely across the broad field of the social sciences. The Census of India stands alone in the world for the volume and scholarship of its publications, a fact that puts all foreign students of the region greatly in their debt, as this writer gladly acknowledges.

In addition to the tabulated results of the 1971 and earlier censuses, reference was made to *Economic and Socio-cultural Dimensions of Regionalisation*, an Indo-USSR Collaborative Study, Census Centenary Monograph No. 7 edited by A. Chandra Sekhar; India, Department of Commercial Intelligence and Statistics, *Monthly Statistics of the Foreign Trade of India; Stastical Abstract*, (annual); Ministry of Information and Broadcasting, Publications Division New Delhi, India: *a Reference Annual 1975*, New Delhi.

It is often difficult to compile time series of statistics owing to the practice of revising figures subsequently.

India, Ministry of Irrigation and Power New Delhi, *Report of the Irrigation Commission 1972;* Indian Council of Agricultural Research, *Proceedings of the Symposium on Cropping Patterns in India*, Delhi 1972; Ministry of Agriculture, Directorate of Economics and Statistics, *Agricultural Situation* (Monthly).

BOOKS

Atal, Yogesh, *The Changing Frontier of Caste*, National Publishing House, Delhi, 1968.

Chaudhuri, M. R., *Power Resources of India*, Oxford & I.B.H. Publishing Co., Calcutta, 1970; *Indian Industries: Development and Location*, Oxford & I.B.H. Publishing Co., Calcutta, 1970.

Dandekar, V. M., and Nilakantha Rath, *Poverty in India*, Ford Foundation, New Delhi, 1970.

Epstein, T. Scarlet, *South India: Yesterday Today & Tomorrow*, Macmillan, London 1973.

Farmer, B. H., *Agricultural Colonization in India Since Independence*, Oxford University Press, London, N.Y., 1974.

Gopal, Ram, *Linguistic Affairs of India*, Asia Publishing House, Bombay, 1966.

Johnson, B. L. C., *South Asia: Selective Studies of theEssential Geography of India, Pakistan and Ceylon.*, Heinemann Educational Books, London, 1969. (Note: While the present volume largely supersedes the India Section of 'South Asia' readers will find some useful sample studies of village agriculture pp 59–67. These could supplement Chapter Eight.)

Kapp, K. W., *Hindu Culture, Economic Development and Economic Planning in India*, Asia Publishing House, Bombay, 1963.

Khusro, A. M., *Economics of Land Reform and Farm Size in India*, Macmillan, India, Madras, 1973.

Maloney, Clarence, *Peoples of South Asia*, Holt, Rinehart and Winston, New York, 1974.

Myrdal, Gunnar, *Asian Drama: An Inquiry into the Poverty of Nations*, (3 vols), Pantheon, New York, 1968.

Myrdal, Gunnar, *The Challenge of World Poverty*, Allen Lane and the Penguin Press, London, 1970.

Pattanshetti, C. C., *Dimensions of India's Industrial Economy*, Somaiya Publications, Bombay, 1968.

Poleman, T. T., and Freebairn, D. K., *Food Population and Employment: the Impact of the Green Revolution*, Praegar Publishers, New York, 1973.

Rao, K. L., *India's Water Wealth*, Orient Longman, New Delhi, 1975.

Singh, Jasbir, *An Agricultural Atlas of India: A Geographical Analysis*, Vishal Publications, Kurukshetra, Haryana, 1974.

Singh, Jasbir, *The Green Revolution in India – How Green it is*, Vishal Publications, Kurukshetra, Haryana, 1974.

Suresh Singh, K., *The Indian Famine 1967: a study in Crisis and Change*, Peoples Publishing House, New Delhi 1975.

Sham Lal, (ed), *Times of India, Directory and Yearbook*, Bombay 1976.

Sinha, B. N., *Industrial Geography of India*, World Press Private, Calcutta, 1972.

Spate, O. H. K., and Learmonth, A. T. A., *India and Pakistan: a General and Regional Geography*, 3rd ed., Methuen & Co., Ltd., London, 1967. (Still the 'basic text' for the serious student.)

Srinivas, M. N., *Caste and Modern India*, Asia Publishing House, Bombay, New York, 1962.

Sukhwal, B. L., *South Asia: A Systematic Geography Bibliography*, Scarecrow Press Inc., Methuen, N.J., 1974.

Wilber, C. O. (ed), *The Political Economy of Development and Underdevelopment*, Random House, New York, 1973.

INDEX

Entries thus: 22 refer to text; *22* refer to figures or tables; **22** refer to photographs; n indicates a footnote. All are page numbers.